LANDSCAPE ARCHITECTURE

L'ARCHITECTURE DU PAYSAGE
LANDSCHAFTSARCHITEKTUR
LANDSCHAPSARCHITECTUUR

© 2010 **booQs** publishers bvba
Godefriduskaai 22
2000 Antwerp
Belgium
Tel.: 00 32 3 226 66 73
Fax: 00 32 3 226 53 65
www.booqs.be
info@booqs.be

ISBN: 978-94-60650-27-7
WD: D/2009/11978/028
(Q040)

Editor & texts: Àlex Sánchez Vidiella
Art direction: Mireia Casanovas Soley
Design and layout coordination:
Claudia Martínez Alonso
Layout: LOFT Publications
Translation: Cillero & de Motta
Cover Image: © Turenscape

Editorial project:
LOFT Publications
Via Laietana, 32, 4.º, of. 92
08003 Barcelona, Spain
Tel.: +34 932 688 088
Fax: +34 932 687 073
loft@loftpublications.com
www.loftpublications.com

Printed in China

LANDSCAPE ARCHITECTURE

L'ARCHITECTURE DU PAYSAGE
LANDSCHAFTSARCHITEKTUR
LANDSCHAPSARCHITECTUUR

This book aims to unite the concept of "art" with that of "landscaping" through a series of different projects illustrated with graphics and images.

Landscape architecture, a concept originated by Gilbert Laing Meason in his book *On the Landscape Architecture of the Great Painters of Italy* (London, 1828), is an architectural discipline bringing together a series of aspects such as design, planning, management, conservation, and soil replenishment.

"Green art" or "landscape art" is the most personal physical expression of an idea planned by a designer, architect, or landscape architect. Architectural and decorative features, materials that are both natural (stone, wood) and artificial (steel, concrete), paths and ponds, and vegetation, among others, are resources available to artists wishing to leave their mark in a setting, whether it be urban, suburban or rural.

Contemporary landscape architecture is characterized by the reintroduction of contrasting colors and the contrast created by introducing urban forms and materials in rural settings.

Rapid urbanization has seen the equally rapid development of the urban parks, riverfronts, and green spaces that residents have been clamoring for.

All of these actions are visible examples of this laborious artistic and creative process where the environment and historical heritage are given a place. The final result of a landscape art project has to please its clients and, especially, users. It must be a place for social, contemplative, and recreational use.

Cet ouvrage cherche à établir un lien entre les concepts d'«Art» et de «Paysagisme» en exposant différents projets illustrés à partir de graphismes et d'images.

L'architecture du paysage, terme employé pour la première fois par Gilbert Laing Meason dans son ouvrage *Landscape Architecture of the Great Painters of Italy* (Londres, 1828), est une discipline architecturale regroupant une série d'activités comme le design, la planification, la gestion, la préservation et la réhabilitation du paysage.

L'«Art vert» ou «Art paysagiste» est l'expression physique la plus personnelle d'une idée projetée par le designer, le paysagiste ou l'architecte. Les éléments architecturaux et décoratifs, l'emploi de matériaux naturels (pierre et bois) et artificiels (acier, béton, etc.), les chemins et les bassins, la végétation, etc. sont des ressources exploitées par les artistes pour laisser leur empreinte dans un contexte urbain, périurbain ou rural.

L'architecture paysagère contemporaine est caractérisée par la réapparition de couleurs contrastantes et par la rupture que suppose l'introduction de formes et de matières urbaines dans des espaces ruraux.

La croissance accélérée en matière d'urbanisme a entraîné le développement spontané de parcs urbains, de zones riveraines et d'espaces verts nécessaires au bien-être des habitants.

Toutes ces transformations sont des exemples visibles de ce processus artistico-créatif laborieux, qui tient compte de l'environnement ou du patrimoine historique. Un projet artistique de paysagisme doit donc répondre aux attentes des clients et surtout, des usagers. Un lieu où ces derniers peuvent exercer une activité sociale, de détente et ludique.

In diesem Buch soll das Konzept «Kunst» mithilfe verschiedener, durch Graphiken und Bilder veranschaulichter Projekte mit dem Konzept der «Landschaftsgestaltung» verbunden werden.

Die Landschaftsarchitektur, ein durch Gilbert Laing Meason in seinem Werk *Landscape Architecture of the Great Painters of Italy* (London, 1828) geprägtes Konzept, ist ein Zweig der Architektur, in dem eine Reihe von Themen wie Planung, Verwaltung, Erhaltung und Sanierung der Erde vereint sind.

«Die grüne Kunst» oder «Kunst der Landschaftsgestaltung» ist der persönlichste greifbare Ausdruck einer vom Designer, Landschaftsgestalter oder Architekten vorgestellten Idee. Die architektonischen und dekorativen Elemente, der Gebrauch von natürlichen (Stein, Holz) und künstlichen (Stahl, Beton etc.) Materialien, Wege und Teiche, die Vegetation usw., sind Mittel, mit denen die Künstler ihren Abdruck in einem städtischen, periurbanen oder ländlichen Umfeld hinterlassen.

Die heutige Landschaftsarchitektur zeichnet sich durch die erneut aufgekommene Verwendung kontrastierender Farben und durch den Kontrast aus, der durch den Einsatz von städtischen Formen und Materialien in einer ländlichen Umgebung erzeugt wird.

Das schnelle Wachstum der Städte hat eine lebhafte Entwicklung zugunsten von städtischen Parks, Uferbereichen und Grünzonen, die von den Bewohnern des jeweiligen Ortes gefordert werden, hervorgerufen.

Alle diese Tätigkeiten sind sichtbare Beispiele für den aufwendigen künstlerisch-kreativen Prozess, bei dem die Umwelt oder das historische Erbe berücksichtigt werden. Das endgültige Ergebnis eines künstlerischen Projekts der Landschaftsgestaltung muss den Kunden und vor allem den Benutzern gefallen. Ein Ort, von dem ein gesellschaftlicher, besinnlicher und erholsamer Gebrauch gemacht werden kann.

In dit boek wordt een poging gedaan om de concepten «Kunst» en «Landschapsarchitectuur» te bundelen aan de hand van verschillende projecten geïllustreerd met grafische voorstellingen en afbeeldingen.

Landschapsarchitectuur, een concept dat Gilbert Laing Meason heeft bedacht in zijn boek *Landscape Architecture of the Great Painters of Italy* (Londen, 1828), is een architectonische discipline waarbinnen een aantal eigenschappen zoals ontwerp, planning, beheer, behoud en herstel van de aarde worden bijeengebracht.

«Groene kunst» of «Landschapskunst» is de persoonlijke, fysieke uitdrukking van een door de ontwerper, landschapsarchitect of architect gepland idee. De architectonische en decoratieve elementen; het gebruik van natuurlijke (steen, hout) en kunstmatige (staal, beton, etc.) materialen; wegen en vijvers; planten, etc. zijn de hulpmiddelen waarover de kunstenaar be-

schikt om zijn stempel te drukken op een stedelijke, voorstede-
lijke of landelijke context.

De hedendaagse landschapsarchitectuur wordt gekenmerkt door
het opnieuw gebruiken van opvallende kleuren en door het contrast dat ontstaat wanneer stedelijke vormen en materialen in landelijke omgevingen worden toegepast.

De snelle stedelijke groei heeft op verzoek van de bewoners een
vlotte ontwikkeling ten gunste van stadsparken, oever- en groenzones teweeggebracht.

Al deze maatregelen zijn zichtbare voorbeelden van dit bewerke-
lijke artistiek-creatieve proces, waarbij rekening wordt gehouden
met het milieu of het historische erfgoed. Het eindresultaat van
een landschapskunstproject moet bij de klanten, en met name bij
de gebruikers, in de smaak vallen. Een plek die gebruikt kan worden voor sociale, ontspannende en recreatieve doeleinden.

Westonbirt Metropolis

Westonbirt, United Kingdom

This temporary installation was presented at the Westonbirt International Festival of Gardens. It features a setting made from wooden crates containing different plants scattered over the lawn. It represents a collection "captured" during an imaginary journey around the world.

L'installation temporaire a été présentée à l'occasion du Festival international des jardins de Westonbirt. L'espace a été parsemé de caisses en bois contenant différentes plantes, déposées sur le gazon. Elles représentent une collection « rassemblée » au cours d'un voyage imaginaire autour du monde.

Die temporäre Installation wurde auf dem internationalen Gartenfestival von Westonbirt vorgestellt. Dieses Szenarium zeigt auf dem Rasen verteilte Holzkästen, die verschiedene Pflanzen enthalten. Eine Sammlung, die während einer imaginären Reise um die Welt „eingefangen" wurde.

De tijdelijke installatie werd gepresenteerd op het Internationale Tuinfestival van Westonbirt. Het gaat om een samenstelling van houten kisten met verschillende planten die verdeeld staan over het gras. Die stellen een tijdens een denkbeeldige wereldreis "gevangen"collectie voor.

 Marco Antonini, Roberto Capecci, Raffaella Sini/LAND-I
www.archicolture.com
© LAND-I

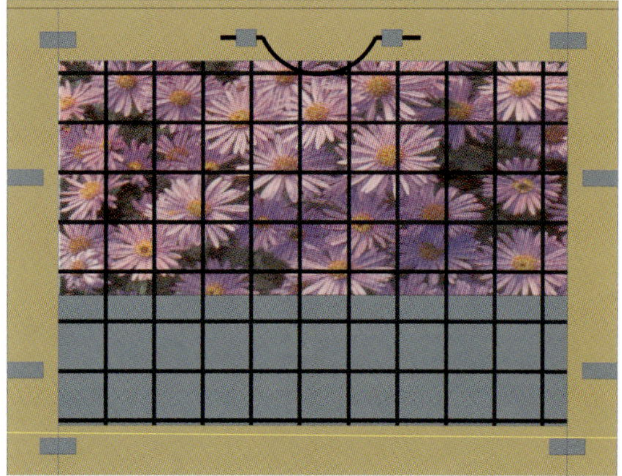

Collages for types of boxes

This installation reproduces the complexity of the contemporary metropolis and its skyline. Each plant has a card showing its name and place of origin.

L'installation reproduit la complexité de la métropole contemporaine et son horizon. Chaque plante est pourvue d'une carte qui indique son nom et sa provenance.

Die Installation gibt die Komplexität von Metropole und Horizont wieder. An jeder Pflanze befindet sich ein Etikett, das Name und Herkunft bezeichnet.

De installatie geeft de complexiteit van de hedendaagse wereldstad en haar horizon weer. Elke plant heeft een kaartje met daarop de naam en afkomst.

Models

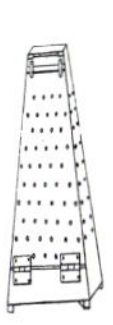

Content of the wooden boxes:

– BOX type B: *Hosta tardiflora*
– BOX type B: *Plumbago capensis*
– BOX type B: *Hyperricum calycinum*
– BOX type B: *Cornus canadiensis*
– BOX type B: *Ceratostigma plumbaginoides*
– BOX type B: *Buxus sempervirens*
– BOX type B: *Leptospermum liversidgei*
– BOX type B: *Ribes alpinum*
– BOX type C: *Lavandula angustifolia*
– BOX type A: *Euphorbia eritrea*
– BOX type C: *Abelia chinensis*
– BOX type C: *Banksia intergrifolia*

– BOX type A: *Cordyline indivisa*
– BOX type D: *Mahonia japonica*
– BOX type D: *Magnolia virginiana*
– BOX type A: *Malus sylvestris*
– BOX type C: *Shibataea kumasasa*
– BOX type D: *Osmanthus delavayi*
– BOX type A: *Trithrinax campestris*
– BOX type D: *Arbutus unedo*
– BOX type B: *Liriope muscari*
– BOX type C: *Cupressus arizonica*
– BOX type A: *Cupressus sempervirens*
– BOX type A: *Pseudopanax ferox*

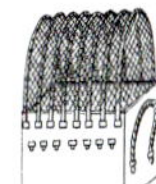

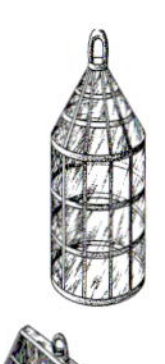

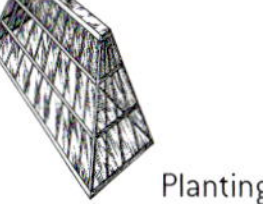

Planting

Eco-boulevard in Vallecas

Madrid, Spain

This project consists of the installation of "three social revitalizing air trees." Each tree is demountable and energy self-sufficient and contains a solar energy collection system. They also act as open structures for many leisure activities.

Ce projet dispose d'une installation à « trois arbres d'air » qui ont un rôle de dynamiseurs sociaux. Chaque arbre est une structure démontable et autonome en termes d'énergie, dotée d'un système photovoltaïque de récupération de l'énergie solaire. En outre, elles fonctionnent comme des supports ouverts pour de multiples activités de loisir.

Dieses Projekt besteht in der Installation von „drei Luftbäumen", die als soziale Beschleuniger dienen. Jede dieser zerlegbaren Strukturen versorgt sich anhand einer Fotovoltaik-Solaranlage selbst mit Energie und dient außerdem als offene Halterung für diverse Freizeitaktivitäten.

Dit project bestaat uit de installatie van "drie luchtbomen" die fungeren als sociale stimuleerders. Elke boom is een energetisch autonome en demonteerbare structuur met een fotovoltaïsch zonne-energiesysteem. Bovendien functioneren ze als open steunen voor veelvuldige vrijetijdsactiviteiten.

Ecosistema urbano arquitectos
www.ecosistemaurbano.com
© Emilio P. Doiztua, Roland Halbe

Site plan

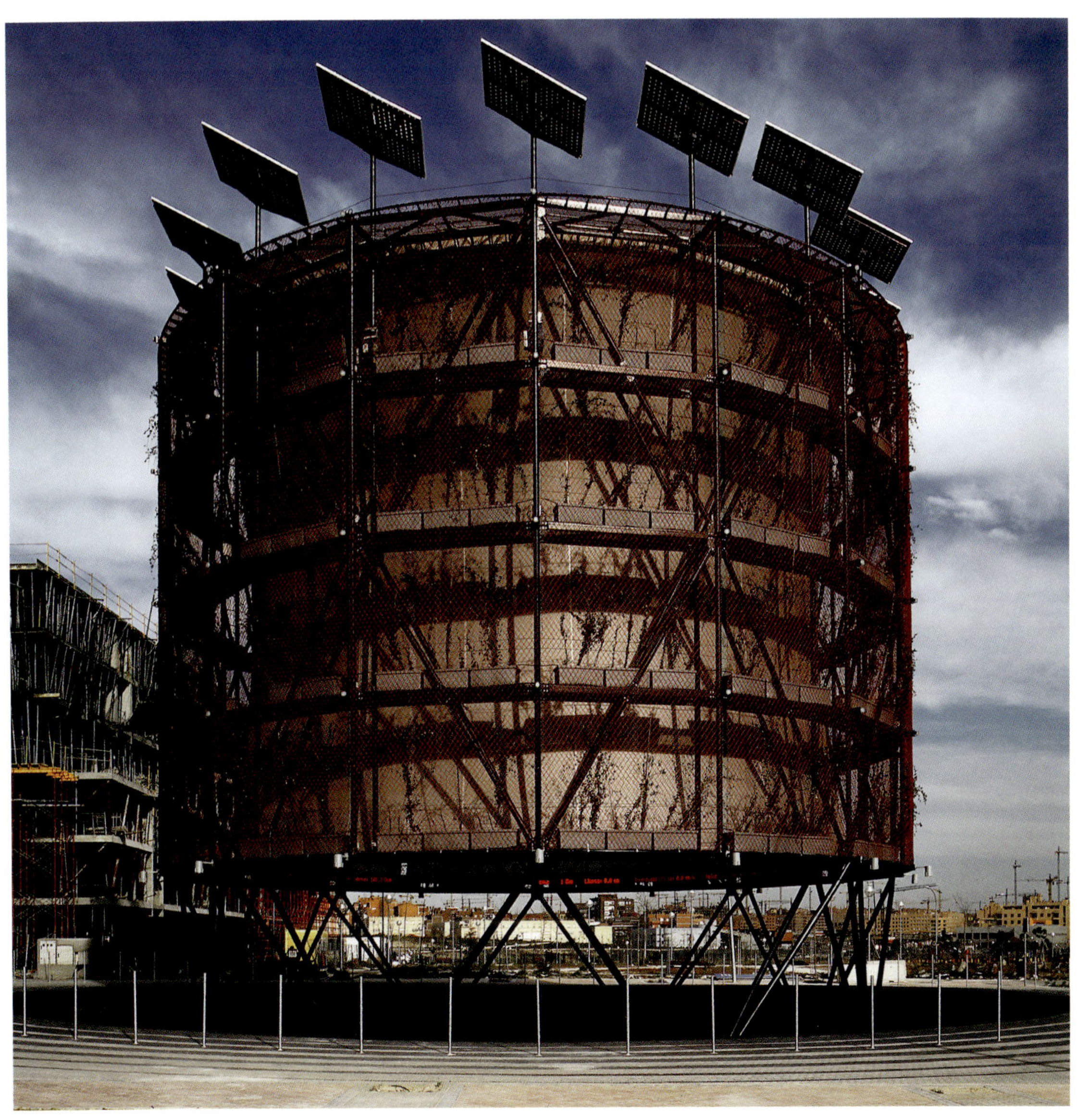

The proposal is an urban recycling operation with structures that consume what they produce as a result of the installation of photovoltaic solar panels.

Le projet est une opération de recyclage urbain avec des structures consommant ce qu'elles produisent grâce à l'installation de panneaux solaires photovoltaïques.

Die Idee entspricht einem städtischen Recyclingprozess mit Aufbauten, die dank des Einbaus der Fotovoltaikplatten das verbrauchen, was sie selbst erzeugen.

Het voorstel is een stedelijke recycleactie met structuren die, dankzij de installatie van fotovoltaïsche zonnepanelen, verbruiken wat ze produceren.

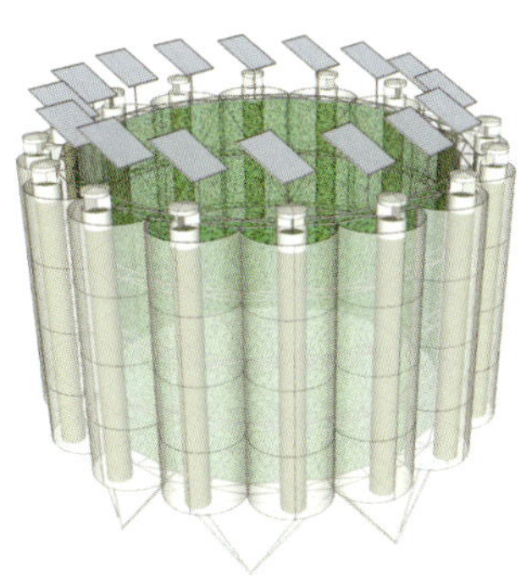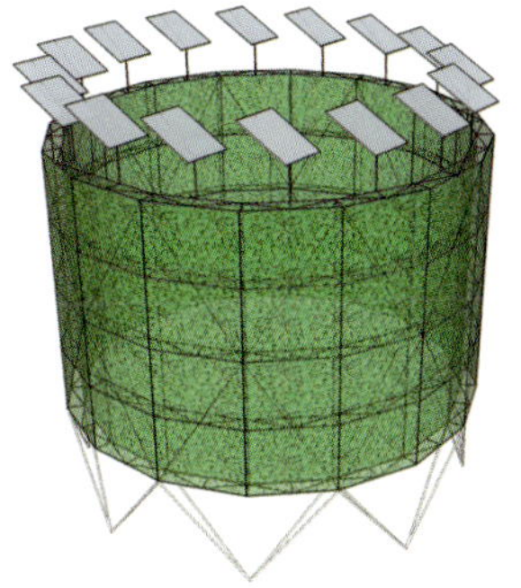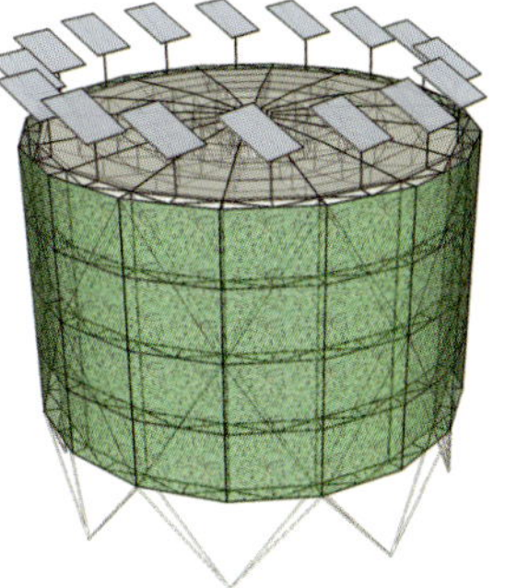

Computer generated renderings

FERCABER

Kielder Belvedere

Northumberland, United Kingdom

The structure made from triangular forms serves as a shelter for visitors and a waiting area for the local ferry. Stainless steel panels partially reflect Kielder Forest and the lake.

Cette structure aux formes triangulaires joue le rôle d'un refuge pour promeneurs et d'une zone d'attente à l'arrivée du ferry local. Une image partielle de la forêt de Kielder et les eaux du lac adjacent se reflètent grâce à des panneaux en acier inoxydable.

Diese Struktur aus dreieckigen Formen dient als Refugium für Ausflügler und als Wartebereich für die Passagiere der örtlichen Fähre. Die Paneele aus rostfreiem Stahl spiegeln einen Teil des Kielder Forest und des angrenzenden Sees wieder.

Deze structuur met driehoekige vormen fungeert als toevluchtsoord voor dagrecreanten en als wachtruimte voor de plaatselijke veerboot. Een gedeeltelijke afbeelding van het Kielderbos en het water van het aangrenzende meer weerspiegelen zich in roestvrij stalen panelen.

Softroom, Forum (construction), Brian Eckersley (structural engineer)
www.softroom.com
© Keith Paisley, Softroom (drawings)

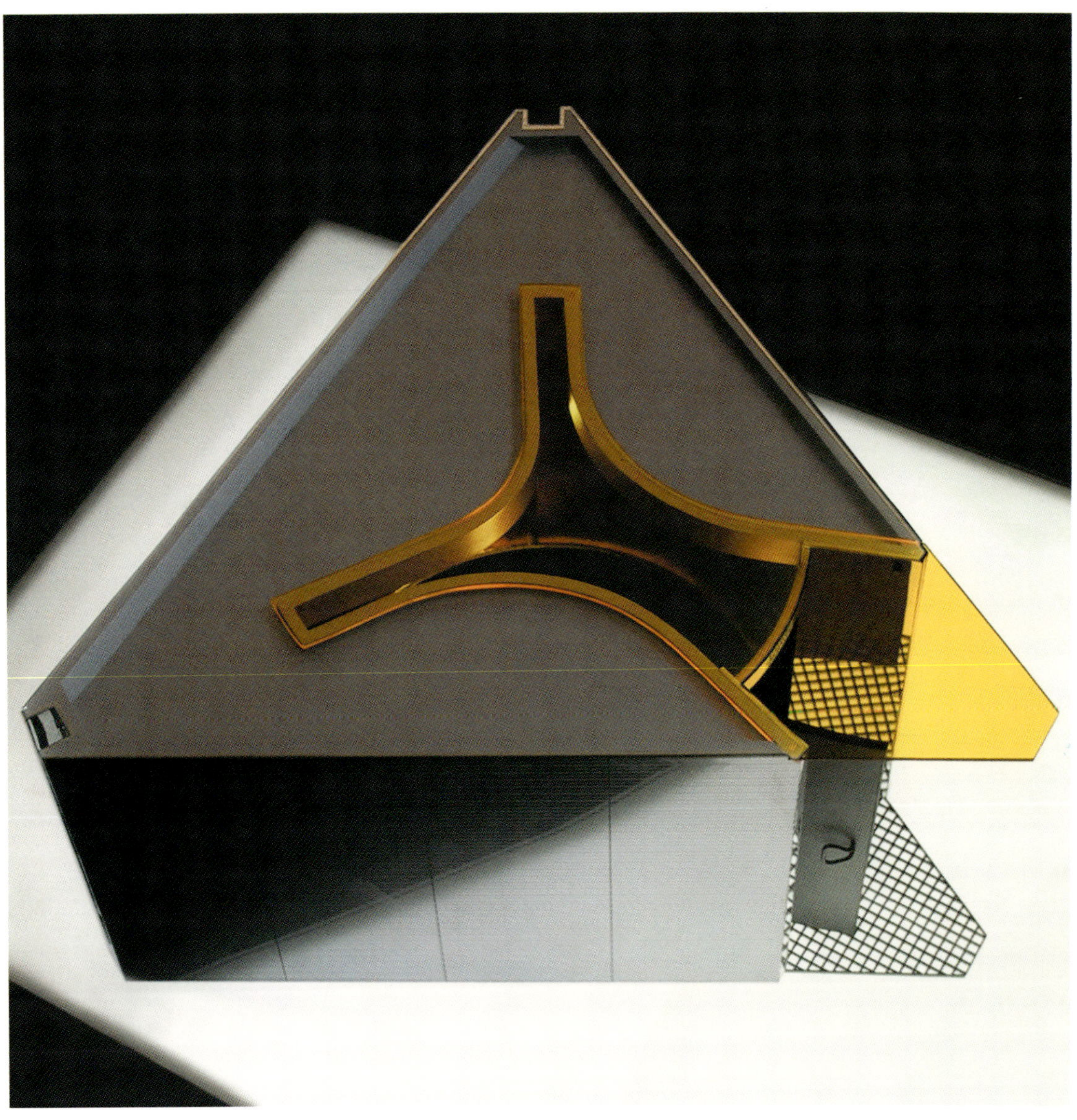

The structure is an integral part of the landscape. The side shapes reflect the adjacent
forest, the convex surface reflects the lake
views, and the curved slot frames views of
the lake.

La structure est intégrée au paysage : les
formes latérales reflètent la forêt voisine,
la surface convexe du miroir reflète les vues
du lac et la rainure courbée les délimite.

Die Struktur ist in die Landschaft integriert:
Die Seitengebilde reflektieren den Wald, der
Spiegel reflektiert den Seeblick, der Schlitz
rahmt die Sicht.

De structuur is in het landschap opgenomen: de zijkanten weerspiegelen het aangrenzende bos, de spiegel kaatst het meer
terug en de gebogen gleuf omlijst een blik
op het meer.

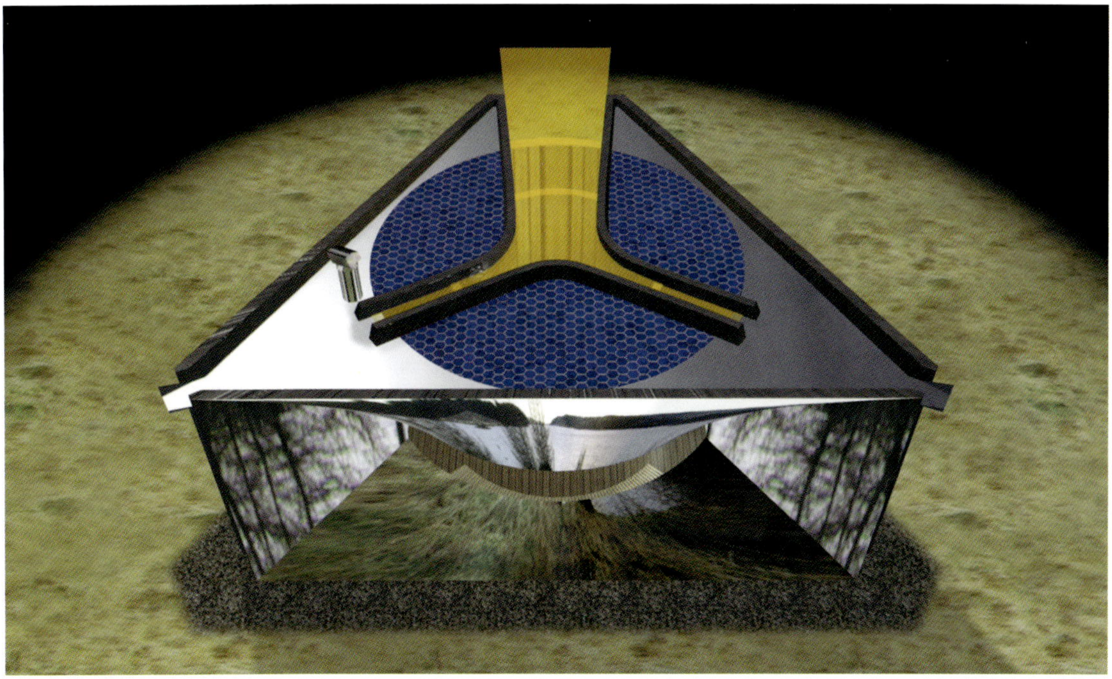

Computer model

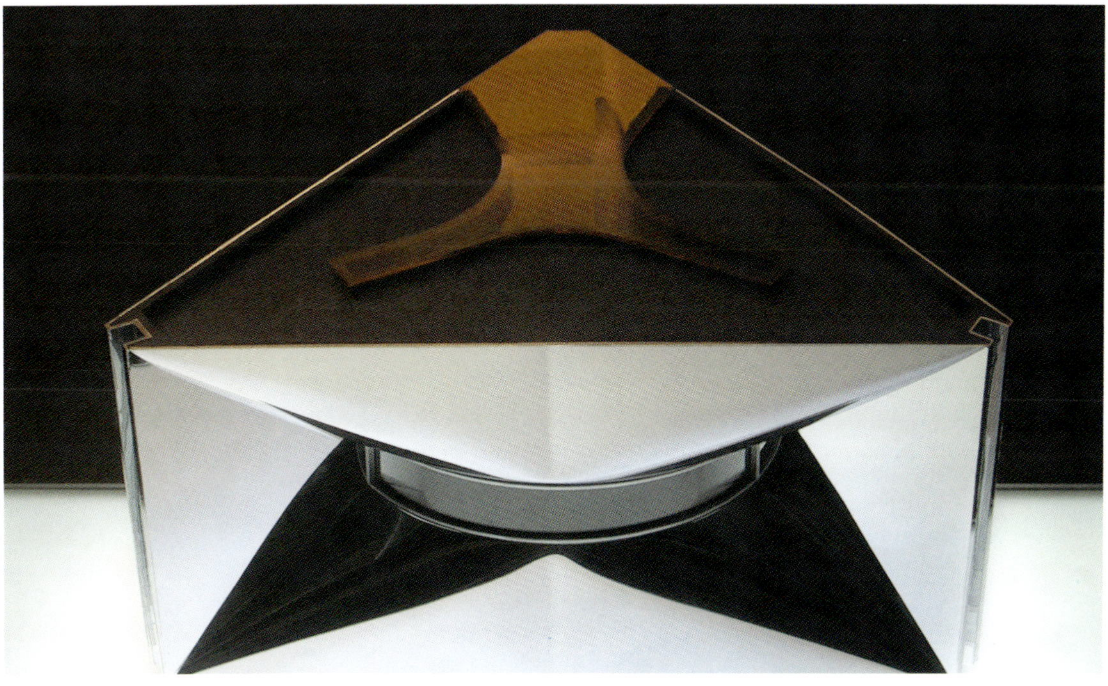

Model

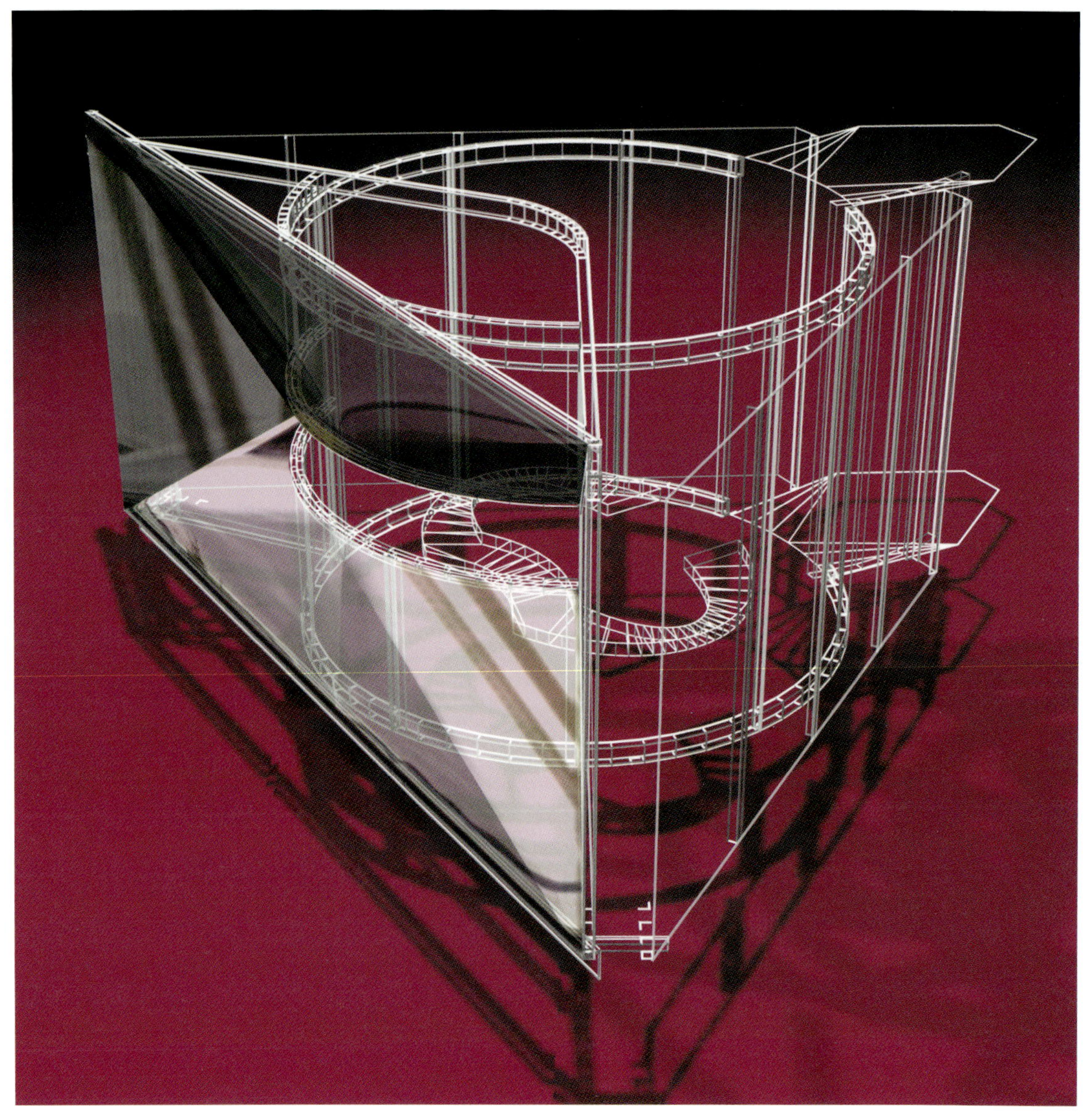

3D model rendering

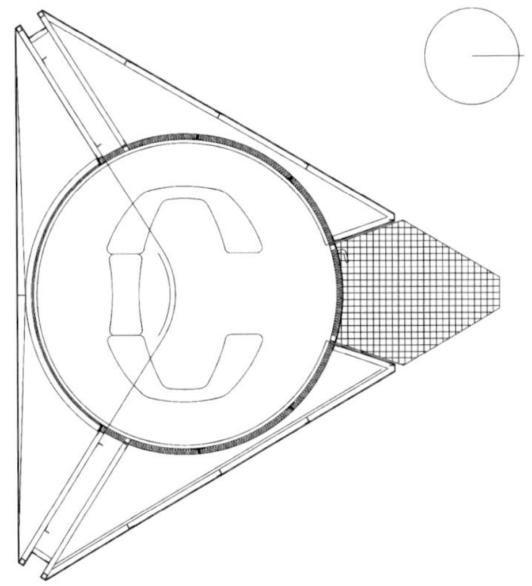

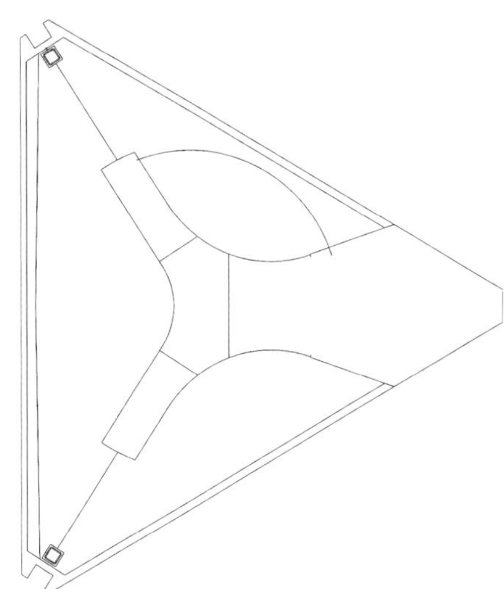

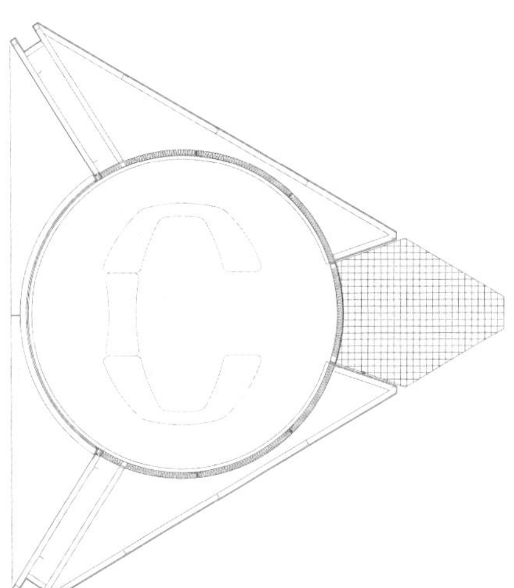

Floor and roof plans

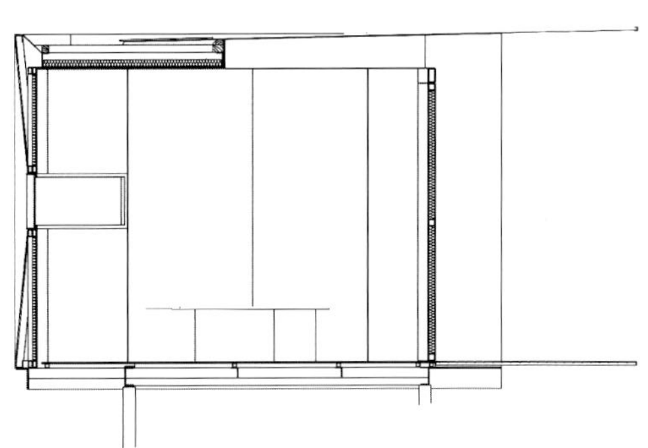

Cross section

Jardins de Metis

Grand-Métis, Canada

This installation was chosen in June 2005 for the International Garden Festival held in the Jardin de Métis. The project is a metaphor of the capillary structure of roots in the ground, symbolically displaying the microhydrology of the place and creating an underground landscape.

Cette installation a été sélectionnée en juin 2005 pour le Festival international des jardins qui a eu lieu dans les jardins de Métis. Le projet est une métaphore de la structure capillaire des racines enfouies dans le sol. Il expose de manière symbolique la micro-hydrologie du lieu et évoque un paysage souterrain.

Diese Installation wurde im Juni 2005 für das internationale Festival der Jardins de Metis ausgewählt. Das Projekt ist eine Metapher der Kapillarstruktur der Wurzeln im Boden, indem es symbolisch die örtliche Mikrohydrologie darstellt und eine unterirdische Landschaft kreiert.

Dit project werd in juni 2005 geselecteerd voor het Internationale Tuinfestival in de Jardins de Métis. Het project is een metafoor van de capillaire structuur van de wortels in de grond. Het geeft symbolisch de microhydrologie van de plek weer en genereert een ondergronds landschap.

 Janet Rosenberg & Associates, CS&P Architects Inc (architects)
www.jrala.ca
© Janet Rosenberg & Associates

Visitors to the garden move by a series of ramps and paths leading to a structure supporting drain pipes.

Les visiteurs du jardin avançaient en empruntant des rampes et des sentiers pour atteindre une marquise qui supportait un enchevêtrement de conduits de drainage.

Die Besucher des Gartens erreichten über Rampen und Pfade ein Schutzdach, das ein Netz von Drainage-Leitungen stützte.

Bezoekers van de tuin wandelden via steigerplanken en wandelpaden naar een luifel dat een netwerk van afvoerleidingen ondersteunde.

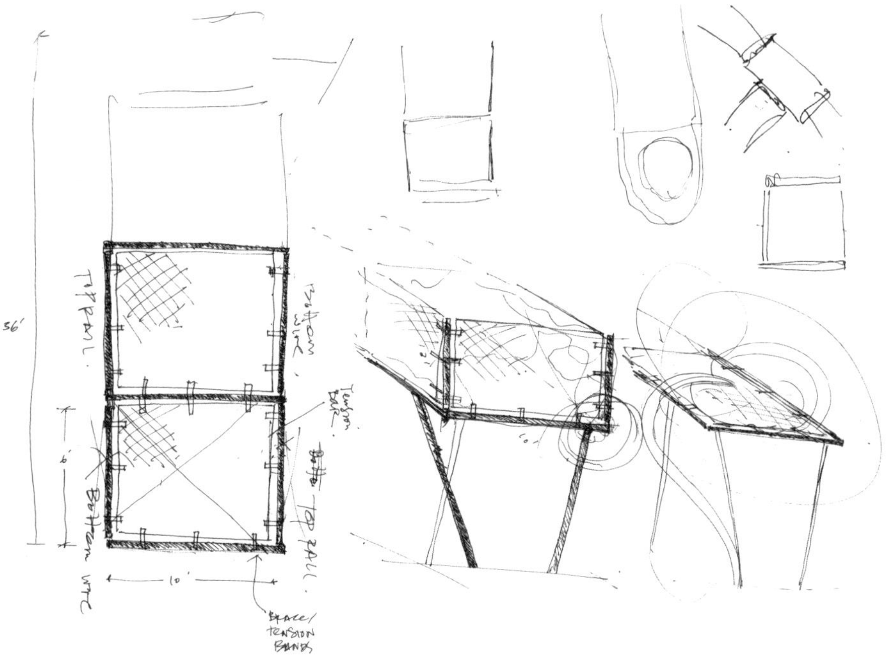

Sketch

Collages for elevations

1. Plexiglass cisterns
2. Suspended root network
3. Aggregate path
4. Tangled panels
5. Tilled textural field

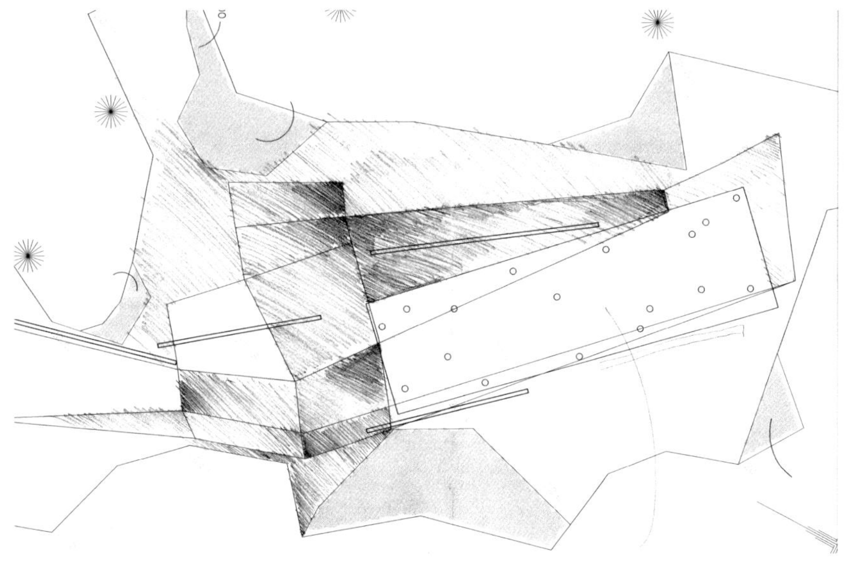

Sketch

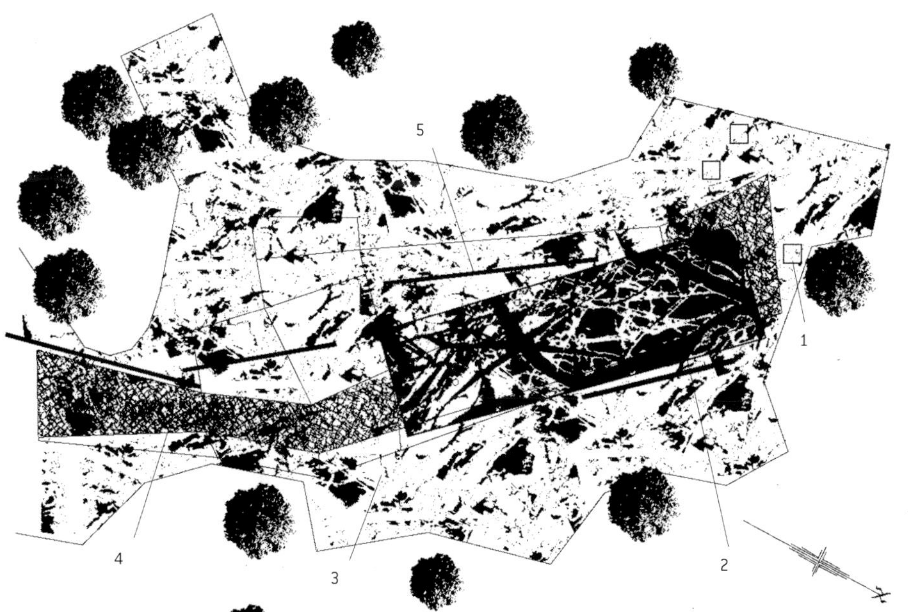

Plan

1. Plexiglass cisterns
2. Suspended root network
3. Aggregate path
4. Tangled panels
5. Tilled textural field

Litlatún

Reykjavík, Iceland

This temporary installation was presented at the Reykjavik Art Museum's "Magma/Kvika" exhibition. It was designed as an alternative to the unbuilt project for connecting the museum and the adjoining park – a tiny meadow in a gray setting.

Cette installation temporaire a été présentée à l'occasion de l'exposition « Magma/Kvika » du musée d'art de Reykjavík. Le projet a été proposé comme une alternative au projet non exécuté concernant la liaison entre le parc adjacent et le musée : une étendue de prairie minuscule dans un environnement gris.

Die temporäre Installation wurde bei der Ausstellung Magma/Kvika des Kunstmuseums Reykjavik gezeigt. Der Entwurf wurde für das nicht realisierte Projekt der Verbindung zwischen angrenzendem Park und Museum vorgeschlagen: Die Erweiterung einer winzigen Wiese in grauer Umgebung.

Op de tentoonstelling "Magma/Kvika" van het Kunstmuseum te Reykjavik werd dit tijdelijke project getoond. Het werd voorgesteld als een optie voor het niet uitgevoerde verbindingsproject tussen het belendende park en het museum: een minuscule grasvlakte te midden van een grijze omgeving.

Landslag ehf
Landslagsarkitektar FÍLA,
Dagný Bjarnadóttir (instalation
and greenhouse furniture
design)
www.landslag.is
© Dagný Bjarnadóttir, Simon Schmid, Friorik Tryggvason, Brynjóflfur Jónsson, Landslag (drawings)

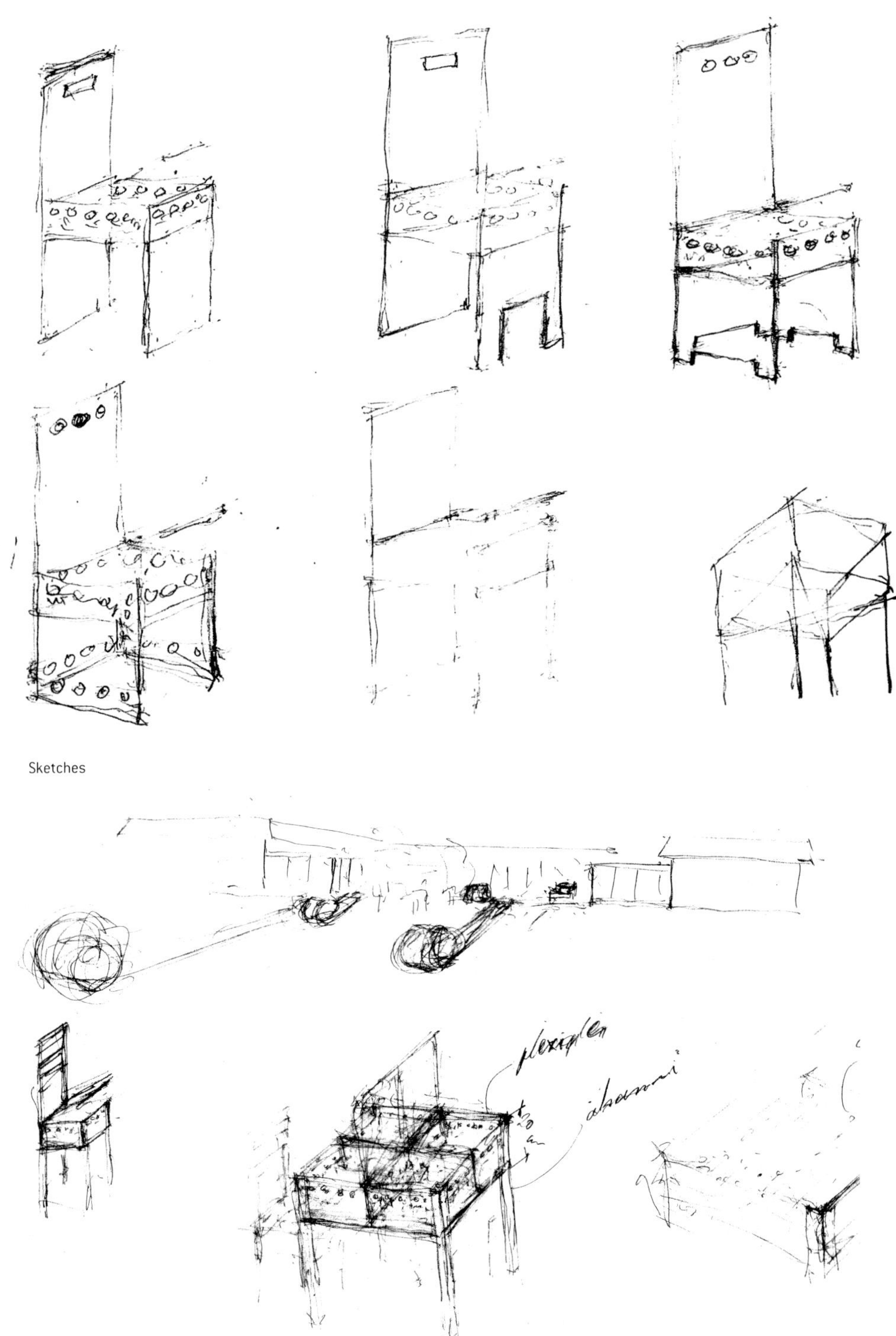

Sketches

Design development studies for greenhouse furniture

Design development studies for greenhouse furniture

The installation features furniture consisting of chairs and tables that act as minia-
ture greenhouses. The vegetation can be
replaced by lights in winter.

*Dans cette installation, il convient de signa-
ler le mobilier composé de chaises et de tables, qui jouent le rôle de serres miniatures.
En hiver, la végétation peut être remplacée
par des lampes.*

*Es sticht das Mobiliar aus Stühlen und Ti-
schen hervor, die als Mini-Gewächshäuser
dienen. Im Winter können die Pflanzen
durch Lampen ersetzt werden.*

*Opvallend is het meubilair bestaand uit
stoelen en tafels die fungeren als minia-
tuurbroeikassen. Tijdens de winter kunnen
de planten vervangen worden door lampen.*

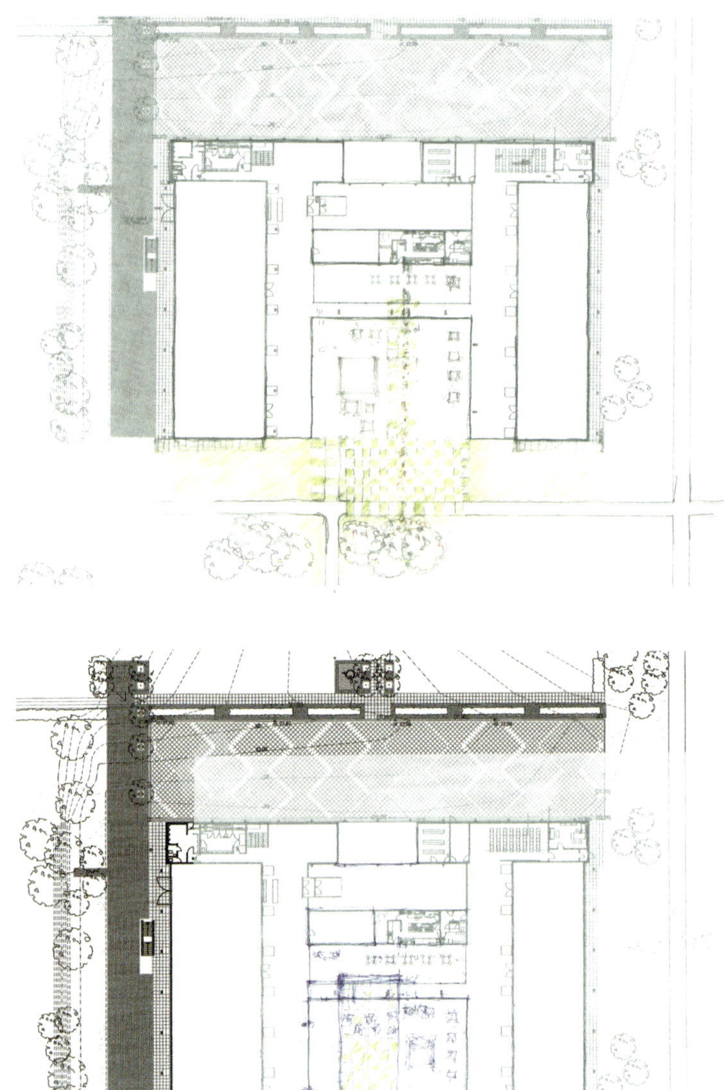

Development plans of square

Color sketch for lawn's grid

Color sketch for wave

3D rendering of greenhouse furniture

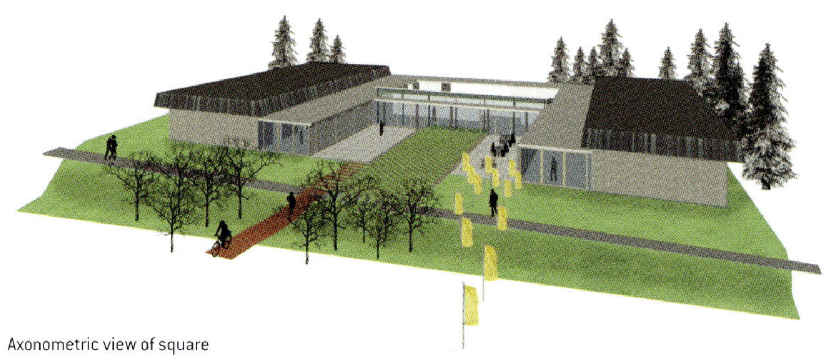

Axonometric view of square

3D rendering of square

3D rendering of terrace

Garden for a plant collector

Bellahouston Park, Glasgow, United Kingdom

This garden is part of the designs presented at the Art Park Glasgow festival. The garden is a tribute to a carnivorous plant and fern collector and shows interest in the relationship between the color and growth of these plants.

Le jardin fait partie des projets présentés à l'occasion du Festival Art Park de Glasgow. Il s'agit d'un hommage à un collectionneur de plantes carnivores et de fougères, qui s'intéresse au rapport entre la couleur et la croissance de ces végétaux.

Der Garten ist Teil der anlässlich des Glasgower Festivals Art Park eingereichten Vorschläge. Er ist der Beitrag eines Sammlers von fleischfressenden Pflanzen und Farnen, der sich für die Beziehung zwischen Farbe und Wachstum dieser Pflanzen interessiert.

Deze tuin behoort tot de voorstellen die zijn ingediend naar aanleiding van het Art Park Festival in Glasgow. De tuin is een hulde aan een verzamelaar van vleesetende planten en varens, die geïnteresseerd is in het verband tussen de kleur en de groei van die planten.

 GROSS. MAX.
www.grossmax.com
© GROSS. MAX.

The garden is located on a structure created with layers of glass and inside which a fiber optic grid and ultraviolet lights hang from the ceiling.

L'endroit choisi pour l'emplacement du jardin est une structure réalisée à partir de couches de verre. À l'intérieur, un treillage composé de fibres optiques et d'ultraviolets est suspendu au plafond.

Der Ort des Gartens besteht aus einer Konstruktion aus Glasschichten. Im Inneren hängt ein Netz aus Lichtleitern und UV-Licht von der Decke.

De plaats waar de tuin is aangelegd is een structuur van lagen glas. Binnenin hangt aan het plafond een net van glasvezels en ultraviolette lichten.

Concept collages

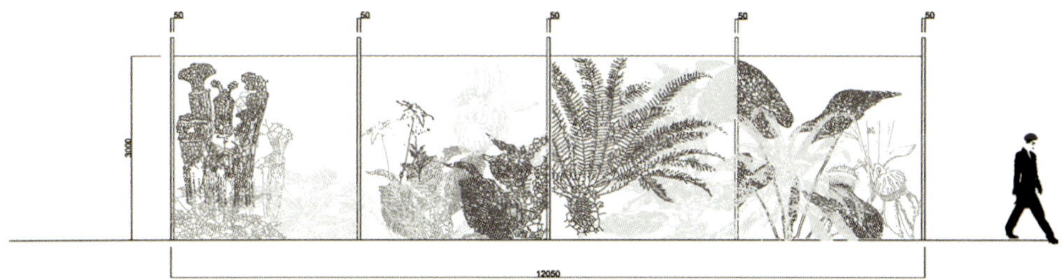

Elevations

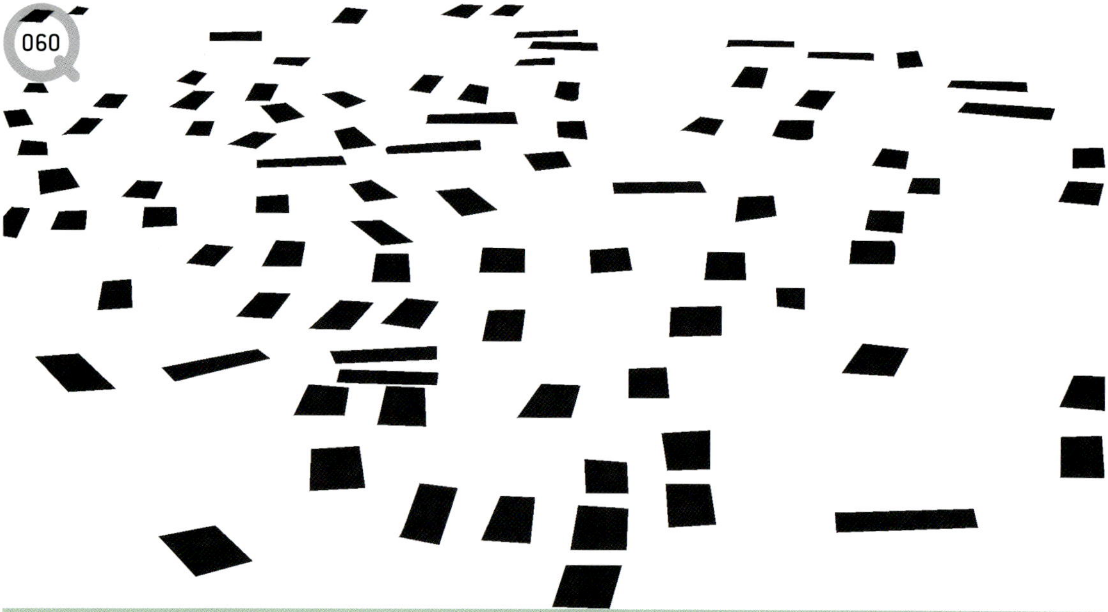

Ombre Grand Metis

Quebec, Canada

This project makes the visitors feel as if they were standing in front of an archaeological excavation. A series of identical and disordered cavities were made in the ground in reference to ancient necropolises. Visitors discover that the cavities are in fact holes with plants.

L'ouvrage donne l'impression au spectateur de se retrouver face à une fouille archéologique. Une série de cavités identiques, faisant allusion aux anciennes nécropoles, sont creusées dans le sol de façon chaotique. Le visiteur découvre que les cavités sont des trous contenant de la végétation.

Das Projekt vermittelt dem Besucher den Eindruck, vor einer archäologischen Ausgrabung zu stehen. Eine Reihe gleichartiger, ungeordneter Hohlräume stellen den Bezug zu antiken Nekropolen her. Der Besucher entdeckt, dass die Hohlräume aus mit Pflanzen bewachsenen Löchern bestehen.

Het project plaatst de toeschouwer voor een denkbeeldige archeologische uitgraving. Er worden een aantal identieke en ongeordende gaten in de grond gemaakt, die naar de oude dodensteden verwijzen. De bezoeker ontdekt dat de gaten planten bevatten.

Marco Antonini, Roberto Capecci, Raffaella Sini/LAND-I
www.archicolture.com
© LAND-I

This installation is a metaphor for the shadows of the past that hang over the present. Shadows are used as a concept to define space, distances, and depth in a garden.

Métaphoriquement, cette installation évoque les ombres du passé qui pèsent sur le présent. Dans un jardin, le concept d'ombre définit l'espace, les distances et la profondeur.

Diese Installation zeigt die Schatten der Vergangenheit, die auf der Gegenwart lasten. Das Konzept Schatten bestimmt Raum, Entfernungen und Tiefe.

Metaforisch verwijst deze installatie naar de schaduwen van het verleden die op het heden drukken. Het schaduwconcept in een tuin bepaalt de ruimte, de afstanden en de diepte.

Plan with plantation

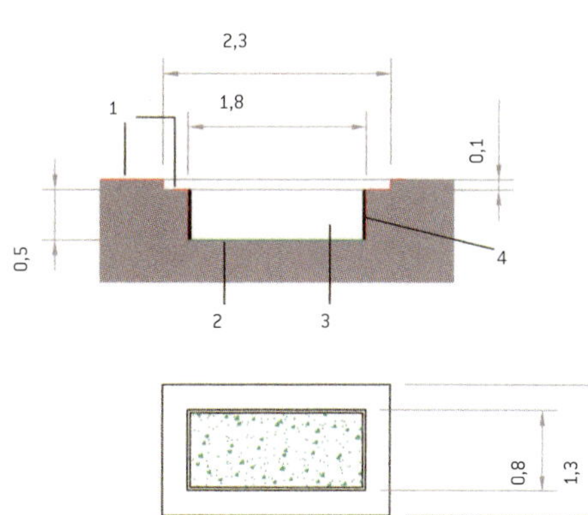

Section and plan

1. Sand
2. Planting
3. Ground excavation
4. Casts of galvanized metal

3D renderings showing cavities impact

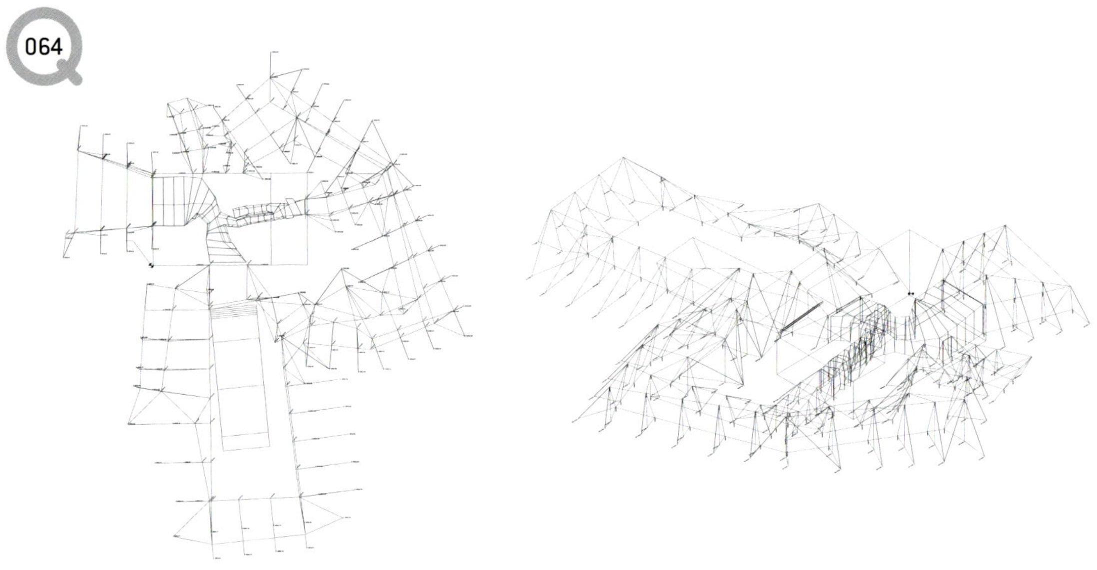

Spidernetthewood

Nimes, France

A long row of trees has been planted on a site covering over 25,000 sq ft that will reach their ideal height in five years. These trees will be covered with a polypropylene mesh to create a maze among the branches. Inside this structure, another, darker, plastic mesh will be created to enable the space to be occupied.

Une longue rangée d'arbres a été plantée sur un terrain de 2 450 m² afin que dans cinq ans, ils atteignent la hauteur idéale envisagée. Cette masse boisée est recouverte d'une maille plastique en polypropylène, qui permet de créer un grand labyrinthe entre les branches. Une autre maille en plastique plus dense est créée à l'intérieur de cette structure afin d'être occupée en toute liberté.

Auf einem 2450 m² großen Grundstück wurde eine lange Reihe von Bäumen gepflanzt, die in 5 Jahren die geplante Idealhöhe erreichen. Diese Baummasse wird mit einem Kunststoffnetz aus Polypropylen bedeckt, um ein großes Labyrinth zwischen den Ästen zu schaffen. Im Inneren dieser Struktur wird ein weiteres dichteres Plastiknetz hergestellt, sodass man sie bewohnen kann.

Op een lap grond van 2450 m² werd een lange rij bomen geplant die in vijf jaar de verwachte ideale lengte zullen hebben. Deze bomenrij wordt bedekt met een plastic net van polypropyleen om tussen de takken een groot labyrint te creëren. Binnenin deze structuur wordt een ander dichter plastic net gemaakt dat de vrijheid biedt om bezet te worden.

 **R & Sie(n) Architects**
www.new-territories.com
© R & Sie(n) Architects

The waiting time for this country house and the outer wooded mesh project to merge with the landscape is five years.

Le temps d'attente nécessaire pour que la maison de campagne projetée et la maille extérieure boisée se fondent avec l'environnement est de cinq ans.

Die Wartezeit für die Verschmelzung des geplanten Landhauses und des baumbestandenen Außennetzes mit der Umgebung beträgt fünf Jahre.

Het duurt vijf jaar voordat de geplande plattelandswoning en het buitennetwerk met bomen in elkaar overvloeien.

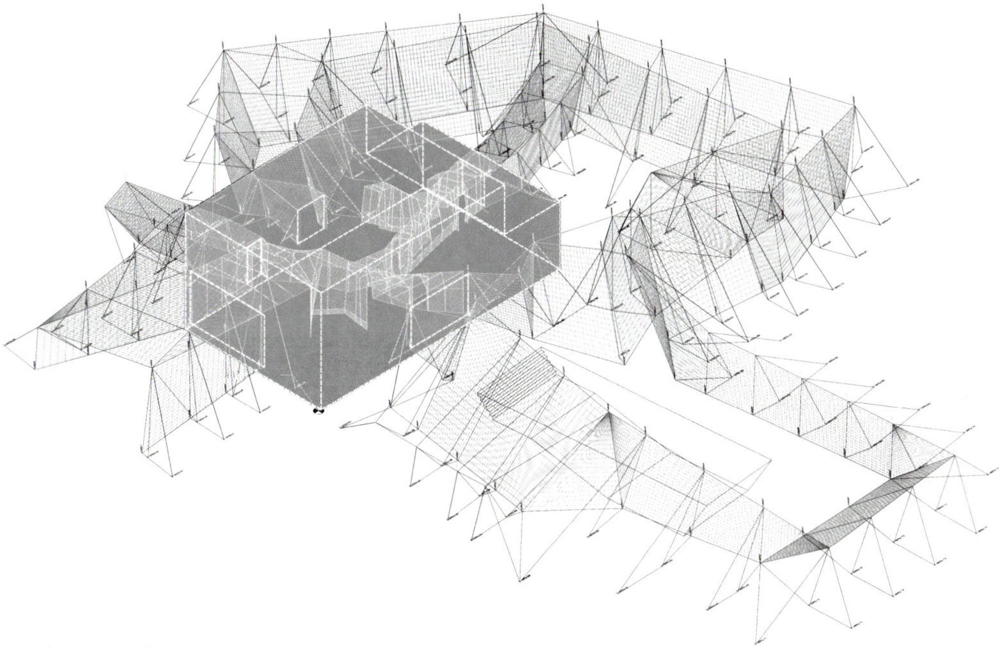

Wire frame perspective

Craigieburn Bypass

This project was installed on the new Craigieburn bypass road. It is the result of a poetic interpretation of the place. It is located on the access highway to Melbourne and is a spectacular landscape action including walls, bridges, and lighting.

Ce projet, installé sur la nouvelle rocade de Craigieburn, est le fruit d'une lecture poétique des lieux. Le site se trouve à l'entrée de Melbourne et constitue une intervention paysagère spectaculaire comprenant des murs, des ponts et des dispositifs d'éclairage.

An der neuen Umgehungsstraße von Craigieburn wurde dieses Projekt, Frucht einer poetischen Lesart des Ortes, errichtet. Der Ort befindet sich kurz vor Melbourne und besteht aus einer eindrucksvollen Gestaltung der Landschaft, die Mauern, Brücken und Beleuchtung umfasst.

Op de nieuwe ringweg van Craigieburn werd dit project aangelegd. Het is ontstaan naar aanleiding van een poëtische lezing van de plek. De plaats ligt bij de ingang van Melbourne en is een spectaculair landschapsproject met muren, bruggen en verlichting.

**Taylor Cullity Lethlean,
Robert Owen (participating artist)**
www.tcl.net.au
© John Gollings courtesy
of Vic Roads, Taylor Cullity
Lethlean (drawings)

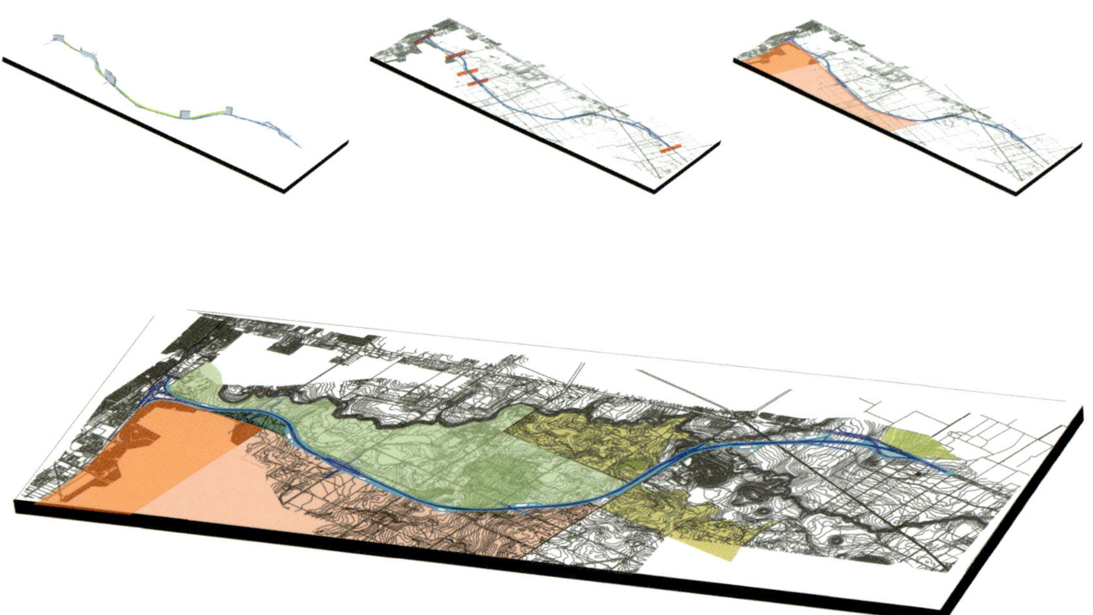

Final plans

The design explores the way static objects take on a dynamic aspect or come to life when viewed at high speed.

Ce concept explore la manière dont les objets statiques semblent être animés ou s'activent lorsqu'ils sont observés en voyageant à grande vitesse.

Das Design erforscht die Art, in der statische Objekte Dynamik erhalten bzw. aktiviert werden, wenn man sie beim Vorbeifahren mit hoher Geschwindigkeit sieht.

Het ontwerp onderzoekt de manier waarop statische voorwerpen dynamisch worden of in actie treden wanneer men opn hoge snelheid langs reist en ze observeert.

Dujiangyan Square

Dujiangyan, China

Dujiangyan Square was inspired by the landscape, irrigation, and local lifestyles. The result is a 27-acre urban space where the population can enjoy art and their local and regional identity. The square features an underground walkway, a central sculpture formed by light columns, a stone wall with carvings, and water features.

La place de Dujiangyan a été construite en s'inspirant des paysages, de l'irrigation et des styles de vie locaux. Le résultat obtenu est un espace urbain de 11 ha où la population profite de l'art et de son identité locale et régionale. Un passage souterrain, des points d'eau, une sculpture centrale composée de colonnes lumineuses et d'un mur de pierre y ont été installés.

Der Platz in Dujiangyan wurde von den Landschaften, der Bewässerung und dem örtlichen Lebensstil inspiriert. Das Ergebnis ist eine 11 ha große städtische Fläche für Kunst und die lokale wie regionale Identität. Angelegt werden ein unterirdischer Weg, eine zentrale Skulptur aus Lichtsäulen und einer gravierten Steinwand und Wasserflächen.

Het plein van Dujiangyan is geïnspireerd op de plaatselijke landschappen, irrigatie en levensstijlen. Het resultaat is een stadsruimte van 11 ha waar de bevolking kan genieten van de kunst en van haar plaatselijke en regionale identiteit. Er is een ondergrondse doorgang aangelegd, met in het midden een beeldhouwwerk gevormd door licht gevende kolommen en een stenen wand met gravures en waterzones.

Turenscape
www.turenscape.com
© Kongjian Yu, Yang Cao, Turenscape (drawings)

Resting boxes
Creek
Sunken water plaza
Underpass
Sunken water plaza
Focal sculpture
Whirl of water
Aquaduit
Creek
Courtyard and well
River walk
Sunken corridor
Sunken water garden
Golden Canopy
Fish mouth
Fountain
Camphor trees
Courtyard
Pedestrian street
Pu Yang River
Bo Tiao River
Zhou Ma River
Jiang An River

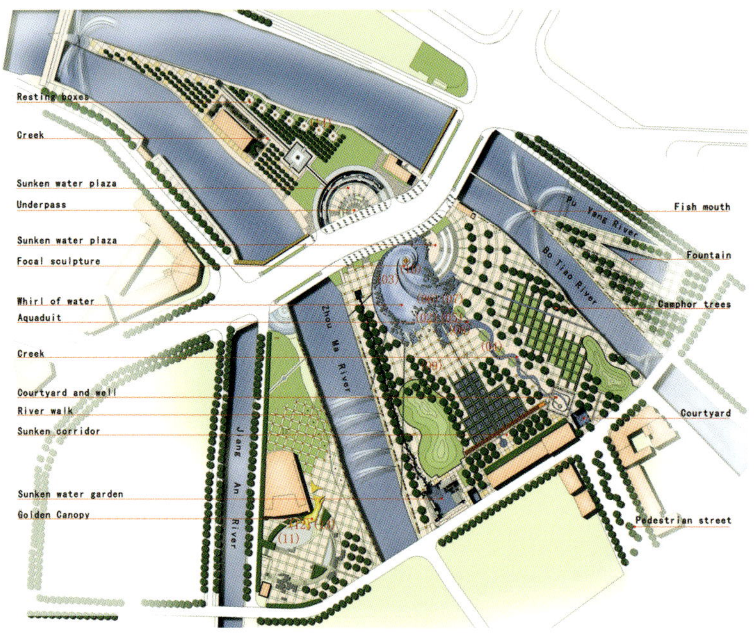

Plan

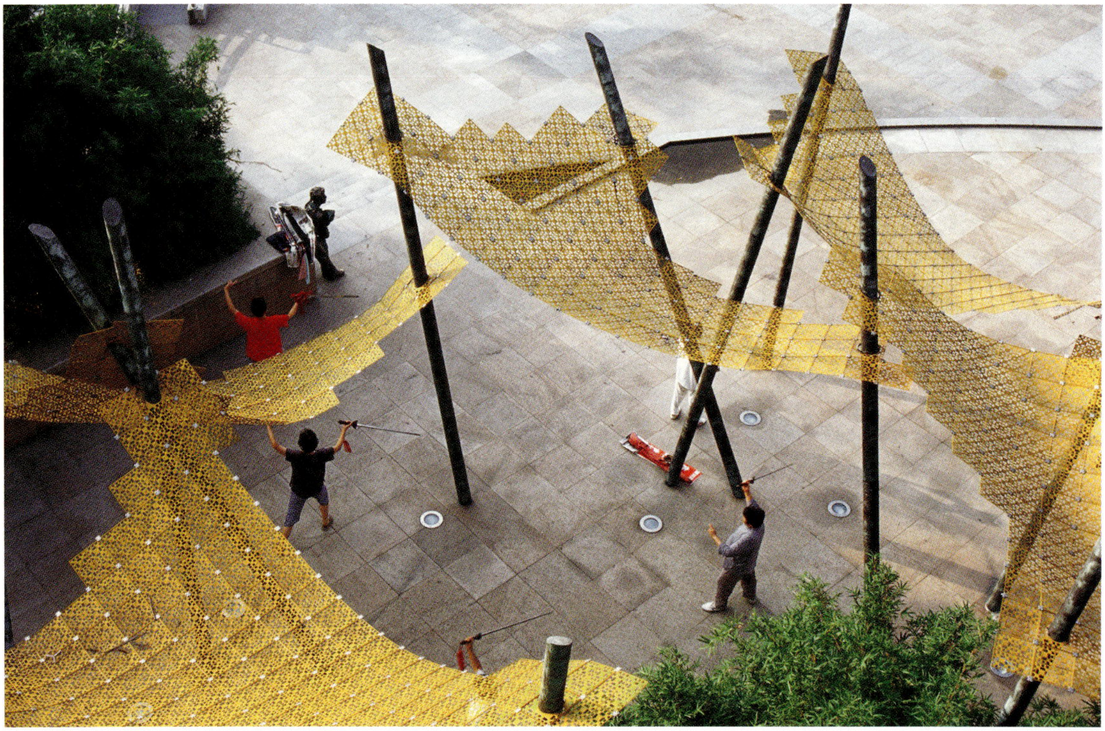

The park and square are defined by art works integrated into residents' daily habits. The focal point is a central sculpture some 100 ft tall.

Le parc et la place sont définis par des œuvres d'art intégrées dans la vie quotidienne de la population. L'élément central du projet est une sculpture de 30 m de haut.

Park und Platz werden durch Kunstwerke geprägt, die in den täglichen Gebrauch durch die Bevölkerung integriert sind. Den Mittelpunkt bildet eine zentrale Skulptur von 30 m Höhe.

Kunstwerken die zijn opgenomen in het dagelijkse gebruik van de bevolking spelen een belangrijke rol in het park en op het plein. Het middelpunt van het ontwerp is een centraal gelegen, 30 m hoog beeldhouwwerk.

Renovation of Čufarjev Square

Jesenice, Slovenia

The Slovenian government wanted a square designed as an open public space with the presence of water. The result was a triangular plaza covering 43,000 sq ft, which has become a landmark in the city of Jesenice. The space is the venue for different events, such as the open-air market, concerts, and art installations.

Le gouvernement slovène voulait faire construire une place conçue comme un espace public ouvert, où l'eau devait être présente. Jesenice a finalement accueilli cette place triangulaire de 4 000 m², qui est devenue un point de référence dans la ville. Divers évènements sont organisés dans cet espace: marché de plein air, concerts de musique et installations d'art.

Die slowenische Regierung wünschte einen Platz, der als offener Raum dienen und das Element Wasser einbeziehen sollte. Das Ergebnis ist ein dreieckiger, 4000 m² großer Platz, der zum Bezugspunkt der Stadt Jesenice geworden ist. Auf dem Platz finden verschiedene Veranstaltungen wie der Markt unter freiem Himmel, Konzerte und Kunstinstallationen statt.

De Sloveense regering wenste een plein als openbare ruimte met water. Het resultaat was een driehoekig plein van 4000 m² dat ondertussen een referentiepunt van de stad Jesenice is geworden. Er worden verschillende evenementen ondergebracht zoals een openluchtmarkt, muziekconcerten en kunsttentoonstellingen.

Scapelab
www.scapelab.com
© Miran Kambič, Scapelab

Water jets shoot up from the asphalt of the center of the plaza painted in white lines that change color, turning bright blue, red, and yellow.

Des jets d'eau jaillissent de la partie centrale bitumée de la place, ornée de lignes passant du blanc à des couleurs vives comme le bleu, le rouge et le jaune.

In der Platzmitte entspringen Wasserfontänen aus dem Asphalt, der mit weißen Linien bemalt ist, deren Farbe sich in ein lebendiges Blau, Rot oder Gelb verwandeln kann.

In het midden van het plein spuiten waterstralen uit het asfalt, dat is geverfd met witte lijnen die kunnen veranderen in felle kleuren zoals blauw, rood en geel.

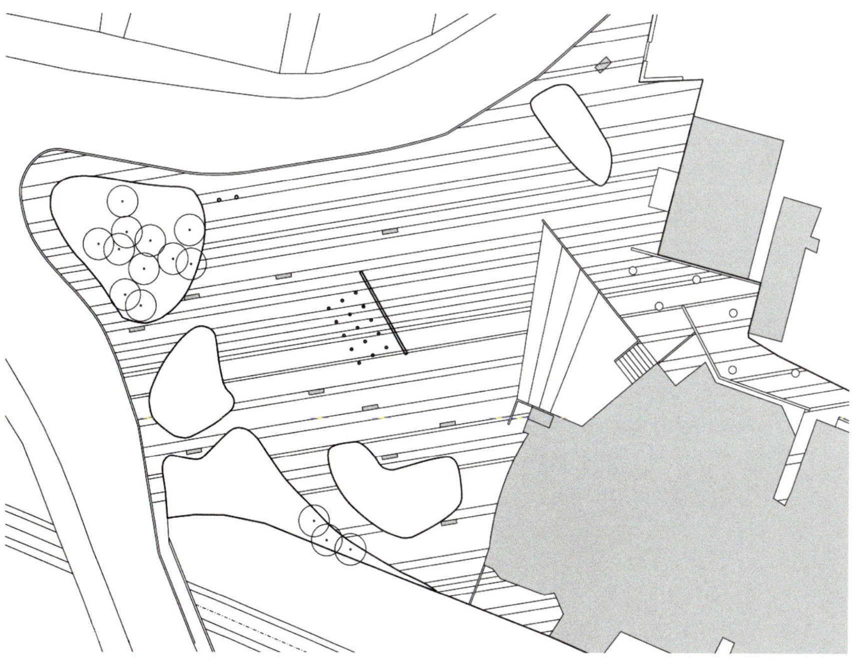

Plan

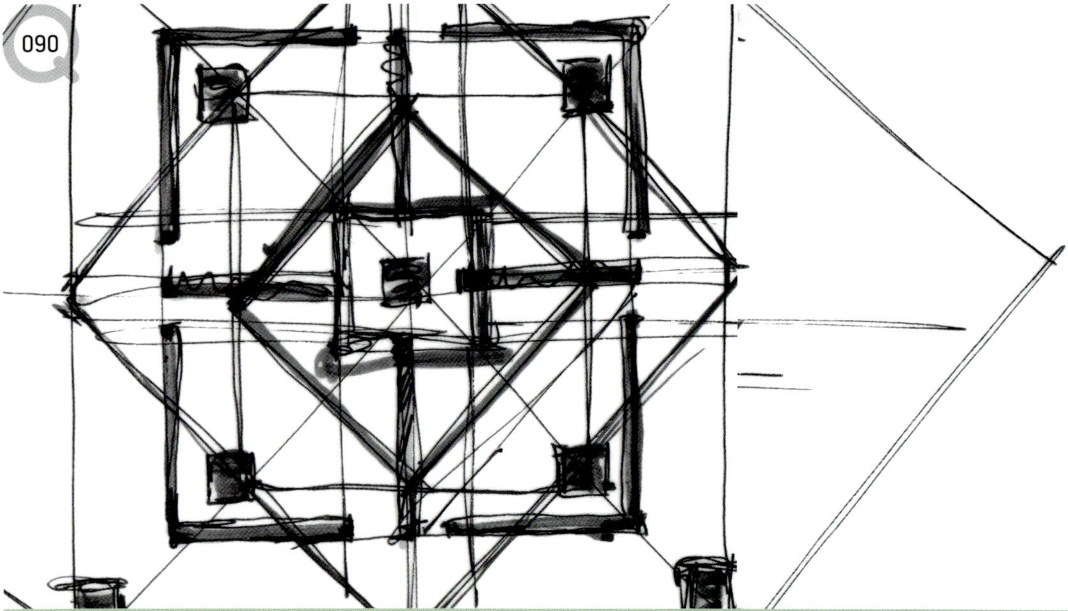

Fountain on Place du nombre d'Or

Montpellier, France

Located at the heart of the Antigone district, this 97,000 sq ft space was designed by the architect Ricardo Bofill. The project is part of a plan for the building of 100 fountains. The winner of the design competition based his idea on the geometry of the golden number "nombre d'or," which gives its name to the square.

Situé au centre névralgique du quartier d'Antigone, cet espace de 9 000 m^2 a été conçu par l'architecte Ricardo Bofill. L'ouvrage fait partie d'un plan relatif à la construction de 100 fontaines. Le lauréat du concours a imaginé son œuvre en se basant sur la géométrie de la section dorée, le « nombre d'or».

Im neuralgischen Zentrum des Stadtteils Antigone wurde das 9000 m^2 große Gebiet von dem Architekten Ricardo Bofill entworfen. Das Projekt ist Teil eines Plans für den Bau von 100 Brunnen. Der Entwurf des Gewinners des Wettbewerbs basiert auf der Geometrie des goldenen Schnitts.

Dit project van 9000 m^2 in het hart van de wijk Antigone werd ontworpen door de architect Ricardo Bofill. Het maakt deel uit van een plan voor de aanleg van 100 fonteinen. De winnaar van de aanbesteding ontwierp zijn werk op basis van de geometrie van de gulden snede, de "nombre d'or".

JLM Arquitectura del agua
www.jeanmaxllorca.com
© JLM Arquitectura del agua

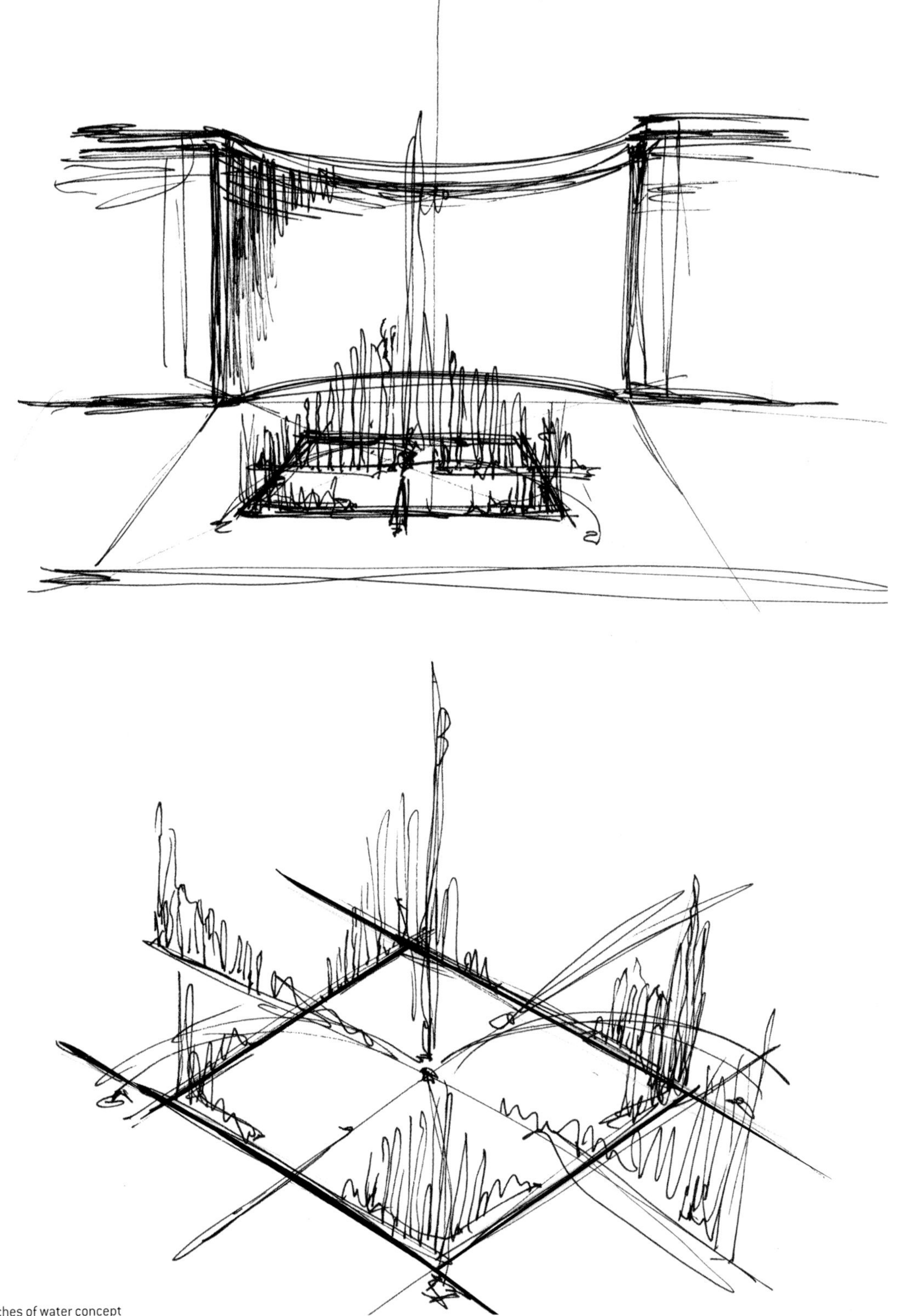

Sketches of water concept

The fountain is an interaction between squares and triangles. Water jets emerge from the ground to form pyramid shapes.

La fontaine est composée de carrés et de triangles qui interagissent entre eux. Des jets d'eau chaude jaillissent du sol en formant des figures pyramidales.

Der Brunnen setzt sich aus Quadraten und Dreiecken zusammen. Aus dem Boden entspringen Fontänen mit heißem Wasser und bilden pyramidenförmige Figuren.

De fontein bestaat uit een wisselwerking van vierkanten en driehoeken. Uit de grond komen warme waterstralen die piramidale figuren vormen.

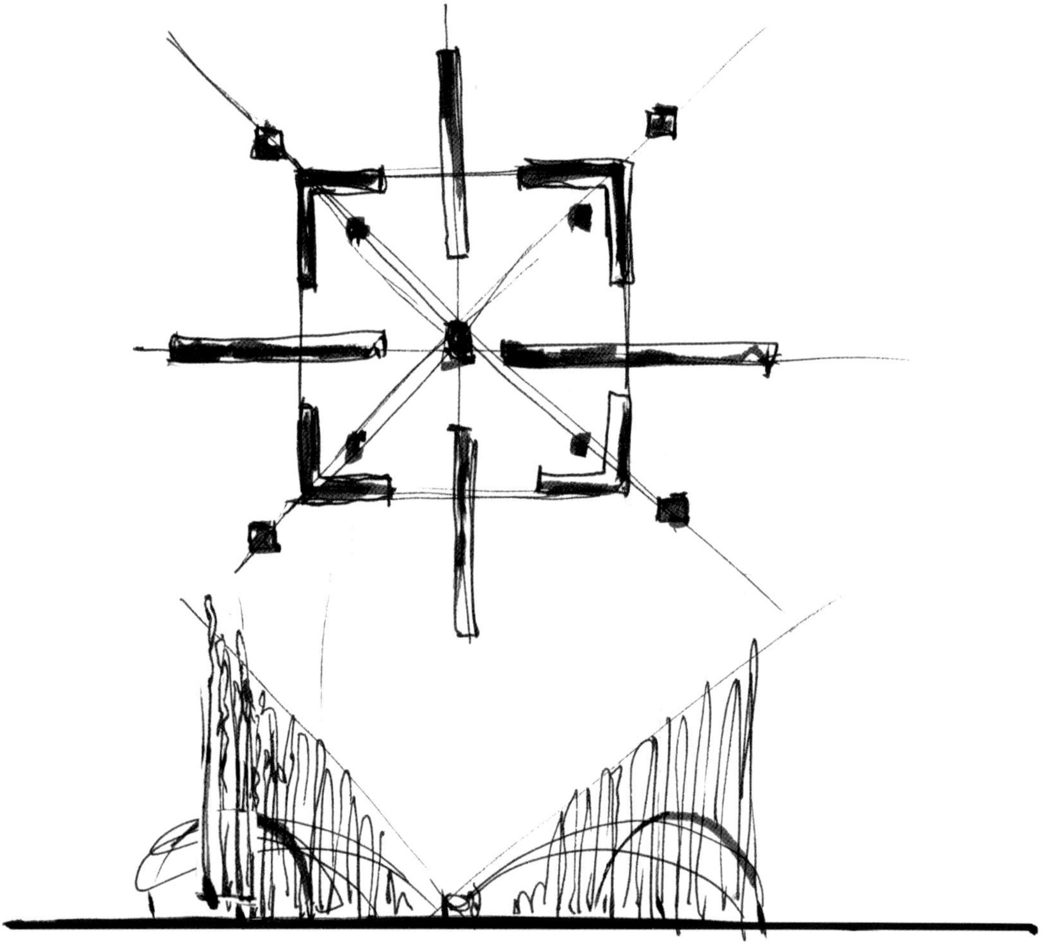

Sketch of plan and section

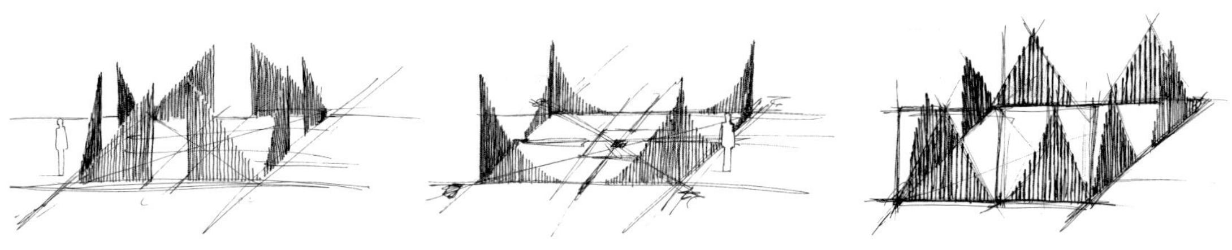

Sketches of water concept

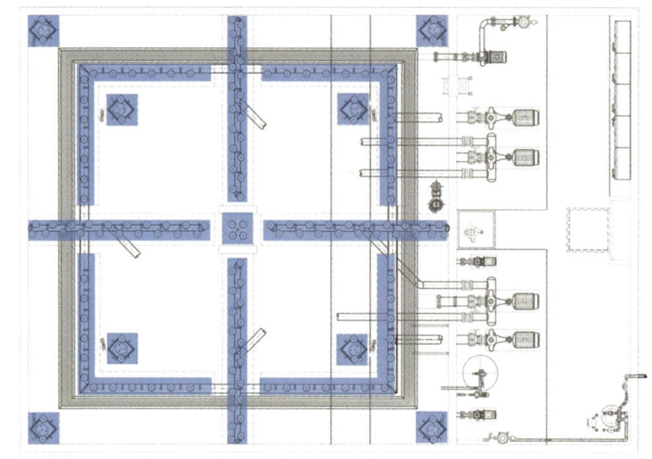

Detailled plan of water inlet

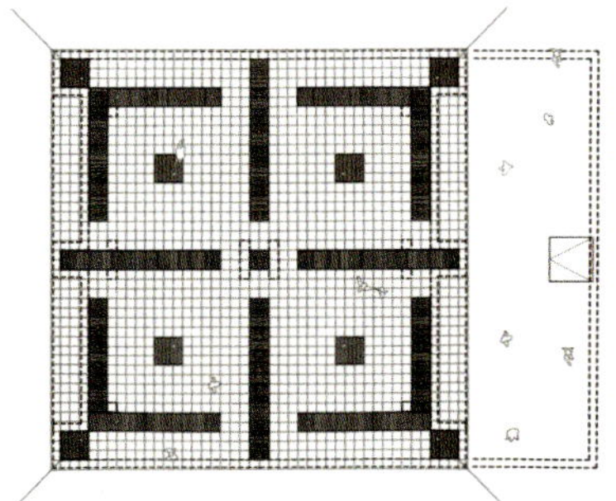

Plan of water inlet

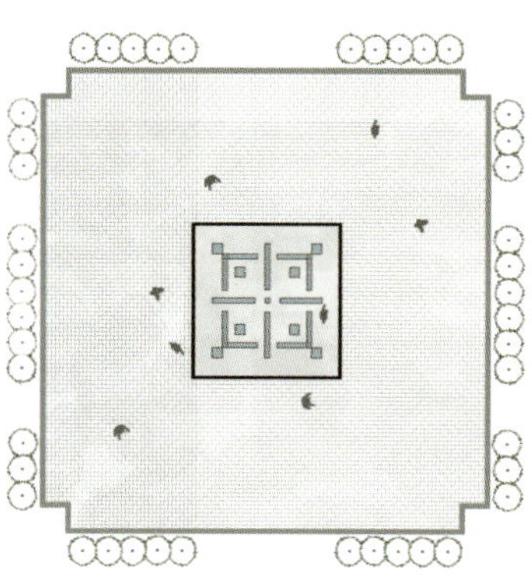

General plan

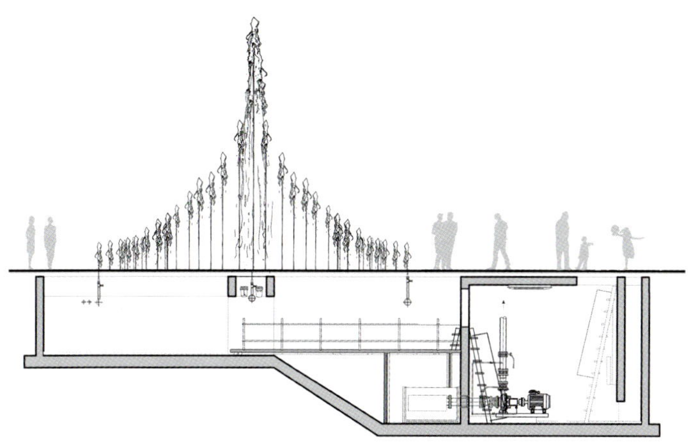

Section of water outlet

Robin Hood children's playground

The Hague, The Netherlands

This project was designed by a teacher for the purpose of providing children over the age of five with a suitable space and which would form part of the natural environment of The Hague Forest. The park was designed around the legendary figure of Robin Hood.

Ce projet a été imaginé par un professeur dont l'objectif était d'offrir un espace adapté à des enfants âgés de plus de cinq ans et pleinement intégré à l'environnement naturel du bois de La Haye. La thématique du parc pour enfants est consacrée au personnage de Robin des Bois.

Dieses Projekt wurde von einem Lehrer mit dem Ziel entworfen, Kindern ab fünf Jahren einen angemessenen Raum zu bieten, der sich in die natürliche Umgebung des Waldes von Den Haag einfügt. Das Leitmotiv für den Spielplatz bildete Robin Hood.

Dit project werd bedacht door een docent. Zijn doel was om een ruimte te bieden die geschikt is voor kinderen vanaf vijf jaar en die in de natuurlijke sfeer van het Haagse Bos past. Het thema van de natuurspeelplaats is Robin Hood.

Jos van der Lindeloof
www.josvandelindeloof.nl
© Ruud van Zwet, Jos van das Lindeloof (drawings)

In the middle of the children's garden there is a wooden throne and a number of chairs, which is the starting point for three play areas: a zip-line, a space with trampolines, and a climbing wall.

Au centre du jardin pour enfants se trouvent un trône en bois et des chaises, point de départ de trois itinéraires ludiques : une tyrolienne, des trampolines et un mur d'escalade.

In der Mitte befinden sich ein hölzerner Thron und einige Stühle, von wo aus drei Wege mit Spielgeräten (Seilrutsche, Trampoline, Kletterwand) ausgehen.

In het midden van de natuurspeelplaats bevinden zich een houten troon met stoeltjes eromheen. Vanuit dit centrale punt vertrekken er drie ludieke routes: een kabelbaan, een trampolinepad en een klimwand.

Drawing made by a child about his vision of a great playgroun (as part a wordshop with surrounding schools)

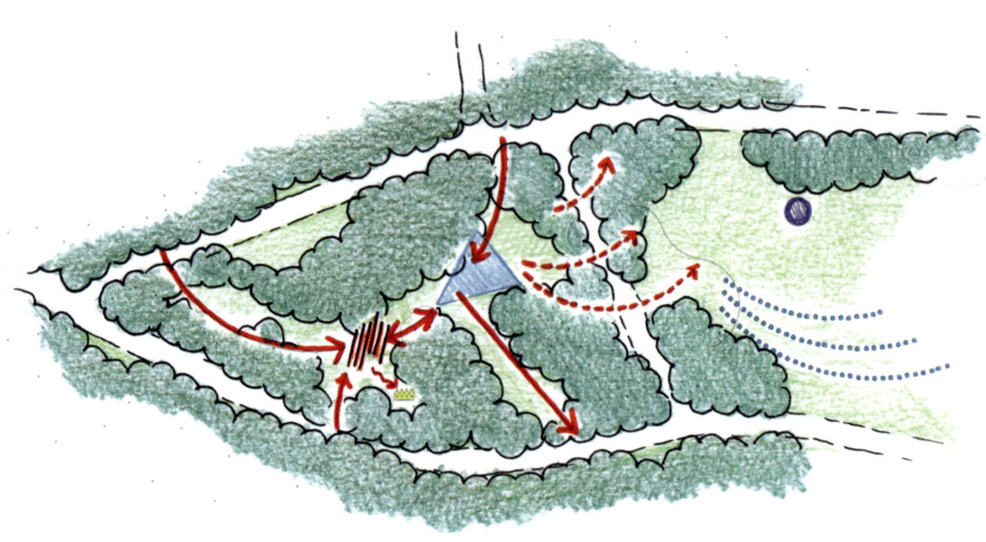

Drawing made by a child about his vision of a great playground

Situation sketch of installations

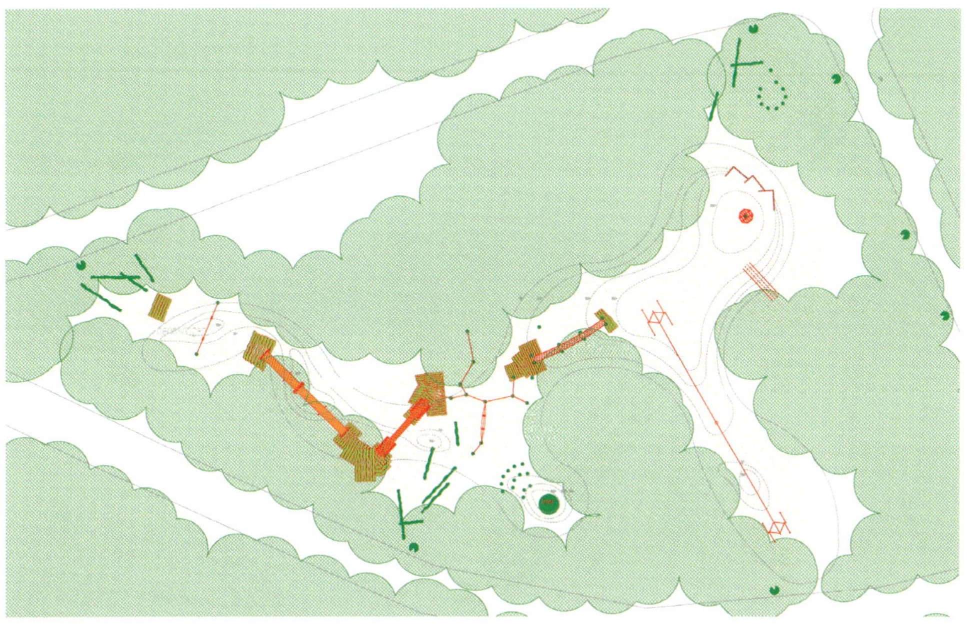

General plan

Robin Hood

in het Haagse Bos

Situation plan

Presentation collage

Hoge Weide Park

Utrecht, The Netherlands

The triangular park area contains different landscapes comprising small hills, slopes, winding paths, and vegetation. In the middle, among the hills, the paths wind through wooded gardens.

La zone du parc de forme triangulaire abrite plusieurs paysages composés de petites collines, de pentes, de chemins sinueux et de végétation. Au centre, les sentiers sillonnent des jardins boisés entre les collines.

Der dreieckig geformte Park umfasst verschiedene Landschaften aus kleinen Hügeln, Abhängen, gekrümmten Pfaden und Pflanzen. Im mittleren Teil, zwischen den Hügeln, befinden sich die baumbestandenen Gärten.

De driehoekige parkzone omvat verschillende landschappen bestaand uit kleine heuvels, hellingen, kronkelige paden en planten. In het midden, tussen de heuvels, lopen de wandelpaden in de tuinen met bomen.

Edwin Santhagens/Buro Sant en Co
www.santenco.nl
© Edwin Santhagens, Monique de Vette, Edwin Santhagens/Buro Sant en Co (drawings)

The recreation areas, designed to be both functional and beautiful, provide the urban area with a living space. A stainless steel oval-shaped ring provides strong visual impact.

Les aires de loisirs, conçues pour apporter fonctionnalité et esthétisme, façonnent un espace vital au cœur d'une zone urbaine. La présence d'une couronne ovale en acier inoxydable provoque un impact visuel fort.

Die mit Augenmerk auf funktionelle und ästhetische Aspekte entworfenen Freizeitbereiche schaffen einen lebendigen Raum. Ein ovaler Edelstahlring ruft einen starken visuellen Eindruck hervor.

De recreatiezones, die het park niet alleen mooi maar ook nuttig maken, creëren een vitale ruimte binnen een stadszone. Een ovaalvormige ring van roestvrij staal maakt een sterke visuele indruk.

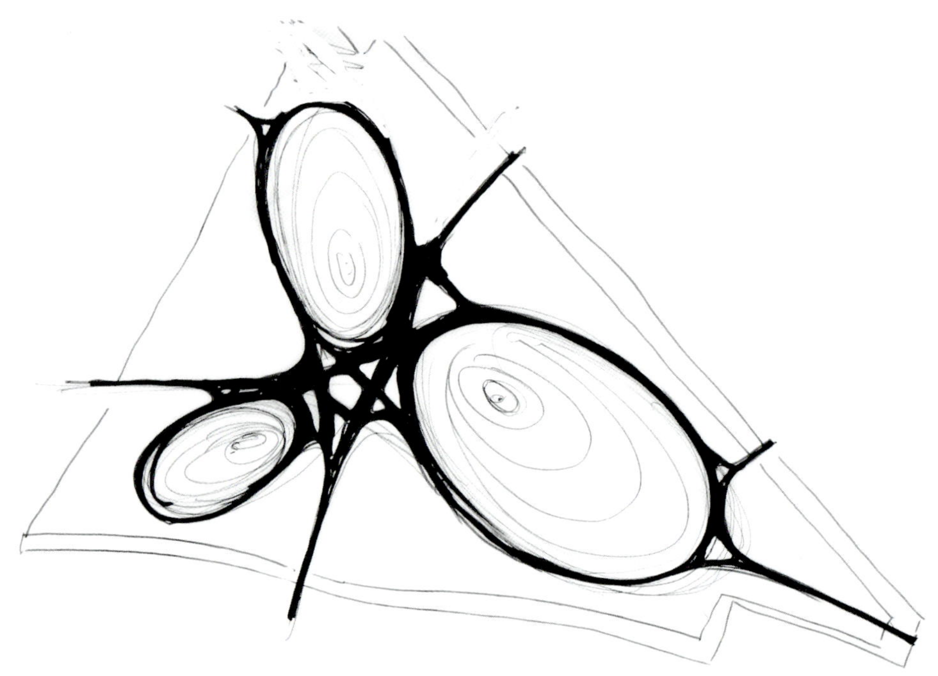

Sketch of general view

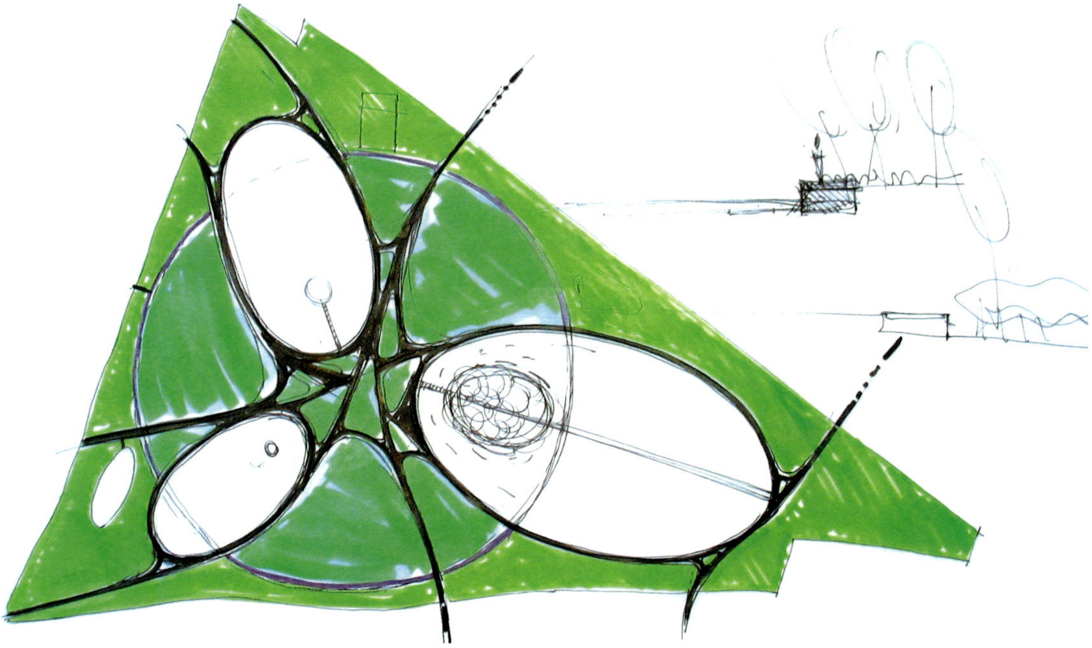

Colored sketch of general view

General plan

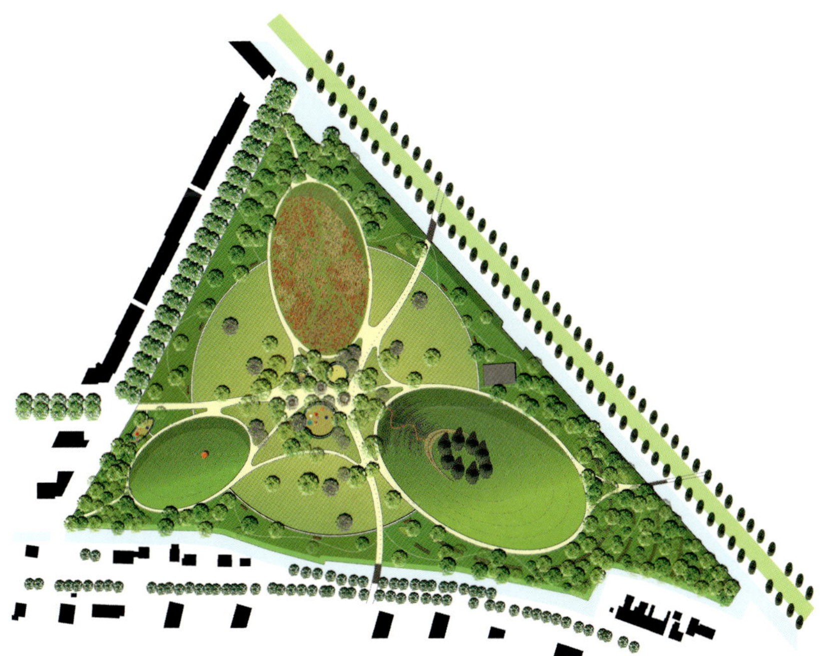

General plan

Model

3D rendering of general view

Sketch of swing

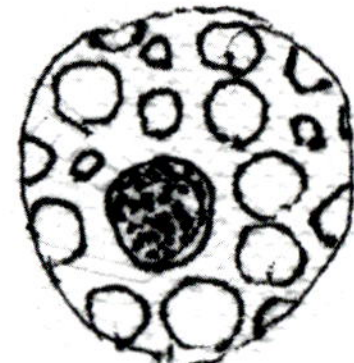
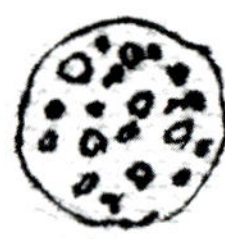
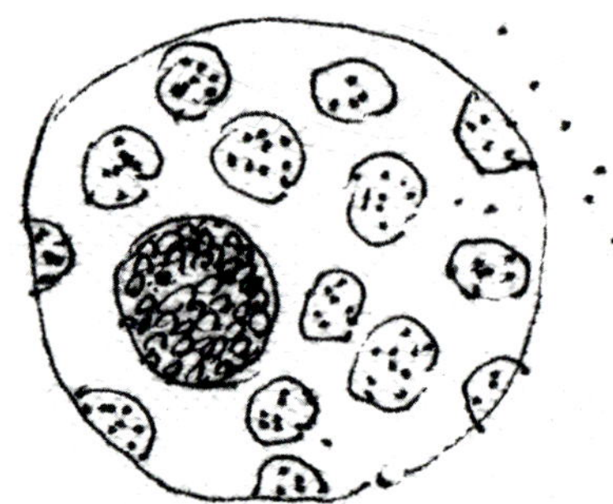

Green Shift

Montreal, Canada

A rubber surface on which a number of huge green buoys are surrounded by plants describes a temporary installation forming part of a biennial exhibition held in Montreal. The project combined a cutting edge garden with a relaxation area.

L'installation temporaire, faisant partie de l'exposition biannuelle célébrée à Montréal, est composée d'une surface en caoutchouc entourée de végétation, sur laquelle sont installées d'énormes bouées vertes. Le projet a permis de combiner un jardin d'avant-garde et une zone de détente.

Eine Fläche aus Kautschuk, auf der riesige grüne Bojen angebracht sind, und die diese umgebenden Pflanzen bilden die temporäre Installation der Biennale von Montreal. Der Entwurf verband einen avantgardistischen Garten mit einer Ruhezone.

Een rubberen oppervlak, met daarop enorm grote groene boeien en begroeiing er omheen, is een tijdelijke installatie die deel heeft uitgemaakt van de tweejaarlijkse tentoonstelling in Montreal. Het project koppelde een avant-gardistische tuin aan een ontspanningszone.

NIPpaysage
www.nippaysage.ca
© NIPpaysage

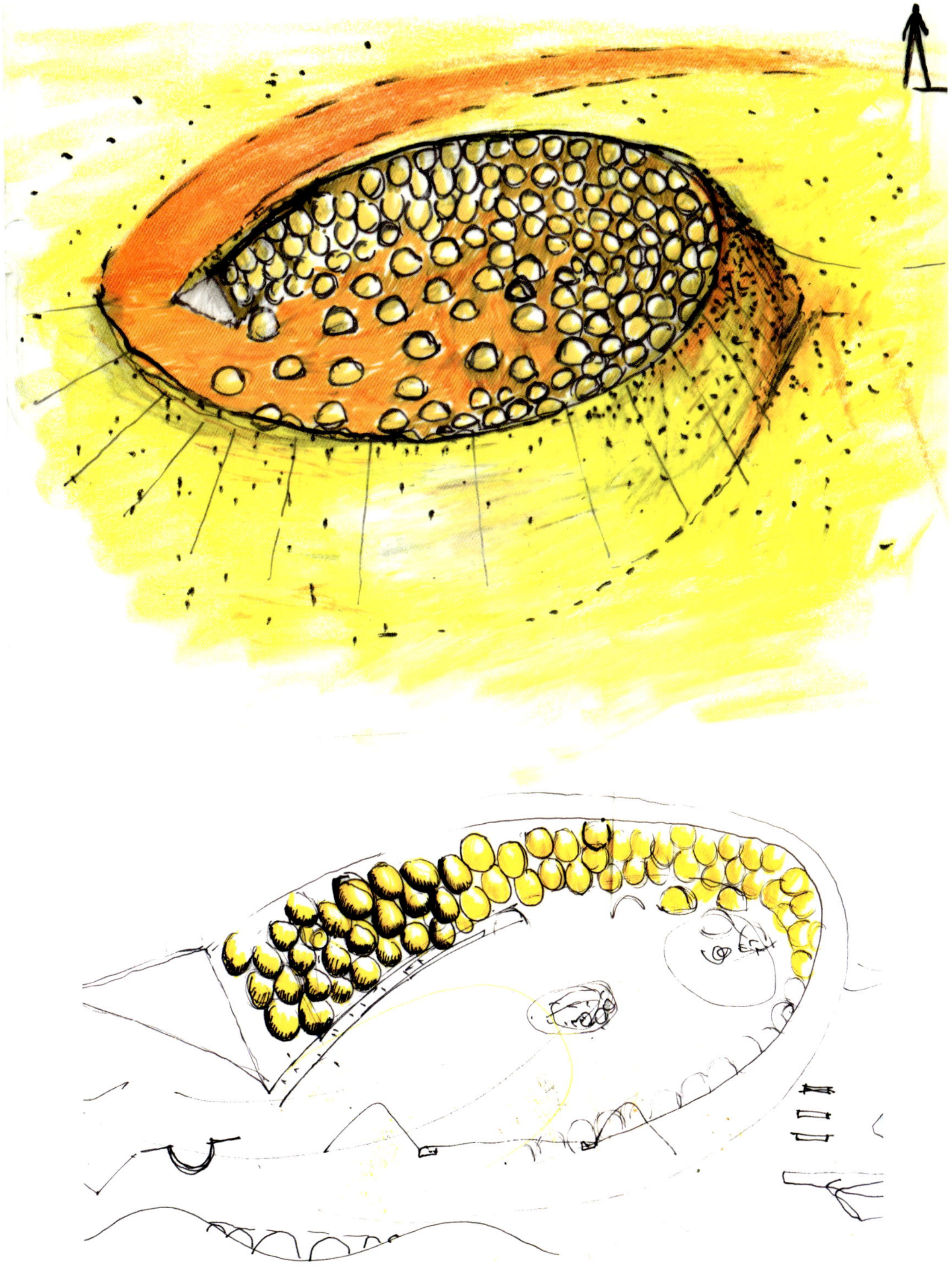

Development studies

contraste
int/ext.
comme ;
ANALOGIE QUI
POURRAIT ÊTRE .

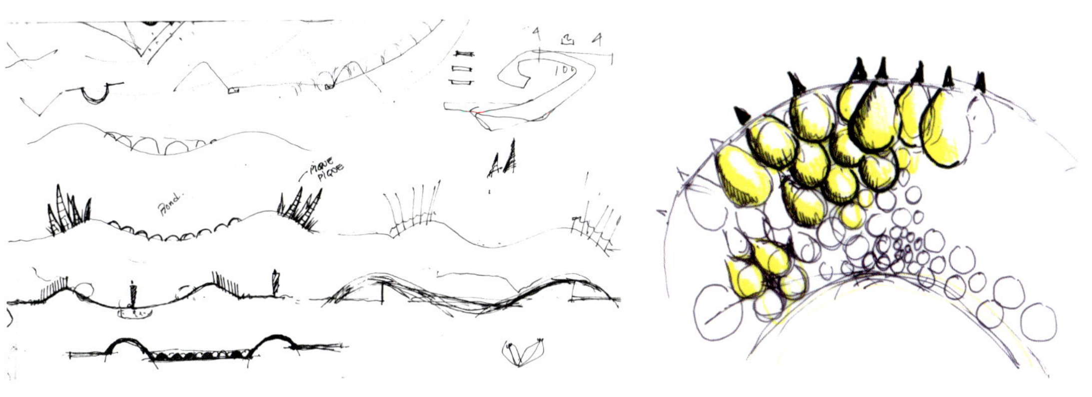

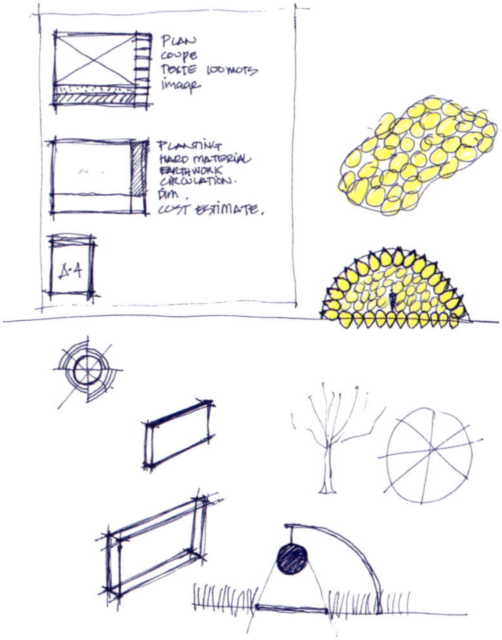

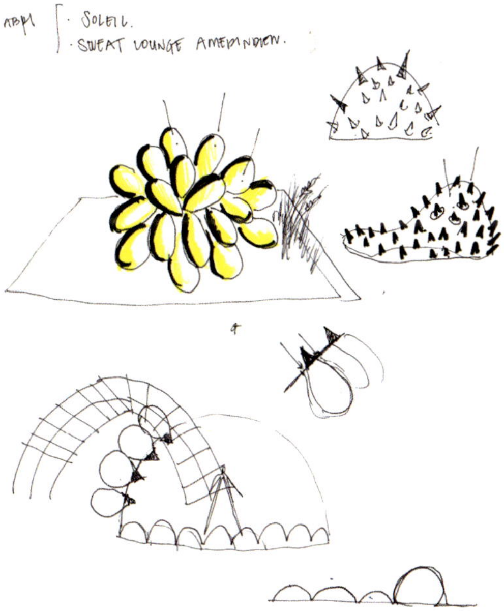

Development studies

Sketch of solar concept

Collage of playground concept

The rubber surface and the buoys created a
buzz with visitors as they were able to sit,
lie, rest, jump, and play on them.

*Les visiteurs sont restés stupéfaits devant
la surface en caoutchouc et les bouées qui
leur ont permis de s'asseoir, de s'allonger,
de se reposer, de sauter et de jouer.*

*Gummibelag und Bojen weckten Erwartun-
gen bei den Besuchern und erlaubten ihnen,
sich auszuruhen, über sie zu springen und
auf ihnen zu spielen.*

*Het rubberen oppervlak en de boeien wek-
ten allerlei verwachtingen bij de bezoekers.
Zij konden erop gaan zitten, liggen, uitrus-
ten, springen en spelen.*

Collage of playground concept

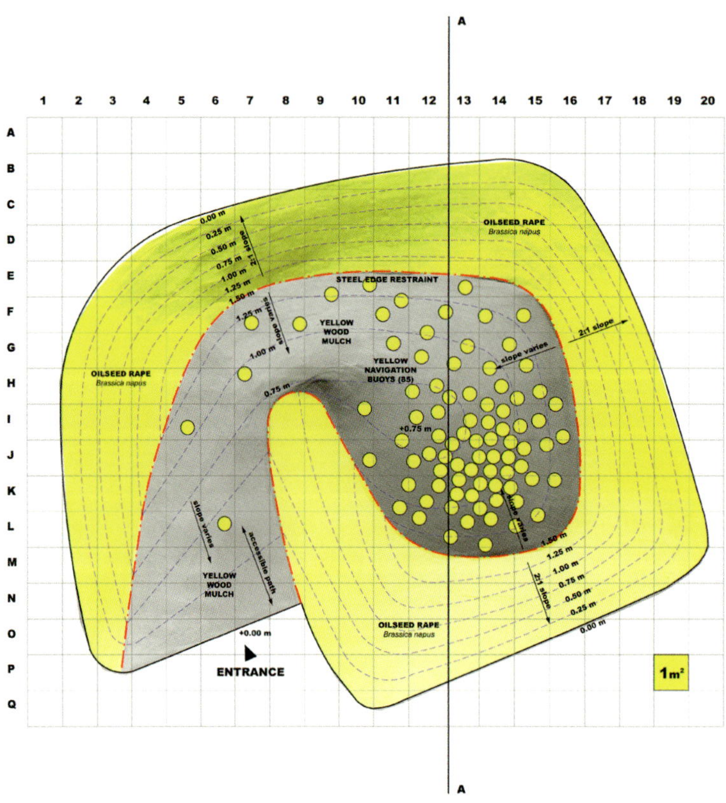

Topographical plan

Collage of playground concept

Green Axis 13

Messestadt Riem, Germany

The park is located between new suburbs built on the site of the old München-Reim Airport in Munich. The project consisted of the building of a green area to join another park in the southern sector, connecting the developed area with another undeveloped area.

Le parc s'étend entre les zones résidentielles construites sur les terrains de l'ancien aéroport München-Riem. Le projet consiste en la construction d'un espace vert qui débouche sur un autre parc par le sud et sert de jonction entre un espace urbanisé et un terrain vague.

Der Park erstreckt sich zwischen den Wohngebieten auf dem Gelände des ehemaligen Flughafens München-Riem. Die Gestaltung besteht aus der Anlage einer Grünzone, die in einen weiteren Park im Süden mündet und als Verbindung zwischen einem bebauten und einem unbebauten Raum dient.

Het park strekt zich uit tussen de woonwijken die zijn gebouwd op het terrein van de voormalige luchthaven München-Riem. Het project bestaat uit de aanleg van een groenzone die in het zuiden uitmondt in een ander park en fungeert als overgang tussen een bebouwde en een onbebouwde zone.

Burger Landschaftsarchitekten
www.burgerlandschaftsarchitekten.de
© Florian Holzherr, Rakete,
Burger Landschaftsarchitekten
(drawings)

A gravel promenade with rest areas, lawns, children's playgrounds, and a pavilion form the main axis of this park in eastern Munich.

Ce grand axe situé à l'est de Munich est composé d'un pavillon et d'une promenade recouverte de gravier le long de laquelle des zones de détente, des pelouses et des aires de jeux pour enfants sont aménagées.

Ein Kiesweg mit Ruhezonen, Rasenflächen, Kinderspielplätzen und einem Pavillon bilden diese große Achse im Osten von München.

Een grindpad met rustzones, grasvelden, speeltuinen en een paviljoen vormen deze grote as ten oosten van München.

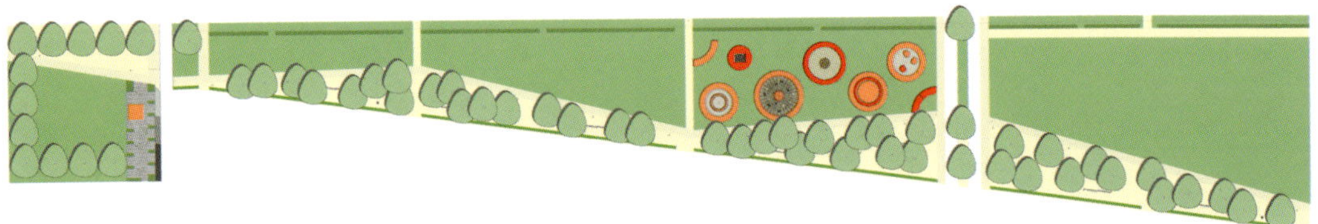

Plan

Queens Botanical Garden and Visitor & Administration Center New York, NY, USA

The Queens Botanical Garden has water as a main feature – different actions were taken to prevent wastage, leading to rainwater to be harvested and reused; and water is combined with different long-lasting materials such as stone, steel, and concrete.

Dans le jardin botanique de Queens, l'eau joue un rôle prépondérant : des mesures ont été prises pour éviter le gaspillage de cette ressource, comme la collecte et la réutilisation des eaux pluviales, ou encore l'emploi de matériaux durables comme la pierre, l'acier et le béton.

Im botanischen Garten von Queens spielt das Wasser eine wichtige Rolle: Um die Wasserverschwendung zu vermeiden, wurden die Entwürfe so ausgeführt, dass Regenwasser aufgefangen und wieder verwendet wird. Dabei wurden dauerhafte Materialien wie Stein, Stahl und Beton verwendet.

In de botanische tuin van Queens speelt water een belangrijke rol: de tuin werd omgebouwd om te voorkomen dat er water wordt verspild. Regenwater wordt opgeslagen en hergebruikt en er wordt gewerkt met duurzame materialen zoals steen, staal en beton.

 Atelier Dreiseitl, Conservation Design Forum, BKSK Architects
www.dreiseitl.com
© Atelier Dreiseitl

Perspective sketch of the Wedding Garden

Sketch

Water-centered settings were designed with different textures and features where water is combined with steel, concrete, and stone.

Des décors aquatiques aux textures et caractéristiques variées prennent forme grâce au mariage entre l'eau, l'acier, le béton et la pierre.

Aufgrund der Kombination von Wasser, Stahl, Beton und Stein zeichnen sich Wasser-szenarien mit unterschiedlichen Merkmalen ab.

Er worden watertaferelen met diverse texturen en eigenschappen gevormd dankzij de combinatie van water met staal, beton en steen.

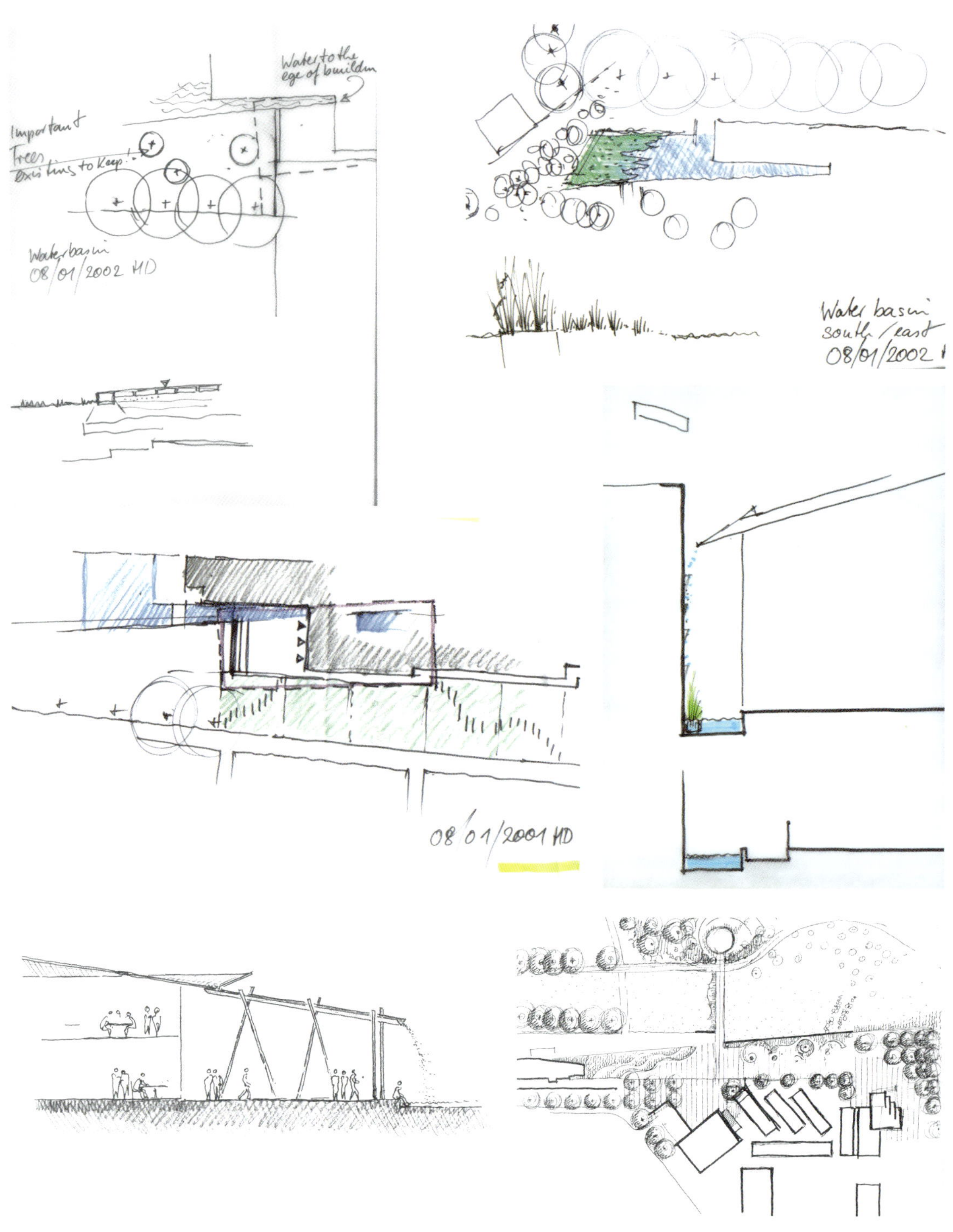

Schematic design of the Adm. Center Building and the water system

Sketch of Central Plaza

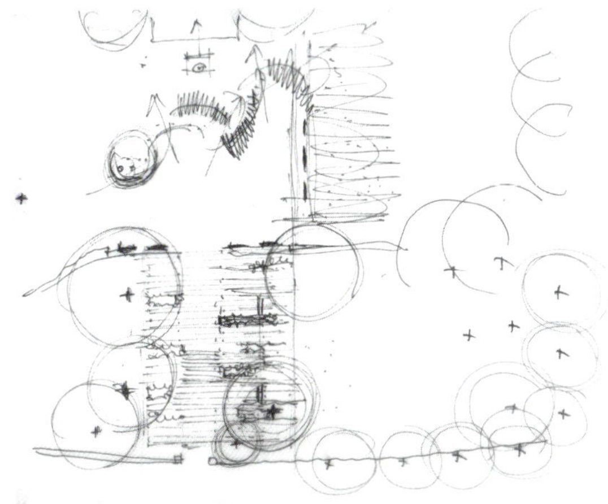

Schematic design of the entrance

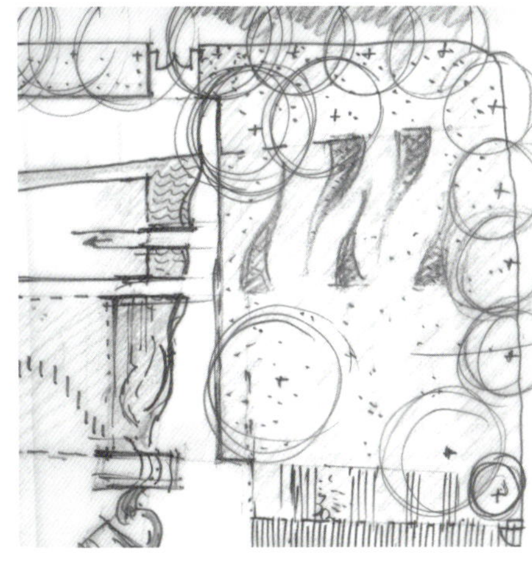

Schematic design of the green roof concept

Perspective sketch of the entrance area

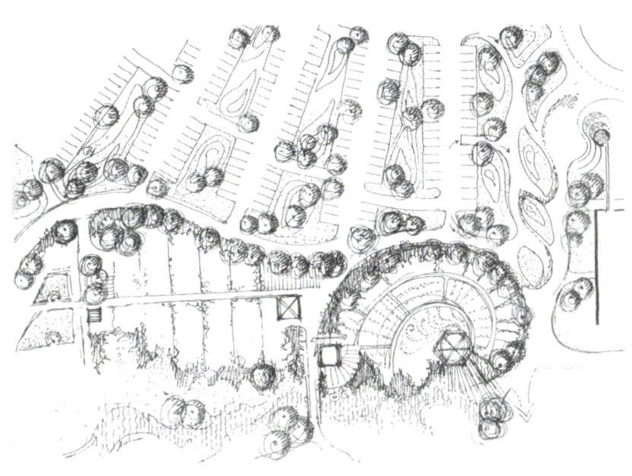

Sketch of the main entrance area

Sketch of an overview perspective

Sketch of irrigation system

Schematic design of the channel wall

Sketch of Sun and Moon Garden

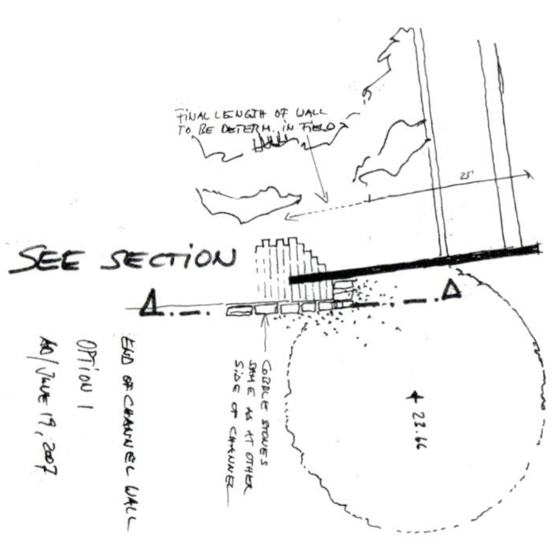

Concep collage of Fog Sails sculpture in Sun and Moon Garden

Schematic design of the channel wall

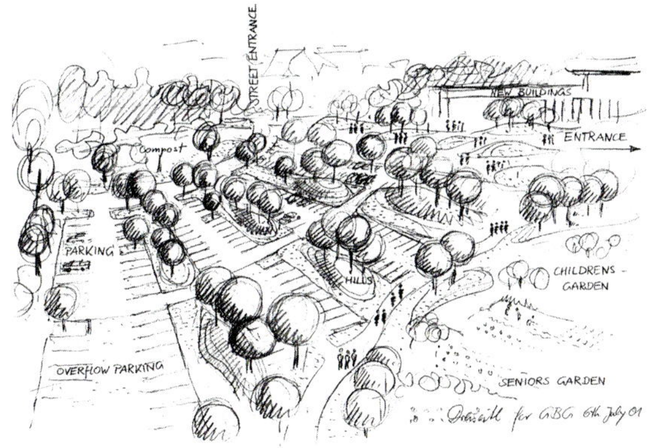

Aerial sketch of the parking area

Aerial color sketch of the parking area

The Parking Concept

The parking is envisioned as green fingers which extend into the Garden and are an integrated part of the landscape. Parking areas are shaped by broad areas of planting (a) which provide character and shade and are in themselves planting displays. Areas of overflow parking are surfaced with grass-gravel (b), which allows the parking spaces to seam with the adjacent landscape when not in use and facitilitates stormwater infiltration. Areas of high use parking are surfaced with permeable paving (c). These surface is hard wearing without the monotony of asphalt, and also allow some infiltration. These paved areas are broken up by areas of planting which extend into the parking bays, emphasizing the overall green character of the parking.

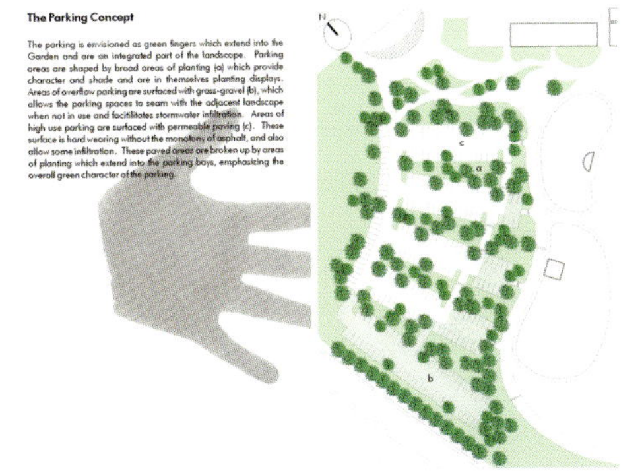

The Parking Drainage

The whole parking surface is composed of permeable to semi-permeable surfaces which allow direct infiltration of rainwater. In cases where there is too much rainfall to be able to all infiltrate directly into the surface (d), it runs into swales (e) - vegetated depressions with high infiltration capacity which run along the planting islands in the parking. These swales have a capacity to handle the majority of rainfalls. In extreme storm events, the swales overflow to the central wetland area (f), ensuring that the parking does not remain water logged.

The planted surfaces of the grass-gravel and swales, and the soil underneath the permeable paving play an important role in treating the surface run-off from the parking. Parked cars drop residues of oil, salt and dirt. This is broken up by micro-bacteria living in the top soil layer.

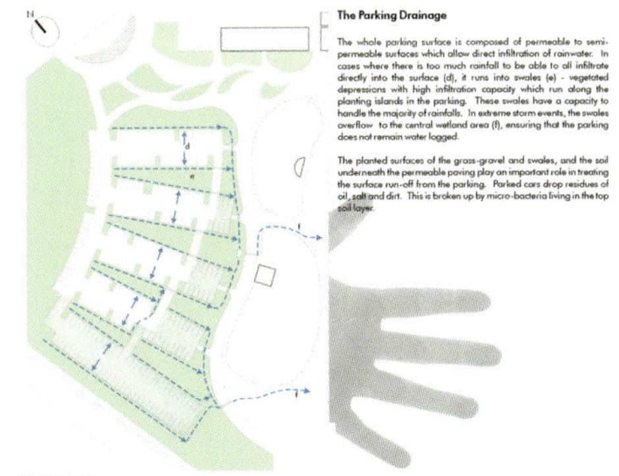

Drawings of the parking concept and the parking drainage system

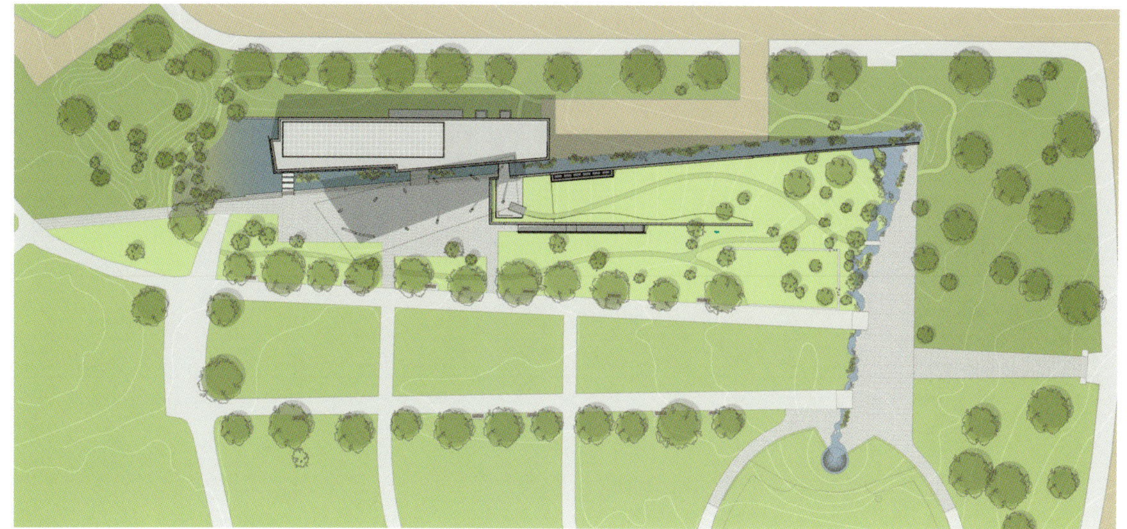

Site plan

Aerial sketch of Hiltop Garden

Master plan

1. Main gate / Tree sculpture	7. Maintenance building	13. Couples garden
2. Administration Building	8. Vehicular drop-off	14. Sun and Moon Garden
3. Green roof	9. Central Plaza/Water play	15. Players green
4. Water collector roof	10. Parking garden	16. Prairie
5. Photovoltaic roof	11. Gardens on parade	17. Wetland
6. Terrace	12. Woodland	18. Bee City / Bird Garden

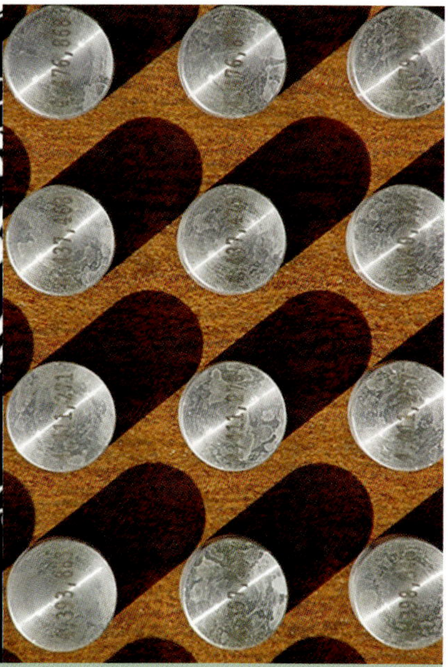

Medtronic Corporation Patent Garden

Fridley, MN, USA

This Zen-inspired courtyard was designed for the Medtronic campus. Located between a car park and a walkway, it was designed as an area for contemplation, inspiration, and celebration for the more than 3,000 patents achieved by the company's teams of scientists and engineers.

La cour intérieure, d'inspiration nettement zen, a été réalisée dans le campus de l'entreprise Medtronic. Elle est située entre une zone de stationnement et une voie piétonne. Elle a été conçue comme un espace de contemplation, d'inspiration et de célébration des quelques 3 000 brevets déposés par l'équipe de scientifiques et d'ingénieurs.

Der Zen-inspirierte Innenhof wurde auf dem Gelände der Firma Medtronic entworfen. Er befindet sich zwischen einem Parkplatz und einem Fußweg. Er wurde als Ort der Besinnung, der Inspiration und zum Feiern der über 3000 Patente geplant, die vom Firmenteam erlangt wurden.

Deze duidelijk op zen geïnspireerde binnenplaats is aangelegd op de campus van het bedrijf Medtronic. Zij is gelegen tussen een parkeerplaats en een voetpad. Zij werd bedacht als ruimte voor overpeinzing en inspiratie en viert de meer dan 3000 octrooien die het team wetenschappers en ingenieurs toegewezen heeft gekregen.

 Oslund.and.assoc.
www.oaala.com
© George Heinrich, Tadd Kreun, Peter Vevang, Oslund.and assoc. (drawings)

The courtyard is rectangular, with two sides measuring 100 ft. It features crushed stone surfaces with a small grassed circle in the center partially enclosed by panels of weathered steel.

De forme rectangulaire, la cour est longue de 30 m. Sa surface est revêtue de pierre concassée et un cercle recouvert de gazon se dresse en son centre, à moitié clôturé par des planches en acier Corten.

Der Hof ist rechteckig mit 30 m Seitenlänge. Er umfasst Flächen aus zerstoßenem Stein, und in der Mitte erhebt sich ein mit Rasen bepflanzter Kreis, der halb durch Corten-stahlplatten geschlossen ist.

De binnenplaats is rechthoekig met zijden van 30 m. Er zijn oppervlakken van fijn-gestampte stenen en in het midden verheft zich een cirkel met gras, half afgesloten door cortenstalen platen.

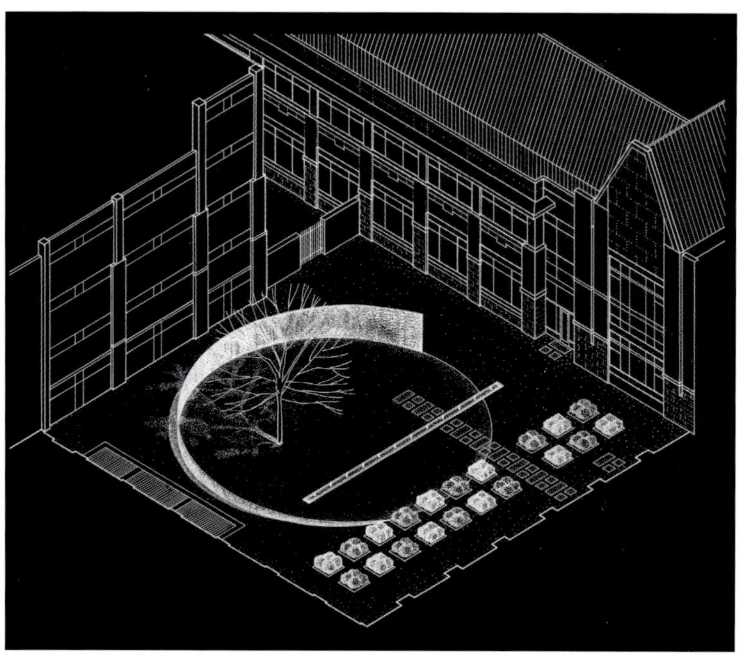

Axonometric view of the garden

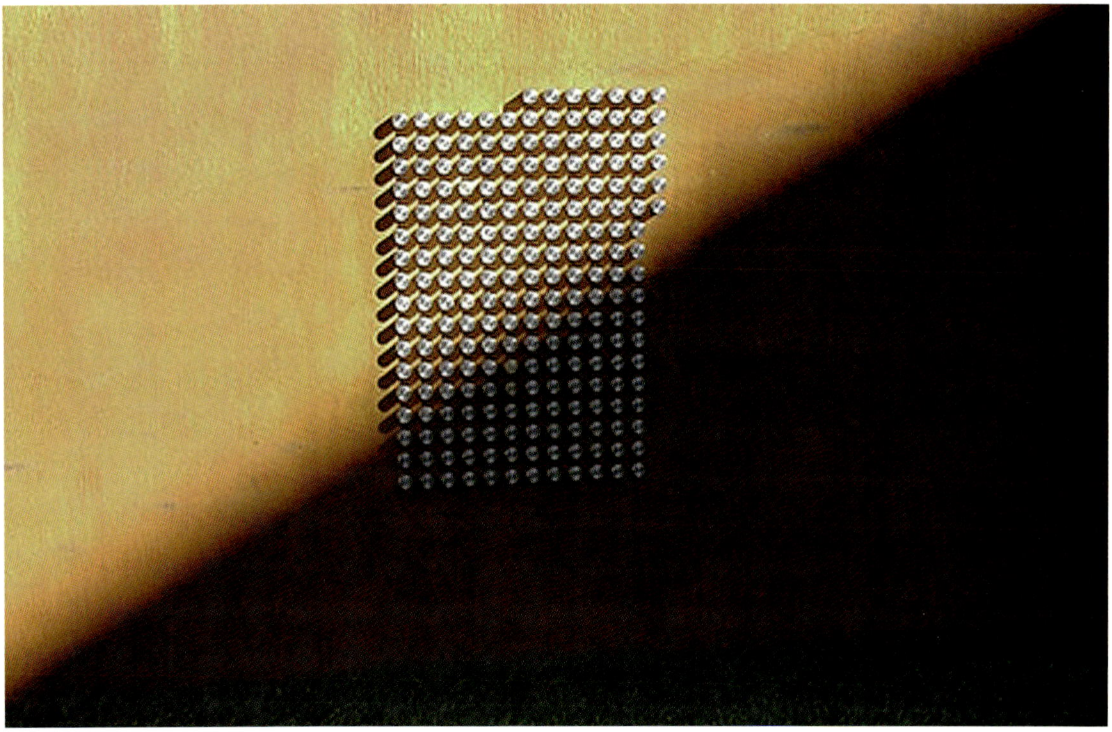

Raglan Street Parkland

Port Melbourne, Australia

The landscape architects' main objective is to revitalize urban areas that are no longer appealing to users and visitors. Raglan Street Parkland is an example of this, as it had become neglected and not very pleasing to the eye. A timber wall was built and several features promoting neighbor interaction were installed.

L'objectif principal des architectes paysagistes est de redonner vie à des zones urbaines qui ne sont plus attractives pour les utilisateurs et les visiteurs. Le parc de Raglan Street en est un exemple, car il était devenu un endroit abandonné et peu attractif. L'intervention s'est traduite par la construction d'un mur en bois et par l'installation de lieux d'interaction entre voisins.

Das Hauptziel der Landschaftsgestalter besteht in der Erneuerung städtischer Bereiche, die für Nutzer und Besucher nicht mehr attraktiv sind. Raglan Street Park, der sich in einen verlassenen und kaum attraktiven Ort verwandelt hatte, ist ein Beispiel dafür. Der Umbau umfasste den Bau einer Holzmauer und die Einrichtung von Punkten für die nachbarliche Interaktion.

Het belangrijkste doel van de landschapsarchitecten is stadsbuurten die voor de gebruikers en bezoekers niet meer aantrekkelijk zijn, nieuw leven in te blazen. Het park in Raglan Street is hier een voorbeeld van, daar het een verlaten en weinig aantrekkelijke plaats was geworden. De ingreep bestond in de bouw van een houten muur en de installatie van buurtpunten.

Site Office Landscape Architecture
www.siteoffice.com.au
© Ben Wrigley

The noise from the adjacent road has been offset by the installation of the timber wall. Indigenous vegetation, a table, a barbeque, a pergola, and several seats have all transformed this neglected urban park.

Le bruit de la route voisine a été atténué grâce à l'installation d'un mur en bois. L'installation de végétation autochtone, d'une table, d'un barbecue, d'une pergola et d'endroits où s'asseoir a transformé ce parc urbain abandonné.

Der Lärm der nebenliegenden Straße konnte mit dem Bau der Holzmauer gedämpft werden. Bodenständige Bepflanzung, Tisch, Grillstelle, Pergola und verschiedene Sitzplätze haben diesen verlassenen Stadtpark verwandelt.

Het lawaai van de belendende weg werd gedempt door de installatie van een houten muur. De aanplant van autochtone vegetatie en de plaatsing van een tafel, barbecue, pergola en verscheidene banken hebben dit verlaten stadspark helemaal omgevormd.

Site plan

Computer generated rendering

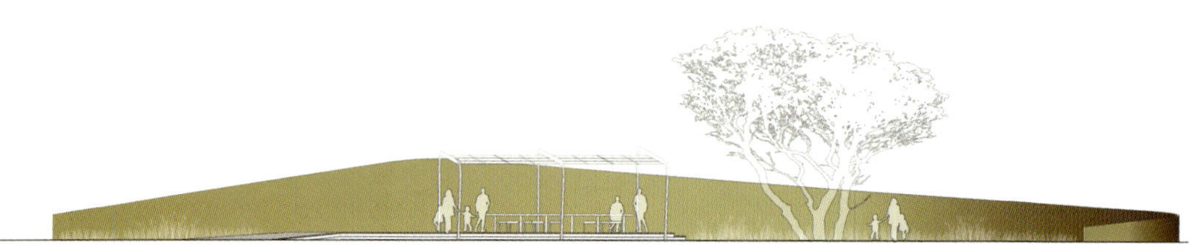

Elevation

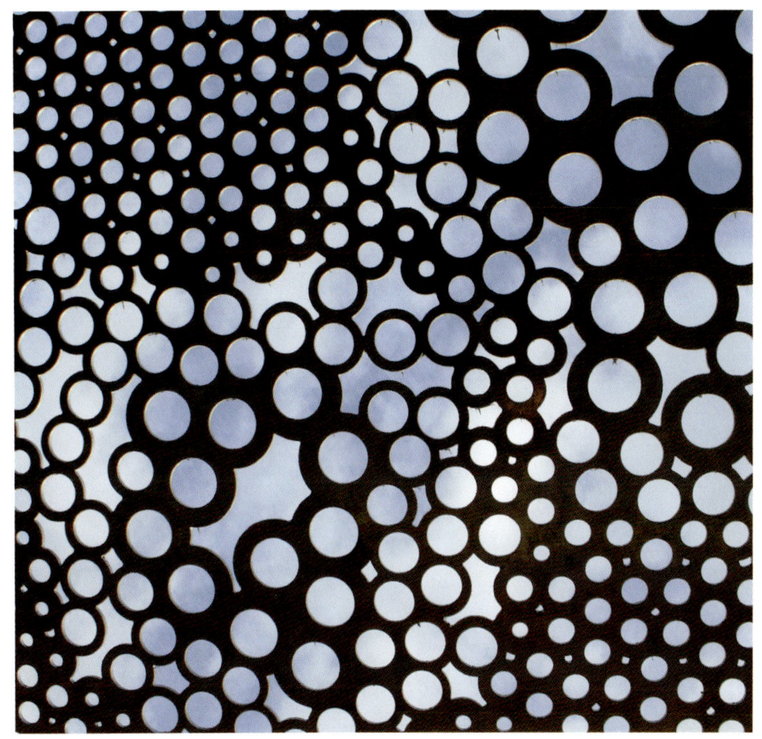

Fluvial Park of Cunella

Cunella, Italy

Nature, a rational design based on mathematical principles, and function are the three basic features of this project. This riverfront park was developed although it had previously been used for spontaneous gatherings and recreation.

La nature, la conception rationnelle basée sur les mathématiques et le fonctionnalisme sont les trois éléments fondamentaux à partir desquels ce projet a été mis en œuvre. Autrefois utilisé de façon naturelle en tant qu'espace de réunion et de loisirs, le parc fluvial a fait l'objet d'une urbanisation.

Die Natur, ein auf der Mathematik basierendes rationales Design und Funktionalität sind die drei Grundelemente, die zur Gestaltung dieses Projekts herangezogen wurden. Der Flusspark wurde urbanisiert, da er schon früher spontan als Treffpunkt und Erholungsort genutzt worden war.

De natuur, het weloverwogen ontwerp gebaseerd op de wiskunde en het functionalisme, zijn de drie peilers waarop dit project steunt. Het rivierpark werd bebouwd omdat het voorheen spontaan werd gebruikt als bijeenkomst- en recreatieplaats.

Gualtiero Oberti
gualtiero.oberti@awn.it
© Gualtiero Oberti

Cement colored with metal oxides to produce an ocher tone contrasts with the greens and browns of the surroundings. Other features of the park are a car park, several open air grills, and a fountain.

Le ciment coloré à partir d'oxydes métalliques en vue d'obtenir une tonalité ocre contraste avec les couleurs vertes et marron du milieu environnant. Une zone de stationnement, plusieurs barbecues et une fontaine sont les autres éléments qui composent le parc.

Der mit Metalloxiden in einem Ocker-Ton gefärbte Zement hebt sich vom Grün und Braun der Umgebung ab. Ein Parkplatz, Grillstellen und ein Brunnen sind ebenfalls vorhanden.

Het cement dat met metaaloxiden oker gekleurd is, vormt een contrast met de groene en bruine kleuren van de omgeving. Verder vindt men in het park een parkeerruimte, diverse barbecues en een fontein.

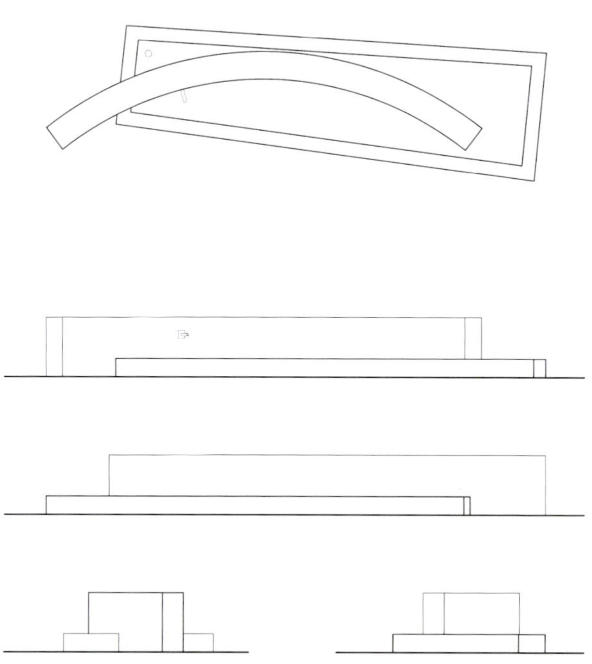

Plan & elevations

Bali Memorial

Perth, Australia

The Australian government commissioned a memorial to the terrorist attacks that occurred on October 12 2002. The project was divided into two parts: the first creating a vista of the Swan River estuary; and the other pointing to the horizon where the sun rises every October 12.

Le gouvernement australien a fait construire un monument commémoratif pour les victimes des attentats terroristes du 12 octobre 2002. La création du projet s'articule autour de deux axes : un axe qui met l'accent sur la vision des eaux de l'estuaire de la rivière Swan et un autre dirigé vers le point de l'horizon où le soleil se lève tous les 12 octobre.

Die australische Regierung gab ein Denkmal zum Gedenken an die Terroranschläge vom 12.10.2002 in Auftrag. Das Projekt ist in zwei Achsen aufgeteilt: Eine, die die Sicht auf die Mündung des Flusses Swan betont, und eine zweite, die sich auf den Punkt am Horizont richtet, an dem jedes Jahr am 12.10. die Sonne aufgeht.

De Australische regering gaf de opdracht om een monument te maken voor de terroristische aanslagen van 12 oktober 2002. Het uiteindelijke project bestaat uit twee assen: één as benadrukt het beeld van het water in de trechtermonding van de rivier de Swan en de andere as richt zich op het punt van de horizon waar de zon elk jaar op 12 oktober opkomt.

Donaldson & Warn Architects
www.donaldsonandwarn.com.au
© Martin Farquharson,
Donaldson & Warn Architects
(drawings)

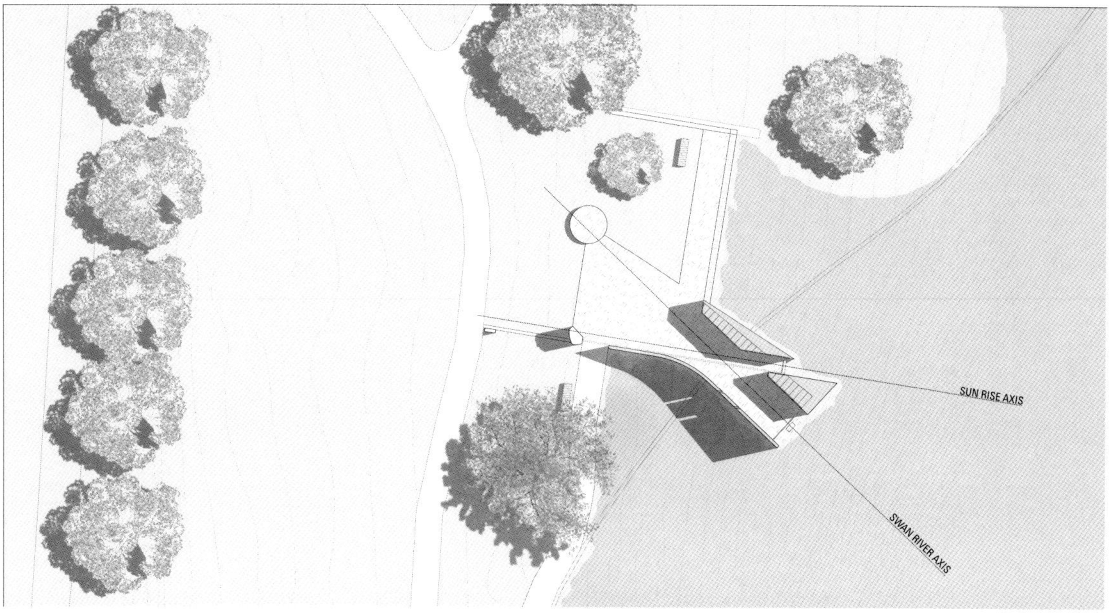

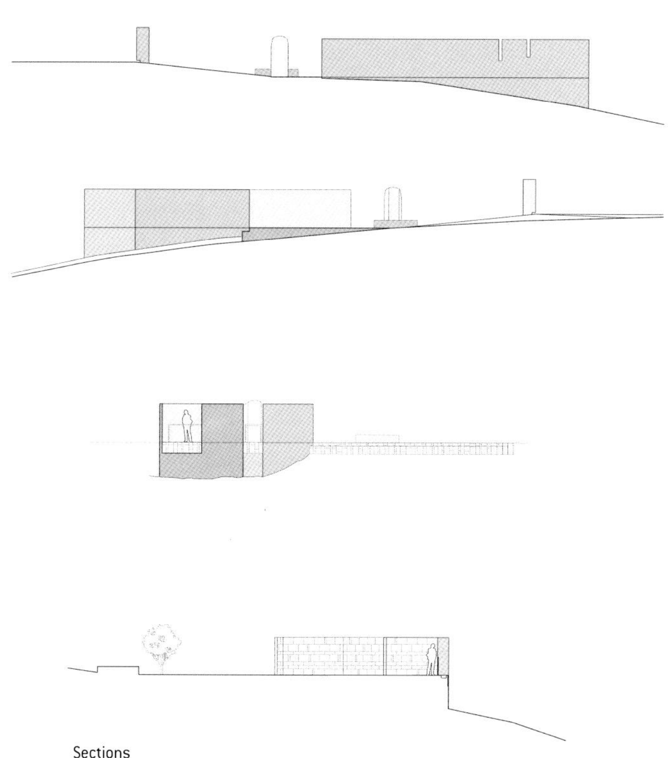

Plan

Sections

Steel, granite, and sandstone walls are the main components of the gateway to the memorial that filters the morning sun, illuminating the plaque commemorating the terrorist attack.

L'acier, le granit et le grès sont les matériaux utilisés pour construire le portail du mémorial, où se concentre la lumière matinale qui illumine la plaque commémorative de l'attentat.

Mauern aus Stahl, Granit und Sandstein bilden das Portal der Gedenkstätte, wo das Morgenlicht durchscheint, welches die Gedenktafel beleuchtet.

Muren van staal, graniet en zandsteen zijn de materialen die werden gebruikt om het portaal van het monument te maken. Daar filtert het ochtendlicht door dat de gedenkplaat van de terroristche aanslag verlicht.

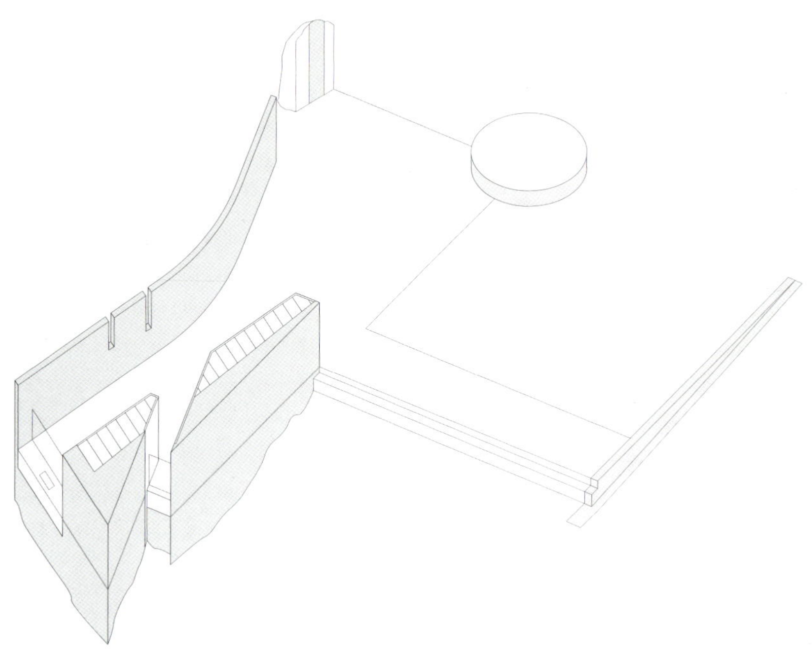

Bali Memorial axonometric

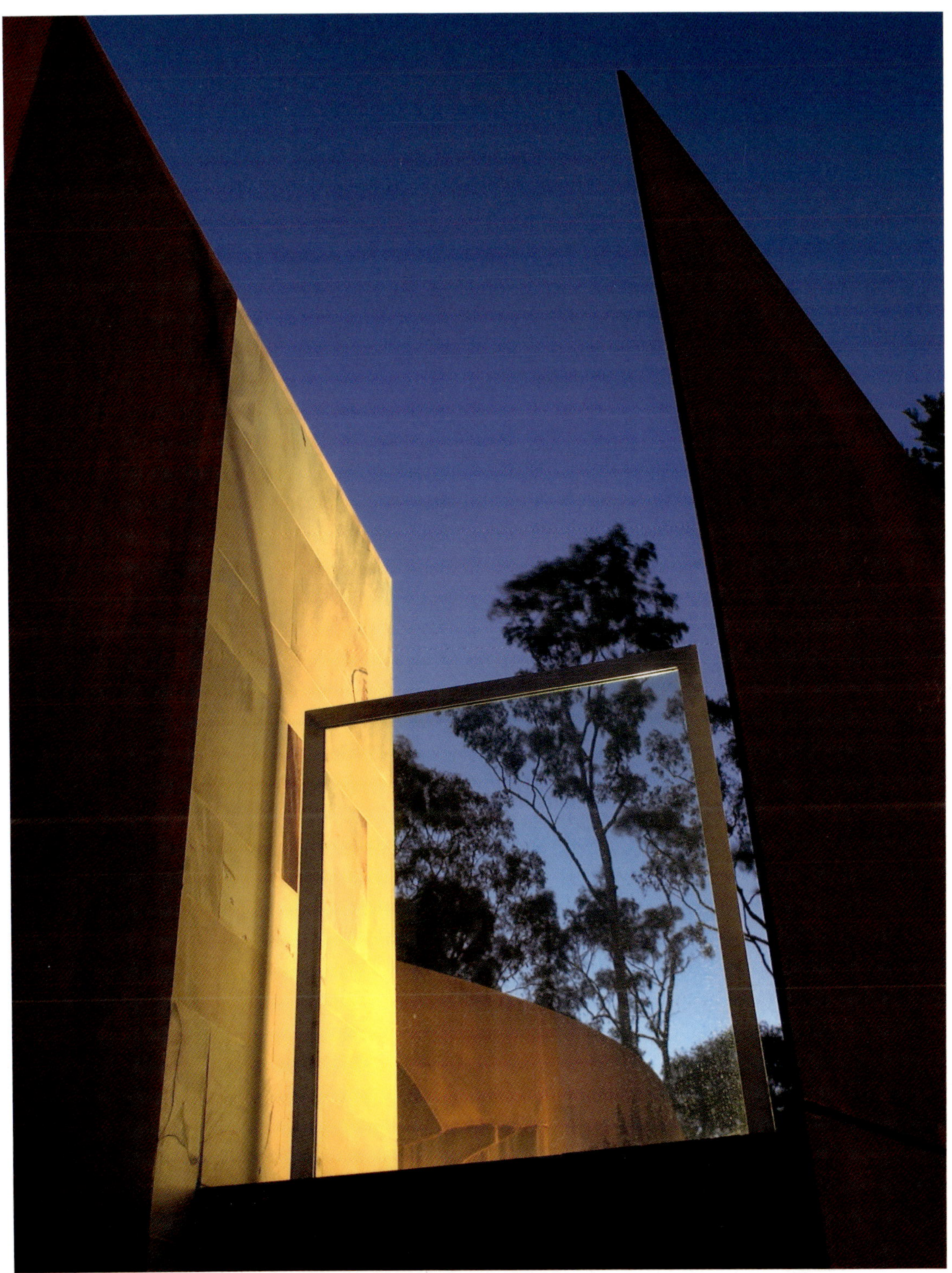

Sungang Central Plaza

Shenzhen, China

The landscape architecture firm brought life back to the plaza by means of curved forms, inspired by the natural texture of the terrain. The surface is clad in a skin of wavy strips that recalls the movement of the tides. This skin serves as a shelter and as a link between the adjoining two car parks.

Le cabinet de paysagisme a redonné vie à la place en faisant appel à une géométrie courbe inspirée de la texture naturelle de la terre. La surface présente un revêtement à bandes ondulées qui rappelle le mouvement des marées. Cette enveloppe fonctionne comme un abri et sert de lien entre les deux zones de stationnement adjacentes.

Das Landschaftsarchitekten-Studio reaktivierte den Platz durch gewölbte Strukturen. Seine Inspirationsquelle war die natürliche Beschaffenheit der Erde. Die Fläche wurde mit einer Schale aus gewellten Bändern überzogen, die an die Gezeitenbewegung erinnern. Die Schale dient als Dach und als Verbindung zwischen zwei angrenzenden Parkplätzen.

Het landschapsarchitectenbureau deed het plein weer opleven door middel van een gebogen geometrie. De natuurlijke textuur van de aarde was de inspiratiebron. Het oppervlak is bekleed met een laag met geribbelde randen die doet denken aan de beweging van de getijden. Die laag fungeert als afdekking en als verbinding tussen de twee aangrenzende parkeerplaatsen.

Urbanus Architecture & Design
www.urbanus.com.cn
© Yan Meng, Jiu Chen, Urbanus Architecture & Design (drawings)

The mosaic created by the curved strips
is broken by small areas with flowers. This
produces an effect of color that contrasts
with the surroundings.

La mosaïque créée par les bandes curvi-
lignes est entrecoupée de petites zones
fleuries. Cette disposition provoque un effet
visuel chromatique, qui contraste avec les
environs.

Das von den gewölbten Bändern erzeugte
Mosaik wird durch kleine Blumenbeete unterbrochen. Dies erzeugt einen farbigen Ef-
fekt, der sich von der Umgebung abhebt.

Het mozaïek dat ontstaat door de kromlij-
nige randen wordt onderbroken door kleine
bloemzones. Dit geeft een optisch kleur-
effect in contrast met de omgeving.

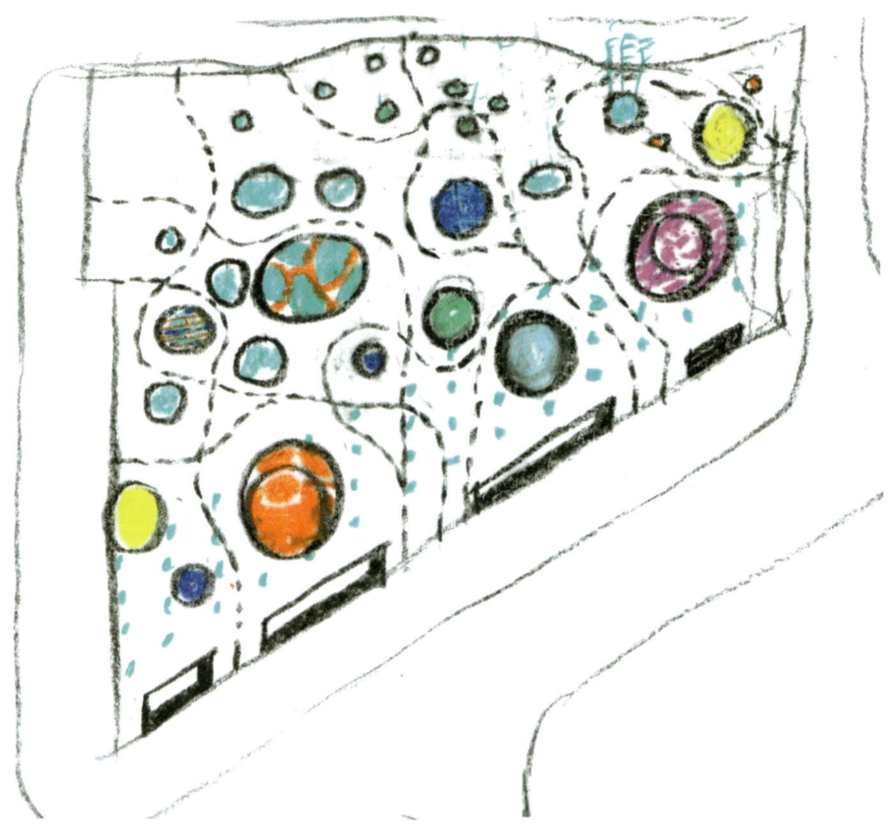

Sketch

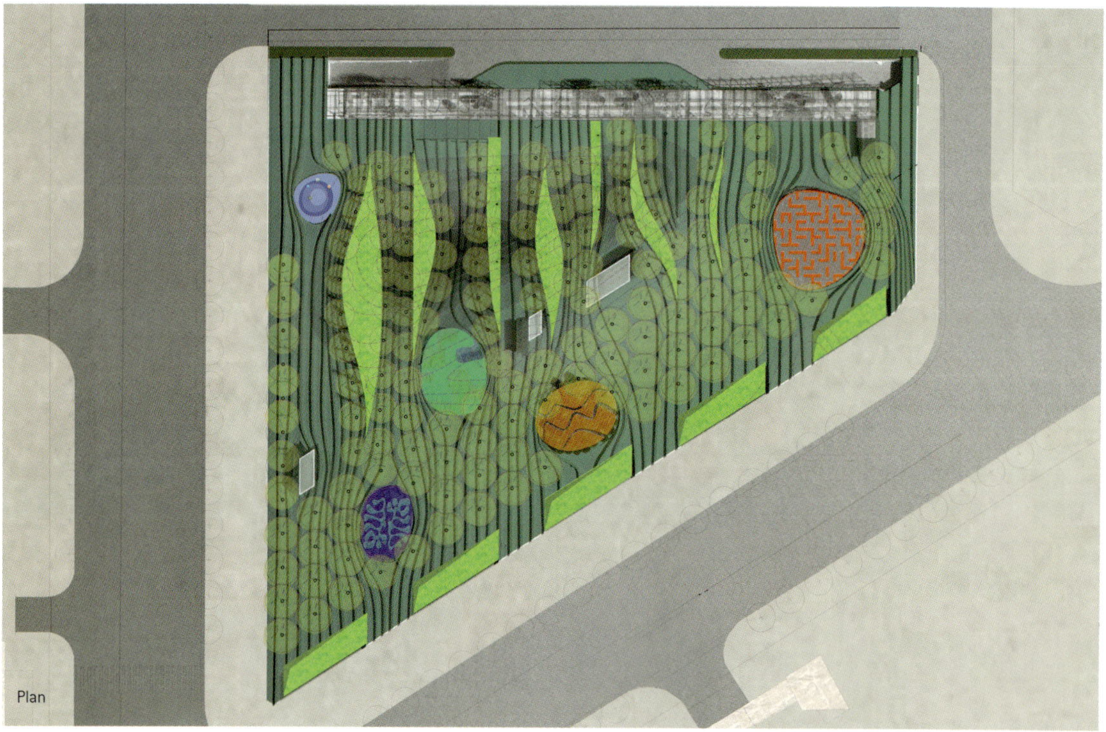

Plan

Rendering

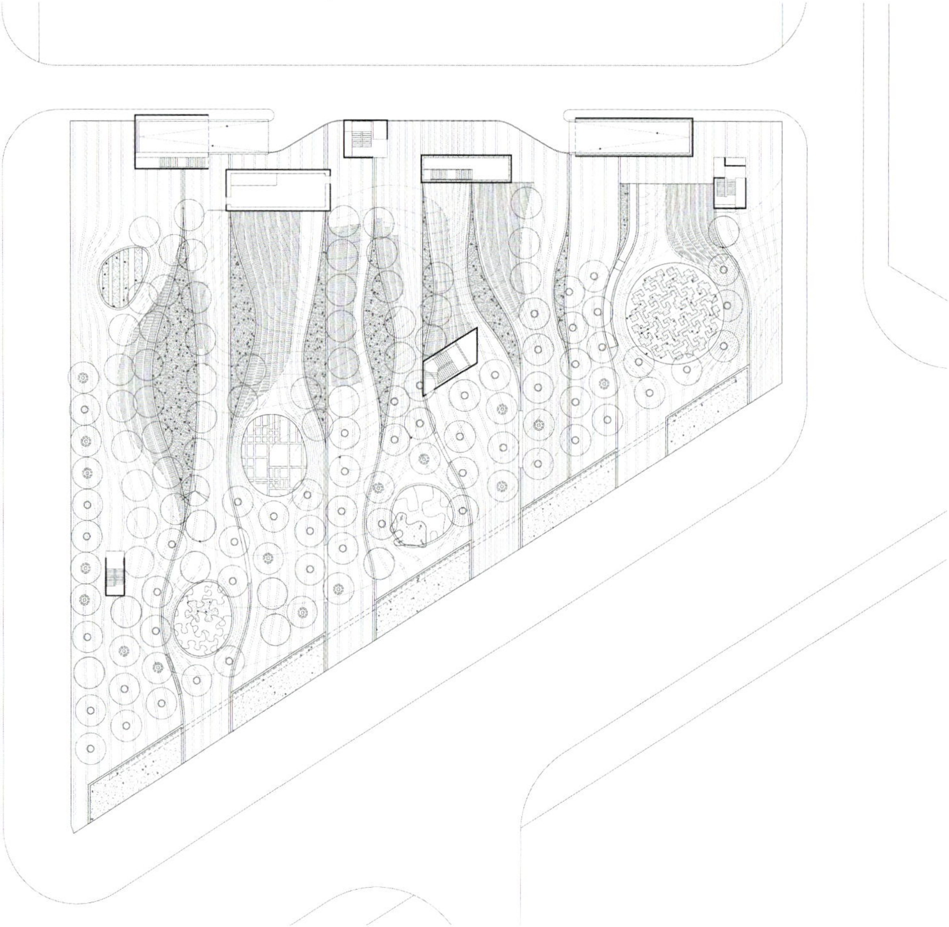

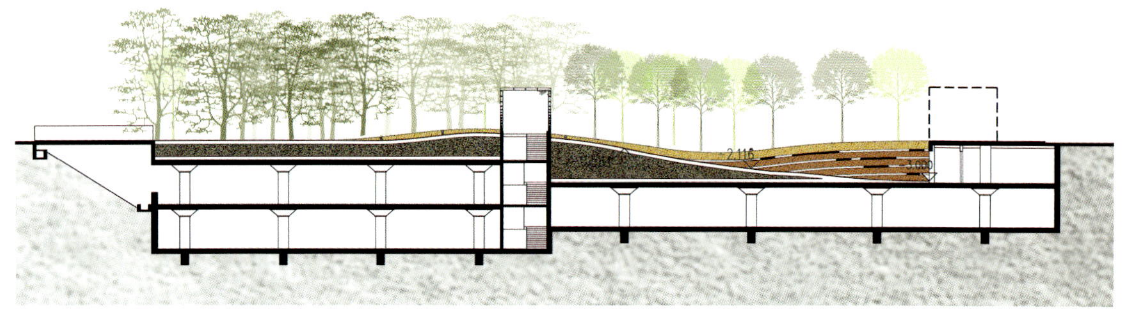

Plan

Section

Rendering

Diwang Park B

Shenzhen, China

The project is surrounded by the main thoroughfares and high-rise buildings of Shenzhen's Luohu district. The landscape architects designed their park from the view of the site provided by the nearby Diwang Tower. This view revealed a movie set landscape of flowing lines, lights, and colors of a busy area.

L'ouvrage, situé dans le district de Luohu de Shenzhen, est entouré de grandes avenues et d'immenses gratte-ciels. Les paysagistes ont planifié la conception du parc en prenant comme point de repère la tour Diwang située à proximité, d'où ils ont une vue panoramique du site. Cette vue révélait une scène cinématographique mélangeant les voies de circulation, les lumières et les couleurs dans une zone de transit.

Die Anlage im Distrikt Luohu von Shenzhen ist von Hauptstraßen und Wolkenkratzern umgeben. Die Landschaftsarchitekten planten ihren Entwurf inspiriert von der Panoramasicht des nahegelegenen Diwang-Turms. Diese Sicht offenbart ein filmreifes Szenario von Fluchtlinien, Lichtern und Farben in einem verkehrsreichen Gebiet.

Dit project wordt omgeven door hoofdlanen en hoge wolkenkrabbers in het Luohu-district van Shenzhen. De landschapsarchitecten planden hun ontwerp voor het park naar aanleiding van een panoramisch uitzicht op de naburige Di Wang-toren. Dit uitzicht suggereerde een filmdecor van stroomlijnen, lichten en kleuren in een zone met druk verkeer.

Urbanus Architecture & Design
www.urbanus.com.cn
© Yan Meng, Jiu Chen, Urbanus Architecture & Design

Solid brick, brick surfaces, lawn, and grass strips are combined to produce a dynamic, movie set-like park design.

La brique solide, les surfaces de brique et de gazon ainsi que les bandes de gazon font partie de la conception dynamique et cinématographique du parc urbain.

Solider Ziegelstein, Flächen aus Ziegel und Rasen und Rasenstreifen sind Bestandteile des dynamischen und filmreifen Designs des städtischen Parks.

Stevige bakstenen, oppervlakken van baksteen en gras en grasranden maken deel uit van het dynamische en cinematografische ontwerp van het stadspark.

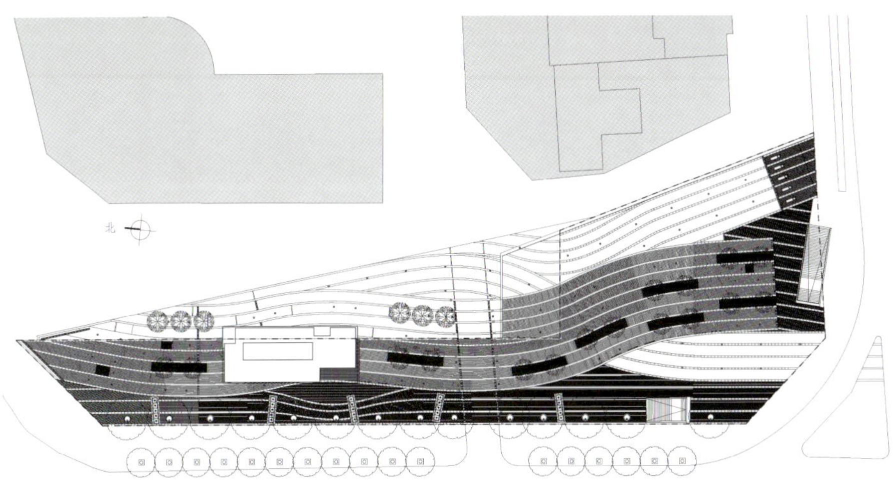

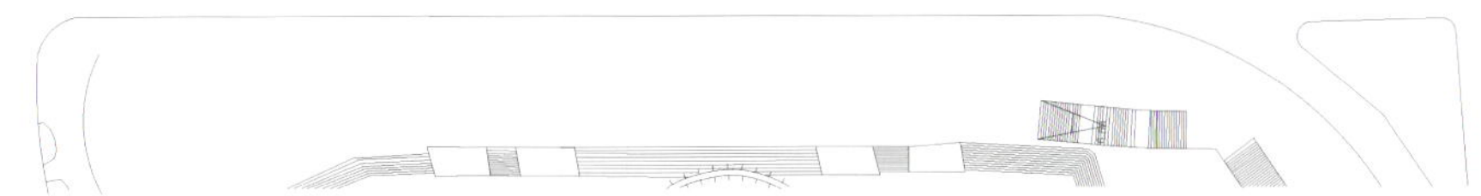

Plan

Prags Boulevard

Copenhagen, Denmark

Prags Boulevard is a 1¼-mile project with a random layout of spaces for traffic, recreation, and rest. The different recreation areas alternate with Prag chair installations, similar to director's chairs, on the different spaces.

Le Prags Boulevard est un ouvrage de 2 km de long où s'alternent de façon aléatoire des espaces de circulation, de loisirs et de détente. Les différentes zones de loisirs se succèdent, entrecoupées par l'installation des chaises Prag, comparables aux fauteuils de cinéma, au niveau des différents parterres.

Der Prags Boulevard ist auf 2 km Länge durch ein zufälliges Verhältnis von Verkehrs-, Erholungs- und Ruhezonen gestaltet. Die verschiedenen Erholungsbereiche, ausgestattet mit Prag-Stühlen, die den Regiesesseln der Filmregisseure ähneln, wechseln sich mit den Blumenbeeten ab.

De Prags Boulevard is een 2 km lang gebied met een willekeurig verband tussen de ruimten bestemd voor verkeer, recreatie en rust. In de verschillende parkjes wisselen de diverse recreatiezones elkaar af met de Prag-stoelen, die op regisseursstoelen lijken.

 **Kristine Jensens Tegnestu**
www.jkristinejensen.dk
© Simon Høgsberg, Christina Capetillo, Kristine Jensens Tegnestue (drawings)

Photomontage

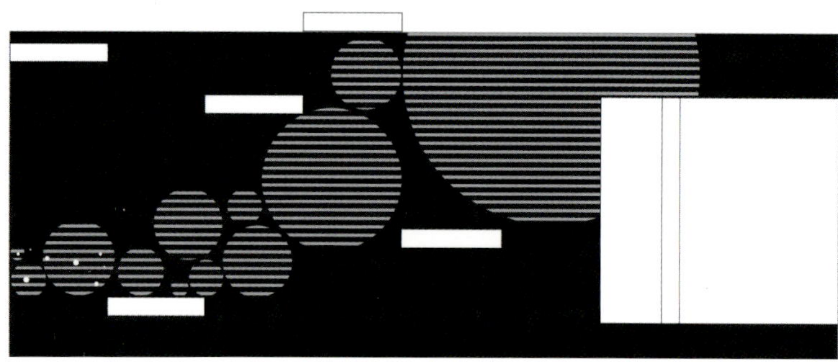

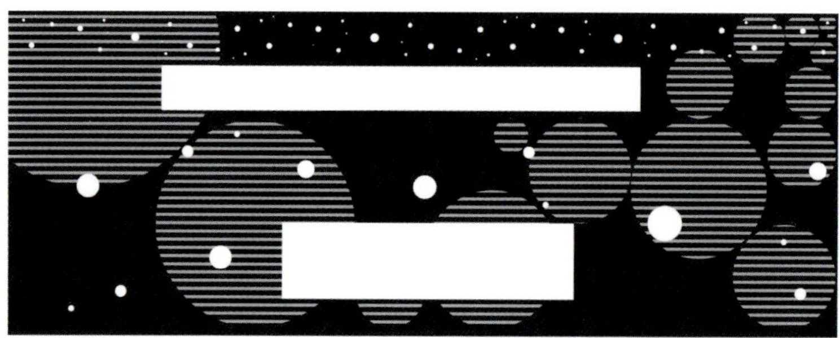

Plans

Besides Prag chairs, Bright colored Prager street lamps were installed to light up and outline the boulevard's length. Pictographs are another facet of the project.

Les lampes Prager, qui s'ajoutent à l'installation des sièges Prag, émettent des couleurs vives qui accentuent graphiquement le long trajet du boulevard. La pictographie est un autre élément phare de ce projet.

Außer Prag-Stühlen gibt es „Prager"-Lampen mit lebendiger Beleuchtung und grafischer Betonung der Boulevardstrecke, wie auch Piktogramme in diesem Projekt.

Er werden Prag-stoelen en felgekleurde Prager-lampen geïnstalleerd die het traject van de boulevard grafisch onderstrepen. Het beeldschrift valt in dit project op.

Rehabilitation of Quinta da Alagoa

Carcavelos, Portugal

The Quinta da Alagoa urban space in the city of Carcavelos was transformed and improved with the creation of a garden with new paths, rest areas, and recreation spaces. Existing elements were mixed with new ones to unify the space.

Dans la ville de Carcavelos, l'espace urbain Quinta da Alagoa a été adapté et amélioré grâce à la création d'un jardin avec de nouveaux chemins, d'espaces de détente et de zones de loisirs. Les nouveaux éléments ont été mélangés aux anciens pour uniformiser l'espace.

In der Stadt Carcavelos wurde die städtische Anlage Quinta da Alagoa durch die Schaffung eines Gartens mit neuen Wegen sowie Erholungs- und Freizeitbereichen umgestaltet und verbessert. Die bestehenden Elemente wurden mit den neuen gemischt, um den Raum zu vereinheitlichen.

In de stad Carcavelos werd de stadswijk Quinta da Alagoa aangepast en verbeterd door een tuin aan te leggen met nieuwe paden, plekken voor ontspanning en recreatiezones. Reeds bestaande elementen werden gecombineerd met de nieuwe om de ruimte tot een geheel te maken.

PROAP Estudos e Projectos de Arquitectura Paisagista Lda
www.proap.pt
© Fernando Guerra, PROAP Estudos e Projectos de Arquitectura Paisagista Lda (drawings)

Sketch of grass land around the lagoon

Canals, rest areas, trees, empty spaces, paths, recreation spaces, and new lighting are the elements involved in this project.

Canaux, aires de détente, arbres, espaces vierges, chemins, zones de loisirs, nouvel éclairage, etc. Tels sont les éléments qui font partie de ce projet.

Kanäle, Ruhebereiche, Bäume, unbebaute Zonen, Wege, Freizeitbereiche und eine neue Beleuchtung sind Elemente dieses Projekts.

Grachten, ontspanningszones, bomen, lege ruimten, wandelpaden, recreatiezones en een nieuwe verlichting zijn de elementen die dit project vorm geven.

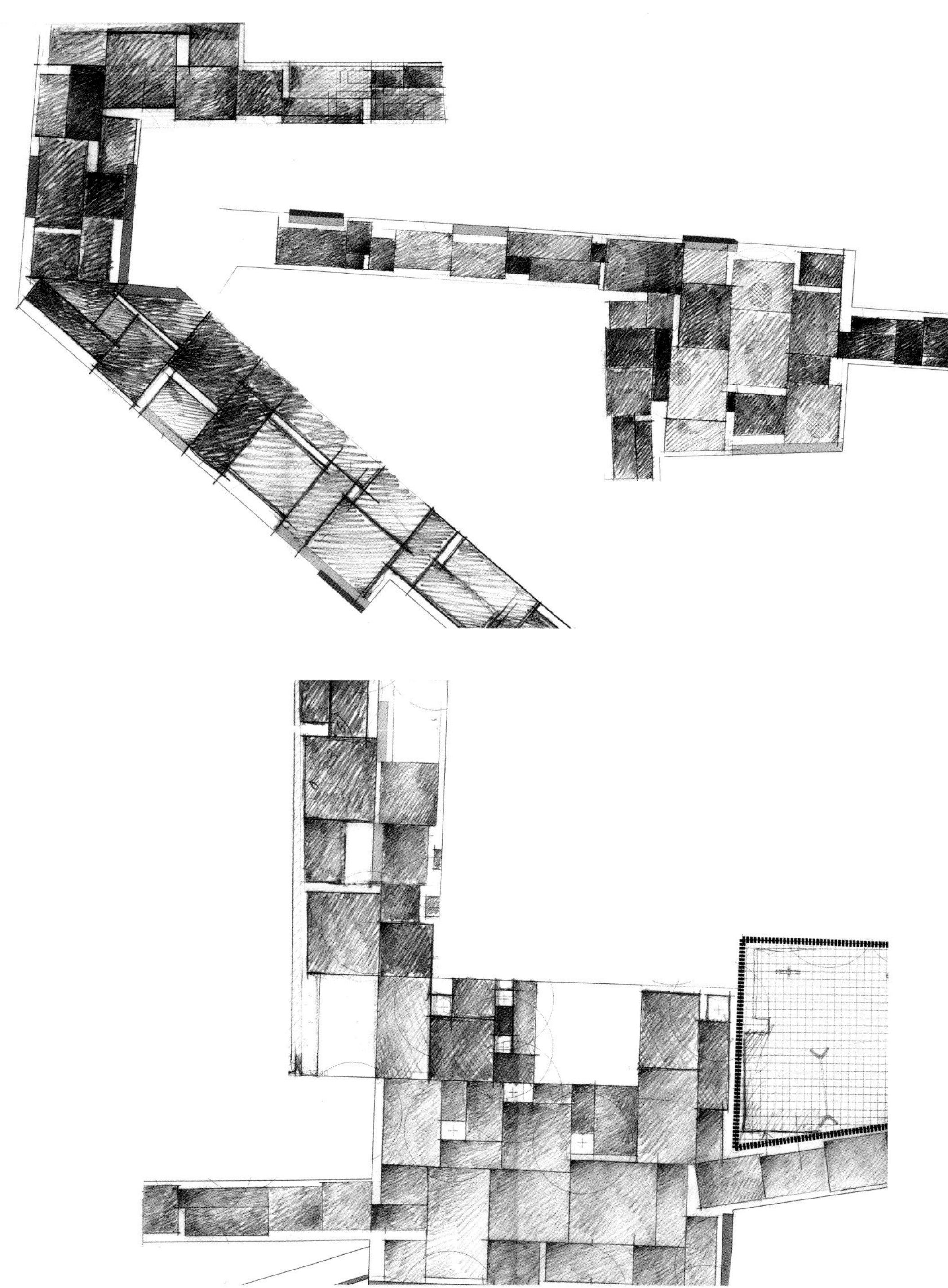

Detail sketch of stereotomy of paths and resting areas

General plan

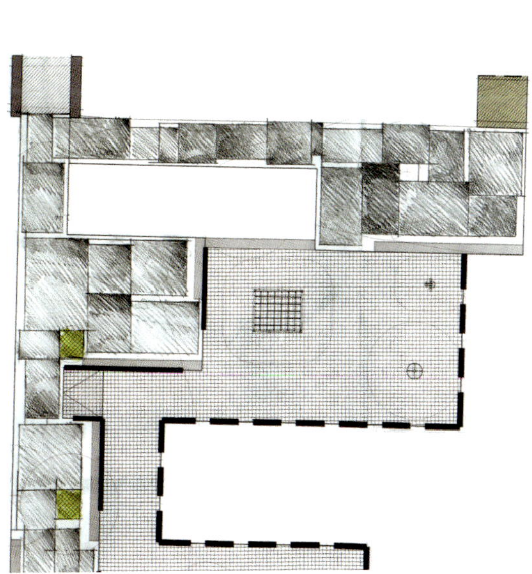

Detail sketch of stereotomy of path and playground areas

Plan and section of the relationship path-plantations

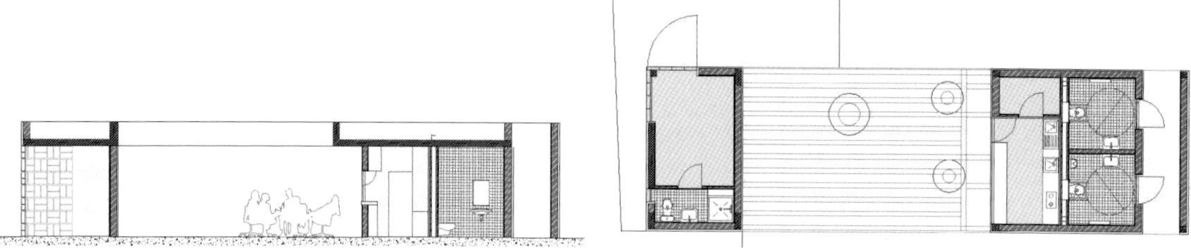

Section and plan of buiding

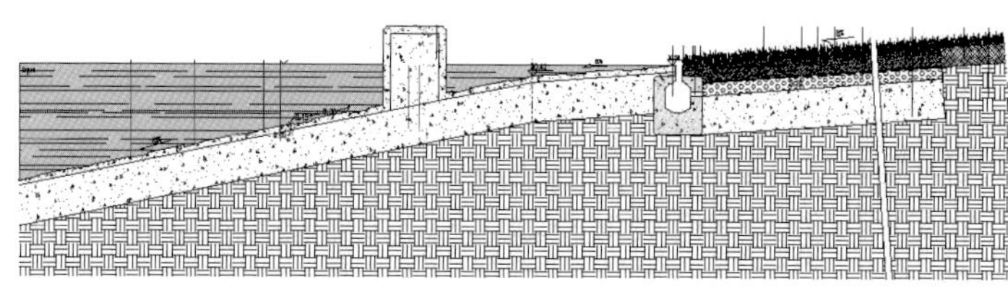

Section through ramp

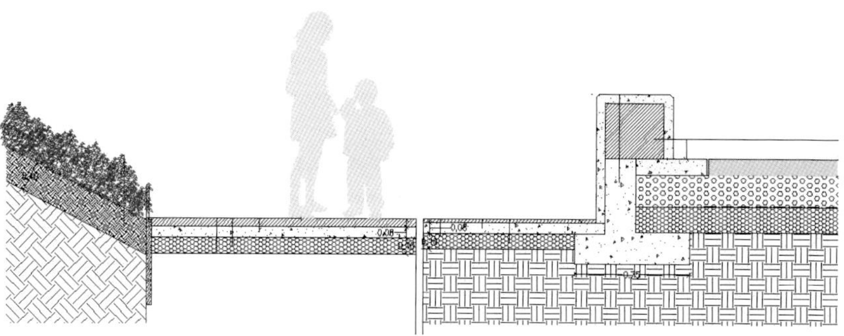

Section through path

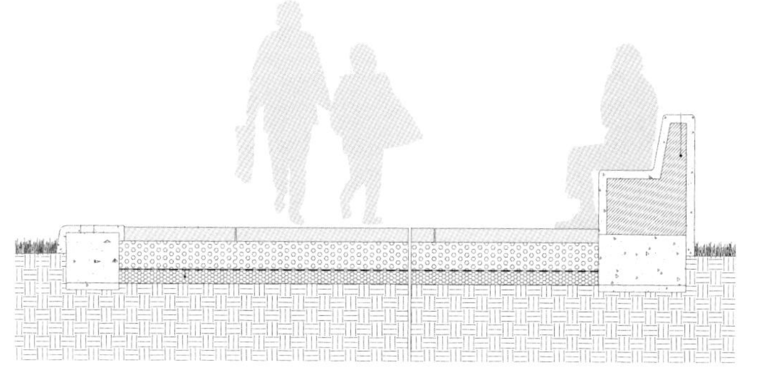

Detailed section of path and bench

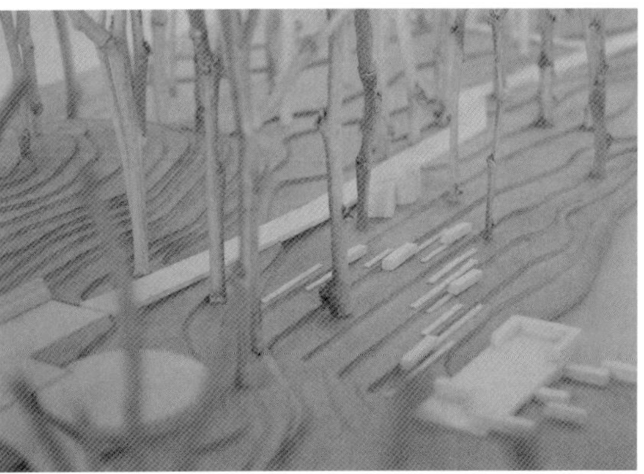

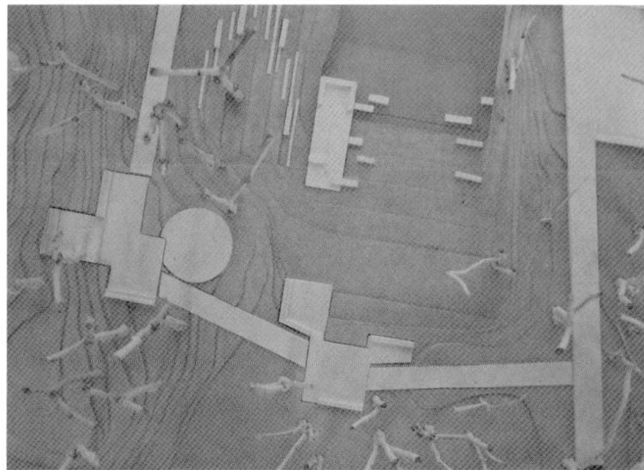

Models

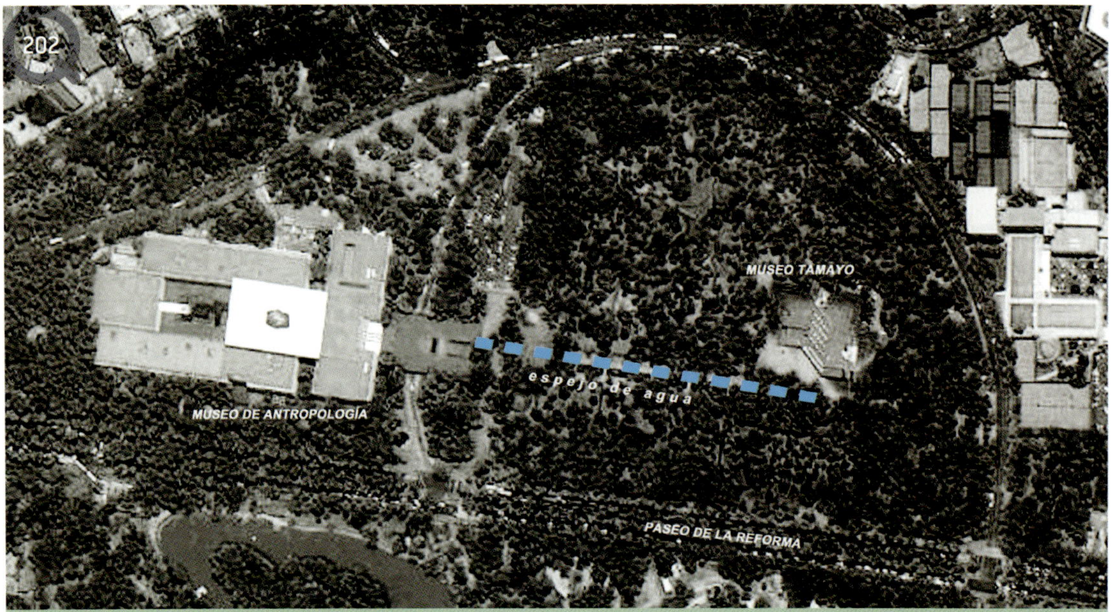

Water Mirrow

Chapultepec Park, Mexico City, Mexico

Chapultepec Park, which is thought to the oldest in the Americas, had certain problems in the gardens, infrastructures, lake water, etc. It was completely remodeled in five different stages, the most important being the improvement of the quality of the water, the irrigation and the pipings.

Le parc de Chapultepec, considéré comme le plus ancien d'Amérique, présentait des problèmes au niveau des jardins, des infrastructures, de l'eau des lacs, etc. Il a été décidé de le réaménager entièrement grâce à cinq interventions. La plus importante a été l'amélioration de la qualité des eaux, de l'irrigation et des conduites.

Der als ältester Park Amerikas bekannte Chapultepec-Park zeigte Probleme in seinen Gärten, Infrastrukturen, Seewasser, usw. Man beschloss seinen vollständigen Umbau in fünf Phasen. Der wichtigste Schritt bestand in der Verbesserung von Wasserqualität, Bewässerung und Rohrleitungen.

Het park van Chapultepec, beschouwd als het oudste van Amerika, had problemen op het gebied van de tuinen, de infrastructuren, het water van de meren, enz. Men besloot het door middel van vijf ingrepen volledig te verbouwen. De belangrijkste was de verbetering van de waterkwaliteit, de irrigatie en het buizennet.

Mario Schjetnan/Grupo de Disñeo Urbano
www.gdu.com.mx
© Francisco Gómez Sosa

The water canal created in the redesign of the park connects two of the main buildings in the enclosure, the National Museum of Archaeology and the Tamayo Contemporary Art Museum.

Le canal d'eau créé lors du réaménagement du parc relie deux des bâtiments les plus importants de l'enceinte : le Musée d'archéologie et le Musée Tamayo.

Der beim Umbau des Parks geschaffene Wasserkanal verbindet zwei der wichtigsten Gebäude der Anlage – das Archäologiemuseum und das Tamayo-Museum.

Het waterkanaal dat bij de verbouwing van het park aangelegd werd, verbindt twee van de belangrijkste gebouwen van het domein, het Museum voor Archeologie en het Tamayo Museum.

Model

Section

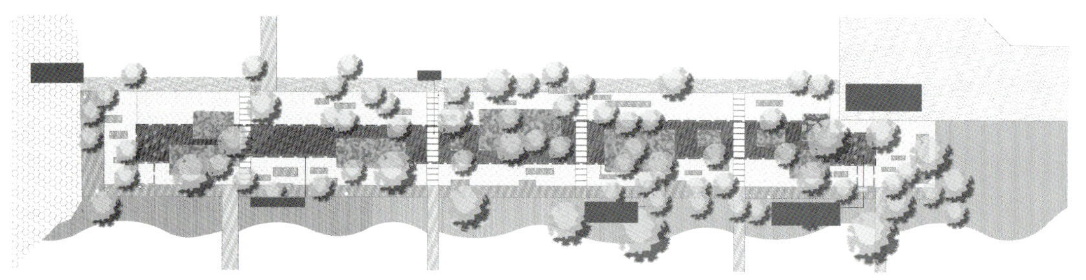

Site plan

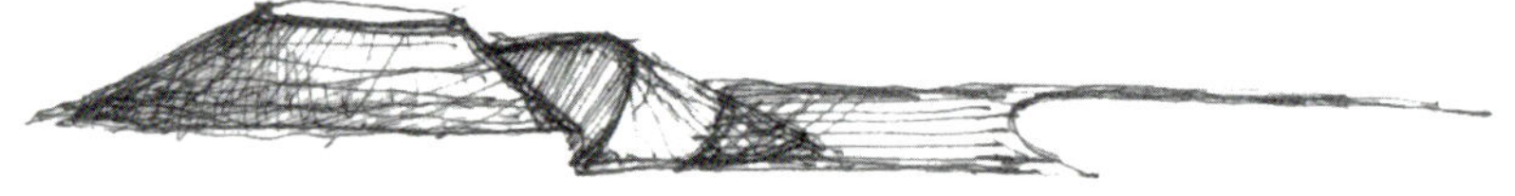

Australian Garden

Cranbourne, Australia

The Royal Botanic Gardens Cranbourne is a space displaying the plant life of Australia in an educational and interactive way. The landscape is used as a source of inspiration for the creation of a sequence of artistic and sculptural experiences.

Le Jardin botanique royal de Cranbourne est un espace qui montre la flore du continent australien de façon éducative et interactive. Le paysage a servi de source d'inspiration pour créer une séquence d'expériences artistiques et sculpturales.

Der Königliche Botanische Garten von Cranburne zeigt die Flora des australischen Kontinents auf lehrreiche und interaktive Weise. Die Landschaft wurde als Inspirationsquelle für die Kreation einer Reihe von künstlerischen und bildhauerischen Erlebnissen genutzt.

De Koninklijke Botanische tuin van Cranbourne is een plek waar de flora van het Australische continent op educatieve en interactieve wijze aan het publiek wordt getoond. Het landschap werd als inspiratiebron gebruikt om een opeenvolging van artistieke en beeldhouwkunstige ervaringen te creëren.

Taylor Cullity Lethlean, Greg Burgess Architects (ArchitectureRockpool Shelter), Kristen Thompson Architects (ArchitectureVisitor Center), Mark Stoner and Edwina Kearney (Sculpture Ephemeral Lake)
www.tcl.net.au
© Ben Wrigley, Peter Hyatt, Taylor Cullity Lethlean (drawings)

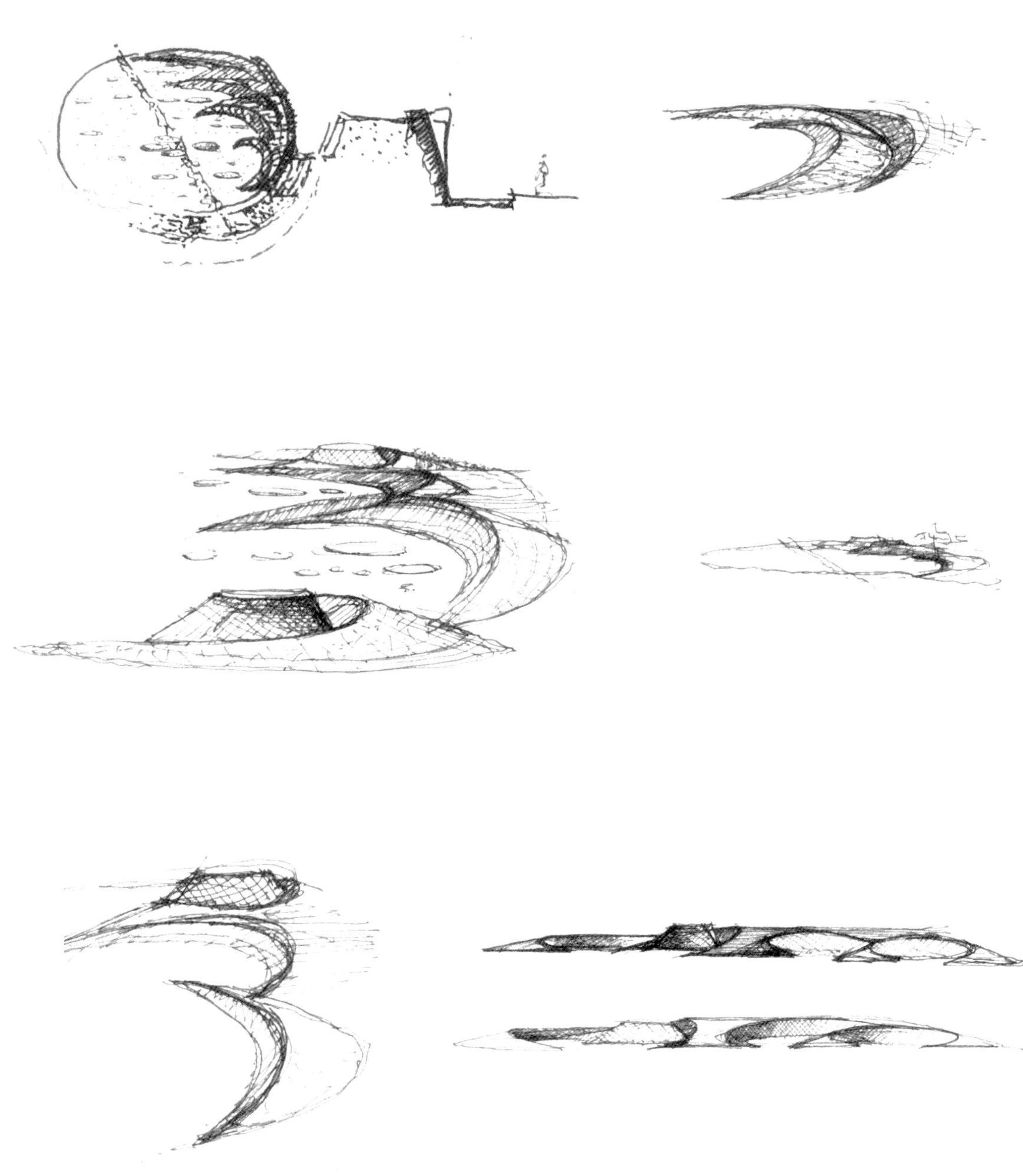

Schematic design sketches

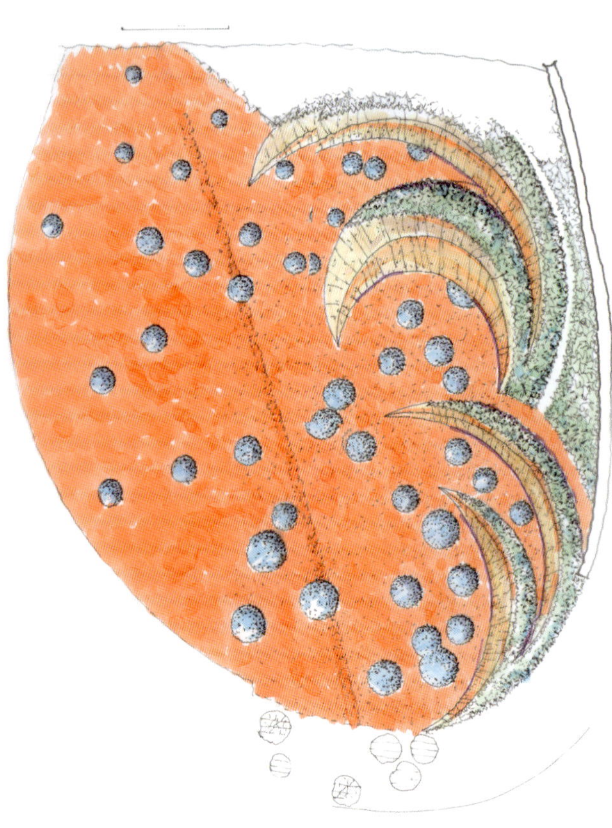

Sketch of definitive design

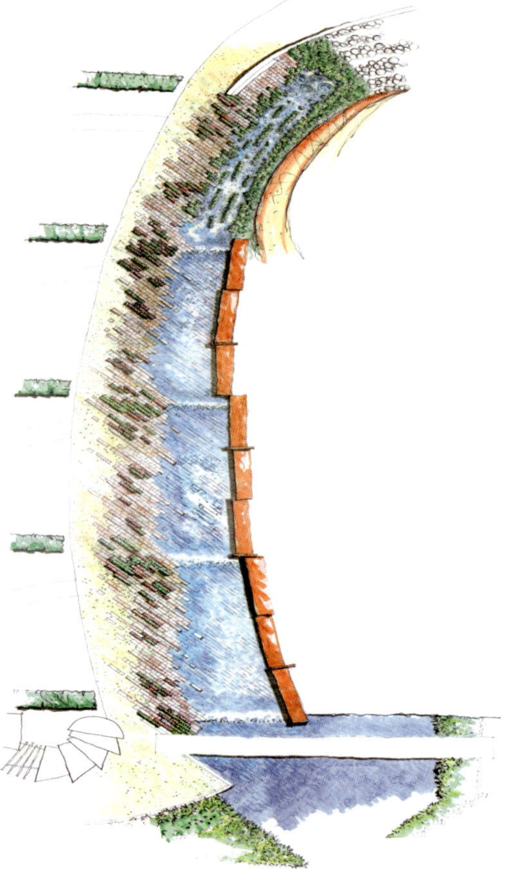

Sketch of rock pool waterway

The project resulted from the desire to provide visitors with knowledge on Australian plant life and its diversity, and to teach the need for its protection.

Le projet est né de la volonté de faire découvrir aux visiteurs les connaissances, la protection et la diversité de la flore australienne.

Das Projekt entstand aus dem Bedürfnis, den Besuchern Kenntnisse über die vielfältige australische Flora und deren Schutz zu vermitteln.

Met het project wil men de bezoekers de kennis en bescherming van de Australische flora en de diversiteit daarvan laten zien.

Sketch of site plan

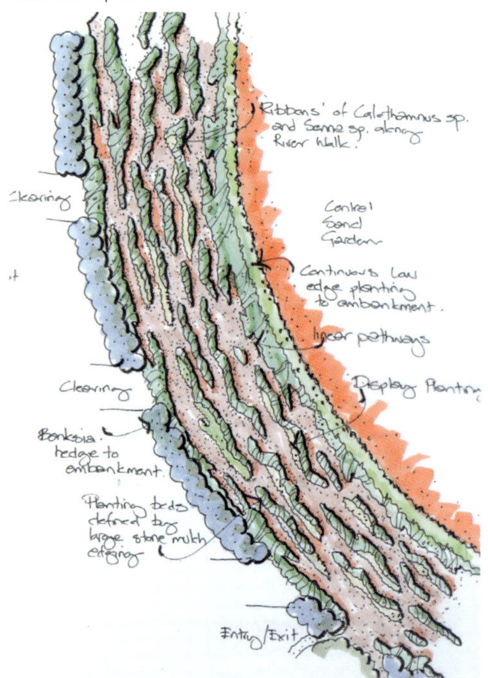

Sketch of the dry river walk

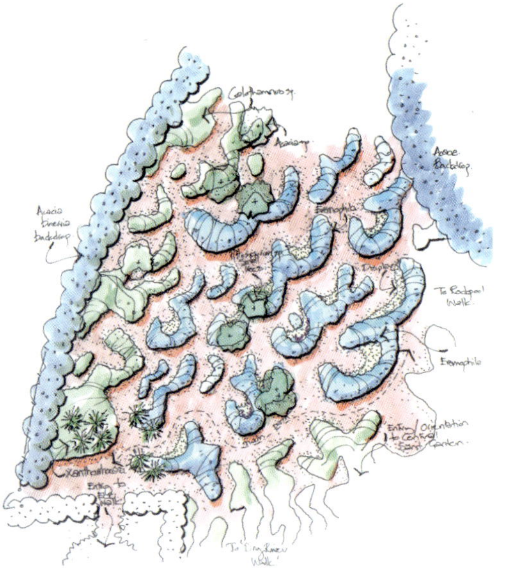

Sketch with plantation key

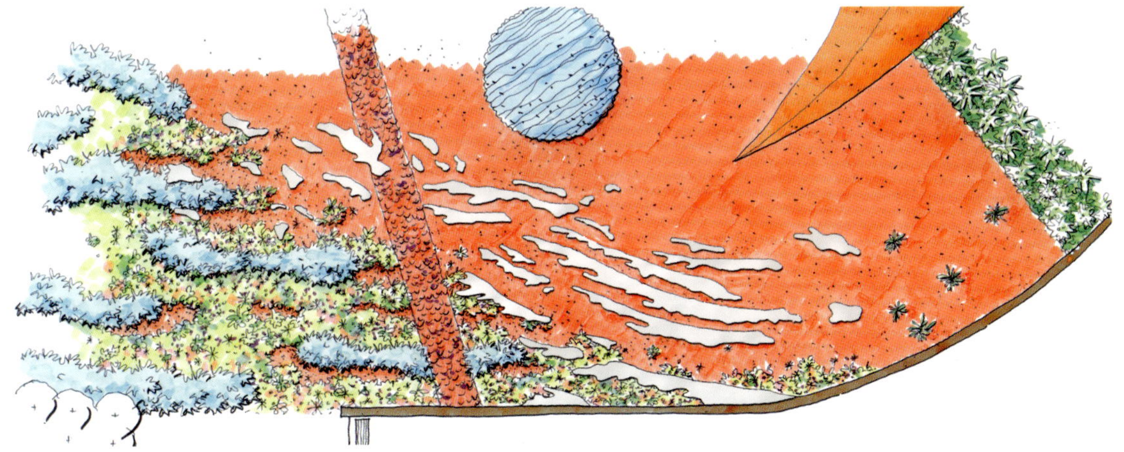

Sketch of plantation detail

Color site plan

Berlin Moabit Prison Historical Park

Berlin, Germany

The site of the old Moabit Prison has been turned into a park and memorial. The park is surrounded on three sides by the old prison walls and some of the original features have been maintained.

Un parc et un monument commémoratif ont été construits sur les terrains où était autrefois situé le centre pénitentiaire de Moabit. Le parc est clôturé sur trois côtés par l'ancien mur de la prison et conserve encore quelques structures d'origine.

Auf dem Gelände, auf dem sich früher das Moabiter Gefängnis befand, wurden ein Park angelegt und eine Gedenkstätte errichtet. Der Park ist an drei Seiten von den alten Gefängnismauern umschlossen. Auch einige Originalschauplätze sind noch erhalten.

Op het terrein waar vroeger de Moabitgevangenis stond, werd een park aangelegd en een gedenkteken gebouwd. Het park wordt aan drie zijden omheind door de voormalige gevangenismuur en heeft nog originele elementen.

Glasser & Dagenbach
www.glada-berlin.de
© Alexander Khomiakov, Udo Dagenbach, Glasser & Dagenbach (drawings)

Second sketch of entrance

Sketch of sculpture for promenade yard

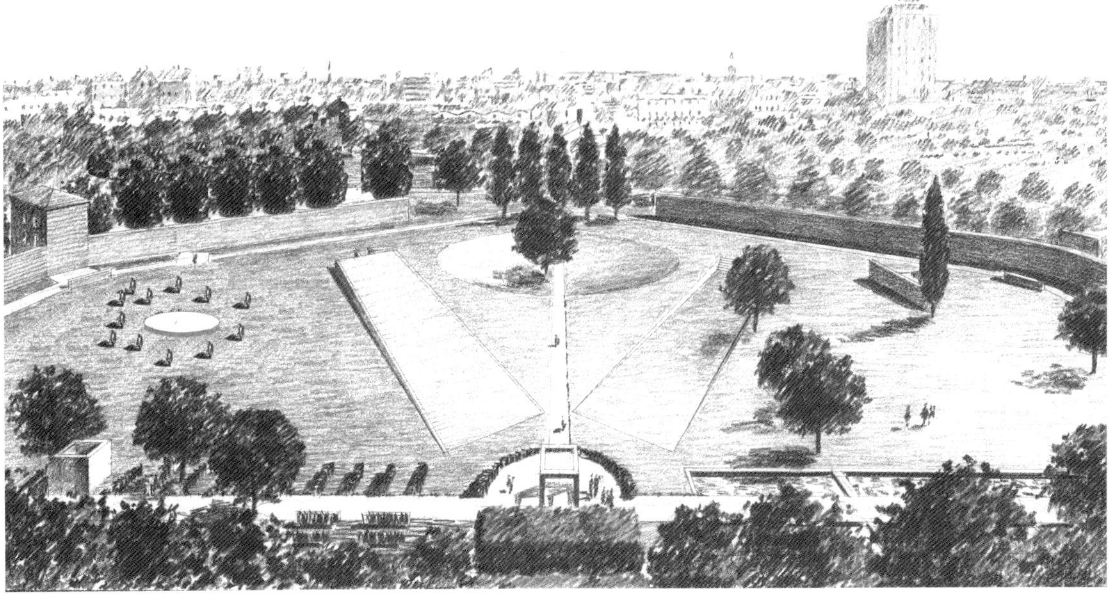

Sketch of perspective view

Sketch of sculpture box

MAUERWERK UND EISEN ... NDIG, EINGEHEIMES ZITTERN...

The project consists of creating a star-shaped layout of raised parterres planted with lawns. The concrete wall features the reproduction of the Moabit Sonnets written by Albert Haushofer while an inmate in the prison.

Le projet consiste en un alignement en forme d'étoile de parterres de gazon surélevés. Les sonnets écrits par Albert Haushofer en prison ont été reproduits sur l'un des murs en béton.

Das Projekt mit erhöhten Rasenbeeten ist sternförmig angelegt. Eine Betonmauer zeigt die Sonette, die Albert Haushofer im Gefängnis schrieb.

Het project is aangelegd in de vorm van een ster met verhoogde grasperken. Op een betonnen muur staan de sonnetten die Albert Haushofer in de gevangenis heeft geschreven.

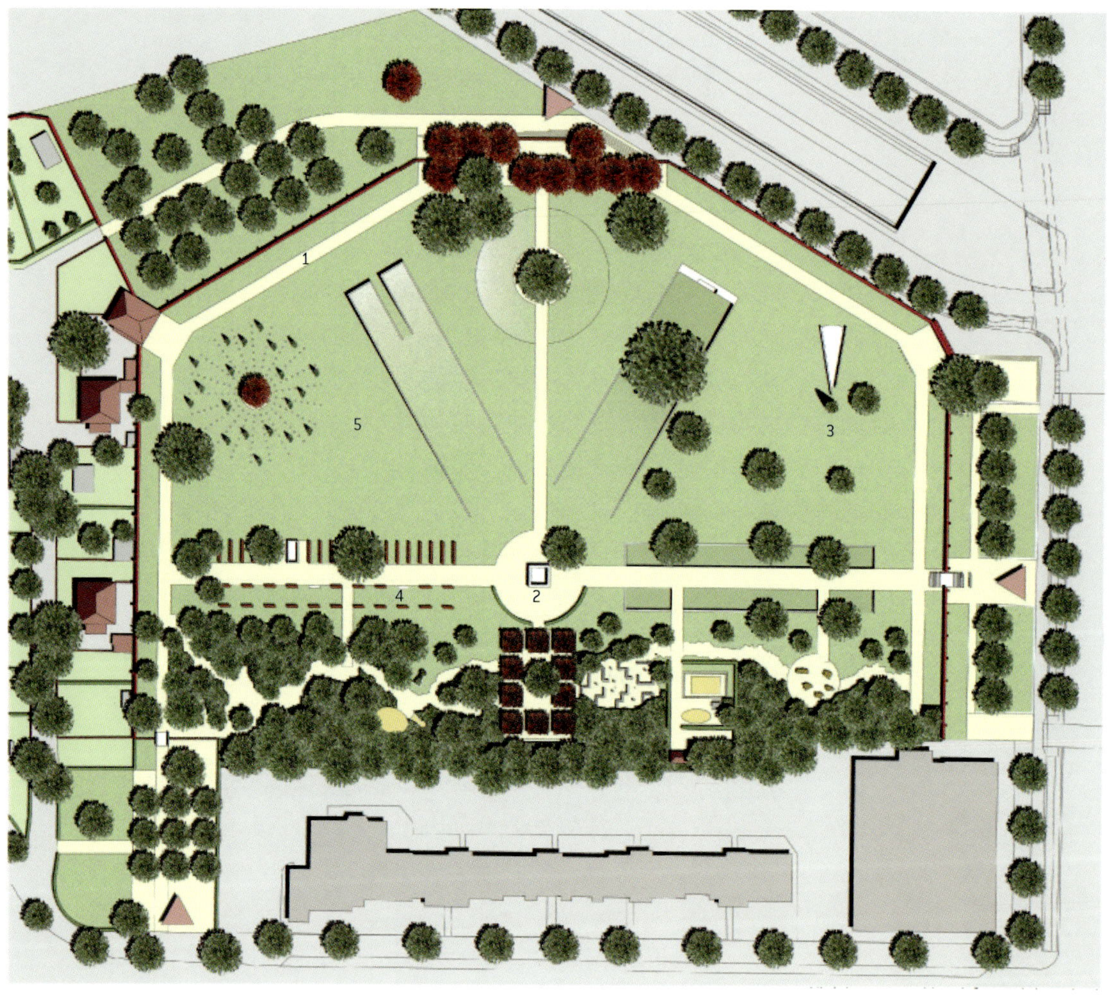

General plan

1. Passage from the sonnet "In Fetters" by Albrecht Haushofer
   inscribed on the preserved prison wall
2. Panoptikum, central surveillance room, symbolized by a cubic
   concrete sculpture
3. Recreation of a former exercise yard where prisoners took solitary
   walks (origina size)
4. Reconstruction of a cell in its original dimensions as a walk-in
   sculpture with a sound installation by Christiane Klepper
5. Depiction of the exercise yard complex. Concrete circles illustrate
   the individual yards. Columnar junipers symbolize the "yardbirds"

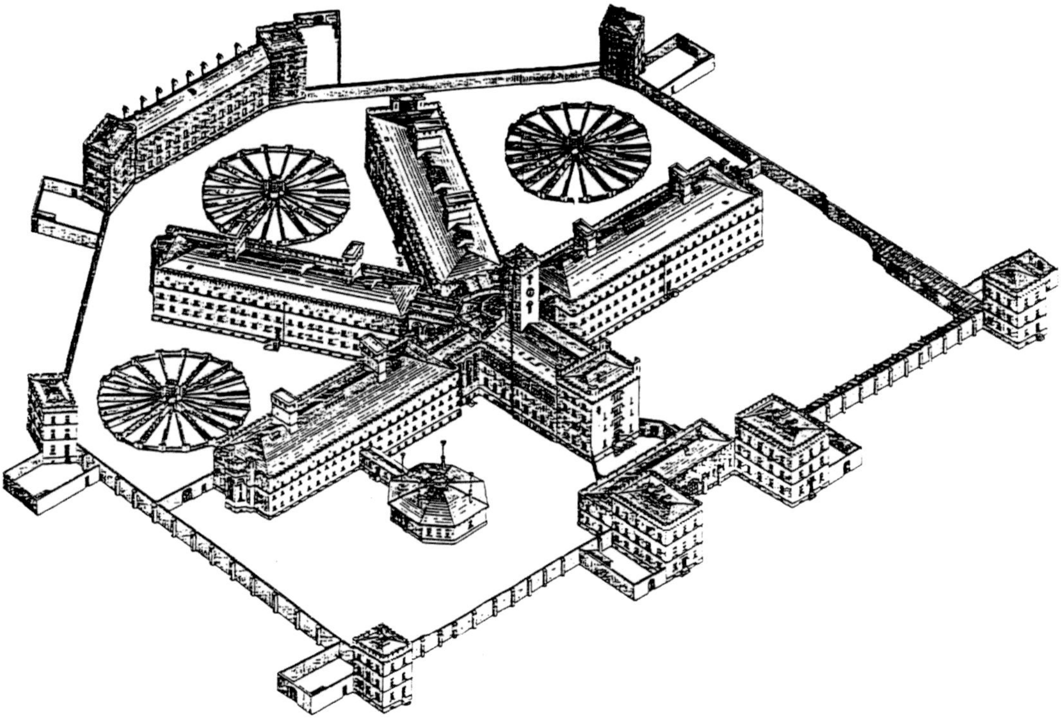

Prison sketch

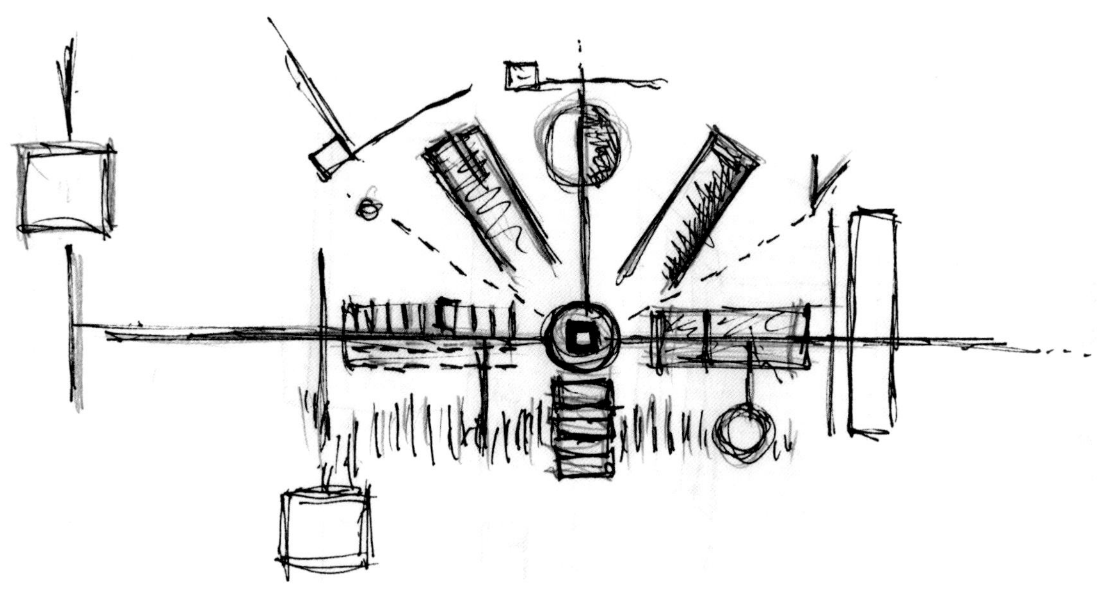

Park sketch

First sketch of Panoptikum

Second sketch of Panoptikum

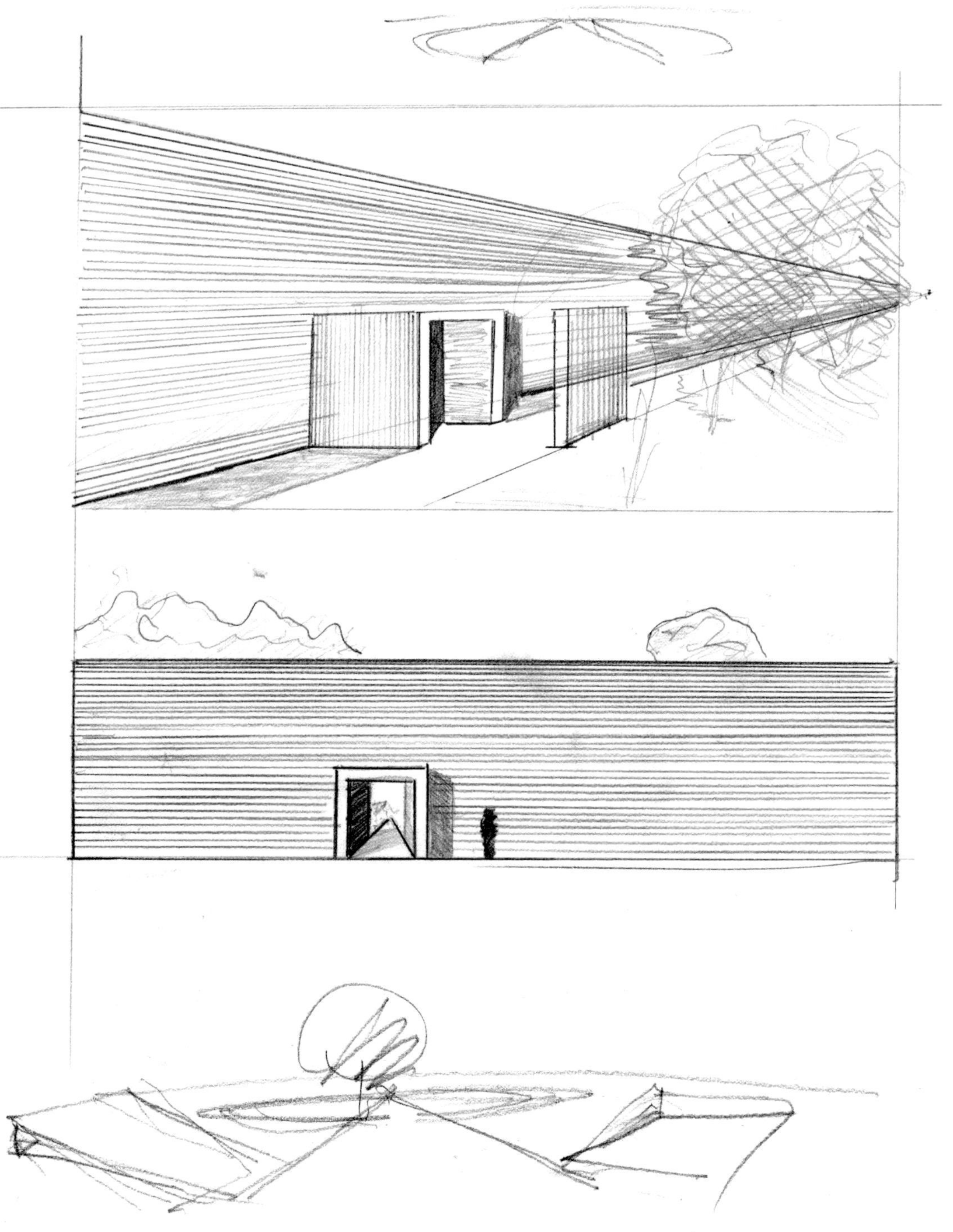

First sketch of entrance

IBM Riekerpolder

Amsterdam, The Netherlands

The Riekerpolder area in Amsterdam's south is the setting for a new urban development that is taking place that includes the new IBM offices. A landscaped courtyard was designed comprising reflecting ponds and canals, in addition to a green slope and a central patio area for resting.

Un plan d'urbanisme, dont fait partie le nouveau bâtiment administratif d'IBM, est mis en œuvre sur la place Riekerpolder, au sud d'Amsterdam. L'espace aménagé en jardin est composé de bassins et de canaux au revêtement réfléchissant, d'une butte verte et d'une cour centrale pour se reposer.

Das neue Bürogebäude von IBM ist Teil des städtebaulichen Plans, der für den Riekerpolder Platz in Amsterdam entwickelt wurde. Es wurde ein begrünter Innenhof entworfen, der Teiche, reflektierende Kanäle, einen grünen Abhang und einen zentralen Hof für die Arbeitspausen umfasst.

Op de Riekerpolder, ten zuiden van Amsterdam, wordt een stadsplan ontwikkeld dat het nieuwe kantoorgebouw van IBM omvat. De binnentuin bestaat uit weerspiegelende vijvers en grachten, een groene helling en in het midden een plein voor ontspanning.

Delta Vorm Groep, William McDonough + Partners
www.deltavormgroep.nl
© Frank Colder, Picture 7, Delta Vorm Groep (drawings)

The focal points of the courtyard are the water and the green space. The landscape architects wanted to create a "green heart" at the center of the office complex.

Les principaux éléments situés au milieu de la cour sont l'eau et l'espace végétal. Le projet des paysagistes consistait à créer un «cœur vert» au centre du complexe administratif.

Die zentralen Elemente sind das Wasser und die Grünzone. Die Landschaftsgestalter wollten eine „grüne Lunge" im Zentrum der Büroanlage schaffen.

De belangrijkste en centrale onderdelen van de binnenplaats zijn het water en de groenzone. De landschapsarchitecten wilden een "groen hart" creëren in het midden van het kantorencomplex.

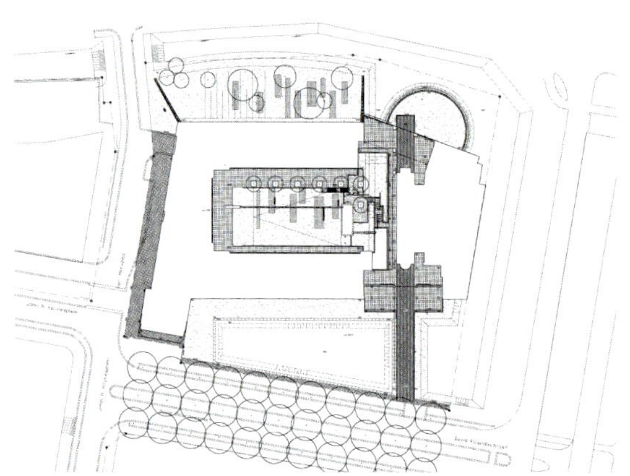

General plan

General color plan

Color sketch for waterfall

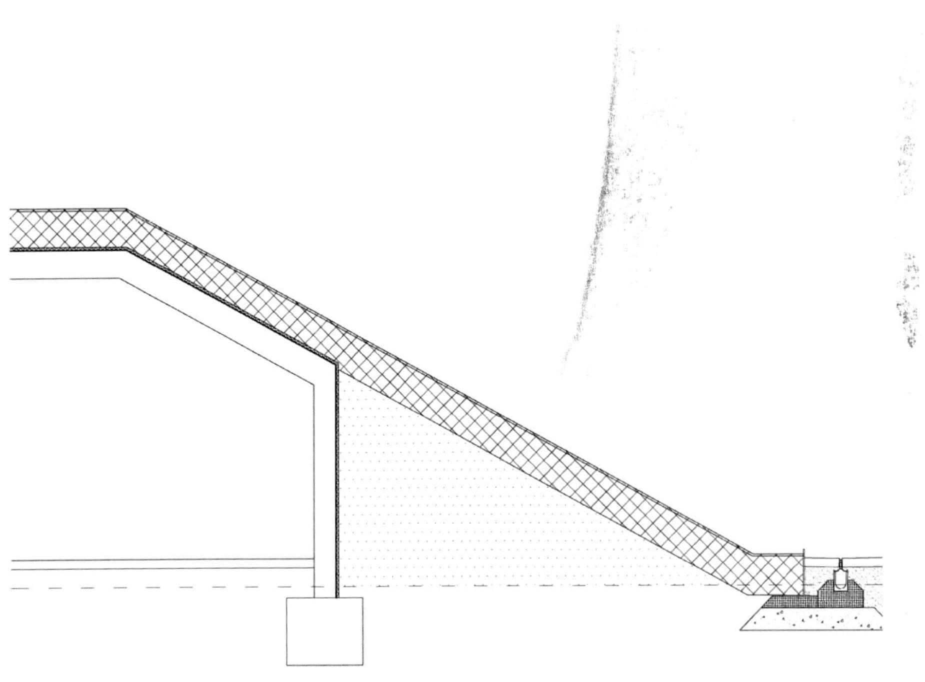

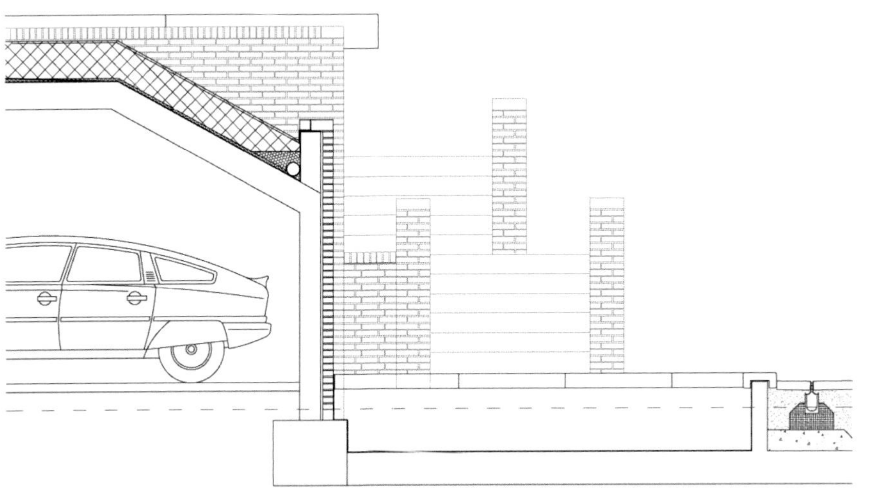

Sections of drop

Court Square Garden

Boston, MA, USA

The remodeling of a factory building as lofts created an open courtyard. A private green space was created for the residents following strict requirements for material (organic and inert), texture (from thick to thin), and values (between light and dark).

La rénovation d'un bâtiment industriel en lofts a laissé une cour intérieure à découvert. Les résidents ont pu donc bénéficier d'un espace vert privé, qui répond à des conditions précises de matérialité (organique et inerte), de texture (grande et petite épaisseur) et de valeurs (ombre et lumière).

Der Umbau eines Industriegebäudes in Lofts gab die Sicht auf den Innenhof frei. Für die Bewohner wurde eine intime Grünzone geschaffen, die von den Regeln der Materialeigenschaften (organisch/unbelebt), der Struktur (dick/dünn) und der Effekte (Licht/Dunkel) beherrscht wird.

Toen een industriegebouw tot lofts werd omgebouwd heeft men een binnenplaats opengelaten. Er werd een groene privézone voor de bewoners gecreëerd die wordt bepaald door nauwkeurige regelingen van (organische en inerte) stoffelijkheid, van textuur (van dik naar dun) en van waarden (tussen licht en donker).

Landworks Studio, AJ Martini (General Contractor), John Cunningham Architects, Office dA (Architects), Emanouil Inc. (Landscape Contractor), DM Berg Consultants (Structural Engineer)

www.landworks-studio.com
© Josh Kuchinsky Photography, Landworks Studio (drawings)

Sketch

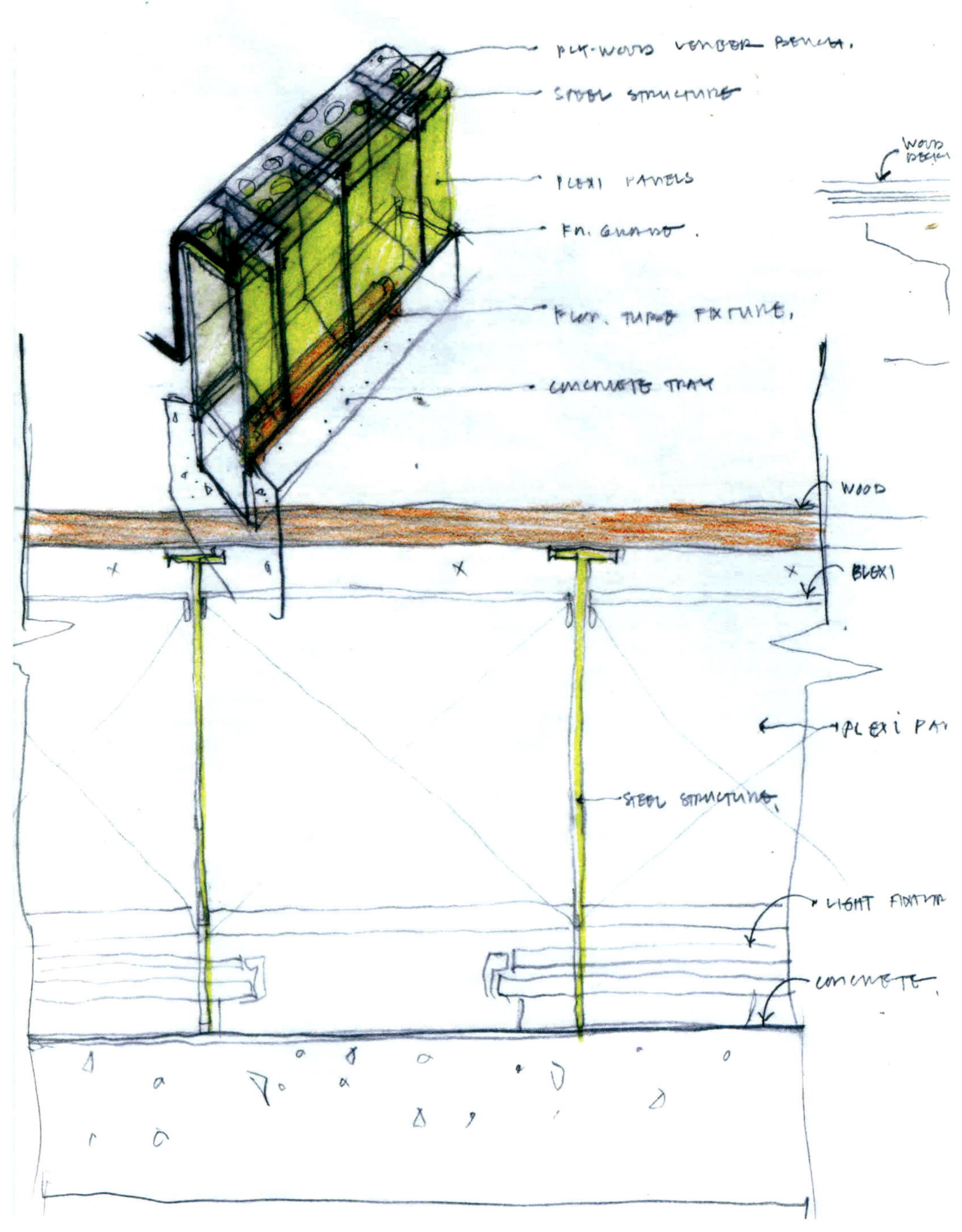

Sketch of bench and detail

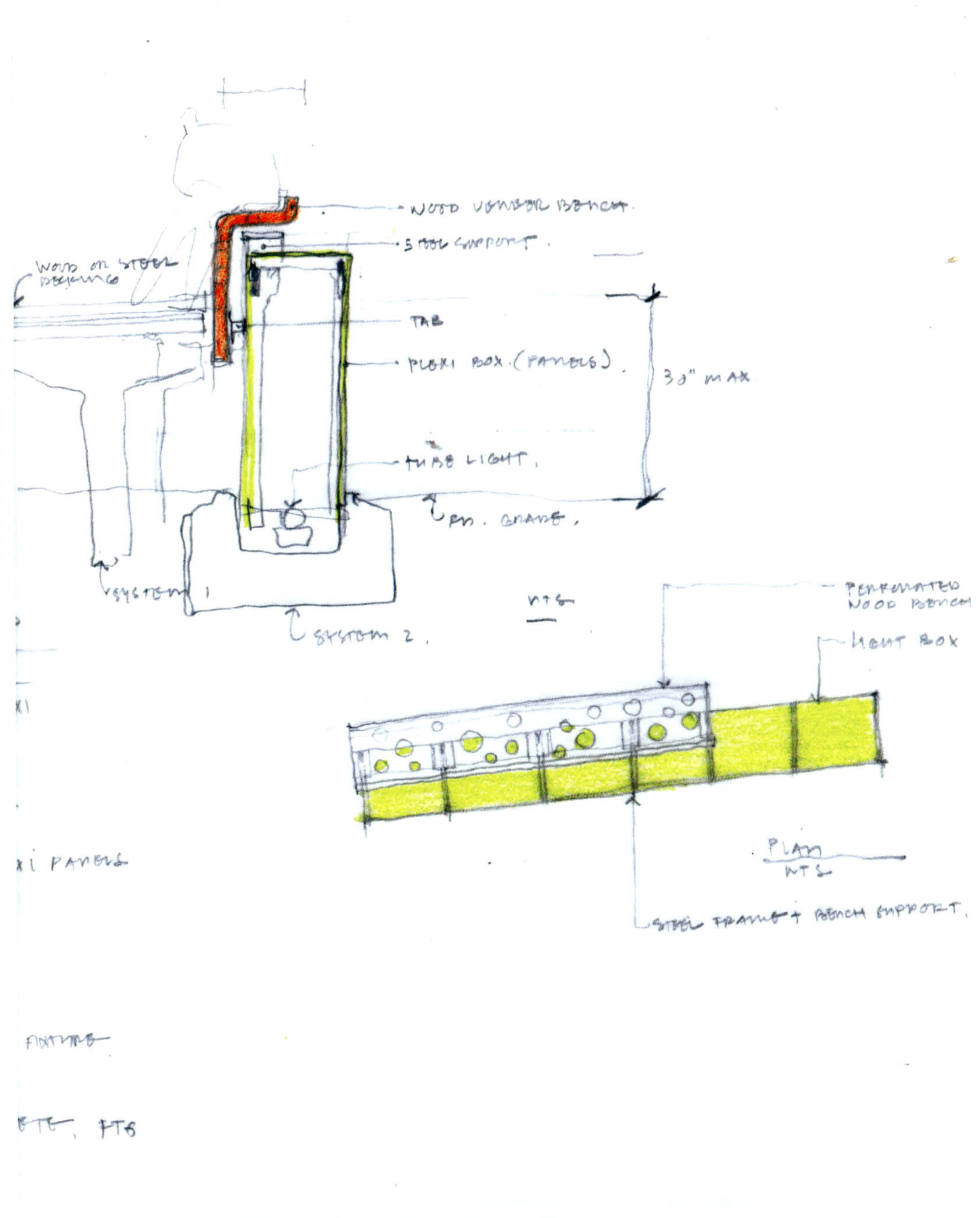

Sketch of bench and detail

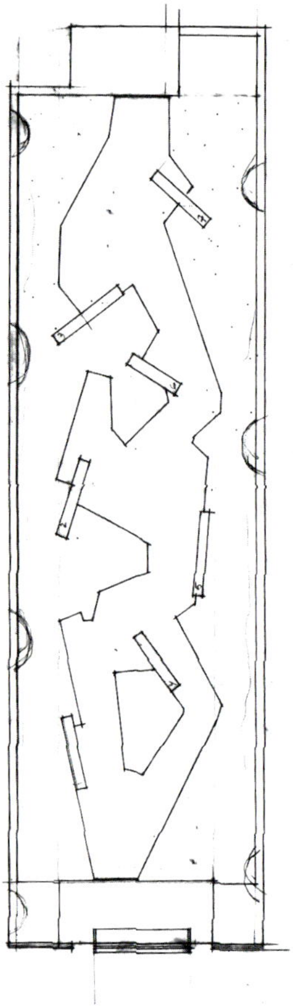

General sketch

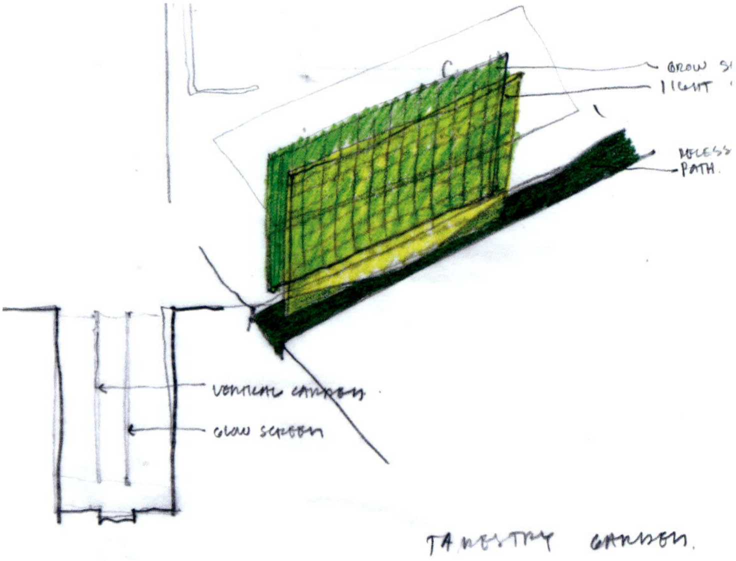

Sketch of light wall

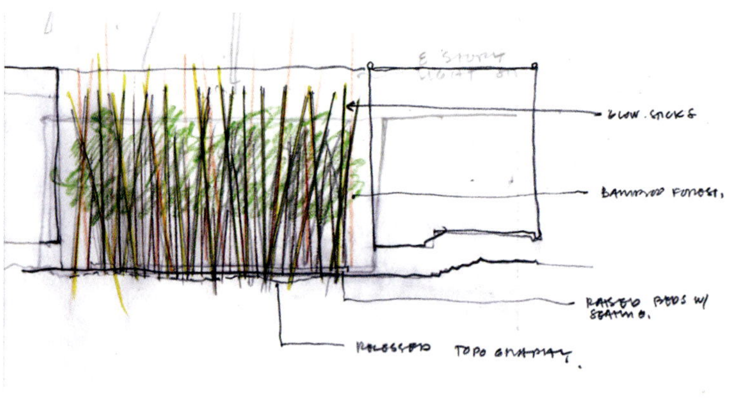

Concept sketch of bamboos web

The windows of the floors have views limited by plants that keep them from being seen from the courtyard. The project is structured around the use of bamboo, optical fiber lighting, and stainless steel.

La vue des fenêtres est limitée par une végétation qui empêche d'être aperçu de l'extérieur. Le bambou, l'éclairage en fibre optique et l'acier inoxydable composent cette structure.

Die begrenzte Sicht der Fenster durch eine Reihe von Pflanzen verhindert den Einblick von der anderen Hofseite. Bambus, Glasfaserbeleuchtung und Edelstahl bilden die Struktur dieses Projekts.

De ramen bieden een beperkt uitzicht: een rij planten voorkomt dat men gezien kan worden. Bamboe, verlichting in glasvezel en roestvrij staal vormen de structuur van dit project.

3D rendering of court square

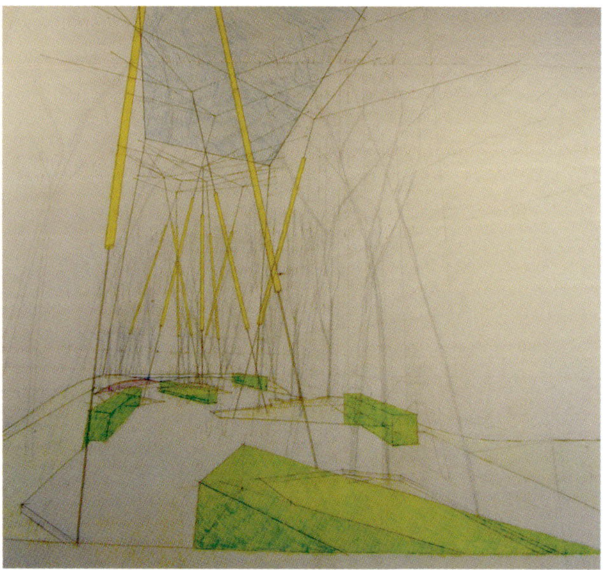

Drawing of court square with bamboos web, benches and light wall

Models

Cross section of court square

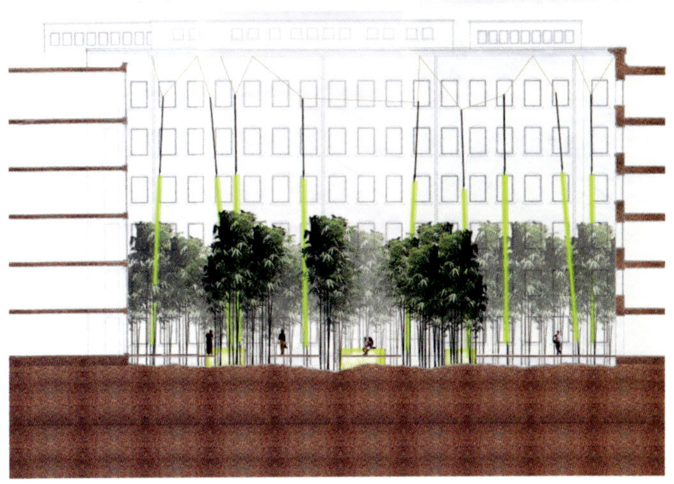

Long section of court square

Danse en Ligne

Montreal, Canada

This project involves the courtyard of an old factory converted into apartments. The landscaped courtyard is paved in cedar wood to contrast with the mineral feel of the surroundings. Raised planter boxes feature next to the stairs leading from the apartments to the courtyard.

Le projet correspond à la cour intérieure d'un ancien bâtiment industriel réhabilité pour y créer des logements. Celle-ci, dotée d'un jardin, est recouverte d'un revêtement en bois de cèdre qui contraste avec la composition minérale des alentours. Des jardinières surélevées ont été installées à côté des escaliers permettant d'accéder des appartements à la cour intérieure.

Das Projekt gehört zum Innenhof eines alten Industriegebäudes, das zu Wohnungen umgebaut wurde. Der Hof mit Garten ist mit Zedernholz ausgelegt, das zum mineralischen Ambiente der Umgebung in Kontrast steht. An den Treppen, die von den Appartements zum Innenhof führen, wurden erhöhte Blumenkästen angebracht.

Het project omvat de binnenplaats van een voormalig industriegebouw dat wordt hergebruikt voor woningen. De binnenplaats met tuin is geplaveid met cederhout dat een contrast vormt met de minerale sfeer uit de omgeving. Er zijn verhoogde bloembakken geplaatst bij de trap van de appartementen naar de binnenplaats.

NIPpaysage
www.nippaysage.ca
© NIPpaysage

A series of green seats are arranged as minimalist dining areas. The rest of the courtyard features cedar wood, crushed stone, and a number of shrubs.

La cour dispose d'un ensemble de sièges verts formant des salons de jardin minimalistes. Le reste de la cour intérieure est composé de bois de cèdre, de gravillons et d'arbustes temporaires.

Ein Ensemble von grünen Sitzgelegenheiten befindet sich in den minimalistischen Gartenlauben. Zedernholz, Kies und einige Sträucher bilden die restlichen Komponenten des Innenhofs.

Groene stoelen werden opgesteld in minimalistische priëlen. De rest van de binnenplaats is voorzien van cederhout, grind en enkele struiken.

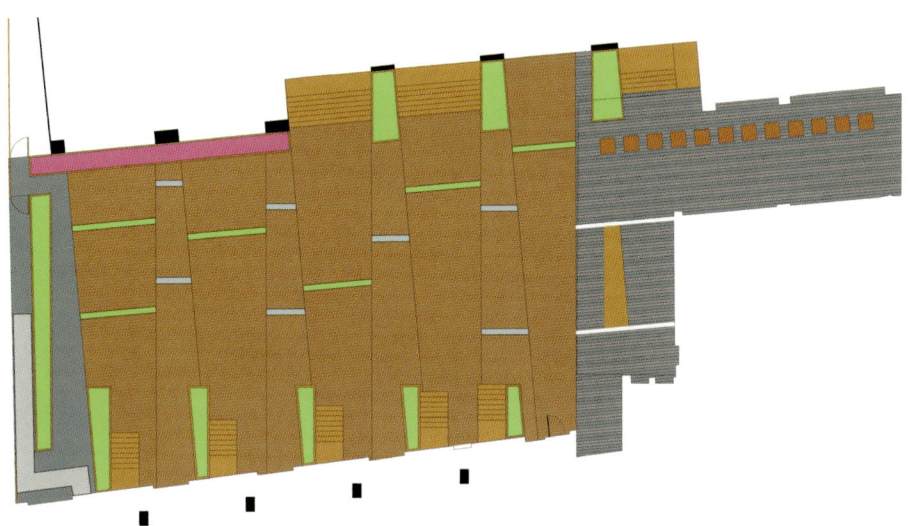

Plan

The Centre for Ideas

Melbourne, Australia

This project involves accentuating the three-dimensional façade of the Centre for Ideas, built in stainless steel. The design is based on geometry and makes use of color contrasts. The geometry is inspired by the book *Order in Space* by Keith Critchlow, which reflects on the connection between mathematics and art in defining space.

L'intervention s'effectue pour mettre en valeur la façade tridimensionnelle singulière du Centre for Ideas, construite en acier inoxydable. La conception se base sur des géométries et des jeux de contrastes chromatiques. Cette géométrie tire son inspiration de l'ouvrage *Order in Space* de Keith Critchlow qui propose une réflexion sur le point de rencontre entre les mathématiques et l'art pour définir l'espace.

Das Projekt wurde in Edelstahl ausgeführt, um die einzigartige dreidimensionale Fassade des „Centre for Ideas" zu betonen. Das Design beruht auf geometrischen Formen und spielt mit Farbkontrasten. Die Geometrie wurde von Keith Critchlows Text *Order in Space* inspiriert, in dem über die Verbindung von Mathematik und Kunst reflektiert wird, um den Raum zu definieren.

Het project wil de nadruk leggen op de bijzondere, driedimensionale, roestvrij stalen gevel van het Centre for Ideas. Het ontwerp is gebaseerd op geometrische vormen en speelt met kleurcontrasten. Deze geometrie is geïnspireerd op de tekst *Order in Space* van Keith Critchlow, waarin wordt nagedacht over het verbindingspunt tussen wiskunde en kunst om de ruimte te bepalen.

Rush & Wright Associates
www.rushwright.com
© Peter Bennetts, Derek Swalwell, Rush & Wright Associates

EXIT

The pavement is designed in black and white stripes that turn into gray and white hexagons. Small pyramid-shaped mounds of synthetic material are also present.

Le revêtement est réalisé à base de rayures noires et blanches qui se transforment en hexagones blancs et gris. Des monticules de matière artificielle en forme de pyramides y sont installés.

Das Pflaster wurde auf der Basis weißer und schwarzer Streifen, die sich in weiße und graue Sechsecke verwandeln, entworfen. Es wurden pyramidenförmige Erhebungen aus künstlicher Materie installiert.

Het plaveisel is ontworpen op basis van witte en zwarte strepen die veranderen in witte en grijze zeshoeken. Er zijn bergen kunstmatig materiaal in de vorm van piramides aangebracht.

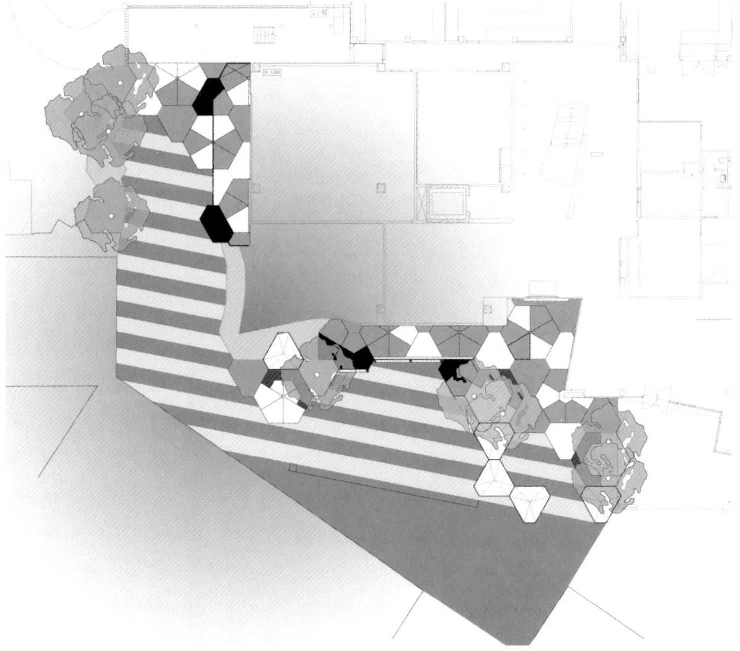

Plan

Cour Bleue

Montreal, Canada

This project is for the new park in the vicinity of the Paul-Bruchési Elementary School in Montreal. The design is spectacular given the great splashes of color used by the landscape architects to lay out and structure the areas depending on their use and the programmed events taking place there.

Le projet correspond au nouveau parc proche de l'école primaire Paul-Bruchési de Montréal. La conception est spectaculaire puisque les paysagistes ont créé un immense étalage de couleurs, distribuées et structurées en zones, en fonction des différents usages et activités programmées.

Das Projekt gehört zum neuen Park nahe der Paul-Bruchési-Grundschule in Montreal. Das Design ist aufsehenerregend, da die Planer eine Vielfalt von Farben entwickelt haben, die verschiedene Bereiche entsprechend ihrer Funktionen und den dort vorgesehenen Aktivitäten strukturieren.

Dit project betreft het nieuwe park dicht bij de basisschool Paul-Bruchési te Montreal. Het ontwerp is spectaculair. De landschapsarchitecten hebben namelijk een grote tentoonspreiding van kleuren gecreëerd waarmee de zones worden georganiseerd en gestructureerd al naargelang de diverse toepassingen en de geprogrammeerde activiteiten.

NIPpaysage
www.nippaysage.ca
© NIPpaysage

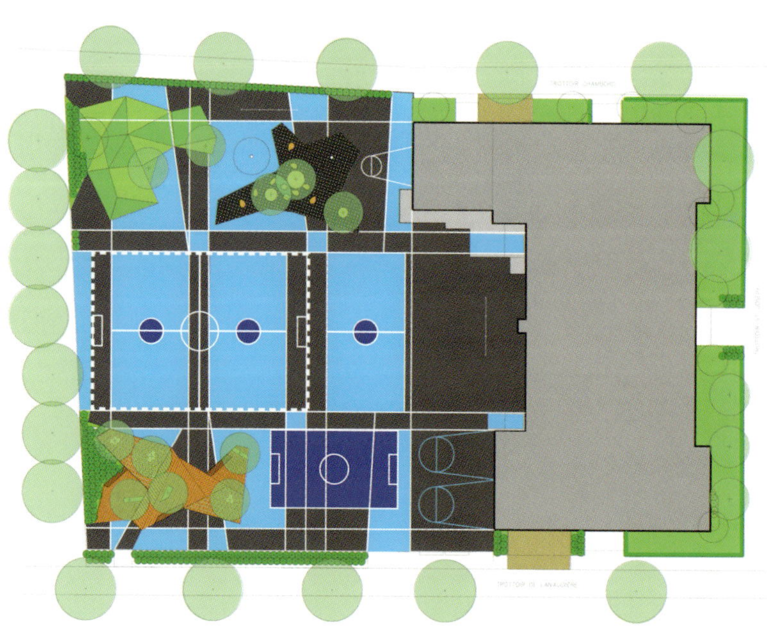

Plan

Large boulders, located in the squares decorated with dots and trees, serve as seats. The remaining space is paved in rubber.

D'immenses galets, utilisés comme des sièges, sont situés sur les quadrillages formés par des cercles et des arbres. Le caoutchouc est utilisé pour revêtir le reste de l'espace.

Große Kieselsteine, liegen als Sitzgelegenheit dienen, befinden sich auf dem aufgemalten Gitternetz, auf dem sich Farbkreise mit Bäumen abwechseln. Der restliche Bodenbelag ist aus Kautschuk.

Grote afgeronde stenen die als stoelen dienen, zijn in ruiten geplaatst en gekleurde cirkels en bomen wisselen elkaar af. voor het plaveisel van de rest van de ruimte is rubber gebruikt.

Katharina Sulzer Platz

Located in one of the most important industrial areas in Winterthur, this space was turned into a 110,000-sq ft development. It combines the feel of its industrial past with contemporary architecture to form shopping areas, studios, and offices.

Situé dans l'une des enclaves industrielles les plus importantes de Winterthour, l'espace a été reconverti en un nouveau site de 10 000 m². Il combine à la fois esthétique du passé industriel et nouvelle architecture pour créer des zones commerciales, des cabinets et des centres professionnels.

In einem der wichtigsten Industriegebiete von Winterthur wurde ein Gelände mit 10.000 m² Fläche neu gestaltet. Dort wurde die neue Architektur in die Ästhetik der industriellen Vergangenheit integriert und man schuf Einkaufszentren, Studios und Fach-Zentren.

Deze ruimte, gelegen in een van de belangrijkste industriegebieden van Winterthur, werd omgevormd tot een nieuwe plek van 10.000 m². Hierin is het aspect van het industriële verleden gecombineerd met de nieuwe architectuur om winkelzones, kantoren en vakcentra te creëren.

Vetsch Nipkow Partner Landschaftsarchitekten
www.vnp.ch
© Ralph Feiner, Vetsch Nipkow Partner Landschaftsarchitekten (drawings)

PIONIERPARK

Metal furniture, concrete paving, water features, colored lighting, and plants feature in the spaces between the buildings.

Des éléments de mobilier en métal, un revêtement en béton, des points d'eau, un éclairage coloré et des espèces végétales ont été installés entre les bâtiments.

Zwischen den Gebäuden wurden Mobiliar aus Metall, Betonpflaster, Bereiche mit Wasser, farbige Beleuchtung und Pflanzen installiert.

Tussen de gebouwen werden metalen meubels, betonnen plaveisel, waterzones, gekleurde verlichting en verschillende planten aangelegd.

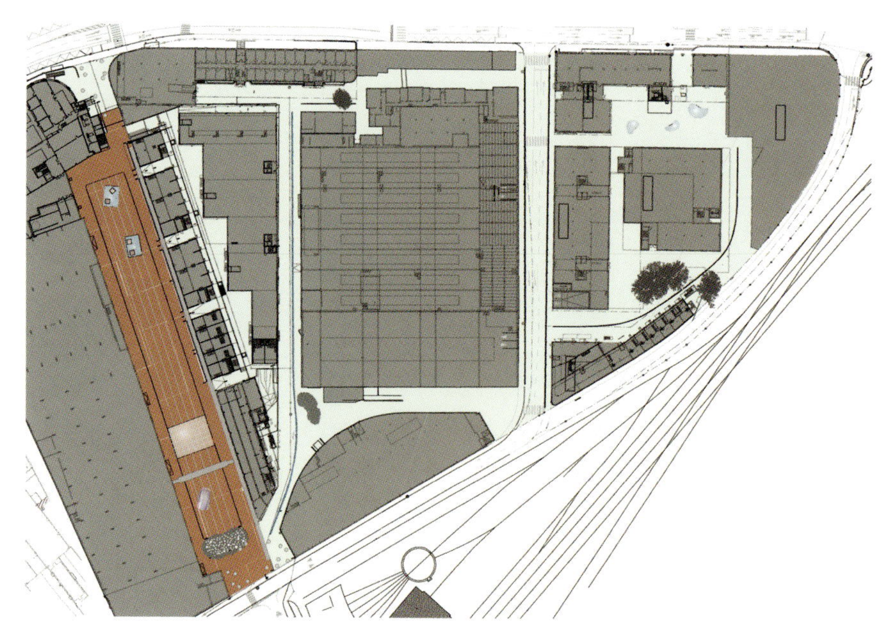

Location plan

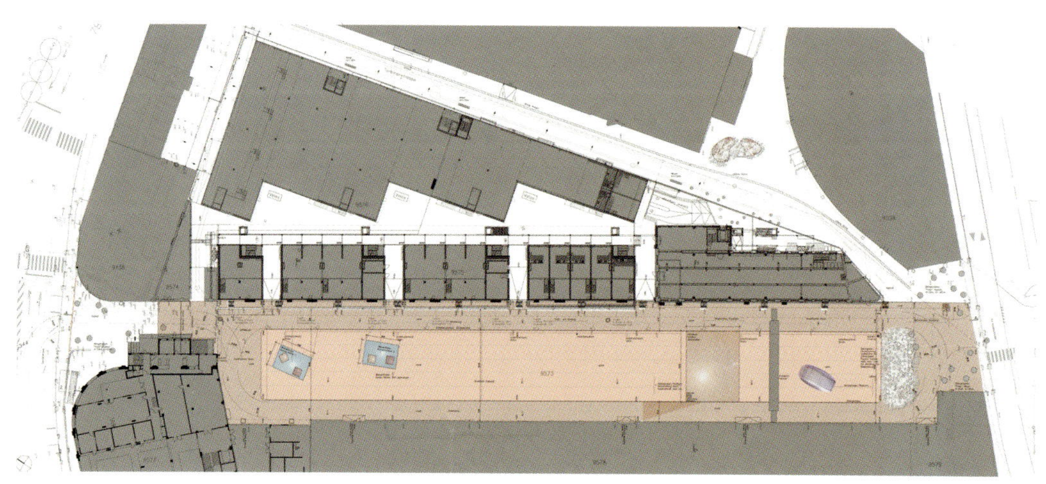

General plan of the square

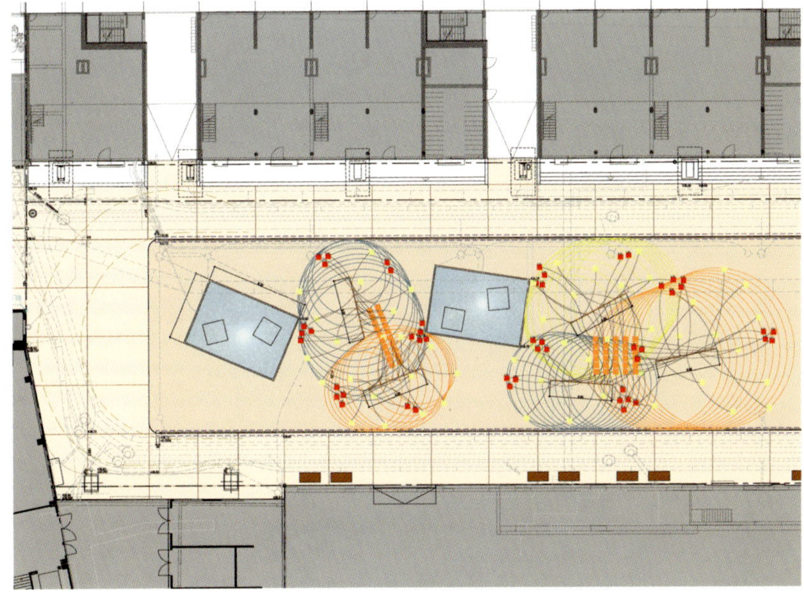

Plan detail

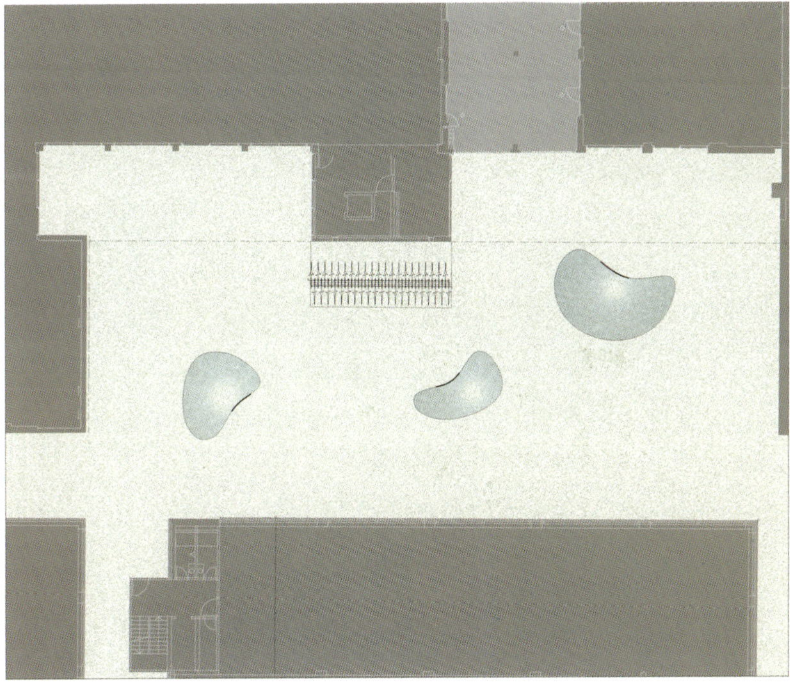

Square plan

Le Jardin Sauvage du Palais de Tokyo

Paris, France

The Palais de Tokyo project was an opportunity to turn an abandoned space into a wild garden. Located on a narrow site, the landscaped area is planted with lush vegetation that transforms the space as it grows.

L'aménagement du Palais de Tokyo a permis de transformer un espace abandonné en jardin sauvage. La zone aménagée en espace vert et située dans un lieu étroit est composée d'une forêt de plantes qui transforment l'espace au fur et à mesure de leur croissance.

Der Umbau des Tokioter Palais ermöglichte die Umgestaltung eines verlassenen Gebietes in einen verwilderten Garten. Die schmale begrünte Zone besteht aus einer Pflanzenwildnis, die das Gebiet, während sie wächst, allmählich verwandelt.

Dankzij de verbouwing van het Palais de Tokyo kon een verlaten ruimte in een wilde tuin worden omgevormd. De tuin ligt op een smalle plek en bestaat uit een oerwoud van planten die de ruimte wijzigen naarmate ze groeien.

Atelier Le Balto, Laurent Dugua (landscape), Robert Milin (artist)
www.lebalto.de
© Yann Monel, Atelier Le Balto (drawings)

Design development collages

The entrance to the garden is by a wood-lined path seen from the walkways leading to the restaurant from the street.

L'accès au jardin s'effectue par un chemin en bois visible grâce aux passerelles qui relient la rue au restaurant.

Der Zugang zum Garten wird über einen Holzweg ermöglicht, der durch die Stege, die von der Straße zum Restaurant führen, zu sehen ist.

Men heeft toegang tot de tuin via een zichtbaar houten pad dankzij de vlonders die vanaf de straat naar het restaurant voeren.

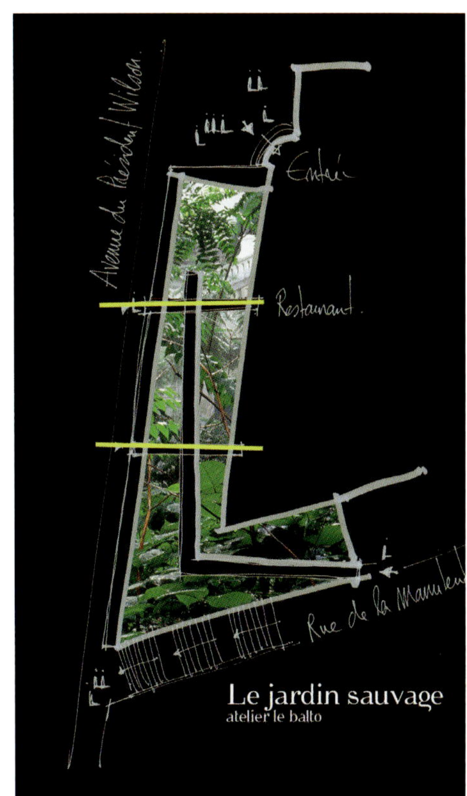

General plan

Design development collages

Pierre Dansereau Sciences Campus, University of Quebec

Montreal, Canada

The need arose to redirect the pedestrian flow between the different buildings of this university campus. The solution was to build paths in triangular patterns to simulate broken glass fragments, between which vegetation was planted.

Il a été nécessaire de redéfinir la circulation piétonnière entre les différents bâtiments de ce campus universitaire. La solution adoptée a été de construire des chemins au milieu de formes triangulaires qui simulent des morceaux de verre cassés sur un sol recouvert de végétation.

Auf dem Gelände dieser Universität war es notwendig geworden, den Fußgängerverkehr zwischen den verschiedenen Gebäuden umzulenken. Die Lösung bestand darin, zwischen dreieckigen Formen, die wie Glasscherben aussehen, Wege anzulegen. Der Boden der Dreiecke wurde bepflanzt.

Op deze universiteitscampus ontstond de noodzaak om het bestaande voetgangersverkeer tussen de verschillende gebouwen in goede banen te leiden. De oplossing waren paden tussen driehoekige vormen die stukken gebroken glas nabootsen. Op de bodem hiervan werd vegetatie geplant.

Claude Cormier Arquitectes paysagistas
www.claudecormier.com
© Annie Ypperciel, CCAPI
(drawings)

The constant flow of students on this university campus led to the creation of transit routes marked out between triangular structures filled with plants.

Le trafic constant d'étudiants sur ce campus universitaire a favorisé la création de voies de circulation insérées entre des structures triangulaires recouvertes de végétation.

Das ständige Hin und Her von Studenten auf dem Campus erforderte die Anlage von gekennzeichneten Wegen zwischen dreieckigen, begrünten Strukturen.

Het constante studentenverkeer op deze universiteitscampus was aanleiding voor de creatie van afgebakende wandelroutes tussen driehoekige structuren vol planten.

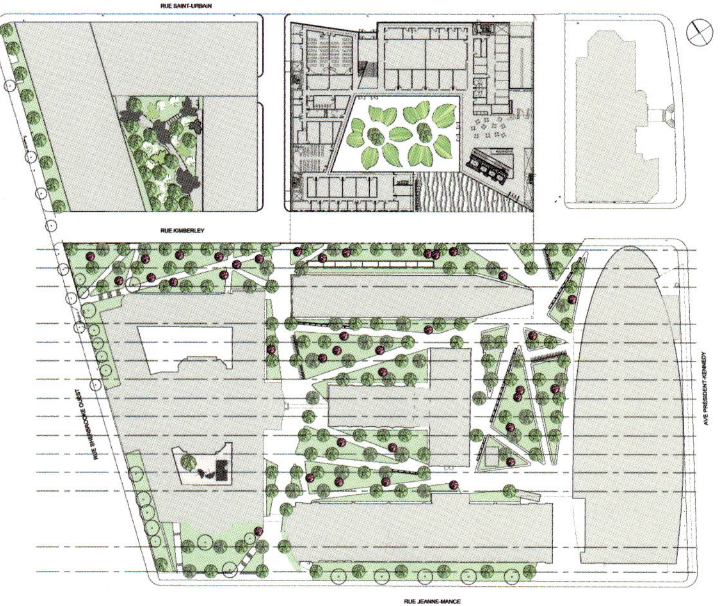

Plan of plantation during spring

Plan of plantation during summer

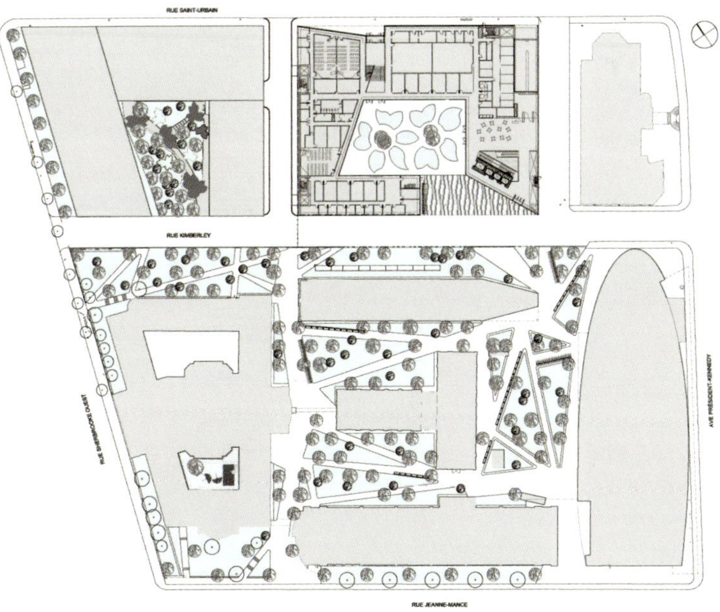

Plan of plantation during winter

Unterföhring Park Village

Munich, Germany

This large-scale project was designed for an office complex consisting of 19 different rectangular buildings. The commission was to unite the different buildings with an open public space. The project covered two areas; the central plaza uniting all of the buildings; and the rooftops, which were given a different and colorful design.

Ce gros projet a été conçu pour une zone administrative composée de 19 bâtiments rectangulaires tous différents. L'objectif consistait à uniformiser la diversité de volumes dans un même espace urbain. L'ouvrage, faisant appel à un design varié et coloré, a été réalisé à deux endroits : la place centrale qui relie tous les bâtiments et les terrasses.

Dieses Makroprojekt wurde für ein Büroviertel geplant, das 19 verschiedene rechteckige Gebäude umfasst. Der Auftrag war, die Vielfalt der Gebäude in einem städtischen Raum zu vereinen. Die Gestaltung wurde an zwei Orten ausgeführt: Auf dem zentralen Platz, der alle Gebäude vereint, und auf den Dachterrassen mit einem vielfältigen und farbigen Design.

Dit macroproject is uitgedacht voor een kantorenpark gevormd door 19 verschillende rechthoekige gebouwen. De opdracht bestond erin de diversiteit van volumes te verenigen met een stedelijke ruimte. Het project werd op twee plaatsen uitgewerkt: op het middenplein dat alle gebouwen met elkaar in verbinding brengt en op de dakterrassen met een divers en kleurrijk ontwerp.

Burger Landschaftsarchitekten
www.burgerlandschaftsarchitekten.de
© Florian Holzherr, Rakete, Burger Landschaftsarchitekten
(drawings)

Plan

The landscape architects worked on two levels: the lower level consisted of a plaza paved in polygonal slabs; while the upper level consisted of landscaped roofs.

Les paysagistes ont travaillé sur deux niveaux : celui du bas, constitué d'une place recouverte de dalles polygonales en pierre, et celui du haut, sur lequel des toitures végétales ont été aménagées.

Die Landschaftsarchitekten arbeiteten auf der unteren Ebene mit einem Platz mit vieleckigen Fliesen und auf der zweiten Ebene, wo begrünte Dächer entworfen wurden.

De landschapsarchitecten werkten op twee niveaus: het onderste, bestaand uit een plein met veelhoekige tegels; en het bovenste waar daktuinen werden ontworpen.

Impluvium

Montreal, Canada

Canadian landscape architects painted concentric circles in different shades of blue on the black asphalt covering the 32,000 sq ft of rooftop on the Belgo building. It was meant to draw attention to the huge potential offered by the large expanses of rooftops in the city.

Les paysagistes canadiens ont peint des cercles concentriques géants en différents tons bleus sur le bitume noir des 3 000 m² de toit-terrasse du bâtiment Belgo. Cette initiative cherche à souligner l'énorme potentiel des gigantesques dimensions des terrasses de la ville.

Auf der 3000 m² großen Dachterrasse des Belgo-Gebäudes malten die kanadischen Landschaftsgestalter riesige konzentrische Kreise in Blautönen auf den schwarzen Asphalt. Dies ist ein Hinweis auf das enorme Potential, das die riesigen Ausmaße der Dachterrassen der Stadt besitzen.

Op het 3000 m² grote dakterras van het Belgo-gebouw hebben Canadese landschapsarchitecten op het zwarte asfalt van het dak gigantische concentrische cirkels in verschillende blauwtinten geschilderd. Hiermee wordt de aandacht gevestigd op het grote potentieel dat verscholen zit in de enorme afmetingen van de platte daken van de stad.

NIPpaysage
www.nippaysage.ca
© NIPpaysage

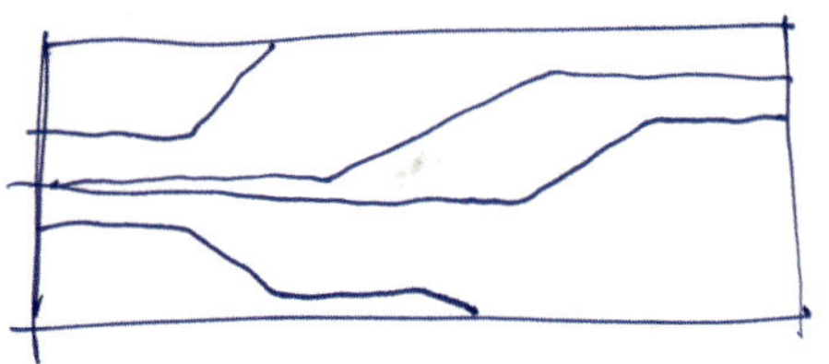
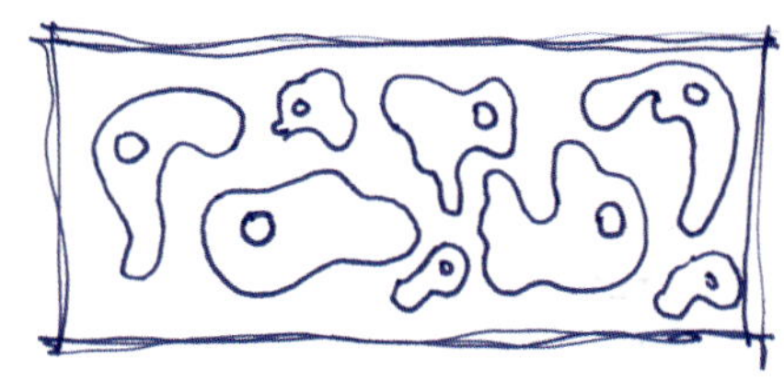

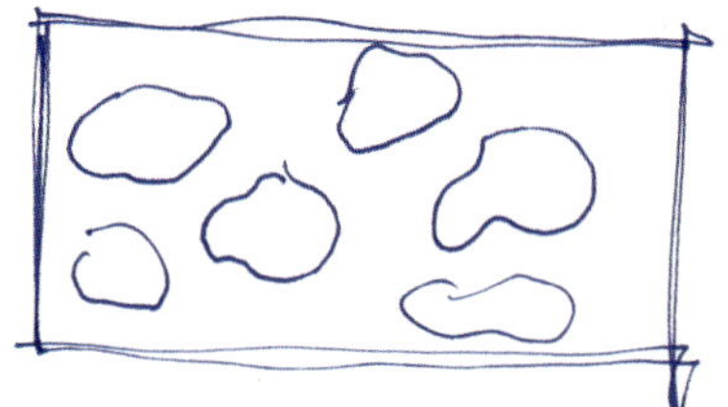

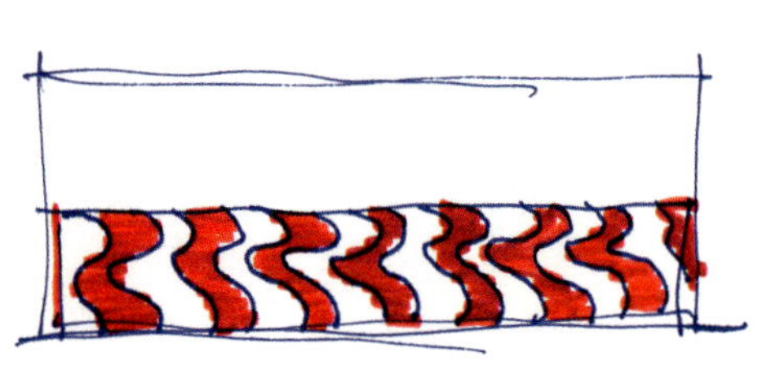

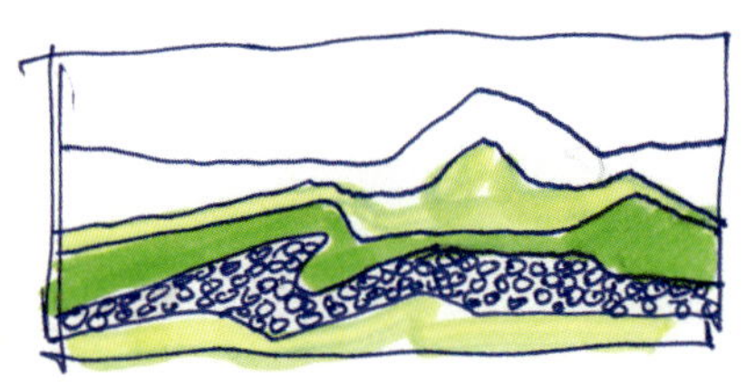
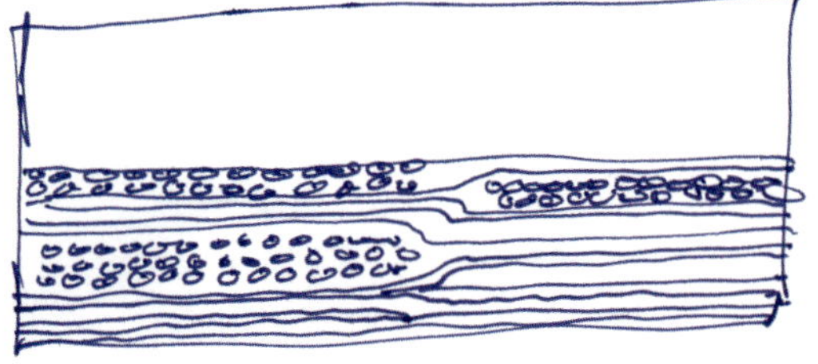

Brainstorming development studies

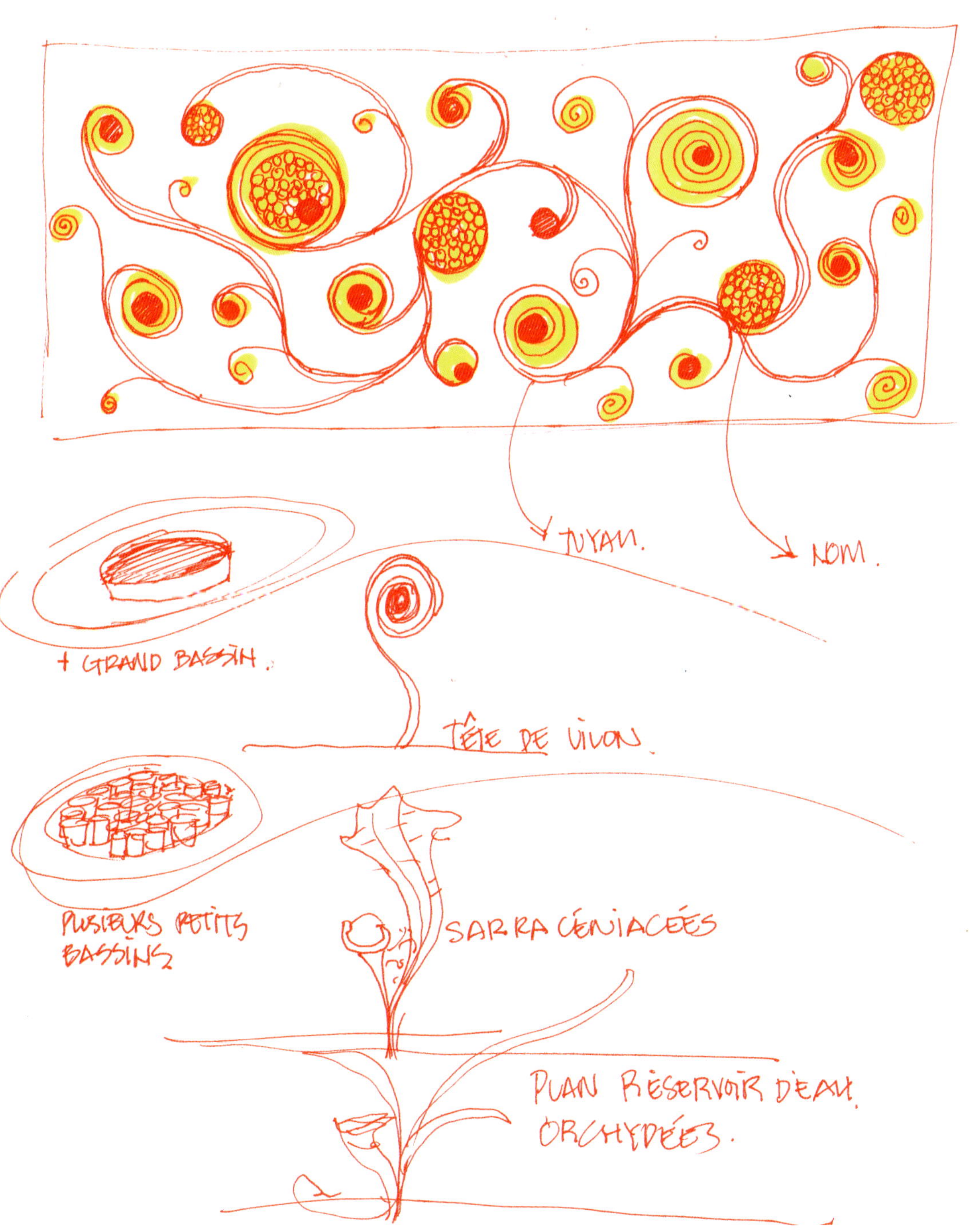

Brainstorming development studies

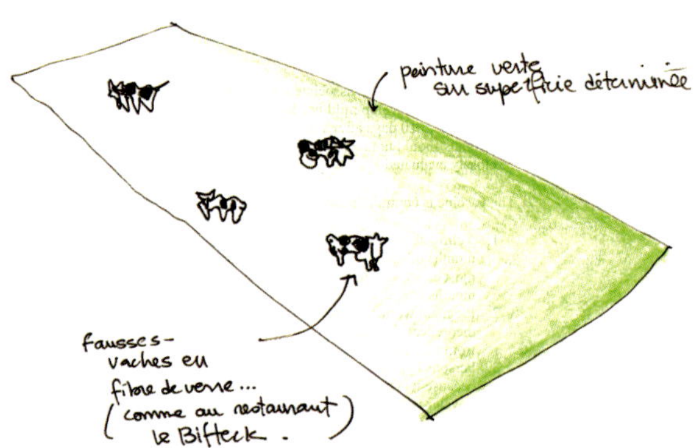

Sketch for a non built idea of synthetic pasture

Brainstorming development studies

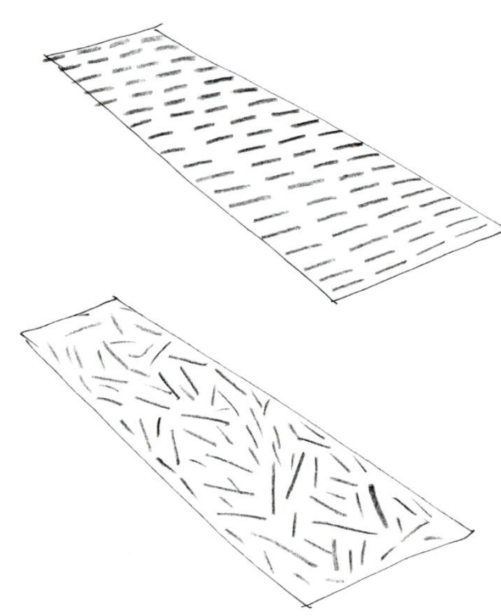

Sketch for a non built idea "Broken Kilometer"

Sketch for a non built idea of a typographic green roof

This project is a reminder that nature continues to exist above the city. The circles represent raindrops, indicating that little use is made of the water falling on these spaces.

Le projet nous rappelle que la nature continue d'exister au-dessus de la ville. Les cercles représentent des gouttes de pluie et dénoncent la mauvaise exploitation de l'eau récupérée dans ces espaces.

Die Aktion erinnert daran, dass über der Stadt die Natur weiterhin besteht. Die Kreise stellen Regentropfen dar, die die schlechte Nutzung des Regenwassers dieser Flächen anprangern.

Het project herinnert eraan dat er bovenop de stad nog steeds natuur bestaat. De cirkels stellen regendruppels voor die de slechte benutting van het water op deze plekken aan de kaak stellen.

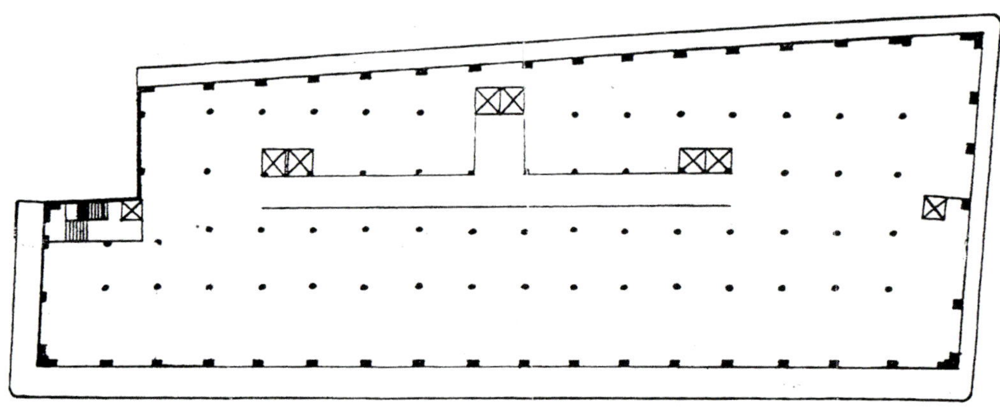

Plan

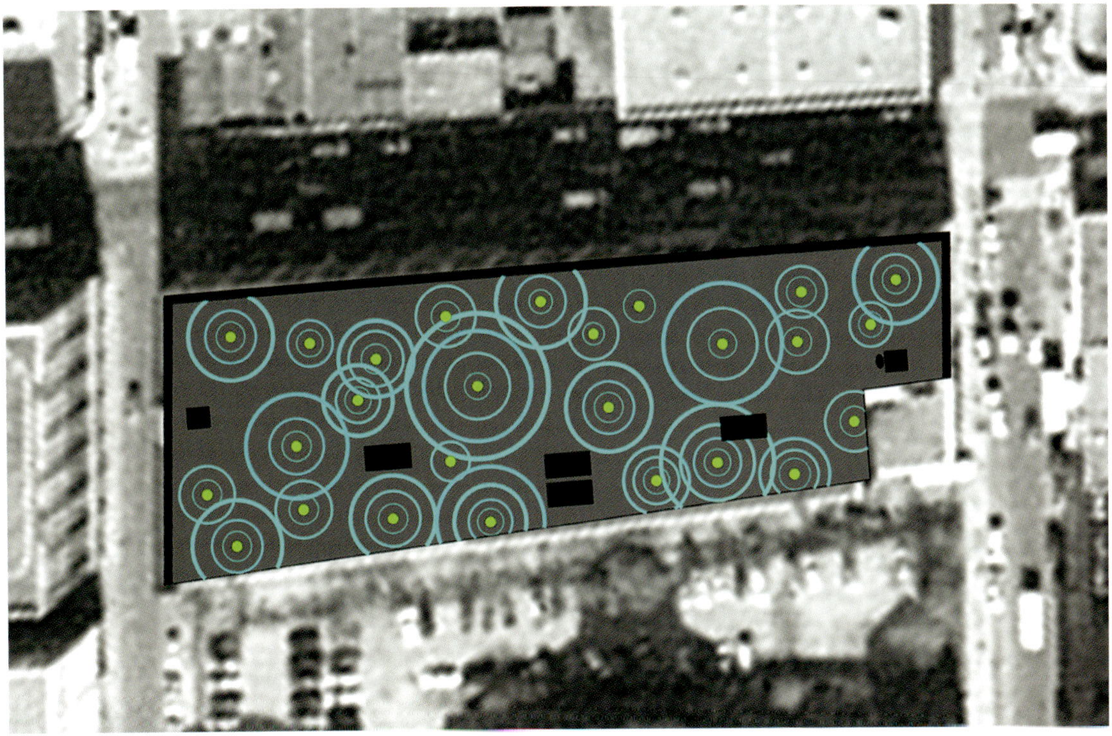

Collage plan

Simulation of aerial view

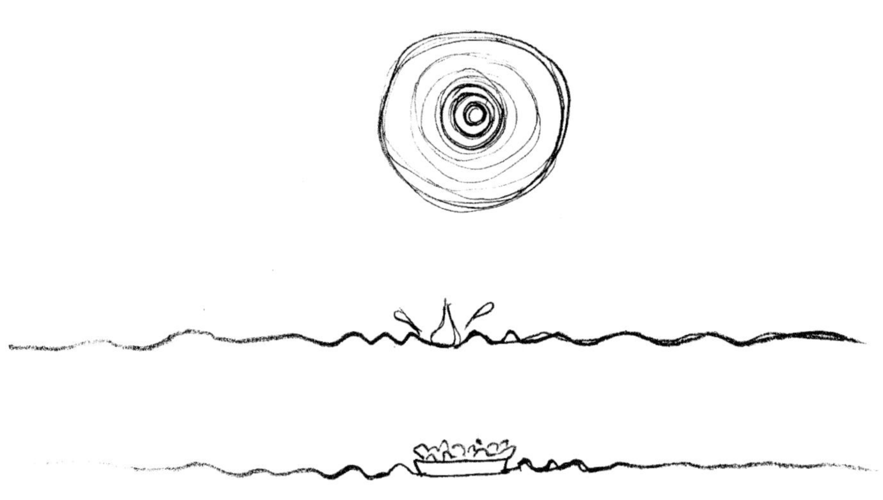

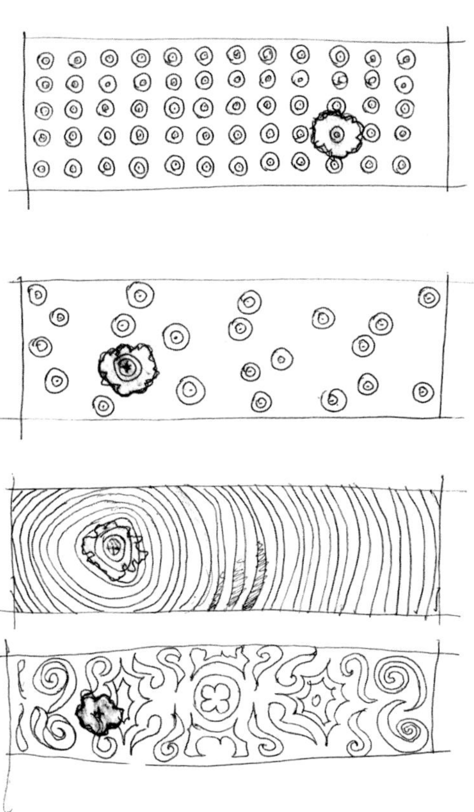

Conceptual sketches

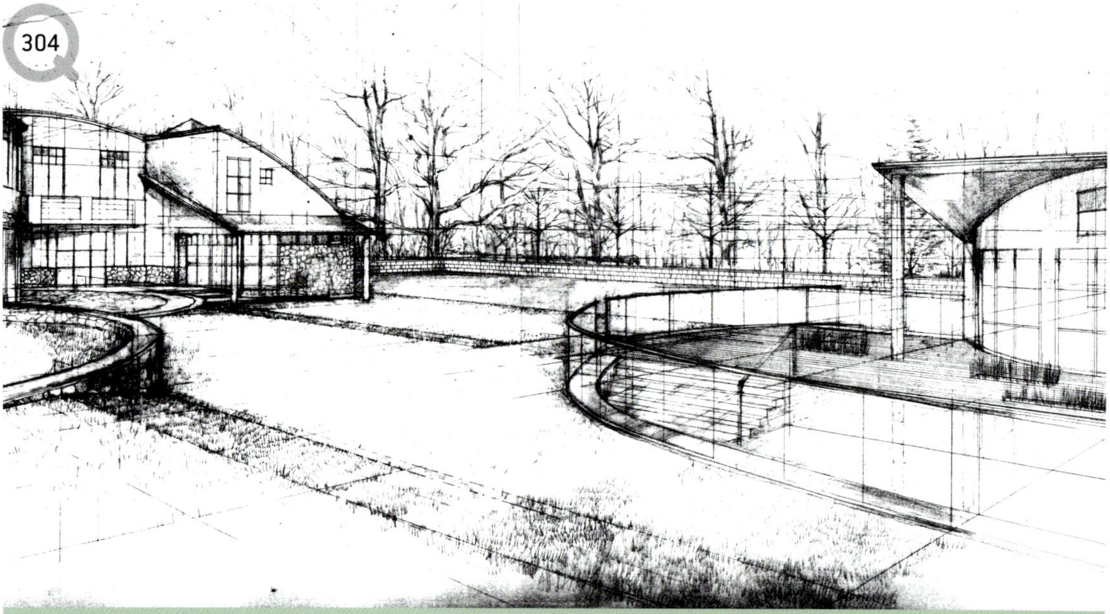

Crackle Garden

Weston, FL, USA

The existence of two oak trees was the inspiration for this garden. Drawings of branches and shadows cast by the trees were made on the granite paving and on the steel fence surrounding the swimming pool. The project blends a modern house into a wooded landscape.

La présence de deux spécimens de chênes a inspiré la création du jardin. Les dessins de branches et d'ombres d'arbres ont été appliqués sur le revêtement en granit et sur la clôture en acier qui entoure la piscine. Le projet intègre une maison moderne dans le paysage arboré.

Das Vorhandensein von zwei Eichen inspirierte die Anlage dieses Gartens. Das Muster von Ästen und Schatten der Bäume wurde auf das Granitpflaster und den Zaun um das Schwimmbecken übertragen. Der Entwurf integriert ein modernes Haus in eine baumbestandene Landschaft.

Twee eikenbomen waren de inspiratiebronnen voor de aanleg van deze tuin. Het patroon van de takken en schaduwen van de bomen werd toegepast op het granieten plaveisel en op het stalen hek rond het zwembad. Het project neemt een modern huis op in het bomenlandschap.

Landworks Studio
www.landworksstudio.com
© Landworks Studio

Site section: north section

Site section: east section

Site elevation: north elevation

Site elevation: east elevation

The design of the stainless steel fence around the garden reproduces the modular system created for the granite with random cracking effects inspired by drawings of the branches and shadows of trees.

Le design de la clôture en acier inoxydable reproduit le système modulaire pour le granit avec un effet de fissuration aléatoire inspiré de dessins de branches et d'ombres d'arbres.

Das Stahldesign des Gartenzauns wiederholt das für den Granit geschaffene Formsystem mit zufällig erscheinenden Rissen, die vom Muster der Äste und von Baumschatten inspiriert sind.

Het roestvrij stalen hek reproduceert het voor het graniet gecreëerde modulesysteem en vertoont een op de takken en schaduwen van de bomen geïnspireerd barstenpatroon.

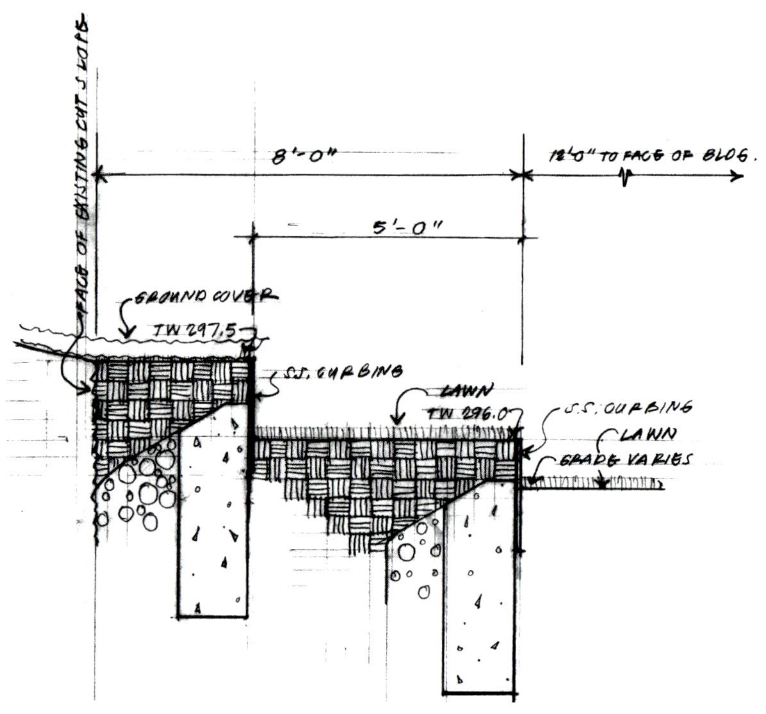

Sketch for lift section

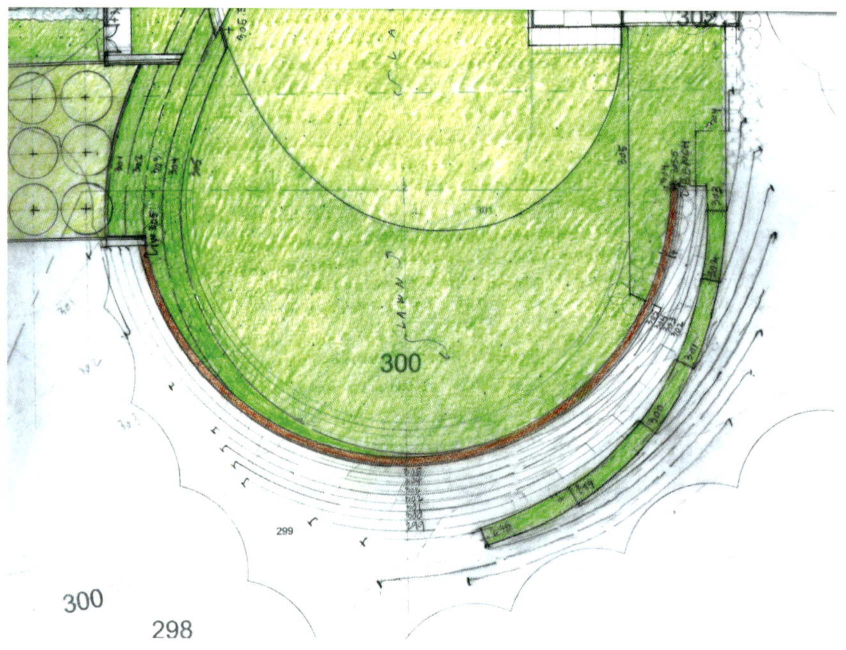

Study for rotation of backyard

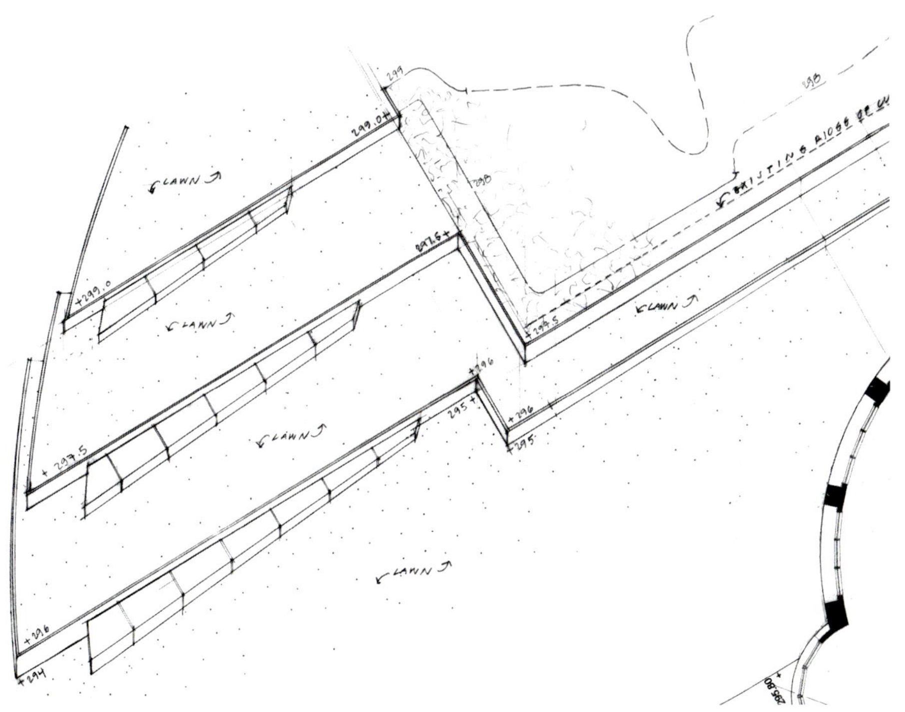

Axonometric study of backyard

Color drawing of backyard

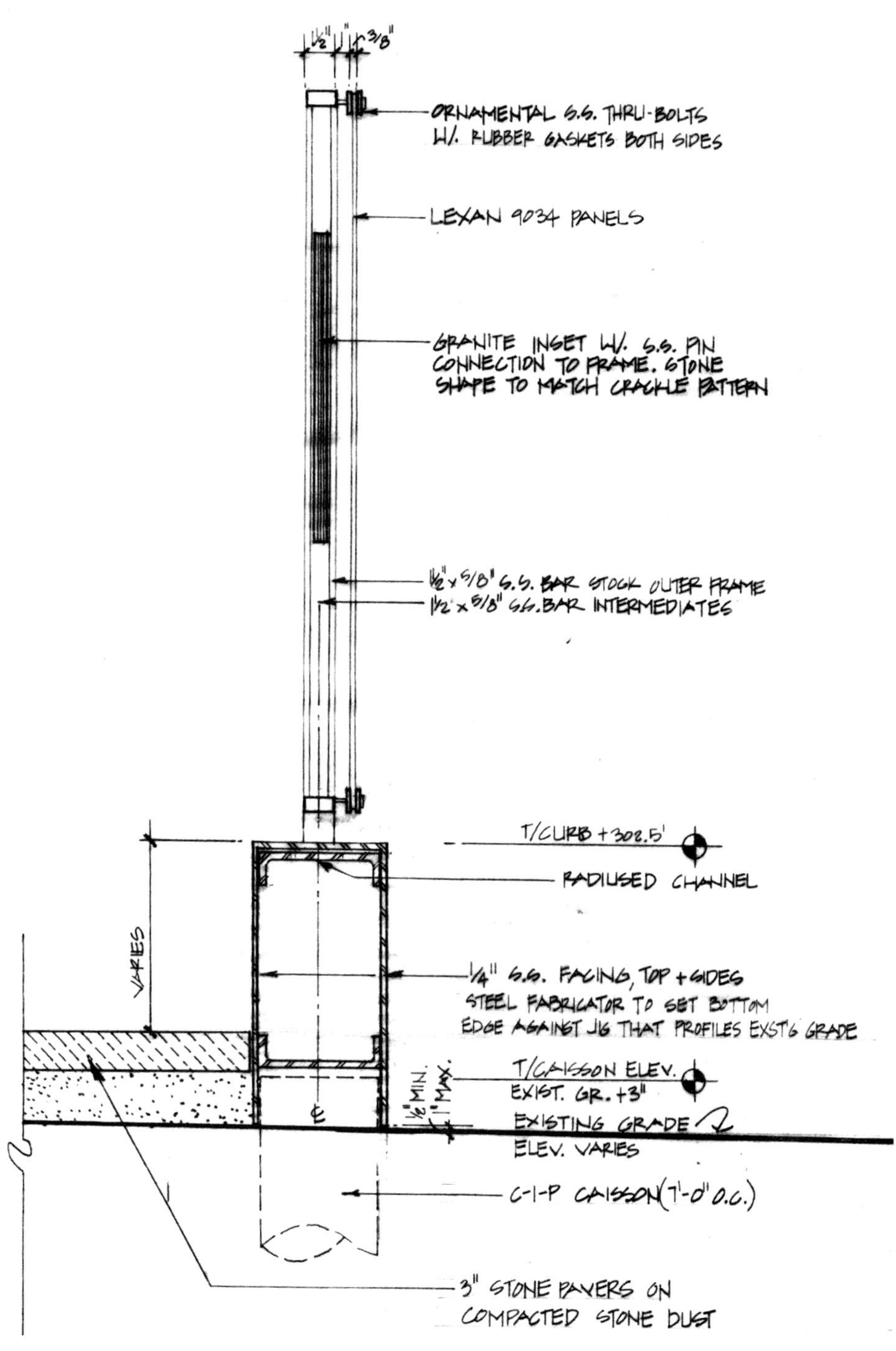

Fence section construction details

Color study for rotation of stairs

Color study for wall

General section

Collage sketch

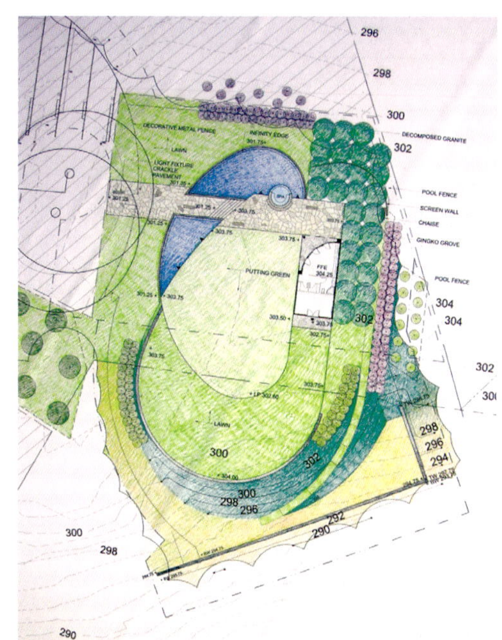

Color plan

Detail plan

Final color plan

Central Park of Nou Barris and Virrei Amat Square

Barcelona, Spain

The project was designed after the 1992 Barcelona Olympics and involves a green area with fragmented geometric spaces to encourage communication. This enables more fluid connections between many of the spaces spread out around the park's 1.8 million sq ft expanse.

Le projet, élaboré après les Jeux olympiques tenus à Barcelone en 1992, est composé d'un espace vert fragmenté en espaces géométriques conçus pour faciliter la communication. La communication entre les nombreuses parties qui s'étendent tout au long des 166 000 m² du parc est ainsi plus fluide.

Das nach den Olympischen Spielen 1992 in Barcelona entworfene Projekt besteht aus einem grünen Areal mit fragmentierten geometrischen Flächen, die die Kommunikation erleichtern sollen. Dadurch wird die Verkehrsverbindung zwischen den vielen Einrichtungen in der 166.000 m² großen Parkanlage flüssiger.

Het project, dat werd ontworpen na de Olympische Spelen van Barcelona in 1992, bestaat uit een groenzone met een splitsing van geometrische ruimten die bedoeld zijn om de communicatie te vereenvoudigen. Op deze manier wordt de verbinding tussen de vele delen die zich langs het 166.000 m² grote park uitstrekken, vloeiender.

Arriola & Fiol Arquitectes
www.arriolafiol.com
© Sergio Belinchón, Beat Marugg, Arriola & Fiol (drawings)

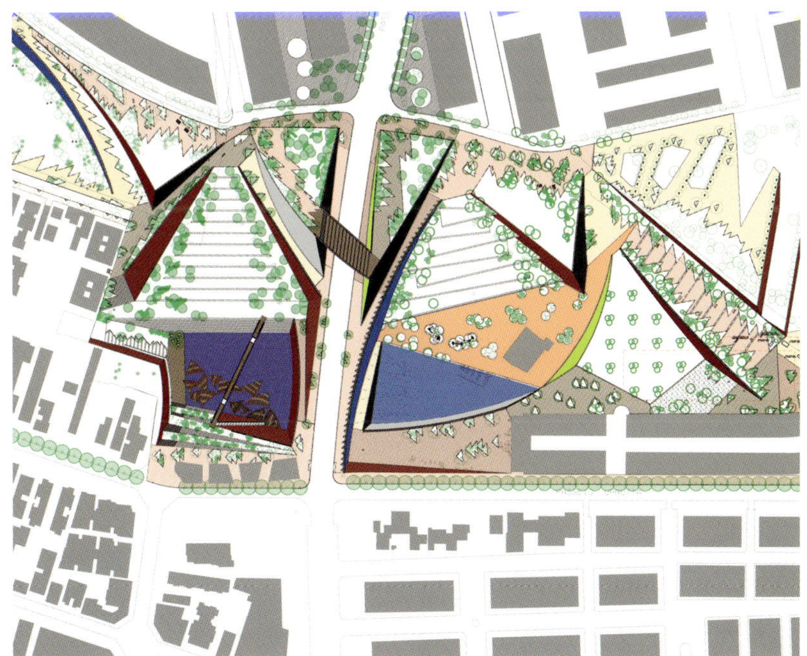

Park plan

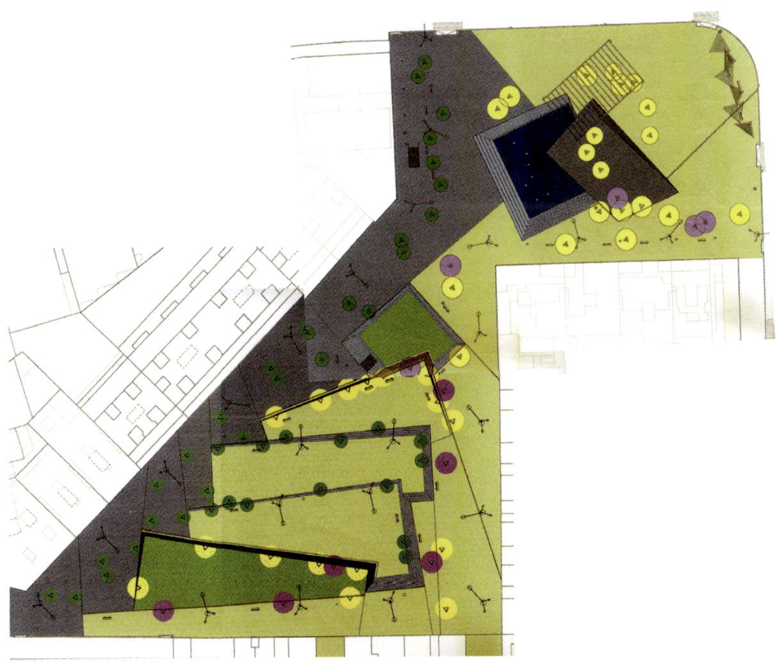

Square plan

Picasso's cubist painting Horta de Sant Joan *was the inspiration for this park. Its many fragmented forms enabled a green space to be created among the buildings.*

Le tableau cubiste Horta de Sant Joan, *œuvre de Picasso, a été la source d'inspiration de ce parc. Ses multiples formes fragmentées ont permis de créer une zone verte entre les bâtiments.*

Picassos kubistisches Gemälde „Horta de Sant Joan" war die Inspirationsquelle für diesen Park. Seine vielfältigen fragmentierten Formen ermöglichten die Schaffung einer Grünzone zwischen den Gebäuden.

Het kubistische schilderij Horta de Sant Joan *van Picasso was de inspiratiebron voor dit park. De vele gefragmenteerde vormen maakten het mogelijk om tussen de gebouwen een groenzone aan te leggen.*

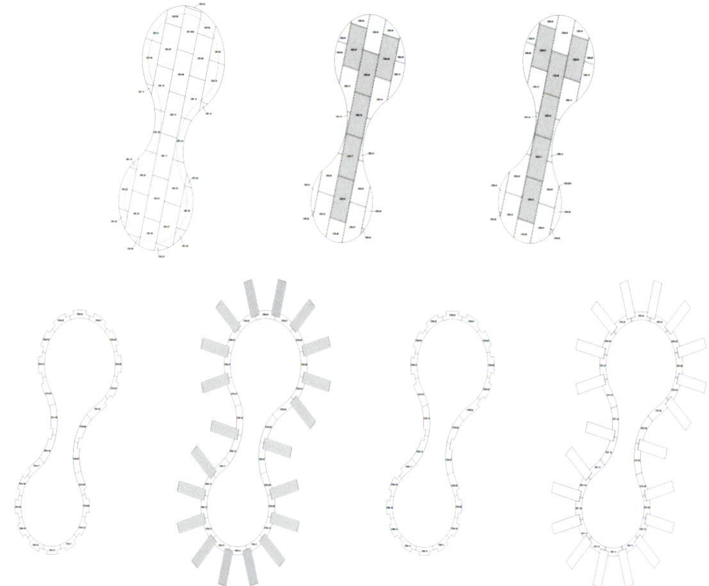

Beatfuse!

In 2006, the Contemporary Art Center PS 1 organized a competition within the Young Architects Program. The winning project consisted of creating a triangular space with seven shell-shaped structures. The structures are made from plywood and polypropylene mesh.

En 2006 le centre d'art contemporain PS 1 a organisé un concours au sein du Programme des jeunes architectes. Le projet gagnant prévoyait la création d'un espace triangulaire doté de sept structures en forme de coquilles. Ces dernières sont composées de contre-plaqué et d'un maillage en polypropylène.

Das Zentrum für Zeitgenössische Kunst PS 1 veranstaltete 2006 im Rahmen des Programms Junger Architekten einen Wettbewerb. Das Siegerprojekt war ein dreieckiger Raum mit sieben muschelförmigen Strukturen aus Furnier und Polypropylennetz.

In het jaar 2006 organiseerde het centrum voor hedendaagse kunst PS 1 een wedstrijd binnen het Programma Jonge Architecten. Het winnende project bestond in de creatie van een driehoekige ruimte met zeven schelpvormige structuren. Deze werden vervaardigd uit gelaagd hout en een maaswerk van polypropyleen.

Obra Architects
www.obraarchitects.com
© Obra Architects

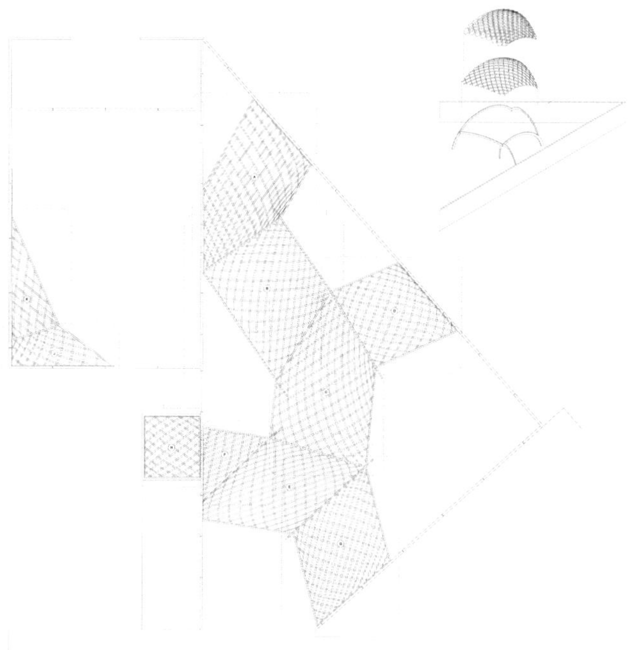

Plans

The space is divided into several areas, most notably that of the Caldarium with sand and barbeques and the Tepidarium with water vaporizers and shade.

L'espace est divisé en plusieurs zones, parmi lesquelles on peut citer le Caldarium, avec son sable et ses barbecues, et le Tepidarium, présentant vaporisateurs d'eau et ombre.

Der Raum wurde in diverse Bereiche aufgeteilt, z. B. ein Caldarium mit Sand und Grillstellen und ein Tepidarium mit Wasserverdunstern und Schatten.

De ruimte werd ingedeeld in meerdere zones, waaronder vooral het Caldarium, met zand en barbecues, en het Tepidarium, met waterverstuivers en schaduw, opvallen.

ART RADIO

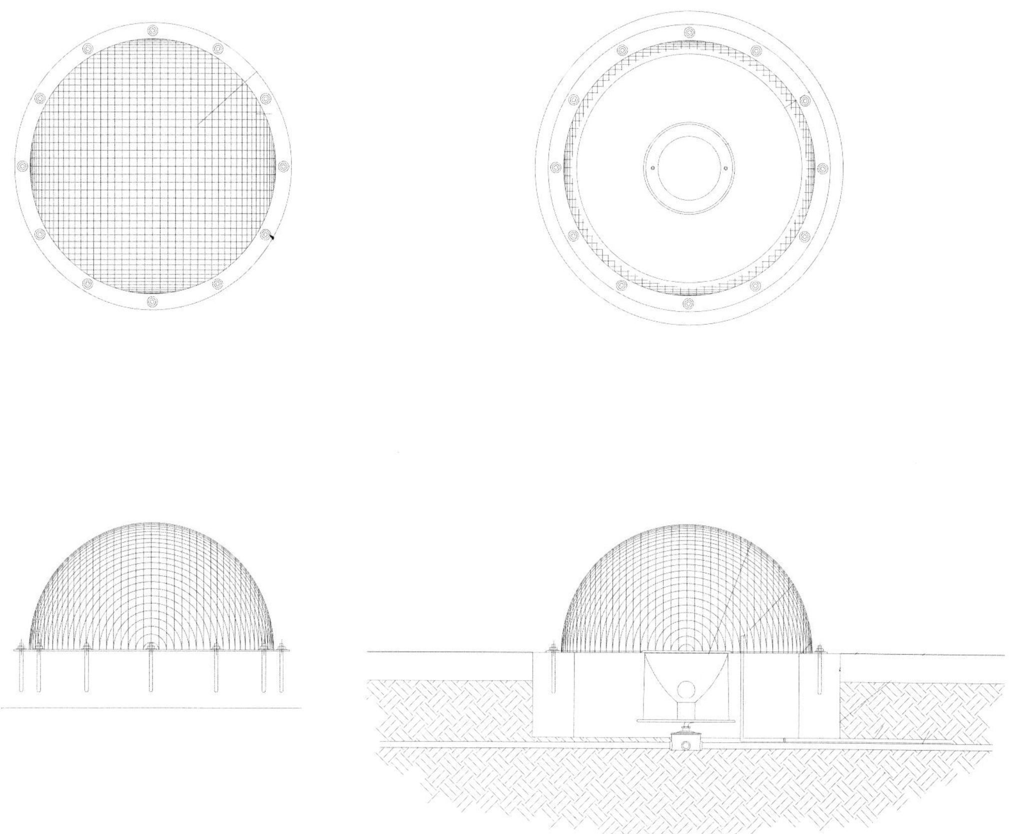

Plan, section & elevations

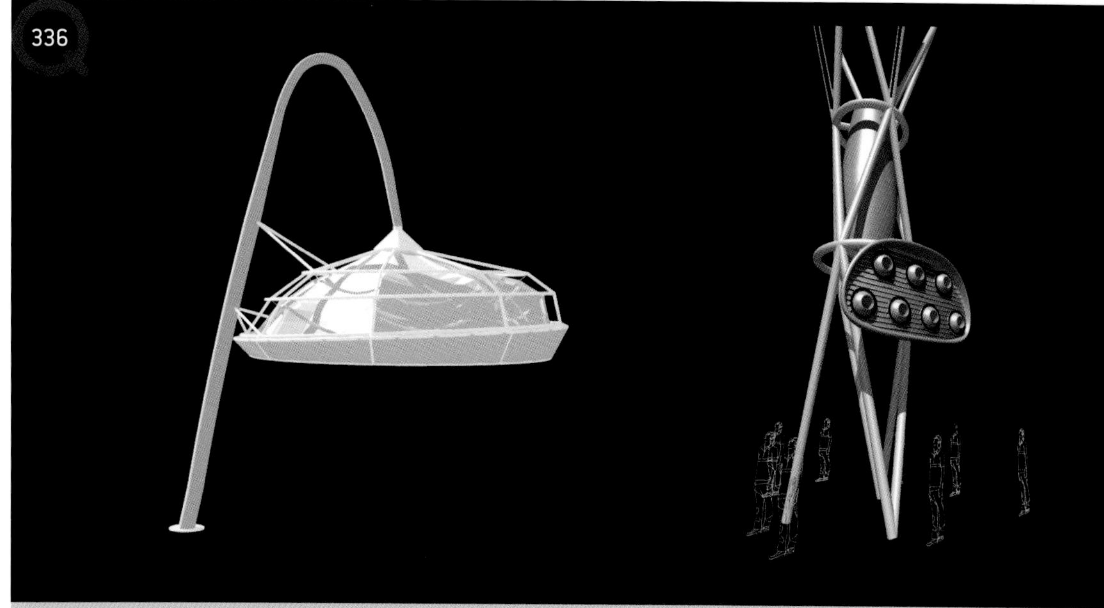

Clare Quay Redevelopment

Singapore, Singapore

The reason behind the remodeling of the historic Singapore River bankside area was the need to revitalize the 7.5-acre diamond-shaped area, which had lost its appeal for tourists and business. The project involved creating a network of colonnades along the four main streets and a central atrium.

La raison pour laquelle la berge historique du fleuve qui traverse Singapour a été rénovée réside dans le besoin de revitaliser une zone de 3 ha en forme de diamant, qui avait perdu son attrait touristique et commercial. Le projet a consisté en la création d'un atrium central et d'un enchevêtrement d'arcades tout au long des quatre rues principales.

Das Motiv für die Renovierung des historischen Ufers des Flusses, der durch Singapur fließt, beruht auf der Notwendigkeit, ein 3 ha großes diamantförmiges Gebiet wiederzubeleben, das seine Anziehungskraft verloren hatte. Das Projekt bestand in der Schaffung eines Geflechts von Arkaden entlang der vier Hauptstraßen und eines zentralen Atriums.

De historische oever van de rivier die door Singapore loopt, moest gerenoveerd worden om een diamantvormige zone van 3 ha, die toeristisch en commercieel niet aantrekkelijk meer was, nieuw leven in te blazen. Het project bestond uit de creatie van een netwerk van bogen langs de vier hoofdstraten en een centraal atrium.

SMC Alsop
www.smcalsopsg.com
© Jeremy San, SMC Alsop
(drawings)

The Singapore riverfront has been given a system made from ethylene tetrafluoroethylene (ЄFTЄ) to protect against the heat and rain. It consists of large suspended steel sunshades that regulate the temperature of the covered area.

Le front fluvial de Singapour a été équipé d'un système de protection contre la chaleur et la pluie composé d'éthylène tétrafluoroéthylène. Il s'agit d'énormes parasols en acier suspendus qui régulent la température de la zone couverte.

Das Flussufer von Singapur wurde gegen Hitze und Regen mit einem Schutzsystem aus ЄTFЄ ausgestattet. Große, stahlgestützte Sonnenschirme regulieren die Temperatur der überdachten Bereiche.

De rivierzijde van Singapore is voorzien van een beschermingssysteem tegen warmte en regen bestaand uit ethyleentetraethyleen. Het gaat om grote hangende parasols van staal die de temperatuur van de overdekte zone regelen.

Plan

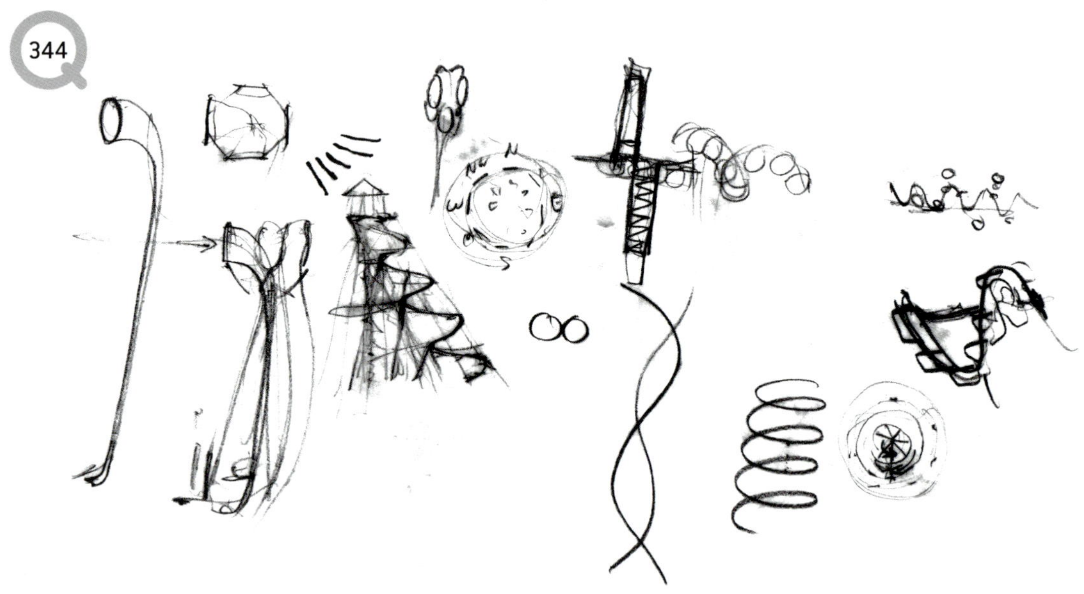

Courtyard in the wind

A ring marked in the ground is the outline of a plate turning slowly in the courtyard of an office building. The ring moves by electricity generated by a wind turbine installed on the office tower. The ring only completes two revolutions per day at a speed of less than half an inch per second.

Une couronne gravée au sol dessine un plateau qui tourne lentement dans la cour d'un bâtiment administratif. Cette couronne se déplace sous l'effet de l'électricité générée par une turbine éolienne installée sur la tour du bâtiment. La couronne n'effectue que deux tours par jour et se déplace de moins d'un centimètre par seconde.

Ein in den Boden eingeschnittener Ring beschreibt eine Scheibe, die sich langsam im Innenhof eines Bürogebäudes dreht. Der Ring, der nur zwei Umdrehungen pro Tag macht und sich weniger als einen Zentimeter pro Sekunde bewegt, wird durch elektrischen Strom, der von einer Windturbine im Gebäudeturm erzeugt wird, angetrieben.

Een in de grond gegraveerde ring tekent een plateau dat langzaam draait op de binnenplaats van een kantoorgebouw. Deze ring beweegt dankzij de stroomtoevoer die wordt opgewekt door een windturbine op de toren van het gebouw. De ring draait slechts twee rondjes per dag en beweegt minder dan een centimeter per seconde.

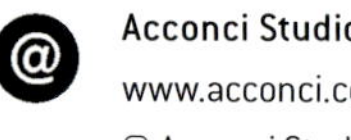

Acconci Studio
www.acconci.com
© Acconci Studio

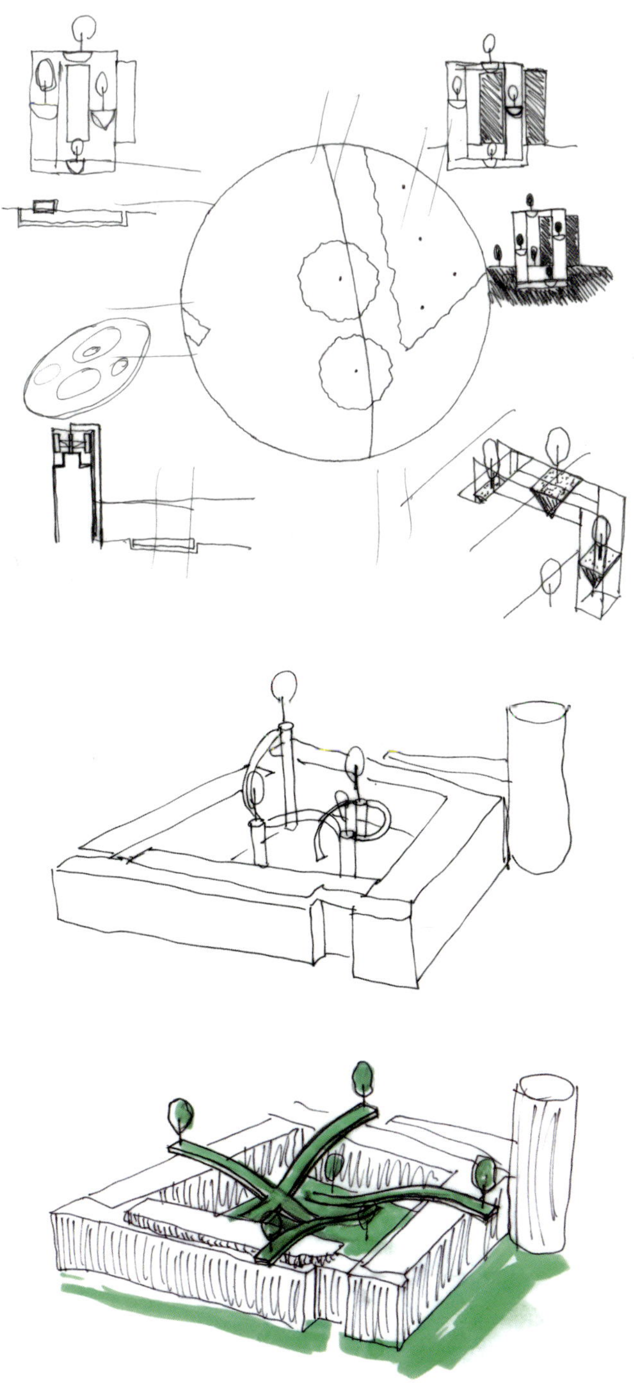

Sketches of concept

Besides the movement produced by the wind turbine, this element also powers a light installation on the tower. Users of this courtyard can feel the earth move when they walk over the ring.

Outre les mouvements qu'elle permet de générer, la turbine éolienne alimente une installation lumineuse mise en place sur la tour. Les usagers de cette cour peuvent sentir le mouvement de la terre en se déplaçant sur la couronne.

Die Windturbine verursacht nicht nur die Ringbewegungen, sondern speist auch eine Lichtanlage im Turm. Wenn die Besucher des Hofs den Ring betreten, können sie fühlen, wie sich die Erde bewegt.

Naast de bewegingen voedt de windturbine eveneens een in de toren aanwezige lichtinstallatie. De gebruikers van deze binnenplaats kunnen voelen hoe de aarde draait als ze op de ring stappen.

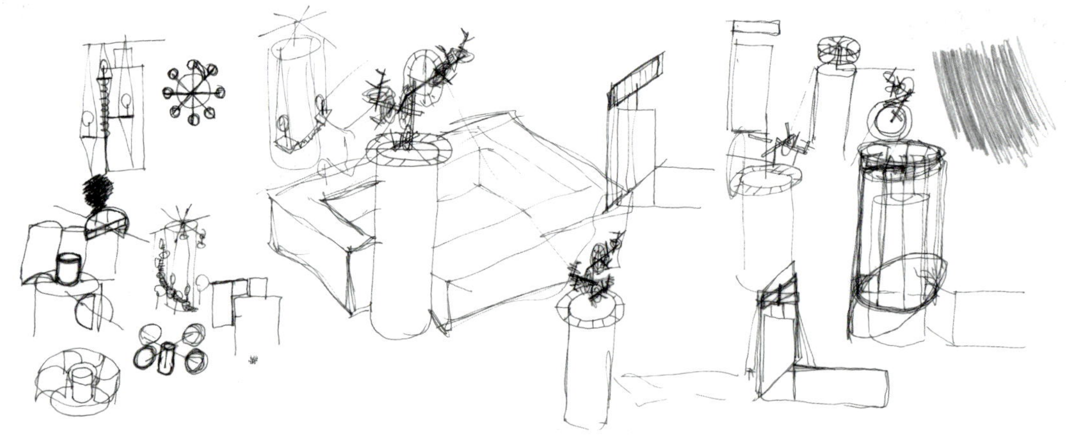

Sketches for helix on tower

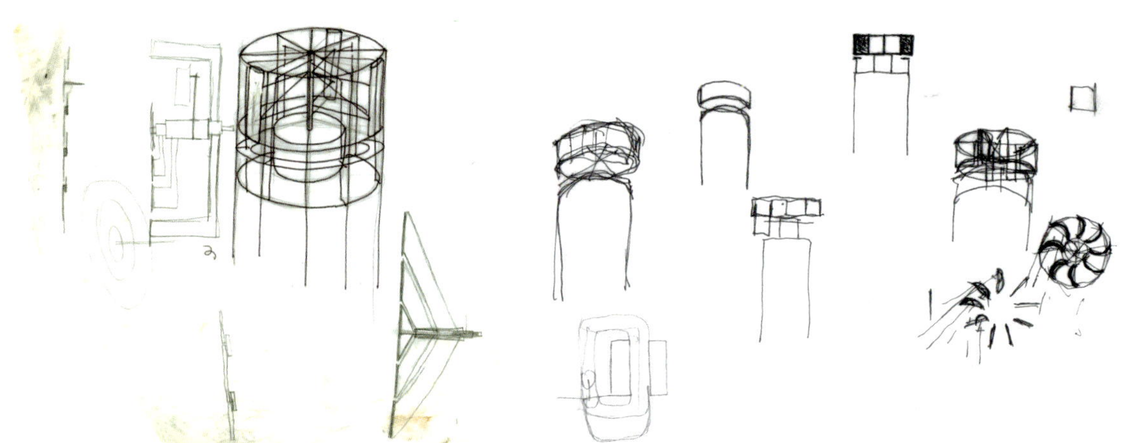

Sketches for helix on tower

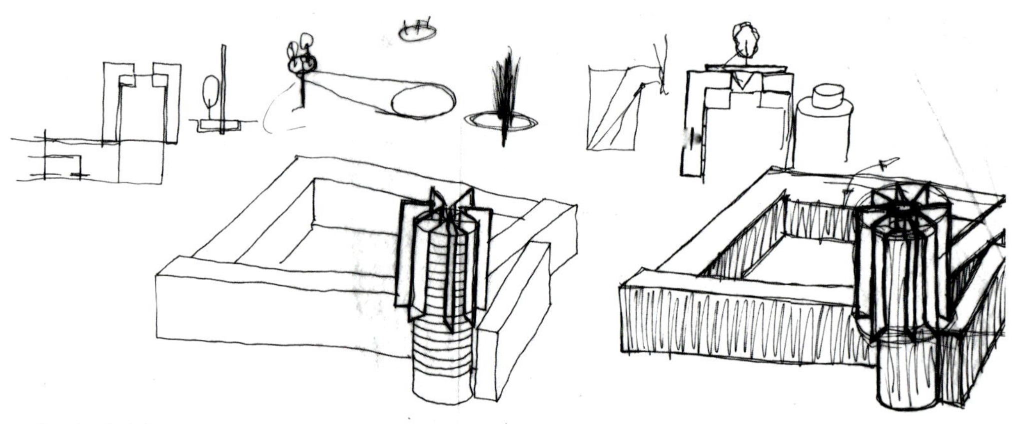

Sketches for helix on tower

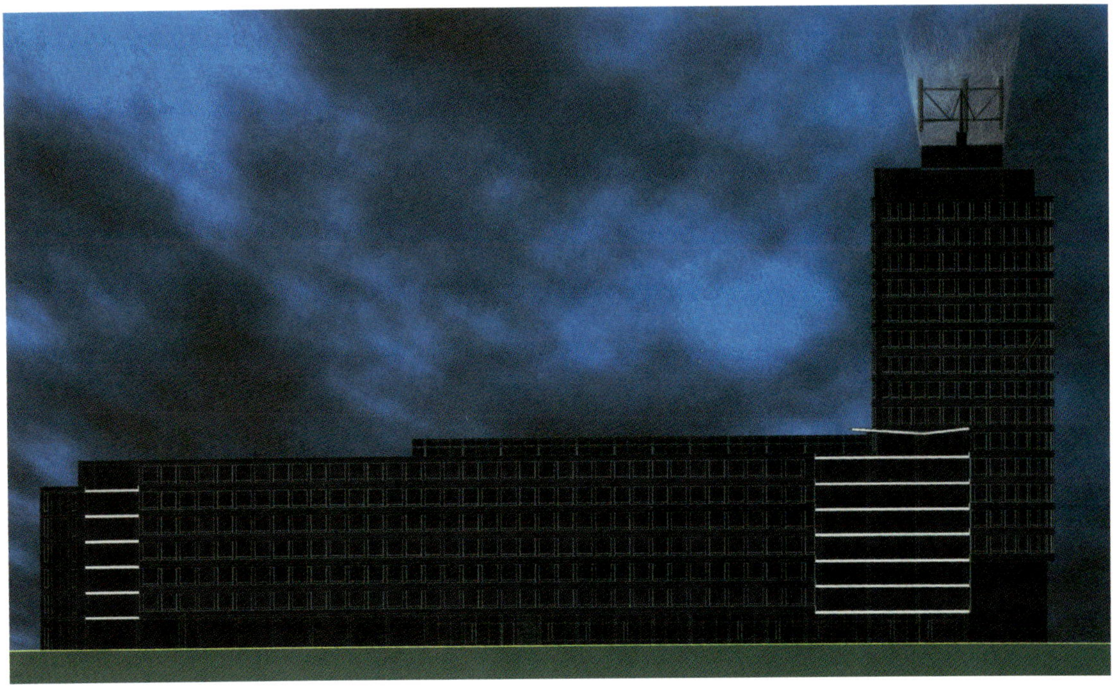

Elevation

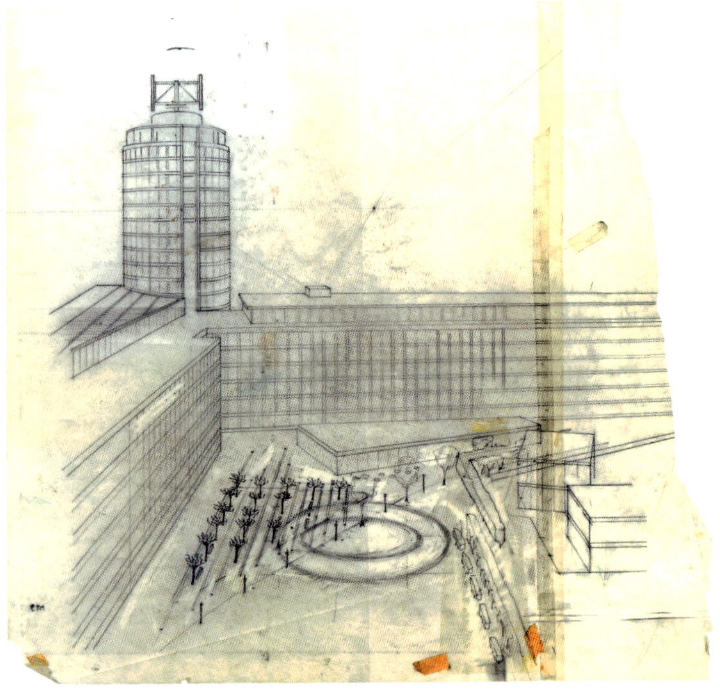

Design development perspective

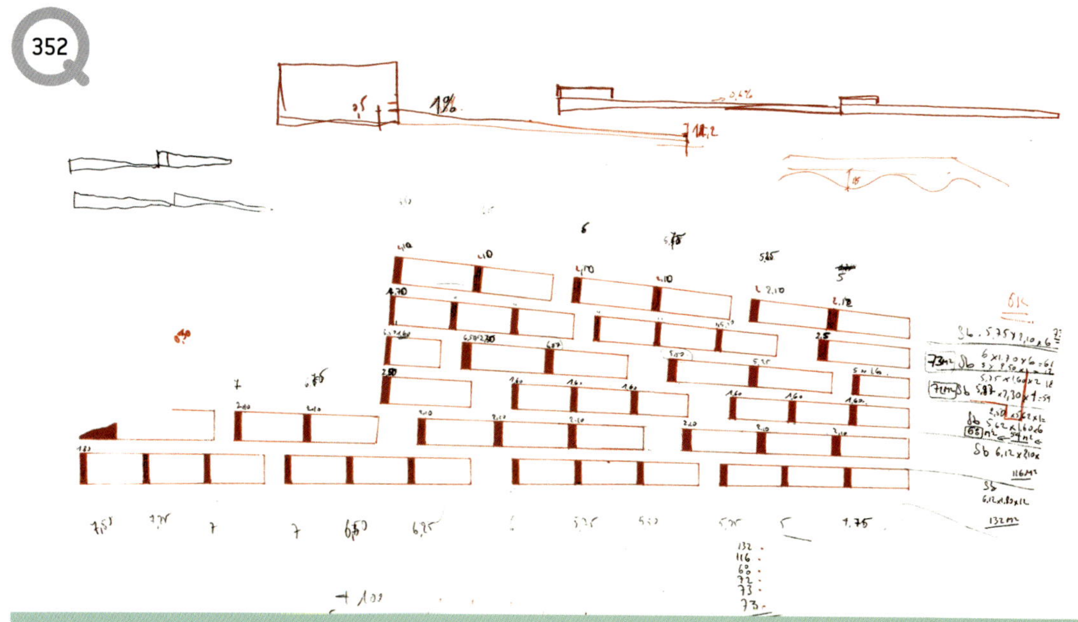

Botanic Gardens in Bordeaux Bastide

Bordeaux, France

The botanical garden was created to house a tropical plant acclimatization center. The new garden connects this area of the bank with the downtown area on the other side of the river. Given the size of the site, six spaces were laid out linked to different crop families.

Le jardin botanique a été créé pour abriter un centre d'acclimatation de plantes tropicales. Le nouveau jardin relie cette zone de la rive au centre situé de l'autre côté du fleuve. L'étendue du terrain a permis de découper la superficie en six espaces consacrés à différentes espèces cultivables.

Der botanische Garten wurde als Zentrum für die Akklimatisierung tropischer Pflanzen geschaffen. Der neue Garten verbindet den Uferbereich und das Zentrum auf der anderen Flussseite. Der Garten wurde in sechs Bereiche mit verschiedenen Pflanzenfamilien aufgeteilt.

De botanische tuin werd aangelegd om er een acclimatisatiecentrum voor tropische planten te vestigen. De nieuwe tuin verbindt deze oeverzone met het centrum dat aan de andere kant van de rivier is gelegen. Het terrein wordt vanwege zijn omvang in zes ruimten opgedeeld die zijn gekoppeld aan verschillende gewasfamilies.

Catherine Mosbach Paysagistes
mosbach.pays@wanadoo.fr
© Catherine Mosbach, Mosbach
Paysagistes (drawings)

The visitor moves along separate, estab-
lished paths through six successive spaces:
the olive grove, the gallery, the trail, the pop-
lar grove, and the water and urban gardens.

Le visiteur se déplace au travers de six espaces thématiques successifs, en suivant
des itinéraires établis et délimités : la zone
de cultures, la galerie, le sentier, la promenade bordée d'arbres et les jardins aquati-
que et urbains.

Durch die 6 Themenbereiche bewegt sich
der Besucher auf festgelegten, abgeteilten
Wegen: Feld der Pflanzenkulturen, Galerie,
Pfad, Allee, Wassergarten und städtischer
Garten.

Aan de hand van zes achtereenvolgende
thematische ruimten beweegt de bezoeker
zich via bepaalde afzonderlijke tracés: het
bouwland, de galerij, het wandelpad, het po-
pulierenbosje en de water- en stadstuinen.

Schematic topographic sketches of Environments Gallery

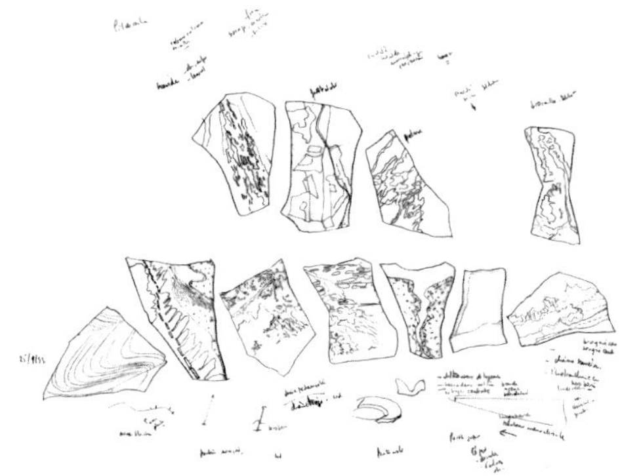

Competion drawing of Environments Gallery

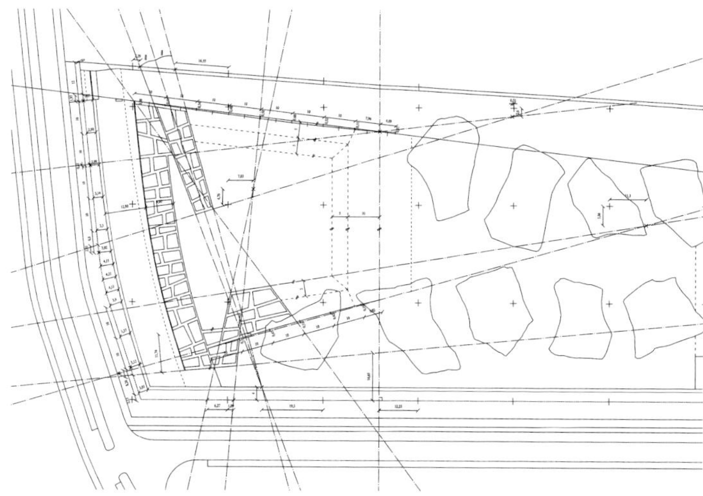

Geometrical reference of Aquatical Garden

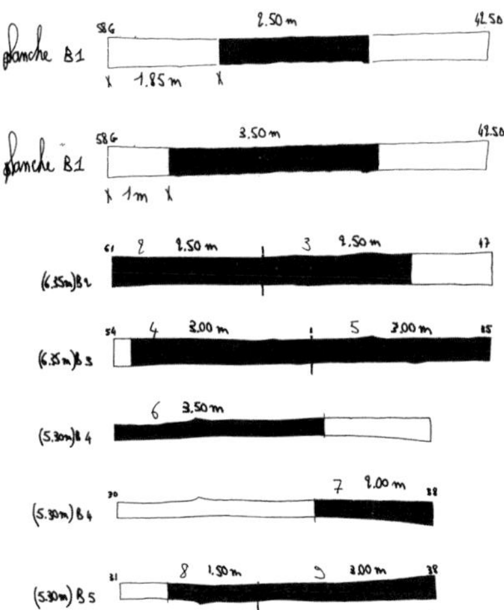
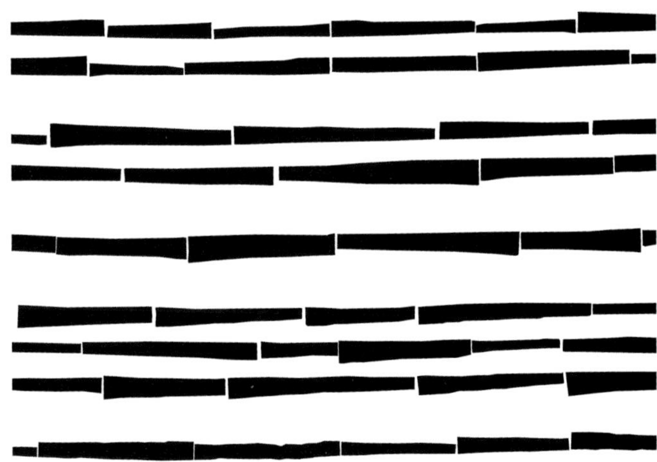

Sketch of plants path, moldel prototype
of oak trunk planks

Scheme of path implantations

Lower portion of gate drawing

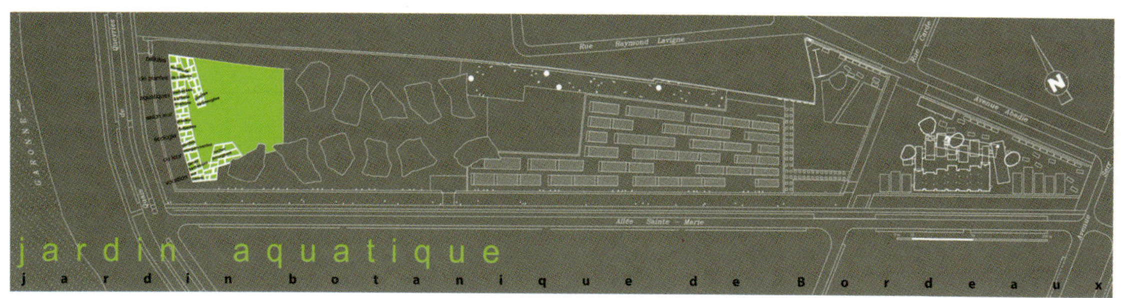

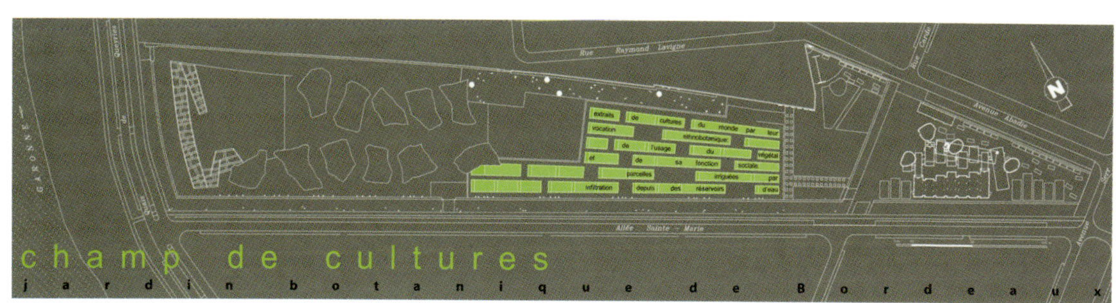

General plans

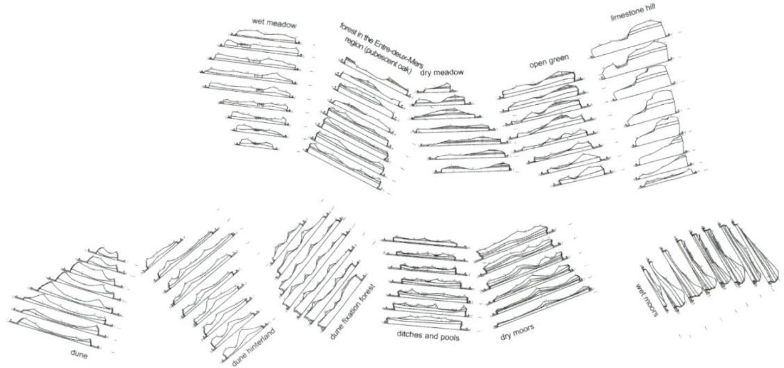

Sketch

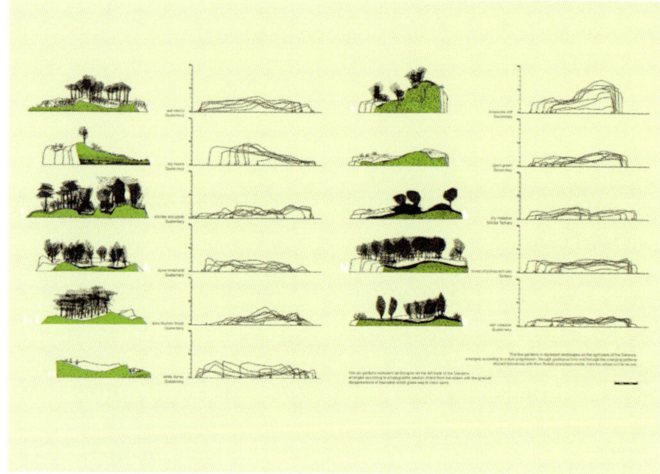

Elevations

Lyon Technology Park

Lyon, France

The Technology Park grew out of the desire to create a network of public spaces that could absorb urban development while offering new green areas for rest and walks. The design is based on respect for nature and the creation of an urban and landscaped structure.

Le parc technologique est né de la volonté de créer un réseau d'espaces publics capables d'absorber l'urbanisation et d'offrir à la fois de nouveaux espaces verts pour la détente et la promenade. Le projet repose sur le respect de la nature et la création d'une structure urbaine et paysagère.

Der Technologiepark sollte ein Netz öffentlicher Räume schaffen, die die Urbanisierung aufnehmen und gleichzeitig neue Grünzonen für Erholung und Spaziergänge bieten. Das Projekt basiert auf dem Naturschutz und der Schaffung einer städtischen, landschaftlich gestalteten Struktur.

Het Technologische Park ontstond vanuit het idee om een netwerk van openbare ruimten te creëren die in staat zijn om de urbanisatie te absorberen en tegelijkertijd nieuwe groenzones te bieden voor ontspanning en wandelingen. Het voorstel is gebaseerd op het respect voor de natuur en op de creatie van een stedelijke en landschappelijke structuur.

ILEX Paysage et Urbanisme, Péré and JeanClaude Durual
www.ilexpaysages.com
© E. Saillet, ILEX (drawings)

The park is laid out following an axis surrounded by thick vegetation made up of different elements that follow a strict order.

Le parc s'articule autour d'un axe, entouré d'une végétation luxuriante, à partir duquel différents éléments se développent dans un ordre strict.

Der Park ist um eine von üppiger Vegetation umgebene Achse angelegt, von der aus sich verschiedene Elemente nach einer strengen Ordnung entwickeln.

Het park ontplooit zich rondom een as, omgeven door een rijke begroeiing, waaruit verschillende elementen zich ontwikkelen volgens een strenge rangorde.

Presentation painting

Presentation painting

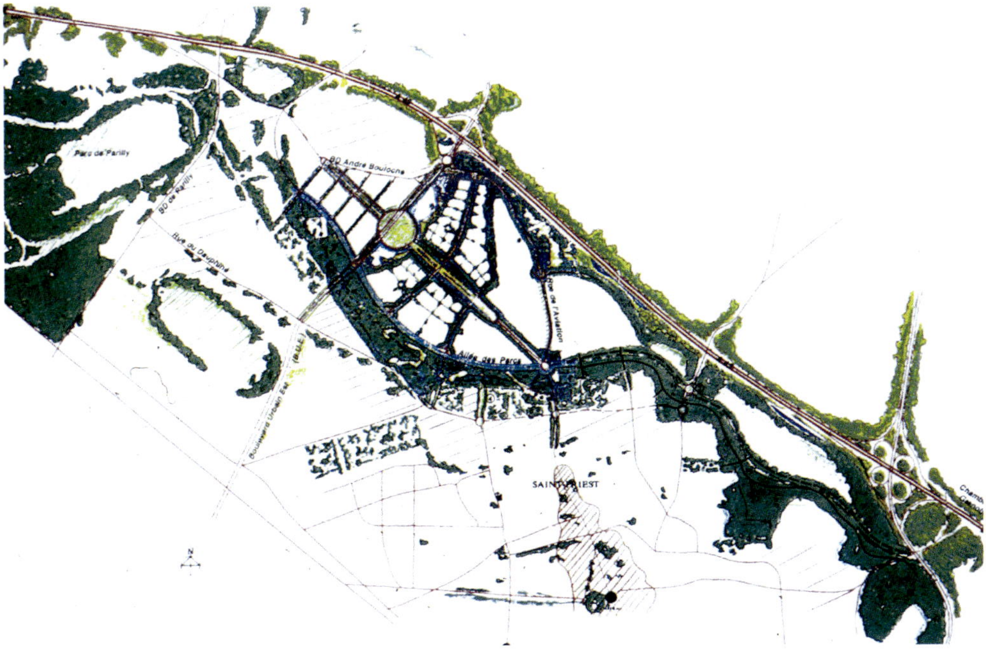

General plan of landscape intervention

Tracce

Lucca, Italy

This installation comprises an action made to the surface of the ground, transforming it into moldable material. It symbolizes the result of a giant hand scraping the ground to expose the naked earth.

L'installation se résume en une action réalisée sur la surface du sol qui se transforme en matière malléable. Symboliquement, elle est le résultat obtenu par le mouvement d'une main gigantesque qui racle le sol pour laisser la terre à nu.

Es handelt sich bei der Installation um eine Aktion auf der Bodenoberfläche, die sich in formbare Materie verwandelt. Sie stellt auf symbolische Weise dar, was sich ergibt, wenn der Boden durch eine riesige Hand abgeschabt wird, um die nackte Erde ans Licht zu bringen.

De installatie bestaat uit een ingreep boven het oppervlak van de grond die verandert in kneedbare materie. Ze stelt symbolisch het resultaat voor dat men zou verkrijgen als een reuzenhand de grond zou schrapen om de blote aarde aan het licht te brengen.

Marco Antonini, Roberto Capecci, Raffaella Sini/LAND-I
www.archicolture.com
© LAND-I

Fragments of ceramic, bones, bottles, and waste materials, among others, emerge from the soil under the torn up lawn. These remind visitors that historical gardens are vulnerable places.

Le gazon arraché à la surface du sol laisse apparaître des morceaux de céramique, des os, des bouteilles, des déchets, etc. Ces éléments rappellent au spectateur que les jardins historiques sont des lieux vulnérables.

Unter dem Rasen kommen Tonscherben, Knochen, Flaschen, usw. zum Vorschein, die daran erinnern, dass die historischen Gärten verwundbare Orte sind.

Onder het geschraapte gras doemen uit de grond stukken aardewerk, botten, flessen, afval, etc. op. Zij herinneren de toeschouwer eraan dat historische tuinen kwetsbare plaatsen zijn.

Materials inspiration

Photo collage

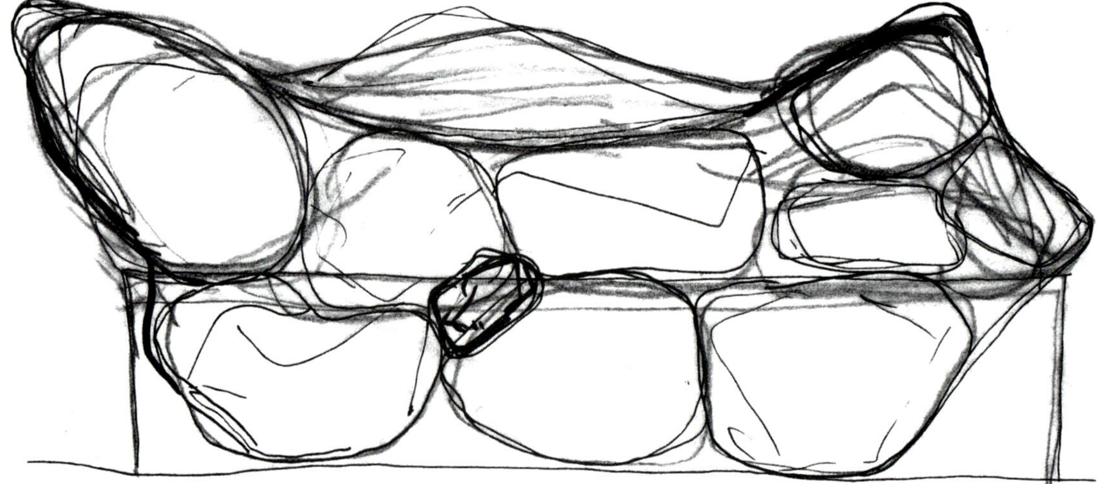

Mente La Menta

Chaumont-sur-Loire, France

The Conservatoire International des Parcs et Jardins et du Paysage de Chaumont-sur-Loire holds an international contemporary garden design festival each year. This project analyzes the uncertain future of the world.

Le Conservatoire international des parcs et jardins et du paysage de Chaumont-sur-Loire organise chaque année un festival international consacré à la création de jardins contemporains. L'incertitude qui plane sur l'avenir du monde est illustrée dans ce projet.

Das Conservatoire International des Parcs et Jardins et du Paysage in Chaumont-sur-Loire organisiert jedes Jahr ein internationales Festival für modernes Gartendesign. Die Unsicherheit in Bezug auf die Zukunft der Erde wird in diesem Projekt analysiert.

Het Conservatoire International des Parcs et Jardins et du Paysage uit Chaumont-sur-Loire organiseert elk jaar een internationaal festival voor het ontwerp van hedendaagse tuinen. In dit project wordt de onzekere toekomst van de wereld geanalyseerd.

Marco Antonini, Roberto Capecci, Raffaella Sini/LAND-I, Gianna Attiani, Daniela Mongini
www.archicolture.com
© LAND-I, Roberto Capecci, Raffaella Sini

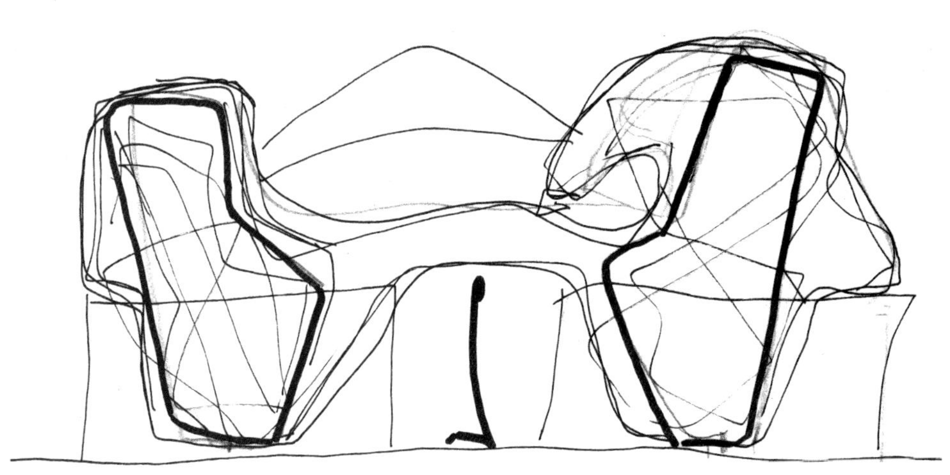

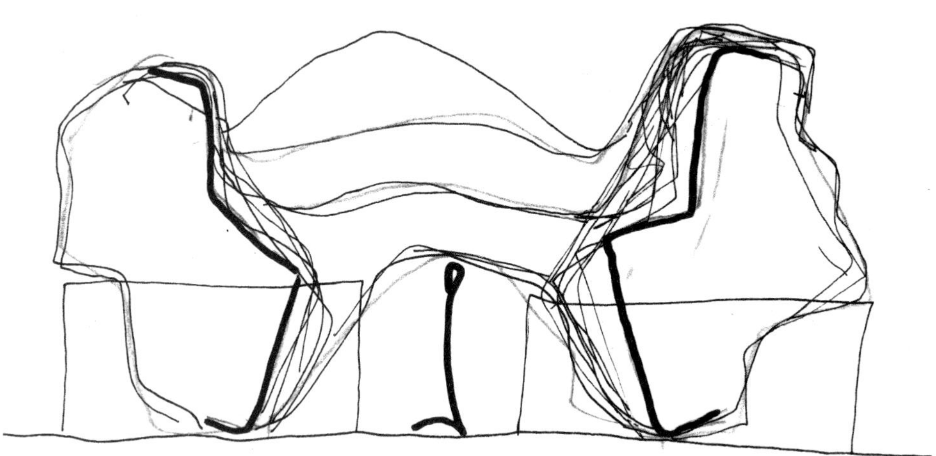

Development sketches

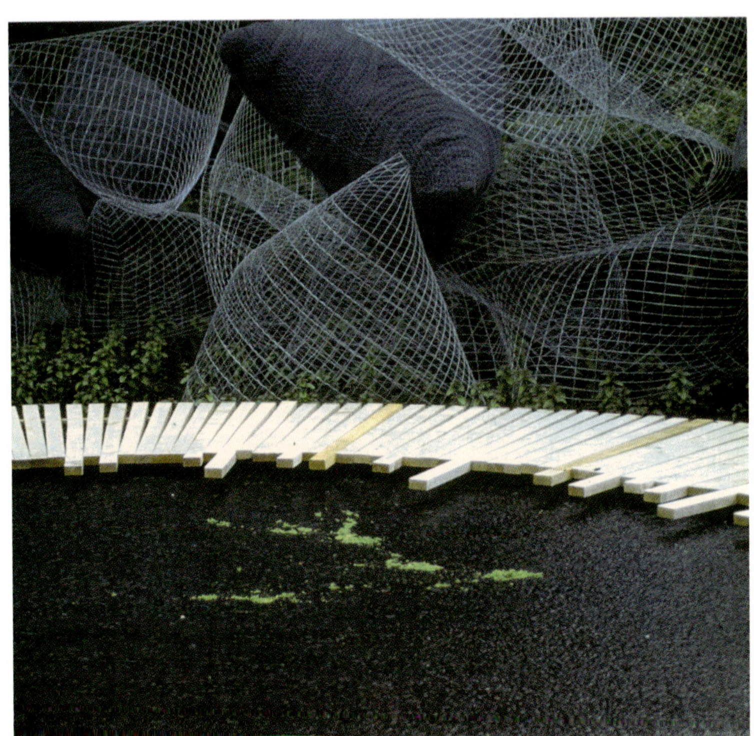

This garden is built around a pool of water surrounded by a wooden walkway. Several metal structures rest on a bed of mint plants.

Le jardin est aménagé autour d'un bassin d'eau entouré d'une passerelle en bois. Des structures métalliques reposent sur une couverture végétale de menthe.

Der Garten ist um einen Teich angelegt, der von einem Holzsteg umgeben ist. Metallaufbauten stützen sich auf ein Beet aus Pfefferminzsträuchern.

De tuin is aangelegd rond een vijver die wordt omgeven door een houten vlonder. Metalen structuren steunen op een perk van muntplanten.

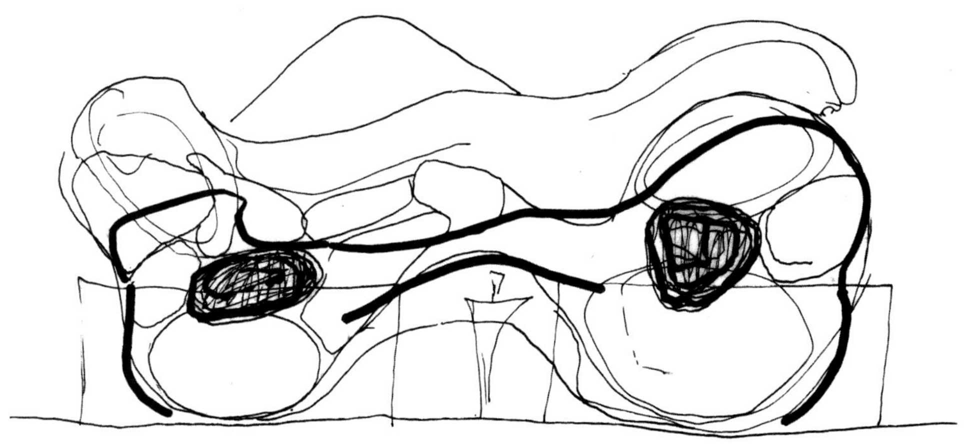

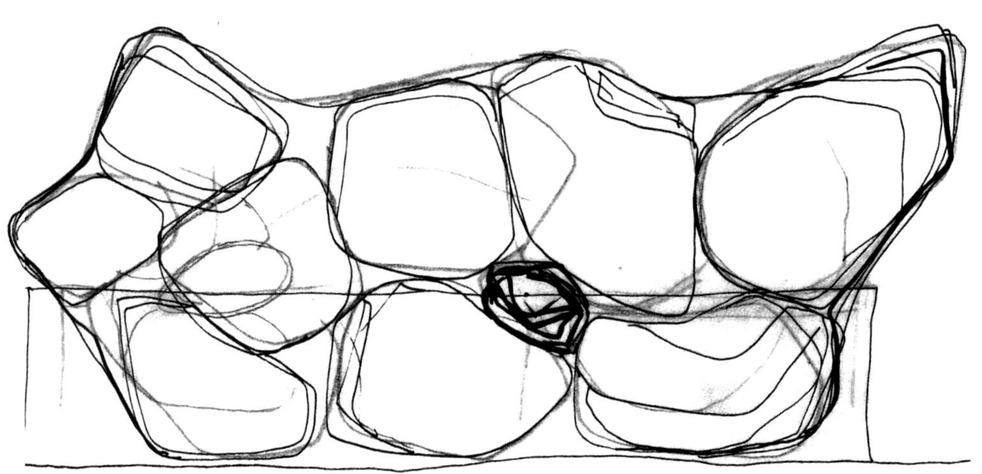

Development sketches

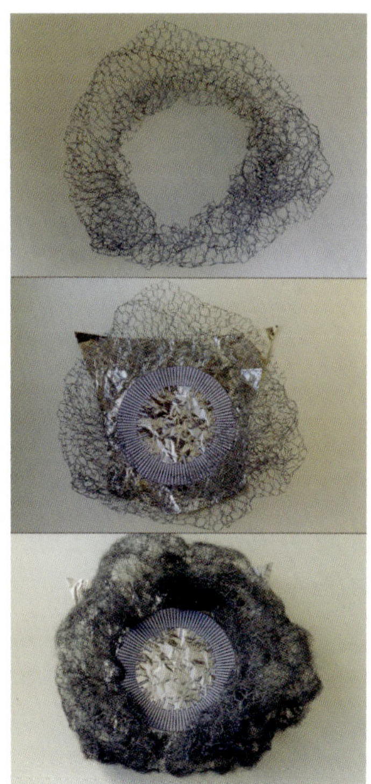

Models

Models

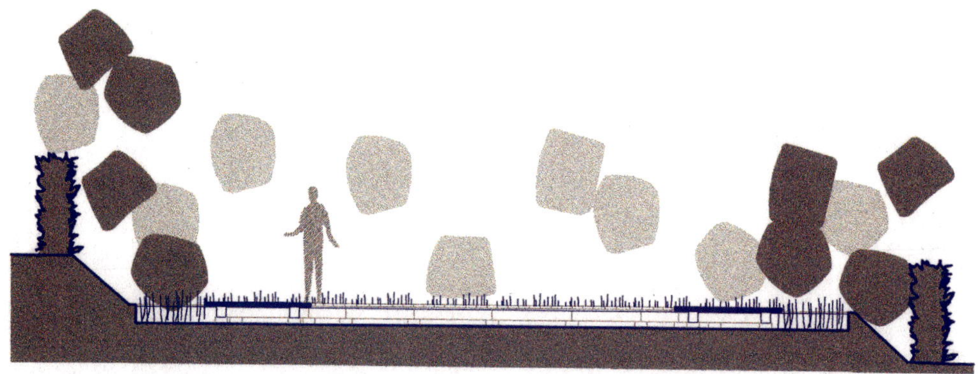

Section

Concept collage

Inspiration: La Solfatara, near Napoli, Italy

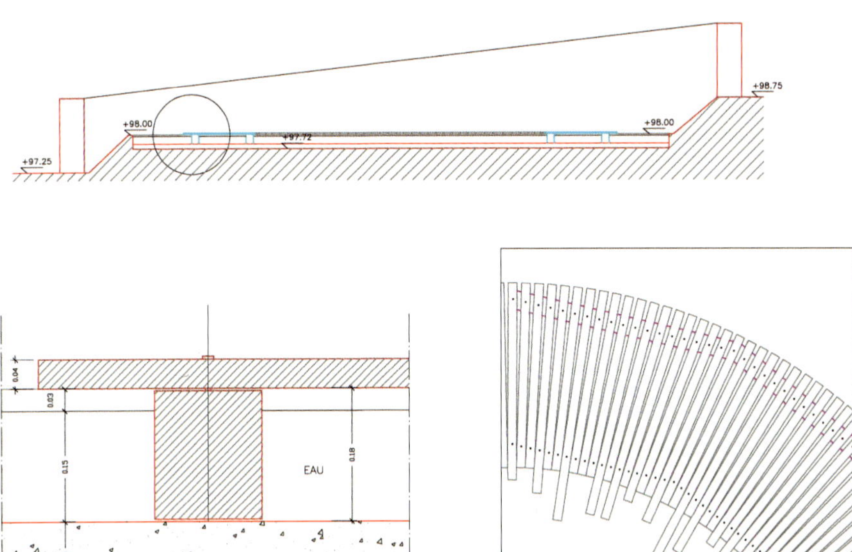

Section and detail of the raft Foot Bridge

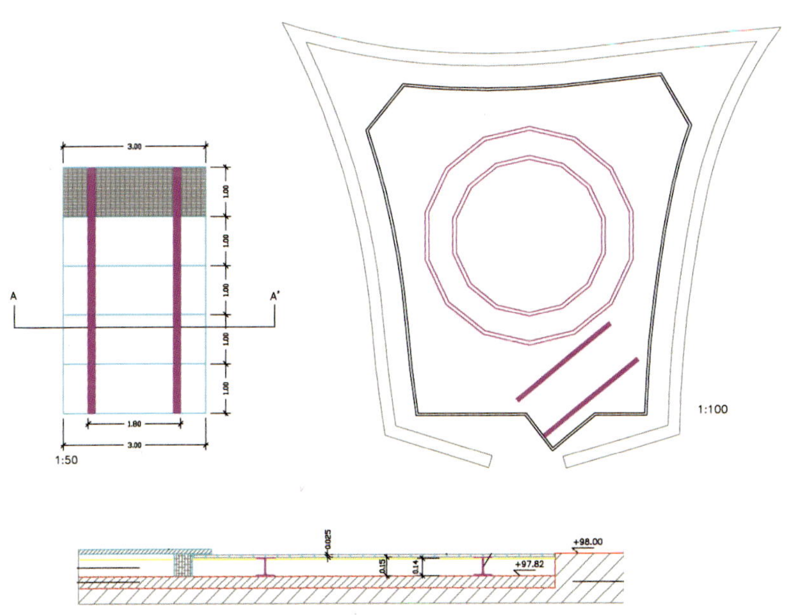

Section, detail and plan of access to raft Foot Bridge

Forest Gallery

The garden is located in a courtyard measuring 164 × 82 ft in Melbourne's new museum complex. The building is surrounded on three sides by Carlton Gardens and is partially covered by a parallel beam structure. This serves as a contemplation space for visitors.

Le jardin est situé dans une cour intérieure de 50 × 25 m du nouveau musée de Melbourne. Le Carlton Gardens est entouré par le bâtiment sur trois de ses côtés et est partiellement recouvert par une structure de poutres parallèles. Il s'agit d'un espace de détente pour les visiteurs.

Der Garten befindet sich in einem 50 × 25 m großen Innenhof des neuen Museumszentrums von Melbourne. Die Carlton Gardens sind an drei Seiten von dem Gebäude umgeben und teils mit einer Struktur aus parallelen Balken überdacht. Die dienen als Ort der Besinnung für die Besucher.

De tuin bevindt zich op de 50 × 25 m grote binnenplaats van het nieuwe museumcentrum van Melbourne. Carlton Gardens wordt aan drie zijden omgeven door het gebouw en wordt gedeeltelijk bedekt door een structuur van parallelle balken. De tuin fungeert als overpeinzingsruimte voor de bezoekers.

Taylor Cullity Lethlean
www.tcl.net.au
© Ben Wrigley, Carla Gottgens, Taylor Cullity Lethlean

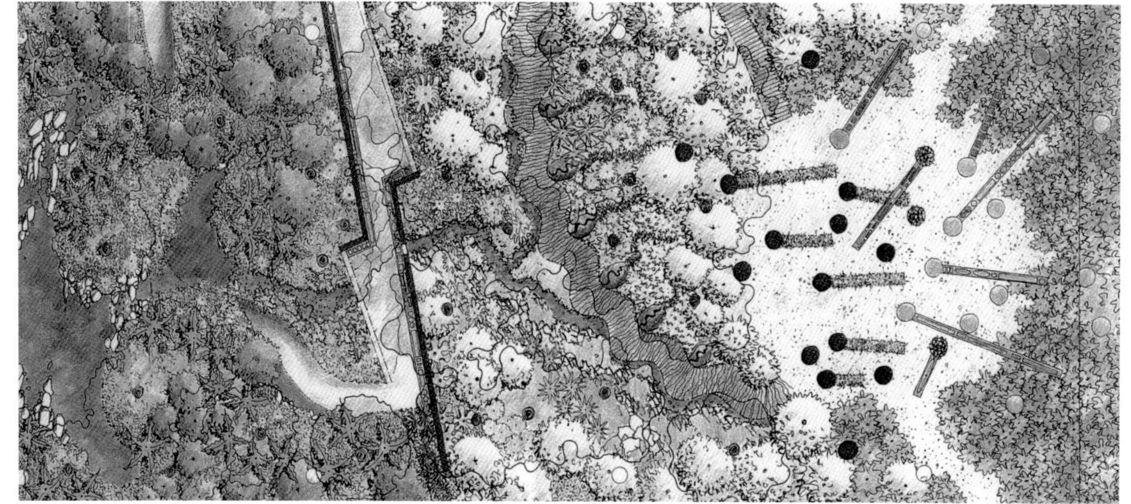

Rendered plan

Rendered elevation

The design is inspired by forests in the mountains near to Melbourne. The space is designed as a living sculpture formed of vegetation, natural and man-made materials.

La conception de ce jardin s'est inspirée des forêts situées dans les montagnes à proximité de Melbourne. L'espace est conçu comme une sculpture vivante composée de végétation ainsi que de matériaux naturels et synthétiques.

Die Inspirationsquelle für den Entwurf dieses Gartens war der Wald auf den Bergen in der Nähe von Melbourne. Der Ort wird als lebendige Skulptur aus Vegetation, natürlichen und synthetischen Materialien aufgefasst.

De inspiratiebron voor het ontwerp van deze tuin was de bergjungle in de buurt van Melbourne. De ruimte is ontworpen als een levend beeldhouwwerk gevormd door planten, natuurlijke en synthetische materialen.

The Red Ribbon – Tanghe River Park

Qinghuangdao, China

The red ribbon stretches for 1,650 ft with a varying width between 1 and 5 ft. The area, covered with lush vegetation and nests for a number of bird species, was once a landfill site with old hydrological structures used for irrigating the land.

Le ruban rouge, dont la largeur varie entre 30 et 150 cm, s'étend sur une longueur de 500 m. La zone était recouverte d'une étendue de végétation et d'un nid de repos pour les différentes espèces d'oiseaux. Ce site, équipé d'anciennes infrastructures hydrologiques utilisées pour cultiver ces terres, servait autrefois de décharge.

Die rote Schleife erstreckt sich auf 500 m mit einer variablen Breite von 30-150 cm. Das Gebiet wurde von einer ausgedehnten Vegetation bedeckt und dient als Ruheplatz für verschiedene Vögel. Früher befand sich hier eine Müllhalde mit einer alten hydrologischen Infrastruktur, die dazu benutzt wurde, das Gelände zu kultivieren.

De rode lus strekt zich uit over een lengte van 500 m en heeft een afwisselende breedte van 30 tot 150 cm. De zone was bedekt door een uitgestrekte vegetatie en er nestelden zich diverse vogels. Vroeger was het een stortplaats met oude hydrologische infrastructuren die werden gebruikt om de grond te bewerken.

Turenscape
www.turenscape.com
© Kongjian You, Yang Cao, Turenscape (drawings)

The new design fulfills the functions of bench, walkway, light source, and lookout. A winding red strip, broken by four buildings, forms the remainder of the project.

Le nouveau design remplit les fonctions de banc, de passerelle, de projecteur d'éclairage et de tour de guet. Le reste du projet est composé d'une bande rouge sinueuse entrecoupée de quatre pavillons.

Das neue Design erfüllt die Funktionen von Bank, Promenade, Beleuchtung und Aussichtspunkt. Ein gewundenes rotes Band, das von vier Pavillons unterbrochen wird, bildet den übrigen Teil des Projekts.

Het nieuwe ontwerp fungeert als bank, bruggetje, verlichting en uitkijktoren. De rest van het project wordt gevormd door een kronkelige rode strook verdeeld door vier tuinhuisjes.

Computer generated 3D rendering

Traffic Junction Odenskog

Odenskog, Sweden

This roundabout in an industrial area of Östersund measuring 460 ft in diameter has been landscaped with low benches, rows of Amelanchier spicata plantings, and small turquoise lighting sculptures.

Sur un rond-point de 140 m de diamètre, situé dans une zone industrielle d'Östersund, des bancs peu élevés ont été érigés, des parterres d'amélanchier en épis ont été plantés et de petites sculptures lumineuses de couleur bleu turquoise ont été installées.

Auf einer Verkehrsinsel von 140 m Durchmesser in einem Industriegebiet von Östersund wurden niedrige Bänke errichtet und Gruppen von Felsenbirnen (Amelanchier Spicata) angepflanzt. Zudem wurden kleine türkisblaue Leuchtkörper installiert.

Op een rotonde met een doorsnede van 140 m in een industriegebied te Östersund, werden lage banken geplaatst, stroken Amelanchier Spicata geplant en kleine turquoiseblauwe lichtsculpturen geïnstalleerd.

GORA Art & Landscape
www.gora.se
© Lennart Jonasson, GORA Art & Landscape (drawings)

These small sculptures are lights made from fiberglass-reinforced polyester. By day they look opaque and solid, while by night they seem semi-transparent and bright.

Ces petites sculptures sont des projecteurs lumineux forgés de polyester renforcé avec de la fibre de verre. D'un aspect opaque et solide en journée, ils sont semi-transparents et brillants pendant la nuit.

Die kleinen Scheinwerfer, hergestellt auf der Grundlage von mit Glasfaser verstärktem Polyester, sind tagsüber undurchsichtig und matt, während sie nachts halbtransparent und glänzend erscheinen.

Deze kleine sculpturen zijn lichtbronnen, gesmeed op basis van met glasvezel versterkt polyester. Overdag zijn ze ondoorzichtig en solide en 's nachts halfdoorzichtig en glanzend.

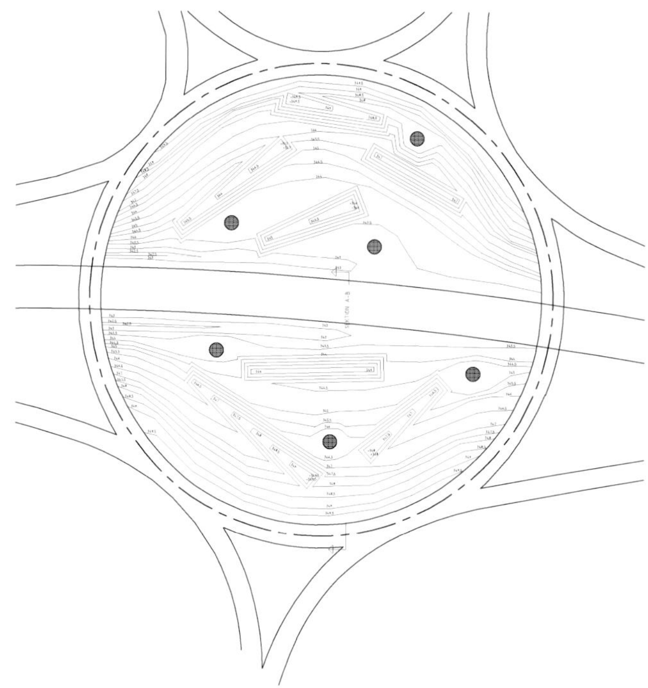

Plan

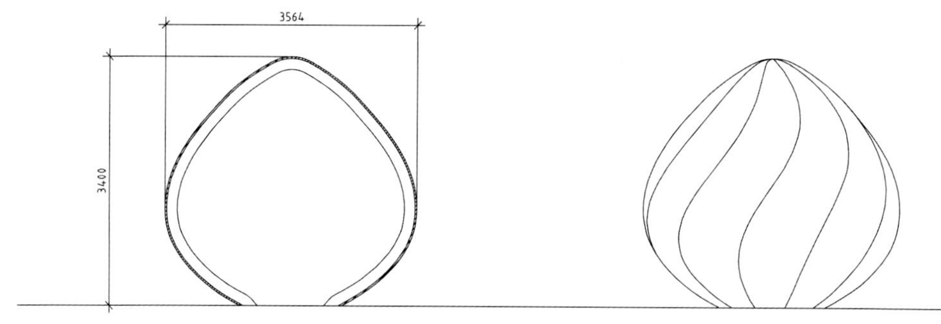

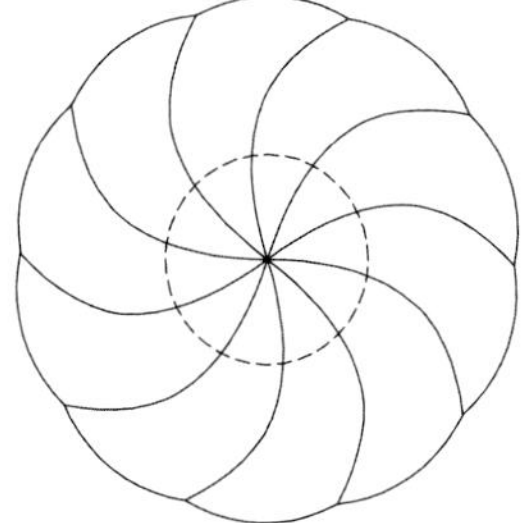

Section, elevation & plan

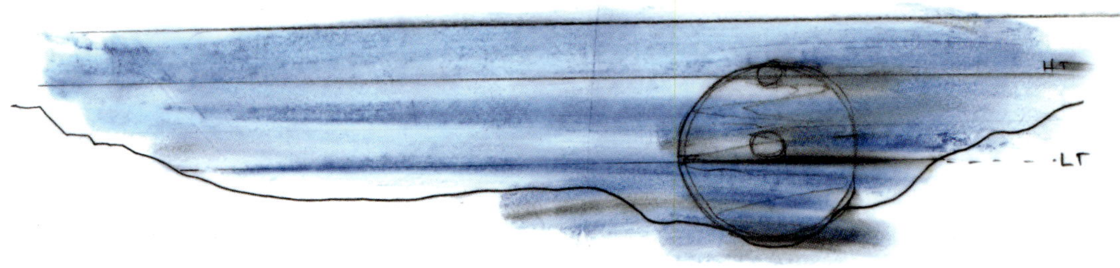

Mur Island

Graz, Austria

This complex project can be interpreted in many ways: it can be a meander, a knot in the river, a walkway, or a bridge. The structure becomes an island; the island becomes a dome; the dome becomes a bowl; and the bowl becomes a dome. The inside of the bowl is used as a theater or as an urban plaza in the middle of the river.

Ce projet complexe peut être interprété de plusieurs façons : il peut s'agir d'un coude, d'un nœud dans le fleuve, d'une voie de circulation ou d'un pont. La structure se transforme en île, qui à son tour devient une coupole, puis un bol, et à nouveau une coupole. À l'intérieur du bol, l'espace devient une scène de théâtre ou une place urbaine au milieu du fleuve.

Dieses komplexe Projekt kann vielfältig interpretiert werden: als Biegung, Schleife im Fluss, Verkehrsweg oder Brücke. Die Struktur verwandelt sich in eine Insel, die Insel in eine Kuppel, die Kuppel in eine Schale und wiederum in eine Kuppel. In der Schale wird der Raum als Theater oder als urbaner Platz in der Mitte des Flusses genutzt.

Dit complexe project kan op vele manieren geïnterpreteerd worden: het kan een bocht, een lus in de rivier, een verkeersweg of een brug zijn. De structuur wordt een eiland, het eiland een koepel, de koepel een kom en die kom verandert weer in een koepel. De binnenkant van de kom wordt gebruikt als theater of als een stadsplein te midden van de rivier.

 **Acconci Studio**
www.acconci.com
© Acconci Studio

Schematic design sketches

The theater terraces are made of perforated metal descending to reach the stage at the bottom. The dome is also used as a restaurant and café.

Les gradins du théâtre sont construits à partir de métal perforé et sont installés de manière plongeante jusqu'à la scène située au fond. La coupole sert également de restaurant et de cafétéria.

Die Theatersitzreihen aus perforiertem Metall steigen bis zur Bühne im Hintergrund ab. Die Kuppel wird auch als Restaurant und Cafeteria genutzt.

De tribune van het theater is gebouwd van geperforeerd metaal dat afdaalt tot aan het toneel op de bodem. De koepel wordt ook als restaurant en café gebruikt.

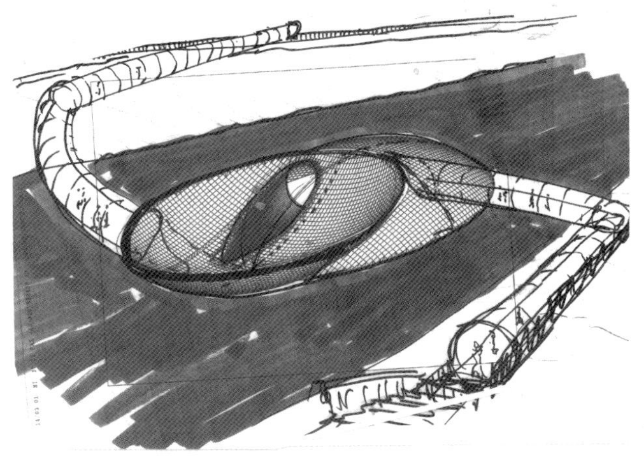

Sketch for general concept

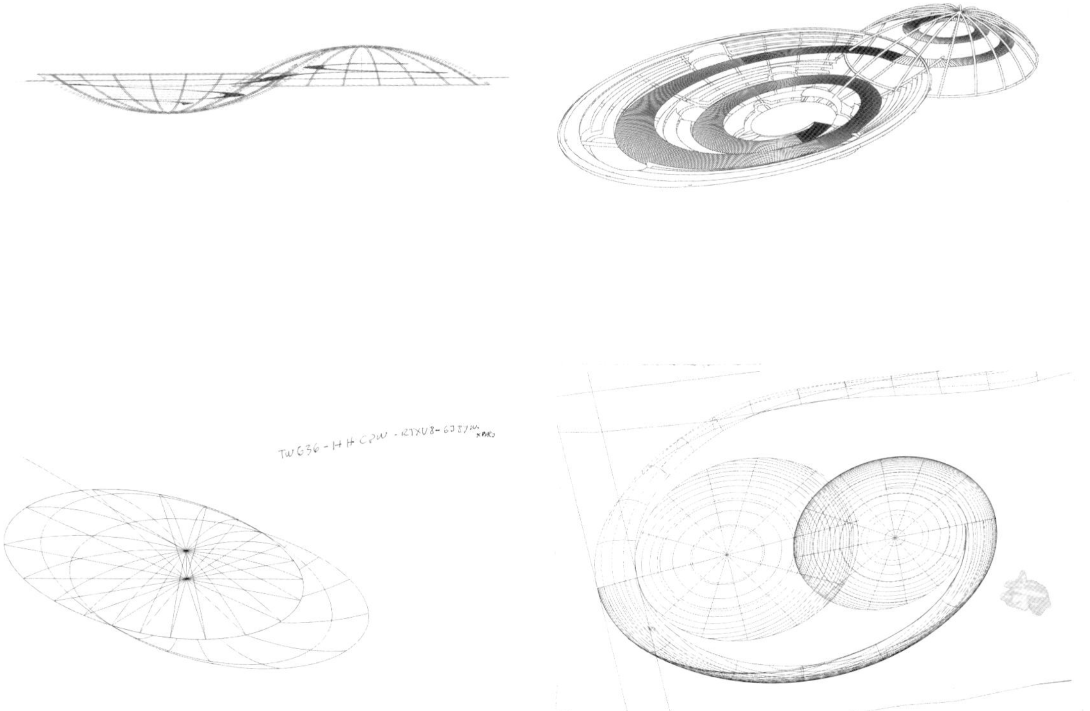

Design development studies

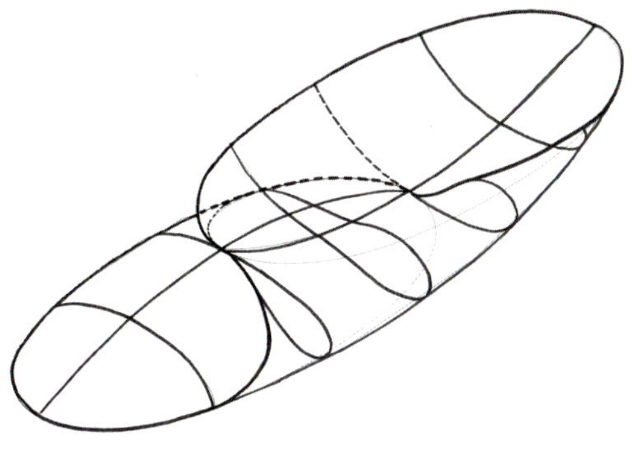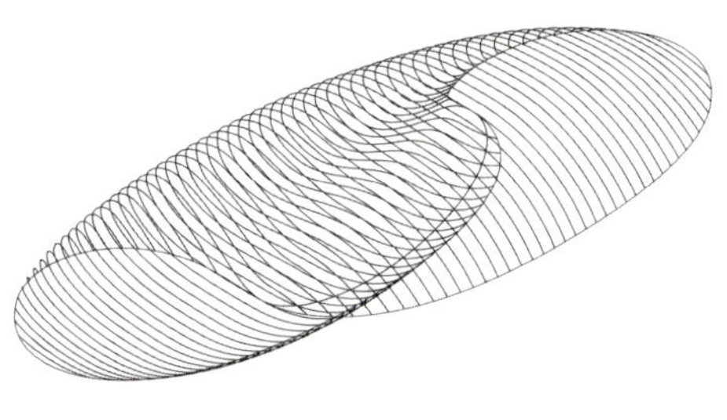

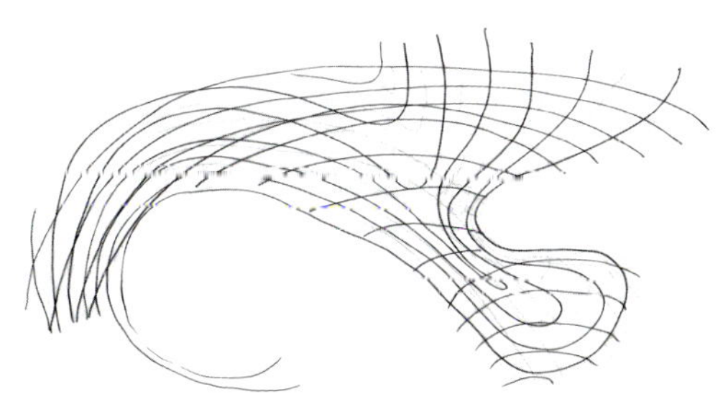

Design development studies

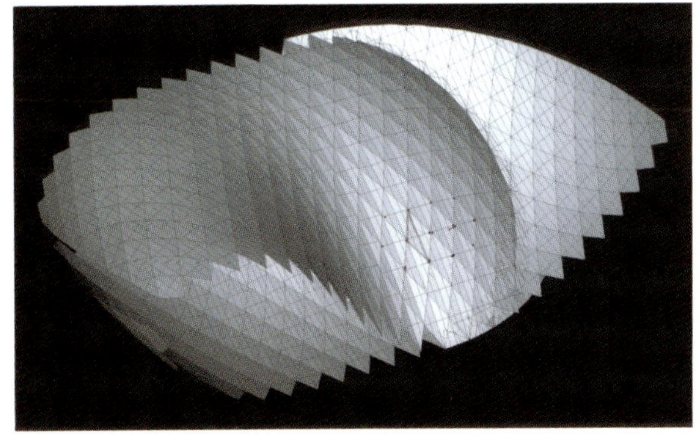

3D studies

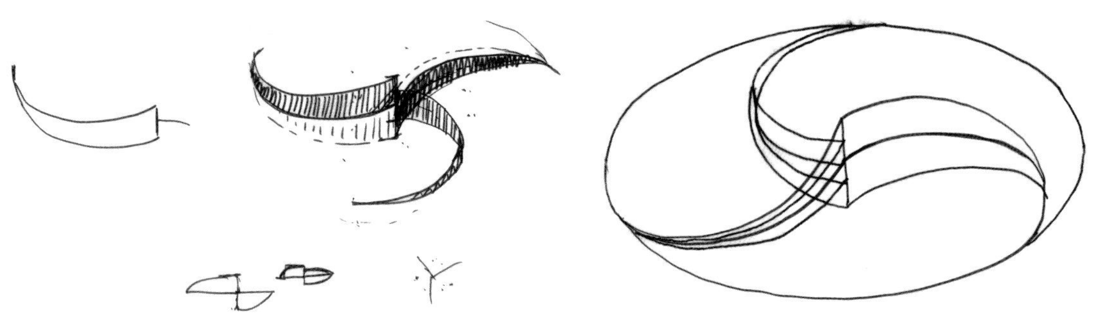

Elevation

Sectional perspective

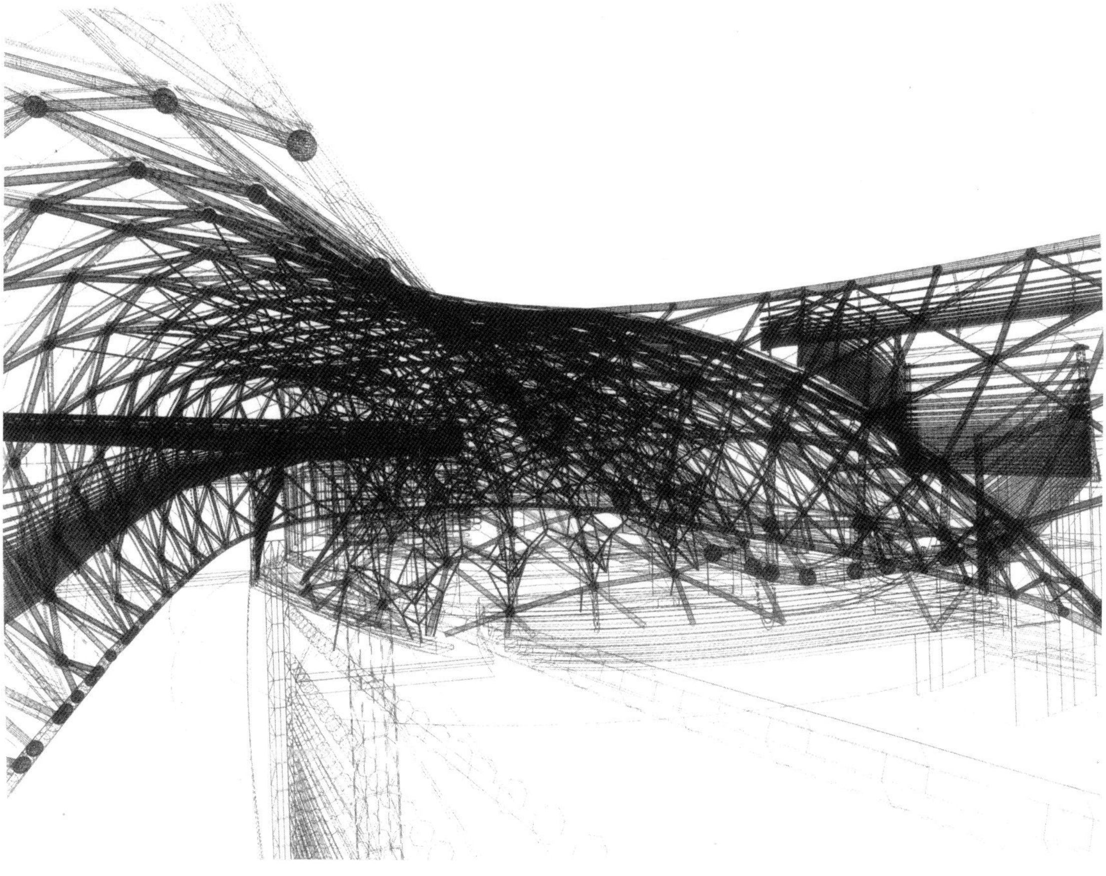

Study for helix

Study for helix

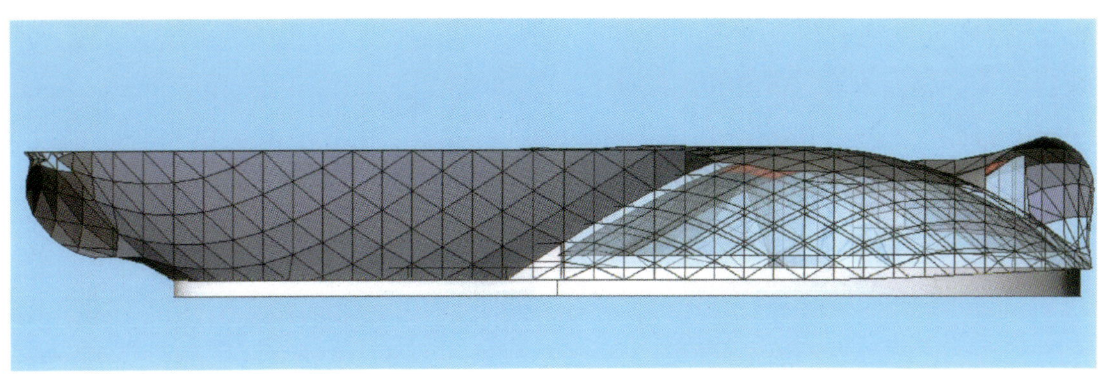

3D renderings

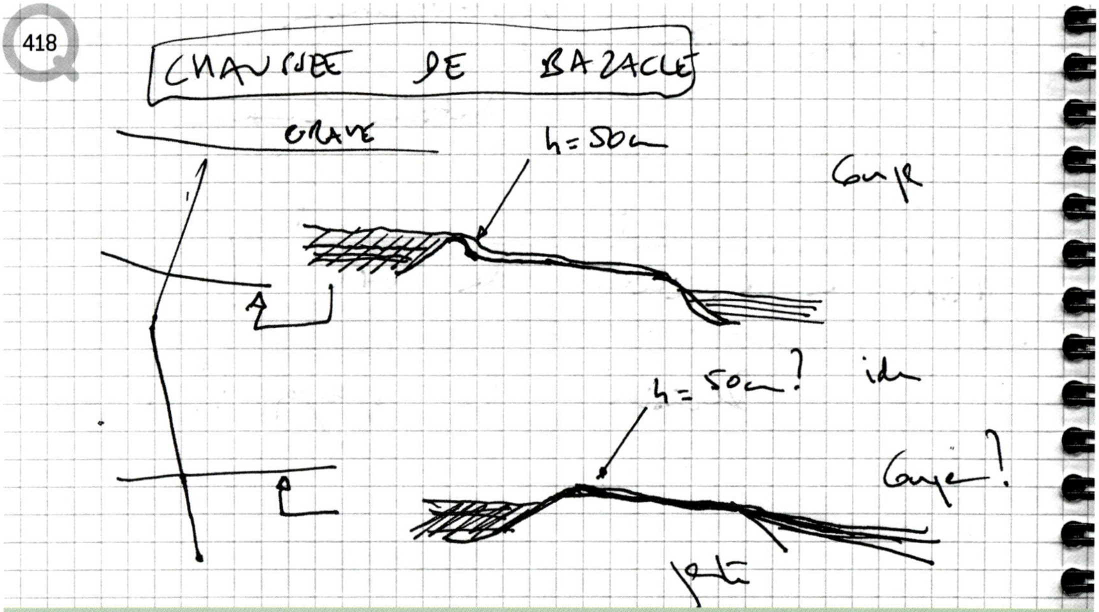

Lighting plan for Toulouse

Toulouse, France

This project consists of lighting the Garonne River as it flows through the city of Toulouse. A series of lights were placed on the river bed to create an original, unusual, and elegant appearance. This project covers a distance of almost one mile.

Le projet consiste en l'éclairage de la Garonne à son passage au cœur de la ville de Toulouse. Une série de dispositifs d'éclairage sont mis en place sur le lit du fleuve afin de conférer un aspect original, insolite et élégant au lieu. Les installations se prolongent sur une distance de 1,55 km.

Bei dem Projekt handelt es sich um die Beleuchtung des Flusses Garonne entlang seines Wegs durch die Stadt Toulouse. Im Flussbett wurde eine Reihe von Leuchtkörpern installiert, die dem Ort ein originelles und elegantes Aussehen verleihen. Die Anlage erstreckt sich über 1,55 km.

Het project bestaat uit de verlichting van de rivier de Garonne waar die door de stad Toulouse loopt. Er wordt een reeks verlichtingsvoorzieningen in de bedding van de rivier geplaatst die de plek een origineel, ongebruikelijk en elegant aspect geven. De installatie strekt zich uit over 1,55 km.

Roger Narboni/Concepto Agency, Sara Castagné and Mélina Votadoro (project managers)
roger.narboni@concepto.fr
© Roger Narboni/Concepto Agency

The 800-ft long raised roadway connecting both banks of the Garonne River becomes an illuminated concrete path with lights that vary in intensity depending on the amount of water flowing in the river.

La chaussée surélevée de 247 m de long, reliant les deux rives de la Garonne, comporte un chemin en béton éclairé, dont l'intensité lumineuse varie en fonction du débit du fleuve.

Auf der erhöhten, 247 m langen Fahrbahn, die beide Garonne-Ufer verbindet, wurde ein beleuchteter Betonweg konstruiert, dessen Lichtintensität mit der Flussströmung variiert.

Op de 247 m lange verhoogde rijbaan, die de twee oevers van de Garonne met elkaar verbindt, wordt een verlichte weg van beton aangelegd, waarvan de lichten een andere intensiteit hebben al naargelang de hoeveelheid water in de rivier.

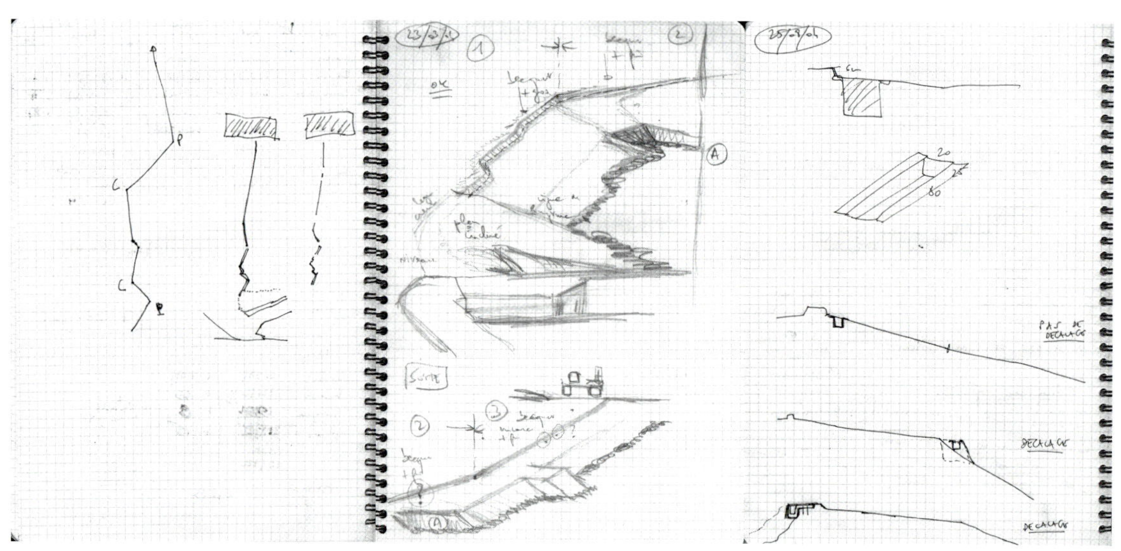

Schematic design sketches

Situation plan

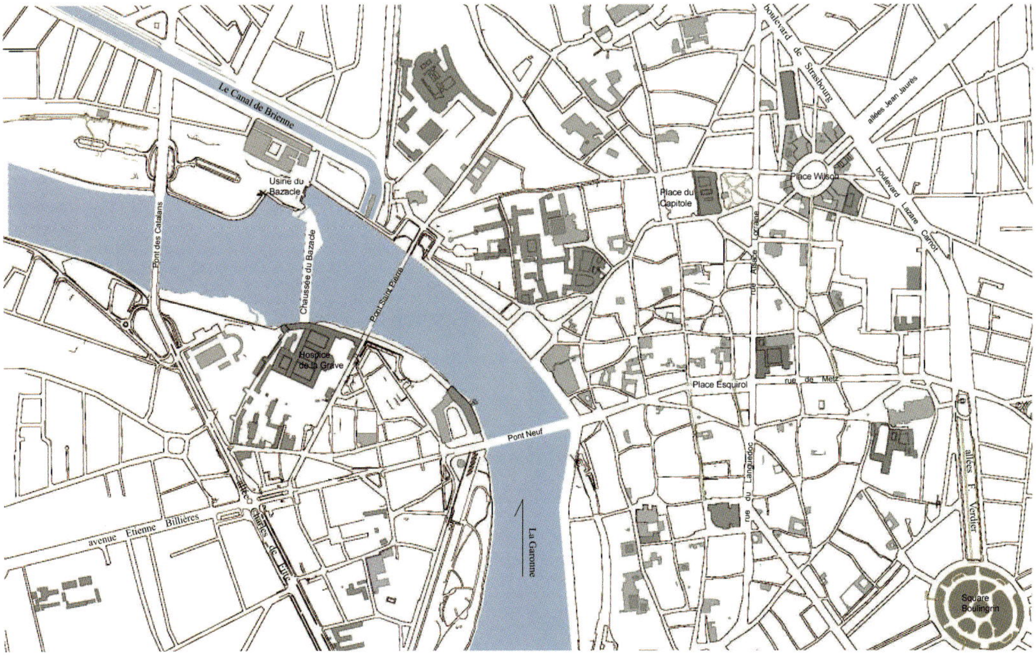

Situation plan on detail

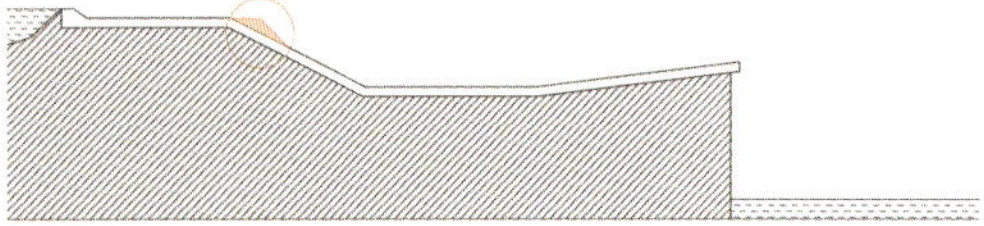

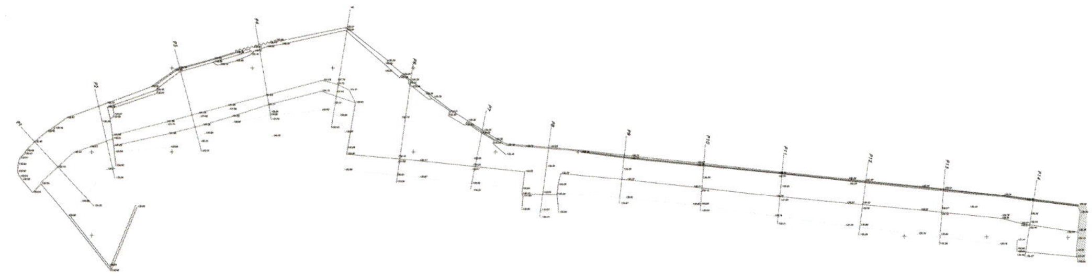

Detail section and plan of river causeway before intevention

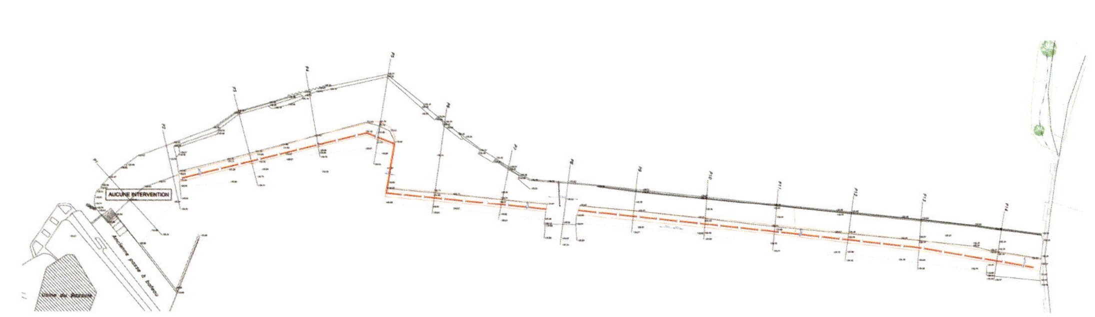

General plan of intervention line

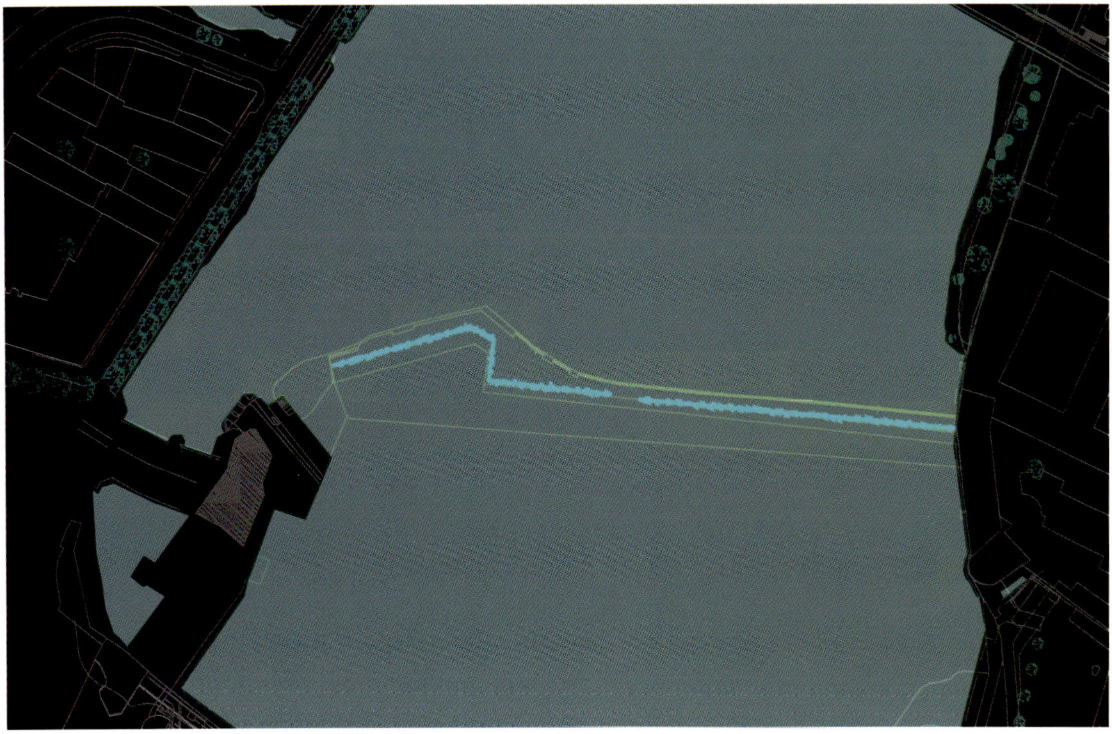

Section and plan of lights arrangement on river causeway

Frederiksberg New Urban Spaces

Frederiksberg, Denmark

For the Danish firm there were several defining points for the final project design: the layout of a number of public squares, the particular climate of the area, the permanent presence of water, and smooth pedestrian flow. The result is a variety of spaces brightened by night illumination, animal noises, and areas with mist.

Pour le cabinet paysagiste danois, plusieurs points de départ ont été pris en compte pour la conception finale envisagée : l'aménagement de plusieurs places publiques, le climat particulier de la zone, la présence permanente d'eau et la fluidité de circulation des piétons. Une variété d'espaces animés sont finalement créés grâce à l'éclairage nocturne, la sonorisation animale et les zones de brouillard.

Für das dänische Landschaftsarchitekten-Studio waren mehrere Punkte für den endgültigen Projektentwurf bestimmend: Die Aufteilung von mehreren öffentlichen Plätzen, das besondere Klima der Gegend, das ständige Vorhandensein von Wasser und der flüssige Fußgängerverkehr. Das Ergebnis ist eine Vielfalt von Räumen, die durch nächtliche Beleuchtung, Geräuschuntermalung durch Tierlaute und Nebelzonen belebt werden.

Voor het Deense landschapsarchitectenbureau waren er diverse bepalende punten voor het eindontwerp: de ordening van diverse openbare pleinen, het bijzondere klimaat van het gebied, de permanente aanwezigheid van water en de vlotte doorstroom van voetgangers. Het resultaat is een keur van gezellige ruimten met nachtverlichting, diergeluiden en zones met mist.

SLA
www.sla.dk
© Jens Lindhe, Torben Petersen, Lars Bahl, SLA (drawings)

Water is featured in a variety of ways in this project – as rain, a waterfall, vapor, and still. Nature was the source of inspiration for this urban experience.

Dans ce projet, l'eau est utilisée de plusieurs façons : pluie, cascade, vapeur ou étang. Cette expérience urbaine puise son inspiration dans la nature.

Das Wasser wird in diesem Projekt in den verschiedensten Formen eingesetzt: als Regen, Wasserfall, Dampf oder stehendes Wasser.

Het water wordt in dit project in diverse vormen gebruikt: als regen, waterval, stoom of stilstaand water. De natuur was de inspiratiebron voor dit stadsproject.

Against and with nature

Siglufjordur, Iceland

The main idea behind the project was to develop structures to protect against avalanches. It consists of a defensive barrier, a prevention system, and environmental and social benefits for the area's inhabitants.

Le projet a pour principal objectif d'aménager les structures nécessaires afin de pouvoir dévier les avalanches. Il apporte ainsi une barrière de défense, un système de prévention et un avantage environnemental et social pour les habitants des lieux.

Das Hauptkonzept des Projekts basiert auf der Idee, die nötigen Strukturen so zu verändern, dass Lawinen umgeleitet werden. So wurde eine Schutzbarriere errichtet, die vorteilhaft für die Umwelt und gleichzeitig von sozialem Nutzen für die Einwohner des Ortes ist.

Het hoofdconcept van dit project is gebaseerd op het idee om lawinewerende structuren een nieuwe vorm te geven. Op deze manier wordt een verdedigingsbarrière en een preventiesysteem gecreëerd met milieuvriendelijke en sociale voordelen voor de plaatselijke bewoners.

**Landslag ehf
Landslagsarkitektar FÍLA,
Reynir Vilhjalmsson (landscape
project manager)**
www.landslag.is
© Omar Ingthorsson, Sigurjon Johsson, Steingrimur Kristinsson, Thrainn Hauksson, Landslag (drawings)

The project consists of two parallel earth walls, one 650 ft in length and the other measuring 2,300 ft, both with heights ranging between 50 and 65 ft, together with 6 additional walls and dykes.

L'ouvrage est constitué d'un système formé par deux murailles en terre parallèles respectivement de 200 et 700 m de long, dont la hauteur varie entre 15 et 20 m, ainsi que de 6 murs et digues.

Die Maßnahme besteht aus zwei parallelen 200 m bzw. 700 m langen Erdwällen mit einer variablen Höhe zwischen 15 und 20 m, sowie sechs Mauern und Dämmen.

Het project bestaat uit een systeem van twee parallelle aardwanden, de ene 200 m en de andere 700 m lang en beide 15 tot 20 m hoog, alsook 6 muren en dijken.

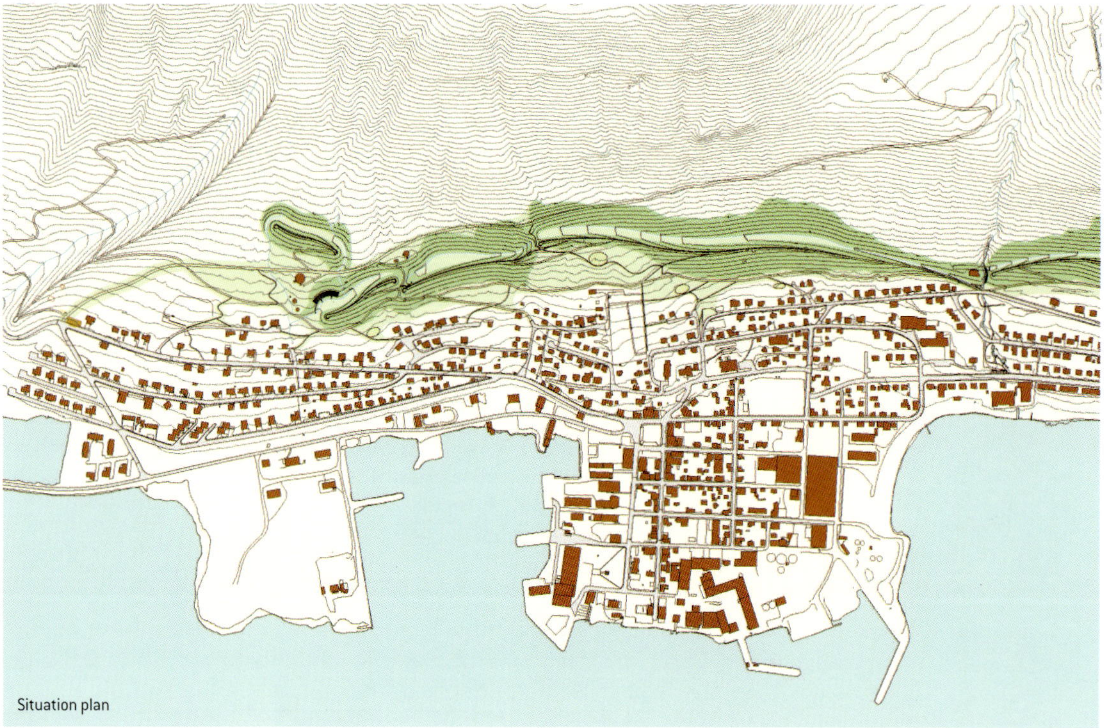

Situation plan

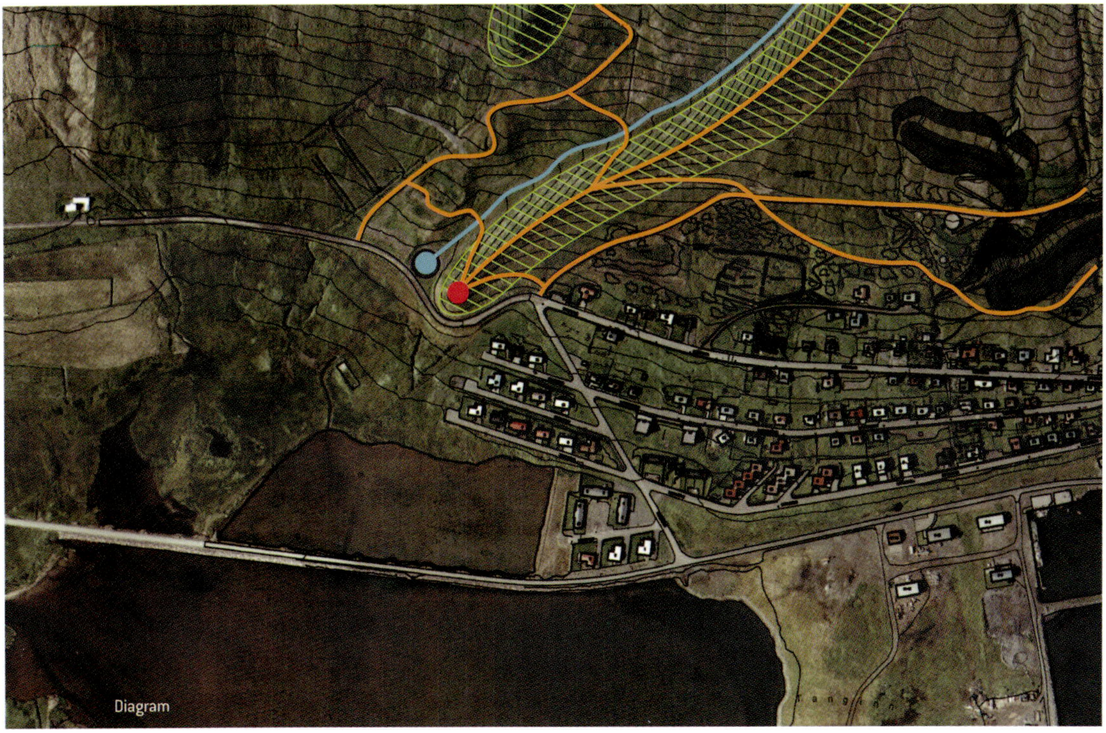

Diagram

Cemetery for the Unknown

Mirasaka, Japan

The construction of a new dam in the north east of Hiroshima prefecture led to the building of a new cemetery to replace the old one that was submerged by the rising water. The local residents requested a memorial for the unmarked tombs that was free of any religious symbols.

En raison de l'aménagement d'une nouvelle digue dans la zone nord-est du département d'Hiroshima, la construction d'un nouveau cimetière venant remplacer l'ancien site englouti par les eaux a été entreprise. La population locale a demandé à ce qu'un monument commémorant les tombes soit érigé et que celui-ci soit exempt de symboles religieux.

Aufgrund der Konstruktion eines neuen Damms auf dem Gebiet nordöstlich der Präfektur von Hiroshima wurde die Anlage eines neuen Friedhofs beschlossen, um den überschwemmten zu ersetzen. Die örtliche Bevölkerung wünschte eine Denkmal ohne religiöse Symbole für die Gräber.

Toen in het noordoosten van de prefectuur Hiroshima een nieuwe dijk werd gebouwd, besloot men om een nieuwe begraafplaats te bouwen ter vervanging van het overstroomde kerkhof. De plaatselijke bevolking had verzocht om een gedenkteken van de graven te plaatsen zonder religieuze symbolen.

Hideki Yoshimatsu & Archipro Architects
www.archipro.net
© Hideyuki Ashiba, Masanori Kato, Earthworks Project, Archipro Architects (drawings)

The memorial consists of 1,500 stainless steel rods each 6¹/₂ ft tall and the replanting of a sacred tree, the tarayoh.

Le monument commémoratif est composé de 1 500 barres en acier inoxydable de 2 m de haut et d'un arbre sacré, le tarayoh, qui a été replanté.

Das Denkmal besteht aus 1500 Edelstahlstangen von 2 m Höhe und der Wiedereinpflanzung des heiligen Baums Taray.

Het monument bestaat uit 1500 roestvrij stalen staven van 2 m hoog. Men verplantte ook een heilige boom, de tamarisk.

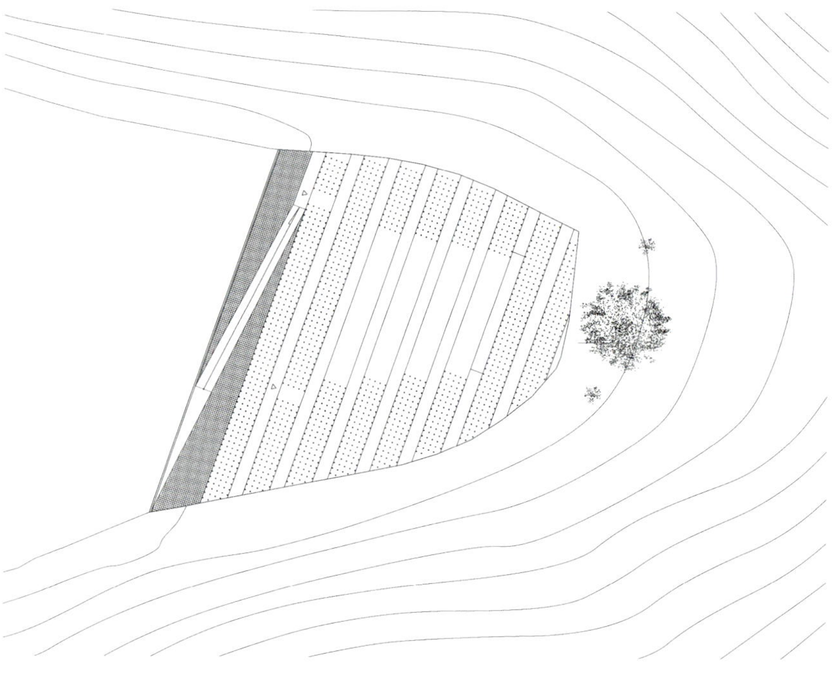

Plan

Bosque de la vida

Leioa, Spain

This spectacular project arose from the search for an open, permeable space as a metaphor for life after death. The project is located in a 14,000 sq ft space on the Leioa campus of the University of the Basque Country. The place meant to hold ashes is designed as a forest, not as a cemetery.

Ce projet spectaculaire est né de la recherche d'un espace ouvert et perméable en tant que métaphore de la vie après la mort. Le projet a été réalisé dans un espace de 1 300 m² aménagé à l'intérieur du campus de Leioa appartenant à l'Université du Pays Basque. Le lieu abritant les cendres est conçu comme une forêt et non comme un cimetière.

Dieser eindrucksvolle Entwurf entstand aus der Suche nach einem offenen, durchlässigen Ort als Sinnbild für das Leben nach dem Tod. Das Projekt befindet sich auf einer Fläche von 1300 m² auf dem Campus von Leioa, der zur Universität des Baskenlands gehört. Die Stelle für die sterblichen Überreste wurde als Wald und nicht wie ein Friedhof entworfen.

Dit spectaculaire project is ontstaan uit de zoektocht naar een open, doordringbare ruimte als metafoor van het leven na de dood. Het project is gelegen op een terrein van 1300 m² binnen de Campus Leioa van de Baskische Universiteit. De plaats waar men de as bewaart, wordt niet als begraafplaats maar als bos opgevat.

Zade & Vilà Associats
zadevila@coac.net
© Mari Carmen Vilà i Espino,
Zade & Vilà Associats (drawings)

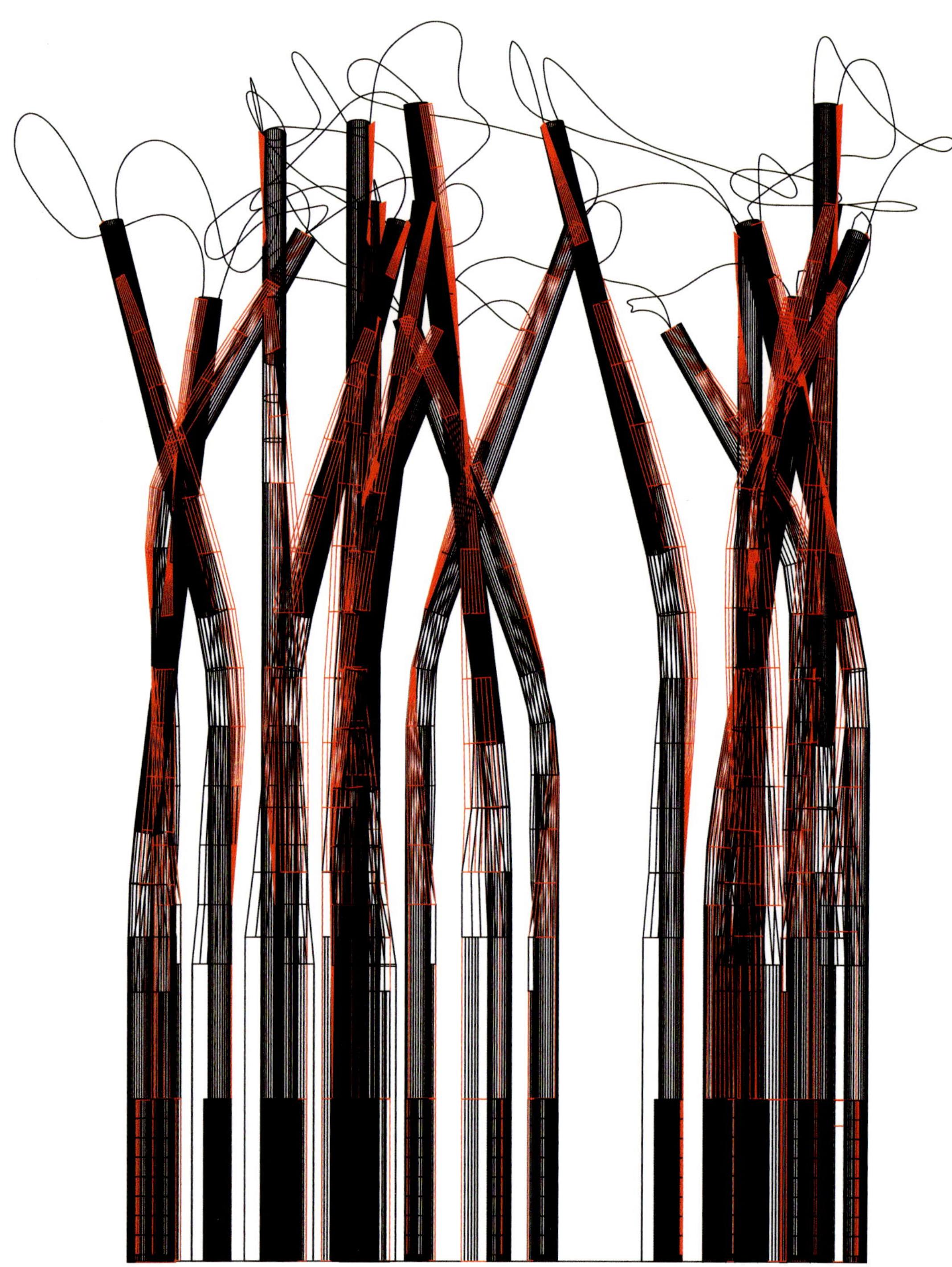

Elevation

The result of the design competition organized by the University of the Basque Country is a sculptural project seen as an open and beautiful sanctuary for depositing ashes.

Un appel d'offres lancé par l'Université du Pays basque a donné lieu à un projet sculptural perçu comme un refuge ouvert, idéal pour y déposer des cendres.

Das Ergebnis eines von der Universität des Baskenlands ausgeschriebenen Wettbewerbs ist ein bildhauerisches Projekt, das als offener und erhabener Zufluchtsort für die sterblichen Überreste betrachtet wird.

Het resultaat van een door de Baskische Universiteit georganiseerde wedstrijd is een beeldhouwproject dat wordt gezien als een open en verheven wijkplaats om de as te bewaren.

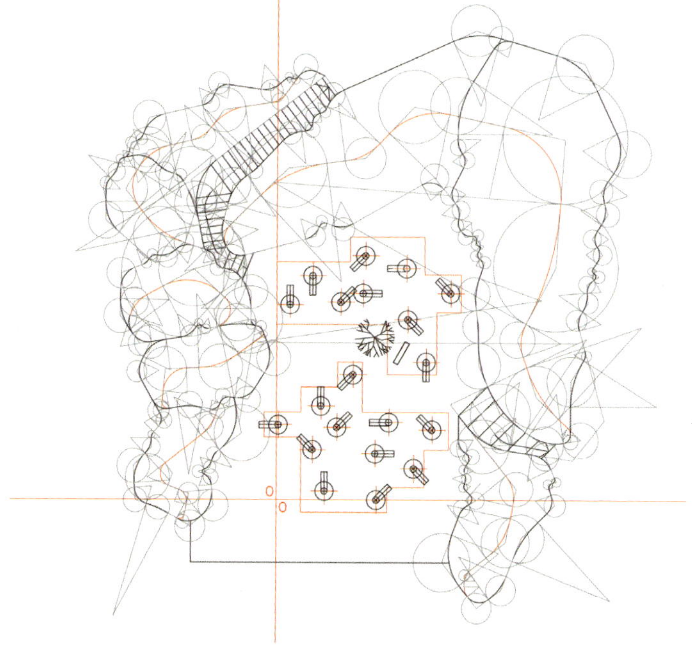

Forest model

Site plan

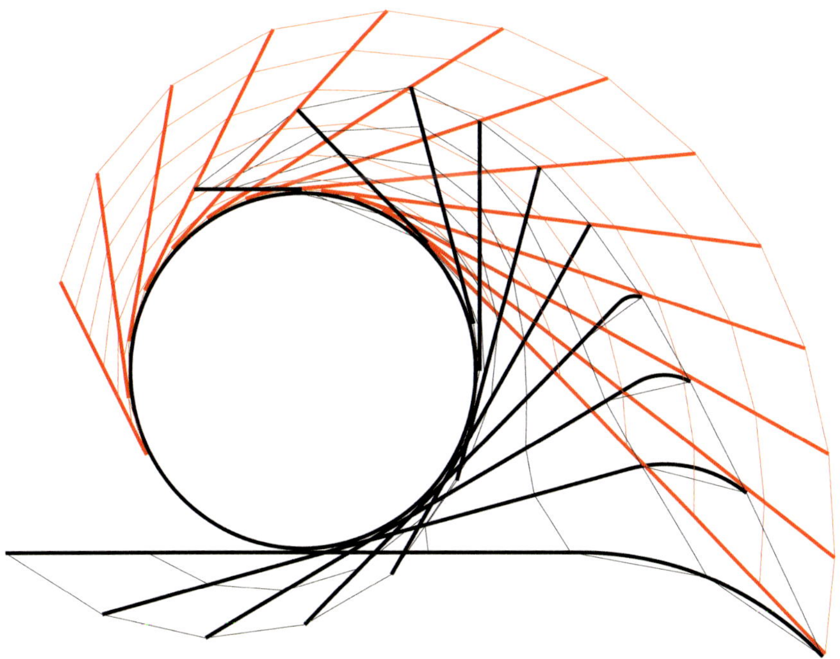

Conceptual drawing

Rice Ocean Breath – The Wetland and Bird Museum

Qinghuangdao, China

The project consisted of regenerating the natural habitat of the site through its reconstruction and the building of a museum of migratory birds. The entrance to the museum and bird observatory is by means of wooden footbridges.

Le projet a consisté en la récupération de l'habitat naturel du terrain grâce à son réaménagement et à la construction d'un musée consacré aux oiseaux migrateurs. Des passerelles en bois servent à accéder au musée et à observer les oiseaux.

Das Projekt bestand in der Wiedergewinnung des natürlichen Lebensraums durch dessen Rekonstruktion und der Errichtung eines Museums, das den Zugvögeln gewidmet ist. Der Zugang zum Museum und die Beobachtung der Vögel werden durch hölzerne Stege ermöglicht.

Het project bestond uit het herstel van de natuurlijke habitat van het terrein door de reconstructie ervan en de bouw van een museum gewijd aan trekvogels. De toegang tot het museum en de vogelobservatie is mogelijk via houten vlonders.

Turenscape, Lin Shihong, Liu Xiangjun, Cheng Cheng, Long Xiang (project team)
www.turenscape.com
© Kongjian You, Yang Cao, Mei Wu (drawings)

Ponds of river water were created on the site with small round islands in the middle of the lake to provide sanctuary to migratory birds.

Des étangs d'eau douce ont été créés sur la terre ferme et de petites îles rondes ont été aménagées au milieu du lac pour favoriser la nidification et le refuge des oiseaux migrateurs.

Auf dem Festland wurden Teiche mit Flusswasser, in der Mitte des Sees kleine runde Inseln konstruiert, die den Zugvögeln als Nistplatz dienen.

Er werden vijvers met rivierwater op het vasteland aangelegd en kleine ronde eilanden midden in het meer, zodat de trekvogels hier gemakkelijk een verblijf- en schuilplaats kunnen vinden.

Concept sketches of Bird Museum

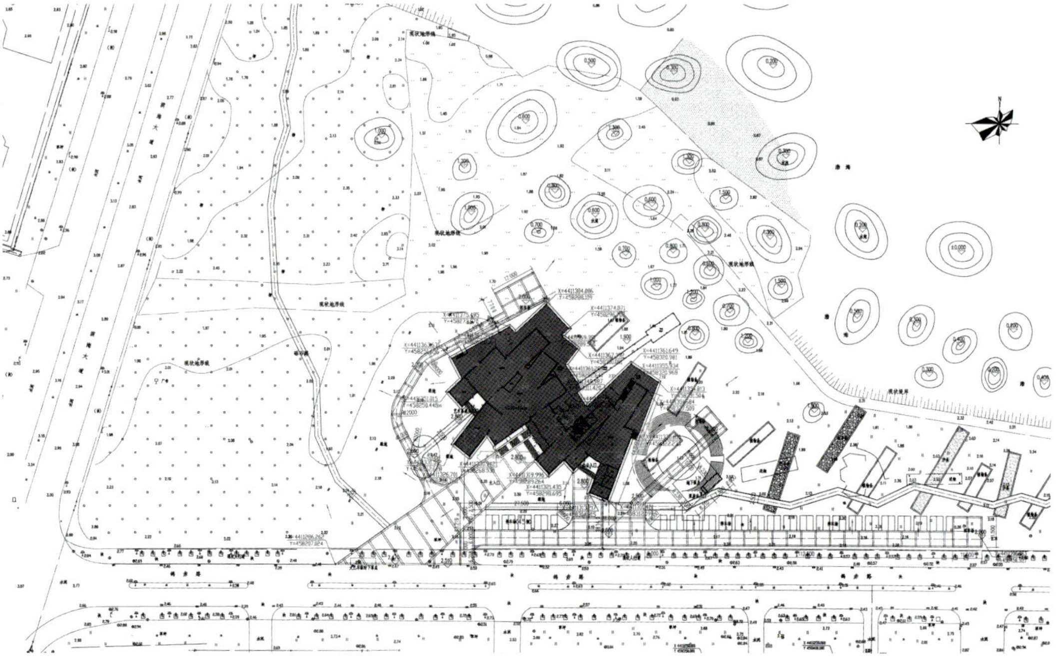

Site plan

Aerial 3D renderings of Bird Museum

Master plan

Parc de la Feyssine

Villeurbanne, France

This project is set in a forest located on the east bank of the Rhone in Villeurbanne. The aim is to create a natural urban space to complement a series of parks already existing along the river banks.

L'intervention a lieu dans la forêt alluviale située sur la rive gauche du Rhône à Villeurbanne. L'objectif consiste à aménager un nouvel espace naturel urbain au sein de l'ensemble des parcs existants sur les berges du fleuve.

Das Projekt wurde im Schwemmwald am linken Ufer der Rhone in Villeurbanne ausgeführt. Das Ziel war es, am Flussufer einen neuen städtischen Naturbereich innerhalb der bestehenden Parks zu schaffen.

Het project wordt uitgevoerd in het aangeslibde bos op de linkeroever van de Rhône in Villeurbanne. Het doel is een nieuwe stedelijke natuurruimte te creëren binnen de bestaande parken aan de oever van de rivier.

ILEX Paysage et Urbanisme, Péré and JeanClaude Durual
www.ilexpaysages.com
© ILEX

The creation of this park arose from the desire to build a natural and urban space for freedom inside the city. It is designed as a space for observing nature.

La création de ce parc est née de la volonté de construire un espace de liberté, à la fois naturel et urbain, au cœur de la ville. Il se veut un lieu d'observation de la nature.

Der Park entstand aus dem Wunsch, einen freien, natürlichen und urbanen Raum in der Stadt als Ort für die Naturbetrachtung zu errichten.

De aanleg van dit park is ontstaan vanuit de wens om een stedelijke en natuurlijke ruimte van vrijheid binnen de stad te creëren. De bedoeling is om een observatieruimte van de natuur te bieden.

Section showing evolution of trees

Watercolor elevation

General plan

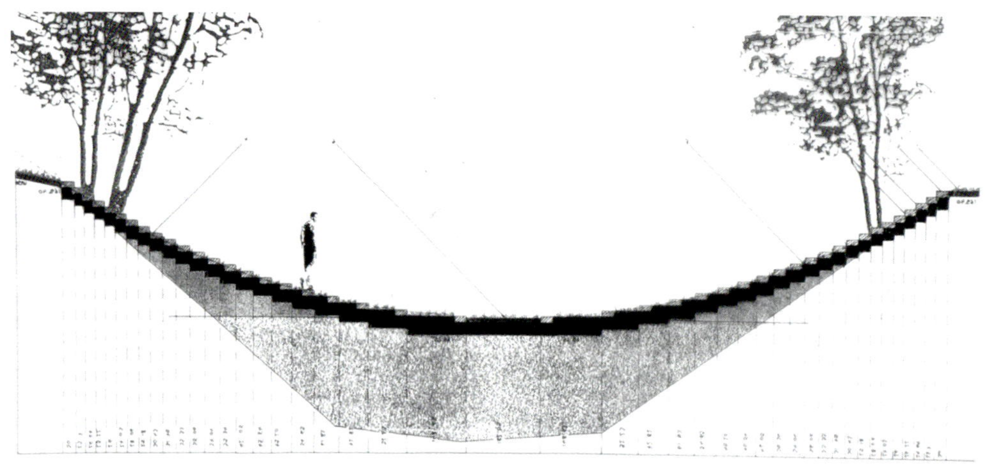

Section of footbridge

Presentation painting

Presentation paintings

Illumination of the Rion-Antirion Bridge

Gulf of Corinth, Greece

This landscaping project consists of the overlapping of shadows and luminous textures along the $1^{1}/_{2}$-mile length of the longest cable-stayed bridge in the world. The Rion-Antirion Bridge crosses the Gulf of Corinth to connect the Peloponnesus Peninsula with mainland Greece.

Le projet paysager consiste en la superposition d'ombres et de textures lumineuses qui sillonnent les 2,3 km du pont à haubans le plus long du monde. Le Rion-Antirion relie la péninsule du Péloponnèse à la Grèce continentale dans le golfe de Corinthe.

Das Landschaftsprojekt besteht aus der Überlagerung von Schatten und hellen Strukturen auf den 2,3 km, entlang der längsten Schrägseilbrücke der Welt. Die Rio-Andirrio-Brücke verbindet die Peloponnes-Halbinsel mit dem griechischen Festland im Golf von Korinth.

Het landschapsarchitectonische project bestaat uit de superpositie van schaduwen en lichttexturen die langs de 2,3 km van de langste hangbrug ter wereld lopen. De Rion-Antirion verbindt het schiereiland Peloponessis met het Griekse vasteland in de Corinthische Golf.

Roger Narboni/Concepto Agency, Sara Castagné and Mélina Votadoro (project managers):
roger.narboni@concepto.fr
© Roger Narboni/Concepto Agency

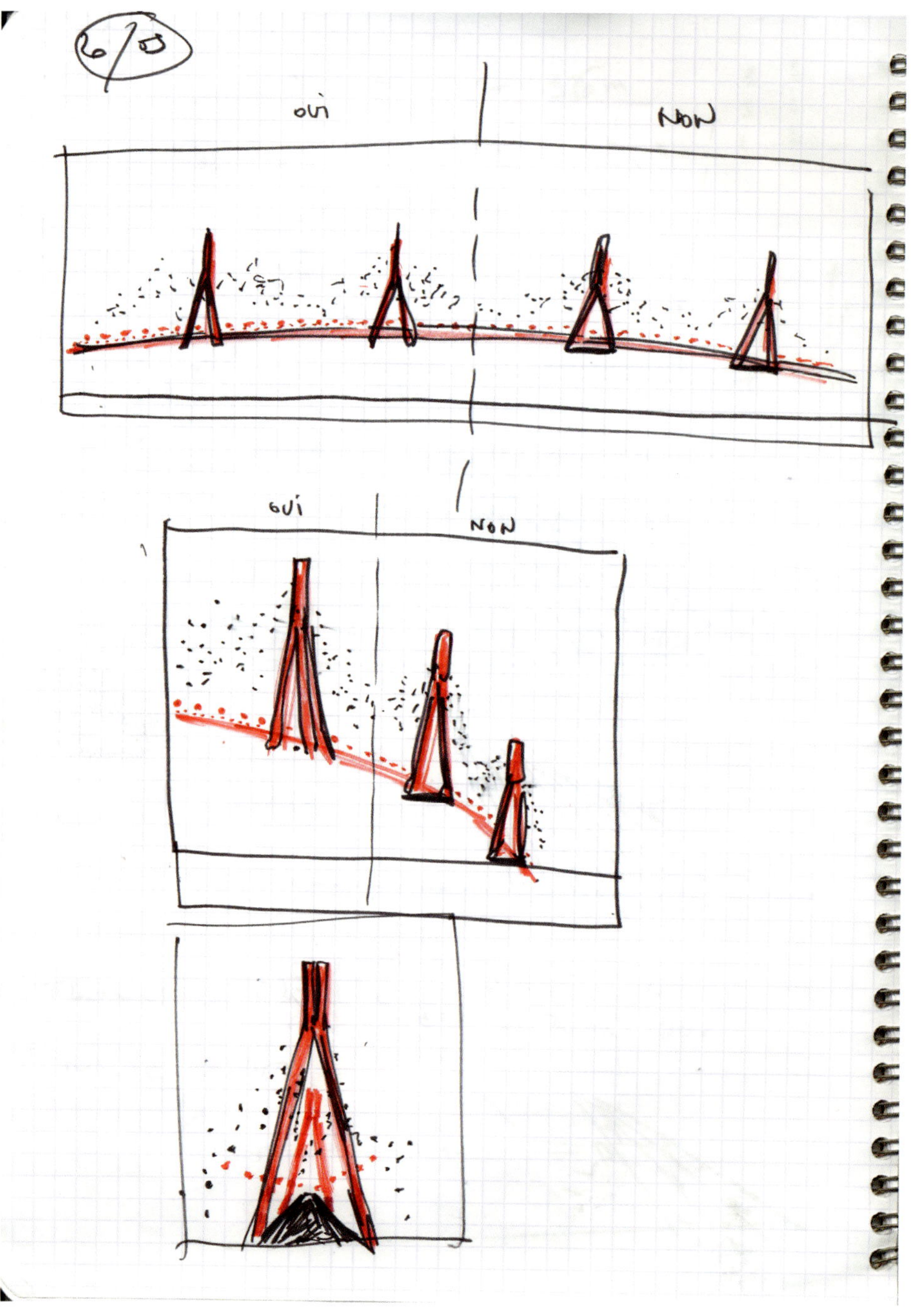

Schematic design sketches

The embankment and submerged structure of the embankment is left dark to emphasize the bridge lighting, which is also reflected in the sea.

Les quais et leurs structures submergées sont plongés dans l'obscurité afin de mettre en valeur la scénographie lumineuse du pont qui, en outre, se reflète dans la mer.

Die Molen und die Strukturen unter Wasser bleiben im Dunkeln, um die Lichtwirkung der Brücke zu betonen, die sich darüber hinaus im Meer spiegelt.

De steigers en hun onder water liggende structuren blijven in het duister om de nadruk te leggen op het lichtdecor van de brug die bovendien in de zee wordt weerspiegeld.

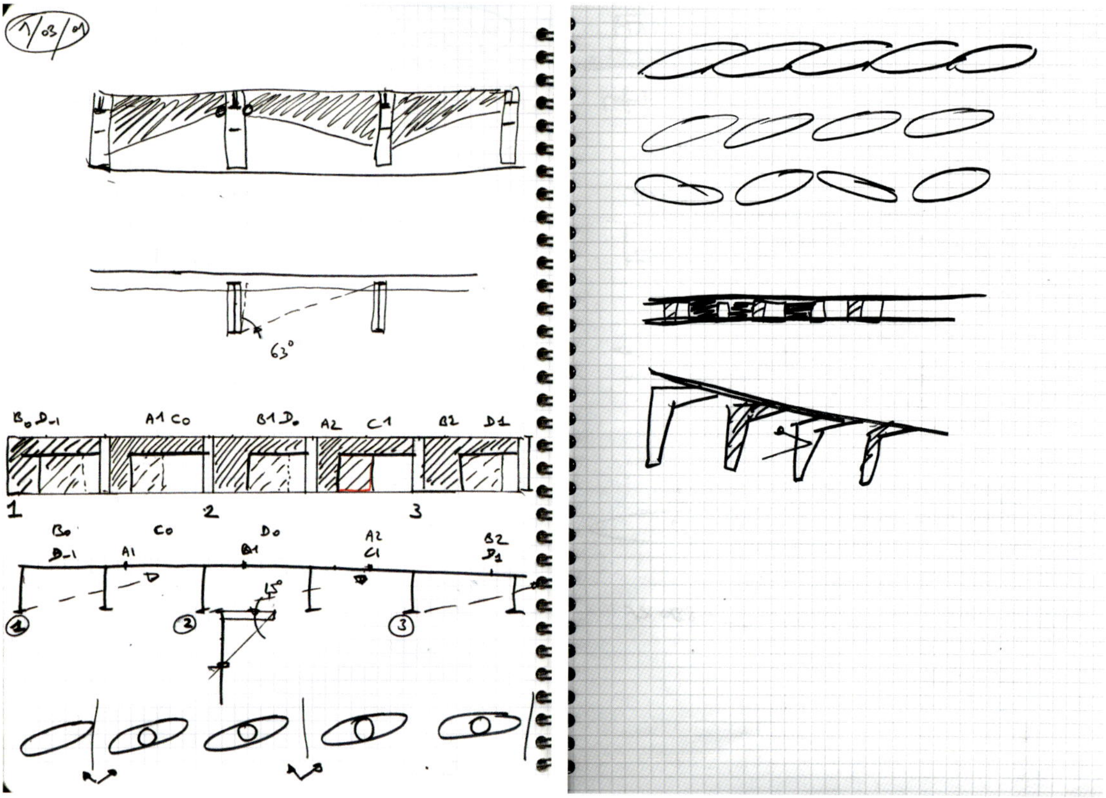

Schematic design skecthes

Section and elevation of bridge deck with spotlight

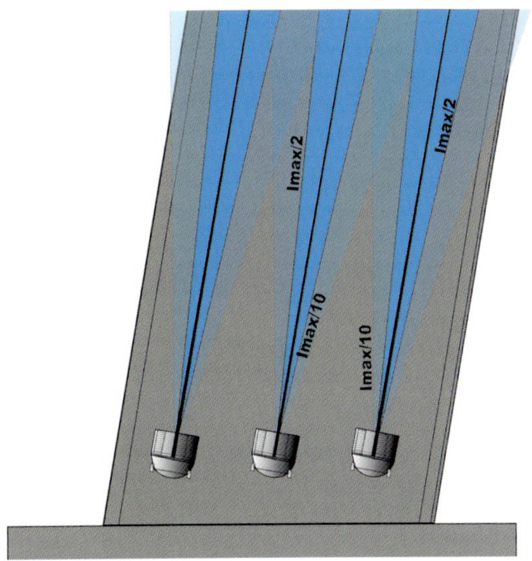

Elevation of spotlights on pylon

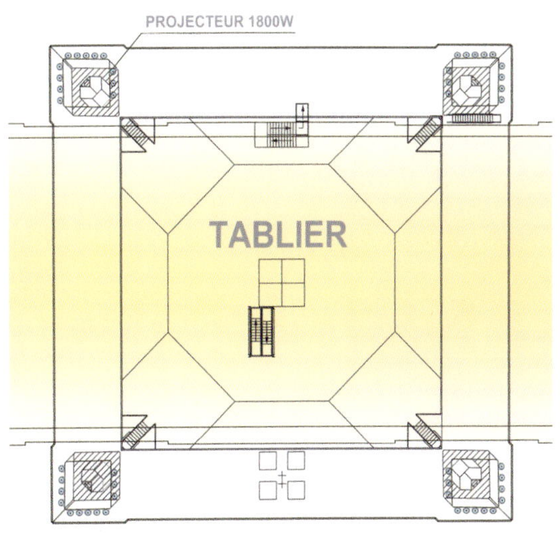

Plan of a pylon with spotlight

Reassess a mountain

This ambitious landscaping project consisted of remodeling the installations of the aerial tramway taking visitors to the top of Mt. Cardada. An esplanade was created at the tramway arrival area, in addition to a recreational route, a suspended footbridge, and an observation deck offering views of the area's geology.

Ce projet paysager ambitieux a consisté en la rénovation de l'infrastructure du téléphérique montant jusqu'au sommet de la montagne Cardada. Une gare d'arrivée du téléphérique, un itinéraire ludique, une passerelle suspendue et un mirador servant d'observatoire géologique ont été créés.

Dieses ehrgeizige Landschaftsprojekt bestand in der Renovierung der Infrastruktur der Seilbahn, die zum Gipfel des Cardada führt. Es wurden ein Zugangsbereich zur Seilbahn, eine Spielstrecke, eine Fußgängerbrücke und ein Aussichtspunkt als geologisches Observatorium geschaffen.

Dit ambitieuze landschapsarchitectonische project bestond uit de renovatie van de infrastructuur van de kabelbaan naar de bergtop van de Cardada. Er werden een aankomstplein voor de kabelbaan, een ludieke route, een hangbrug en een uitkijkplaats als geologisch observatorium aangelegd.

Paolo L. Bürgi
www.burgi.ch
© Giovanna Crivelli,
Montagnola CH,
Jean Michel Landecy,
Paolo L. Bürgi (drawings)

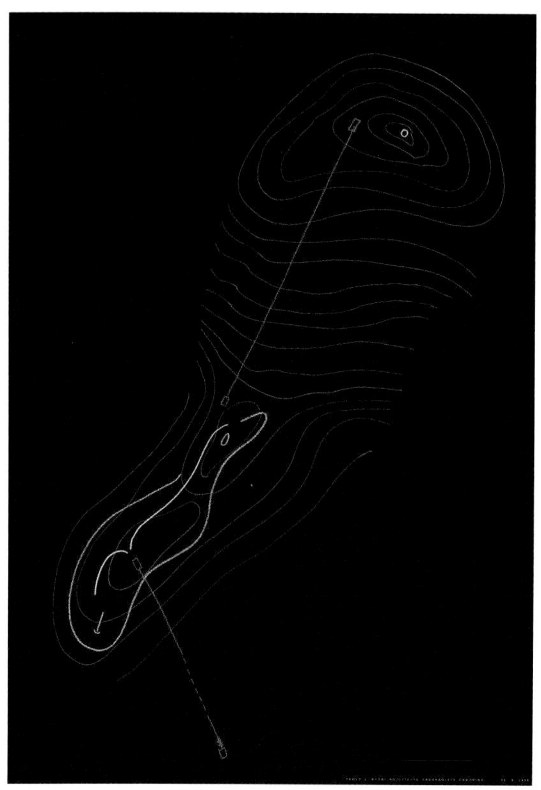

General concept

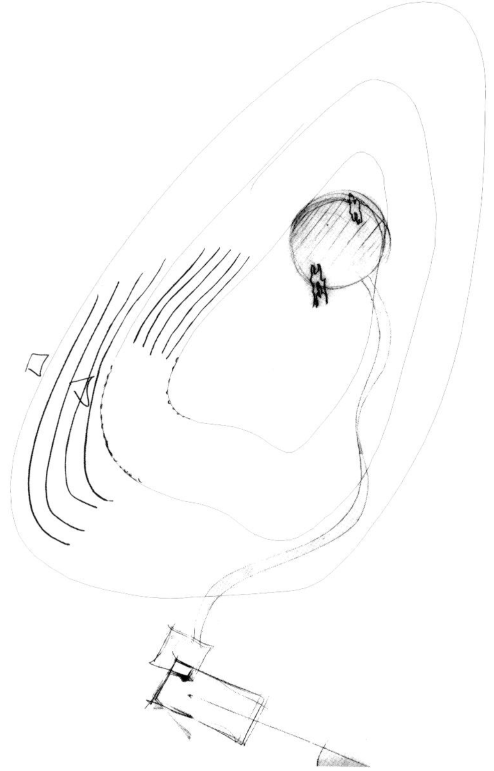

Sketch

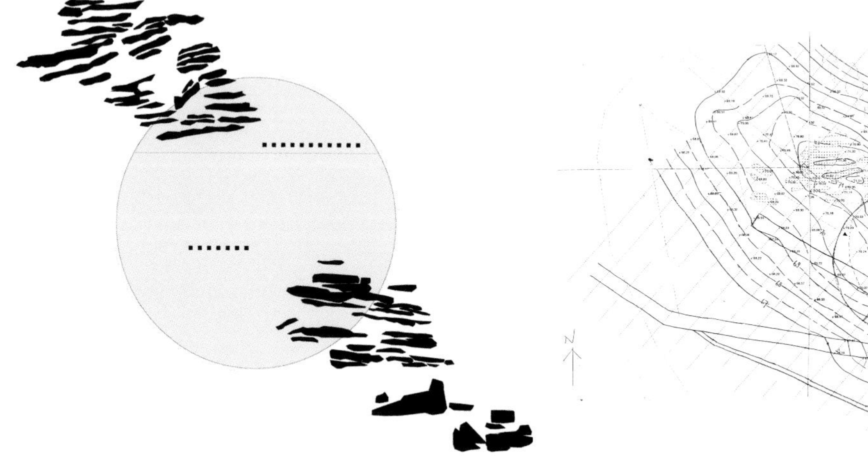

Drawing of geological observatory

Topographical plan

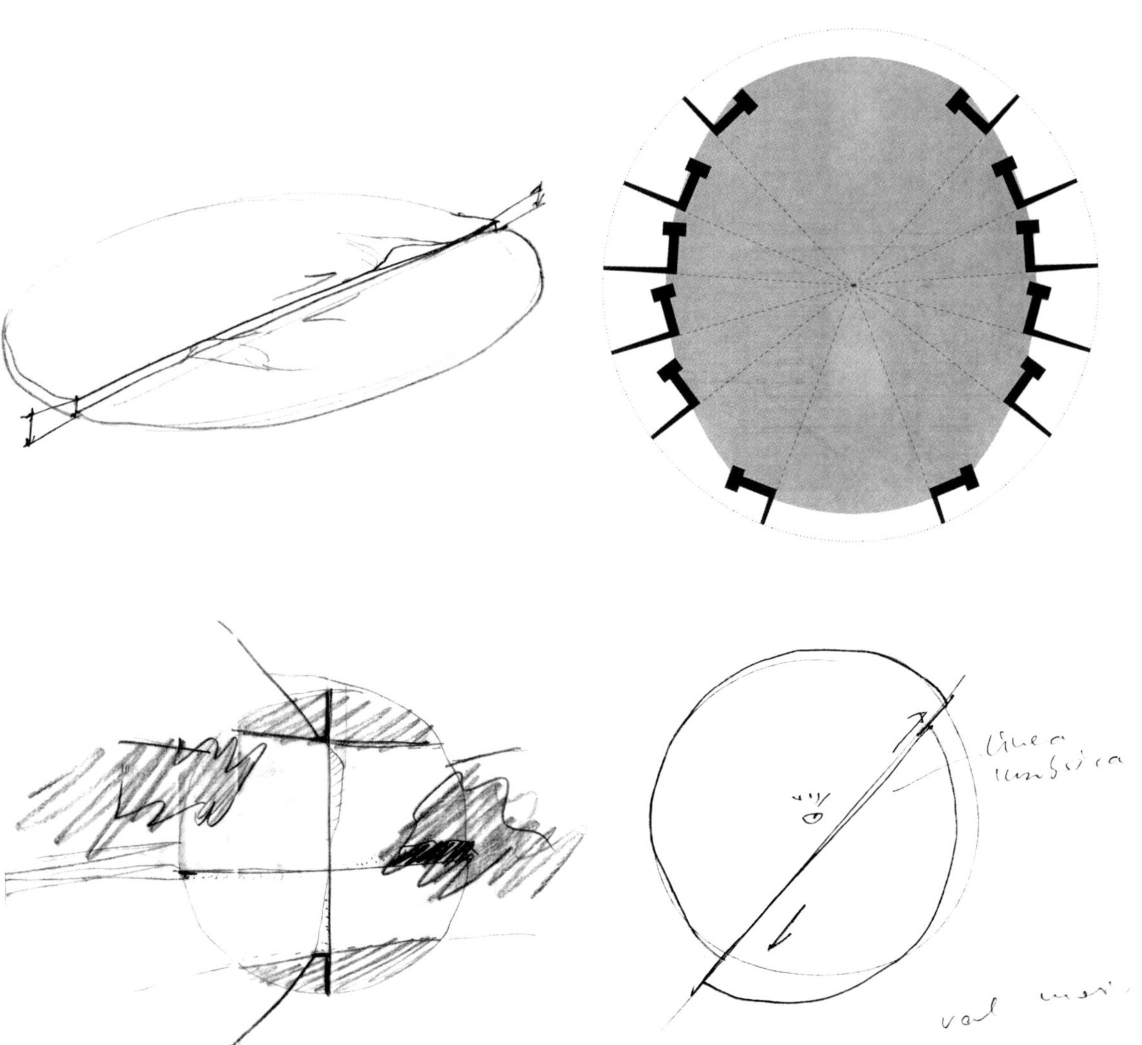

Development studies

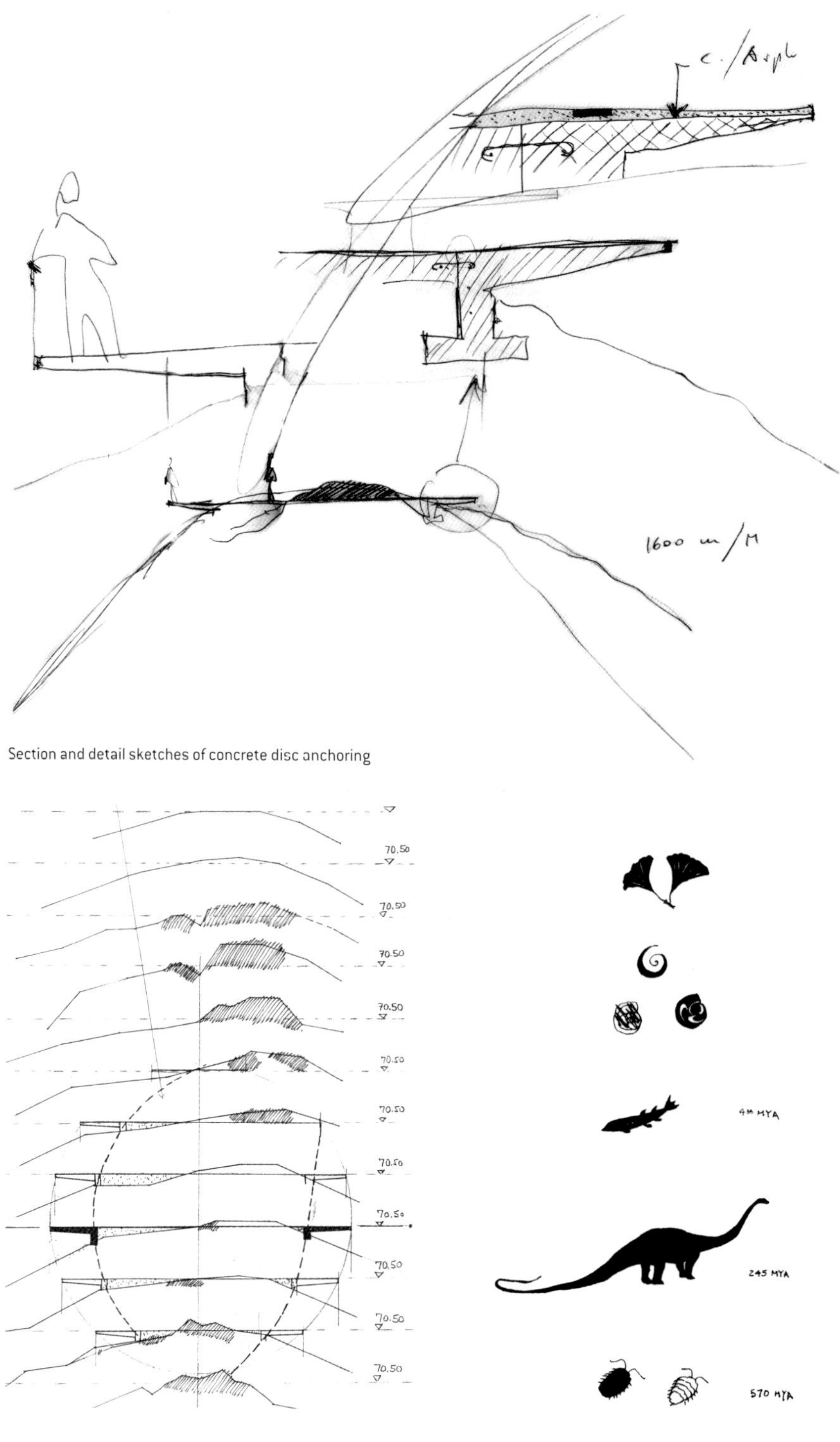

Section and detail sketches of concrete disc anchoring

Sections

Drawings of ground-stamps

Perspective drawings of path and concrete disc

Collage of a starry Cimetta night

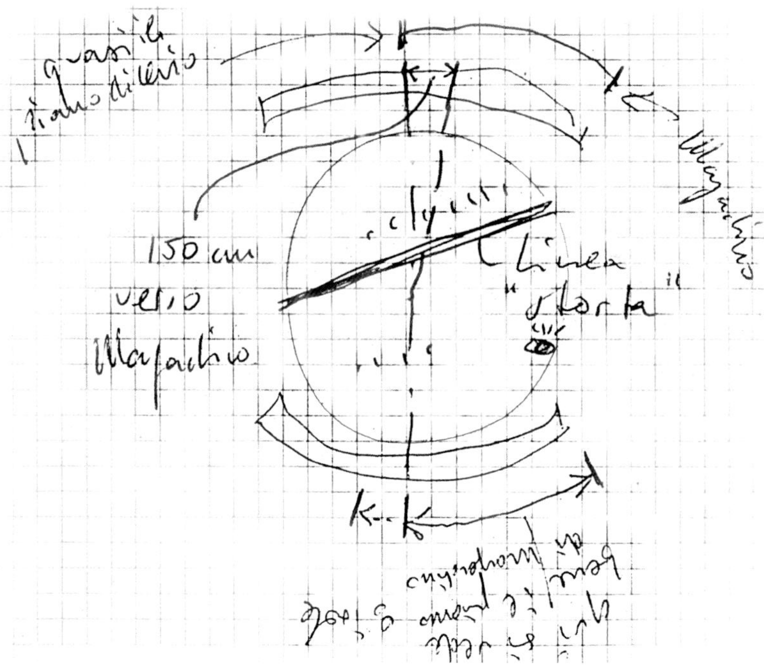

Sketch

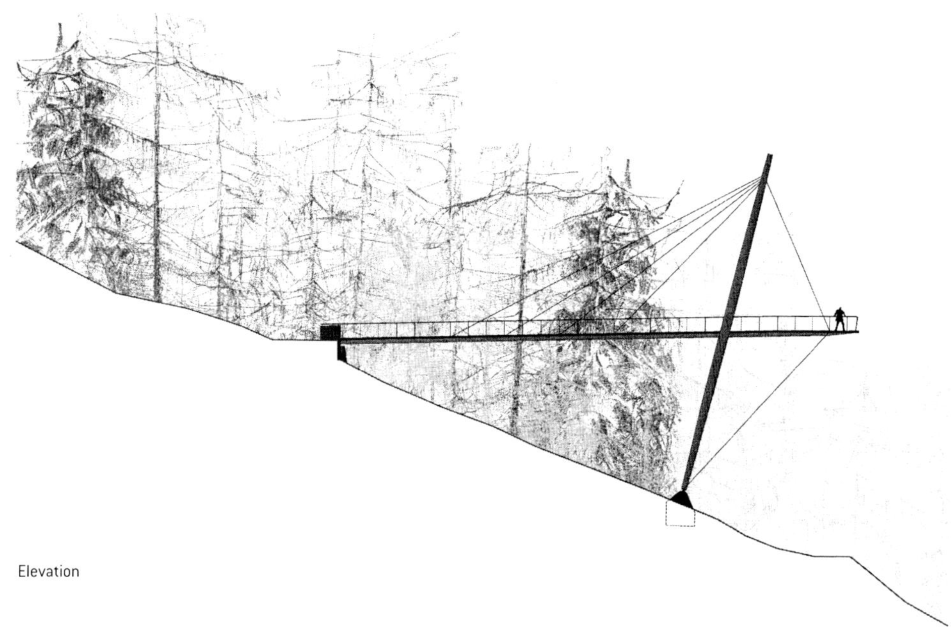

Elevation

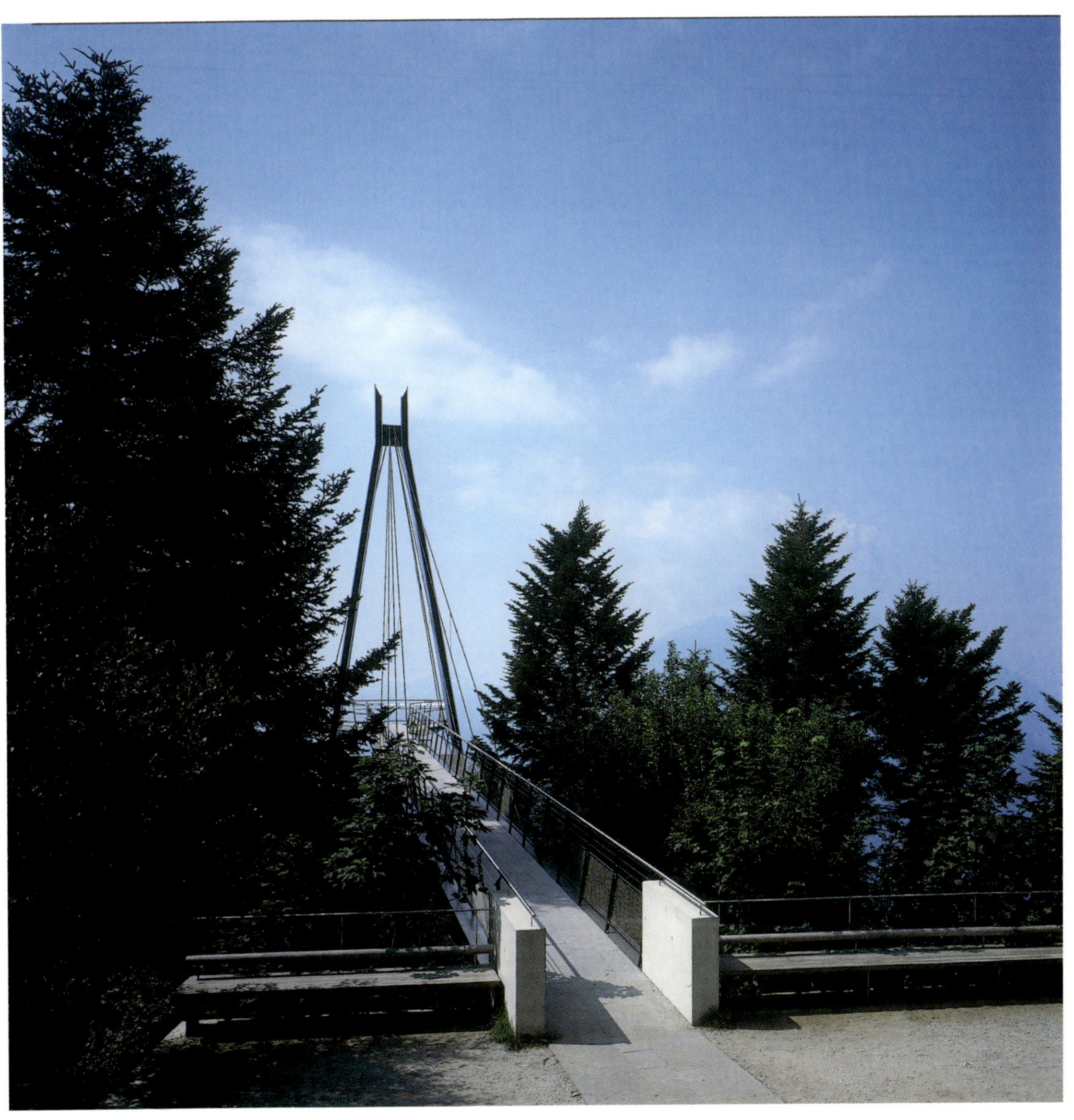

The steel and titanium footbridge leads to the observation deck: a circular platform 50 ft in diameter offering an educational and contemplative viewing space overlooking Lake Maggiore.

La passerelle en acier et en titane permet d'accéder au mirador : une plateforme circulaire de 15 m de diamètre avec une vue permettant de connaître et d'admirer les environs du lac Majeur.

Die Fußgängerbrücke aus Stahl und Titan führt zum runden Aussichtspunkt mit 15 m Durchmesser, der einen lehrreichen Blick auf den Lago Maggiore bietet.

De toegangsbrug van staal en titanium van de uitkijkpost: een cirkelvormig platform met een doorsnede van 15 m dat een didactische en ontspannende blik werpt op het Lago Maggiore.

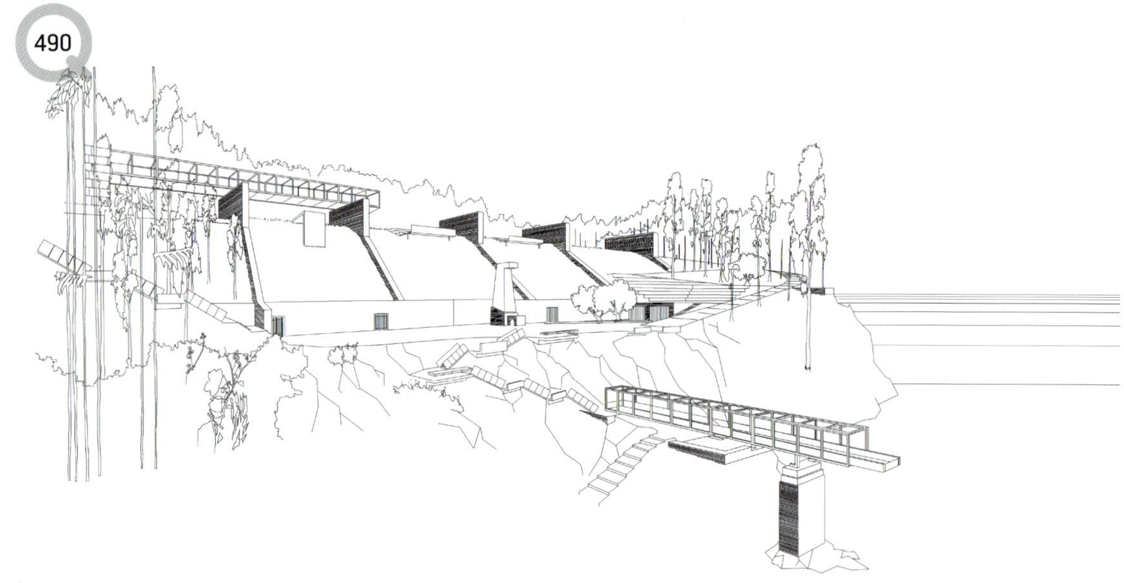

Ethnographic Park in Insua

This project involves the remodeling of a former iron loading dock in the Ría de Viveiro harbor. Industry, ethnography, environment, and recreation are the main features of the project. The platform is built from iron, steel, and stone, and is a new place for walking and recreation.

Le projet consiste en la reconversion d'un ancien lieu de chargement de minerai de fer dans la ria de Viveiro. Industrie, ethnographie, environnement et loisirs sont les principaux éléments de l'intervention. La plateforme, fabriquée à base de fer, d'acier et de pierre, offre un nouvel endroit pour la promenade et les loisirs.

Das Projekt besteht aus der Umwandlung eines ehemaligen Verladeplatzes von Eisenmineralien an der Ria de Viveiro. Industrie, Ethnografie, Umweltschutz und Erholung sind die Hauptgestaltungselemente. Die Plattform aus Eisen, Stahl und Stein bietet einen neuen Ort für Spaziergänge und Freizeitgestaltung.

Het project is de herstructurering van een voormalige laadplaats voor ijzererts in de ria de Viveiro. Industrie, etnografie, milieu en recreatie zijn de hoofdelementen van dit project. Het met ijzer, staal en steen vervaardigde platform is een nieuwe plek voor wandelingen en vrijetijdsbesteding.

Estudio Felipe Peña & Francisco Novoa
fepena@arquired.es
© Juan Rodríguez, Estudio Felip Peña & Francisco Novoa (drawings)

Plan & site plan

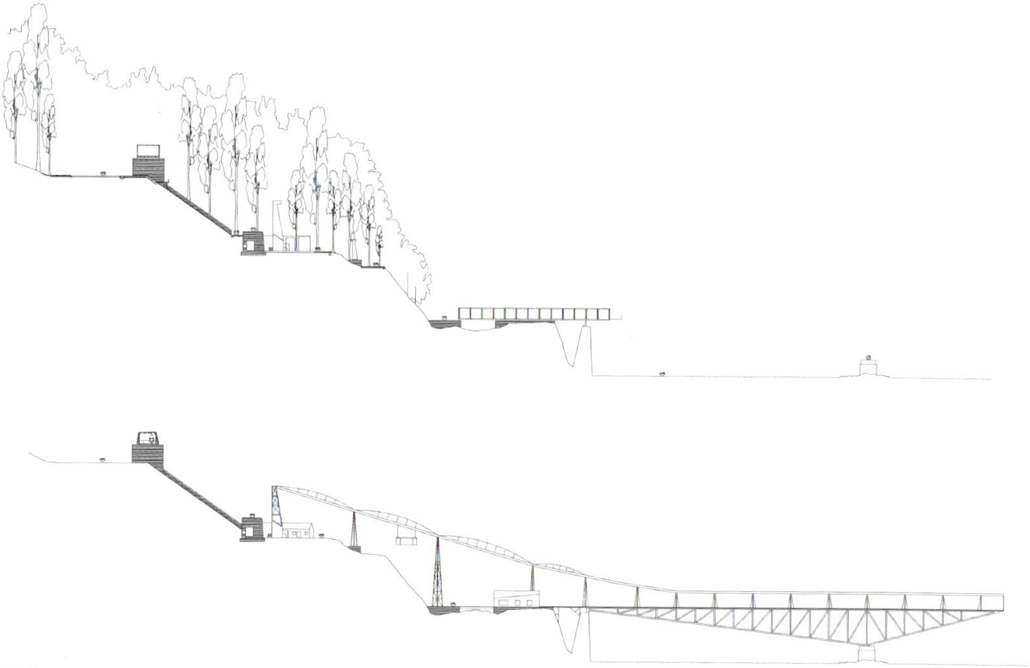

Sections

The remains of the 13 ft original iron structure and stone wall are elements from the past that formed the observation platform, complemented with an upper iron structure.

Les restes de la structure en acier et des murs de pierre de 4 m sont des éléments du passé utilisés pour créer un mirador, complétés par une structure supérieure en fer.

Die ursprünglichen Stahlkonstruktionreste und 4 m hohen Mauern sind für den Aussichtspunktbau anhand einer höheren Stahlstruktur ergänzte Elemente aus der Vergangenheit.

De resten van de oorspronkelijke stalen structuur en de 4 m hoge stenen muren dienden als basis voor de uitkijkplaats die is aangevuld met een ijzeren bovenstructuur.

Sohlbergplassen Viewpoint

Stor-Elvdal, Norway

The landscape architects' main achievement was to create a structure that did not harm the forest where it is located and without causing a large impact on the landscape. They used concrete to build a walkway with a 1-ft slope.

Les architectes paysagistes ont réussi à créer une structure qui ne dégrade pas la forêt luxuriante dans laquelle le projet a été mis en œuvre et ne provoque pas d'impact visuel important sur le paysage. C'est pour cette raison que le béton a été choisi pour construire une passerelle avec une pente de 0,3 m.

Das Hauptziel der Landschaftsarchitekten war die Schaffung einer Struktur, die den dichten Wald nicht beeinträchtigen und auch keine starke visuelle Wirkung in der Landschaft auslösen sollte. Aus diesen Gründen wurde ein Betonweg mit einem Gefälle von 0,3 m angelegt.

De grootste verdienste van de landschapsarchitecten is hier de creatie van een structuur die geen schade toebrengt aan het lommerrijke bos waar deze zich bevindt en die evenmin een visuele impact op het landschap maakt. Daarom werd beton gebruikt om een brug met een helling van 0,3 m aan te leggen.

CarlViggo Hølmebakk
holmebakk.cvh@getmail.no
© Rickard Riesenfeld, Ellen Ane Krog Eggen, Helge Stikbakke, CarlViggo Hølmebakk (drawings)

The concrete structure holding the platform
is connected to the ground by metal tubes
anchored to the rocks. This design did away
with the need for digging, which would have
damaged the tree roots.

La structure en béton de la plateforme est
ancrée au terrain par le biais de tubes en
acier logés dans les rochers. Cette méthode
a permis d'éviter les travaux de terrasse-
ment qui auraient endommagé les racines
des arbres.

Die Betonstruktur des Unterbaus ist durch
in den Fels eingelassene Stahlrohre verbunden. Dadurch wurden Grabungen, die
die Baumwurzeln geschädigt hätten, verhindert.

De betonstructuur van het platform wordt
door middel van in de rotsen aangebrachte
stalen buizen met het terrein verbonden.
Hierdoor waren er geen uitgravingen
nodig die de boomwortels zouden hebben
beschadigd.

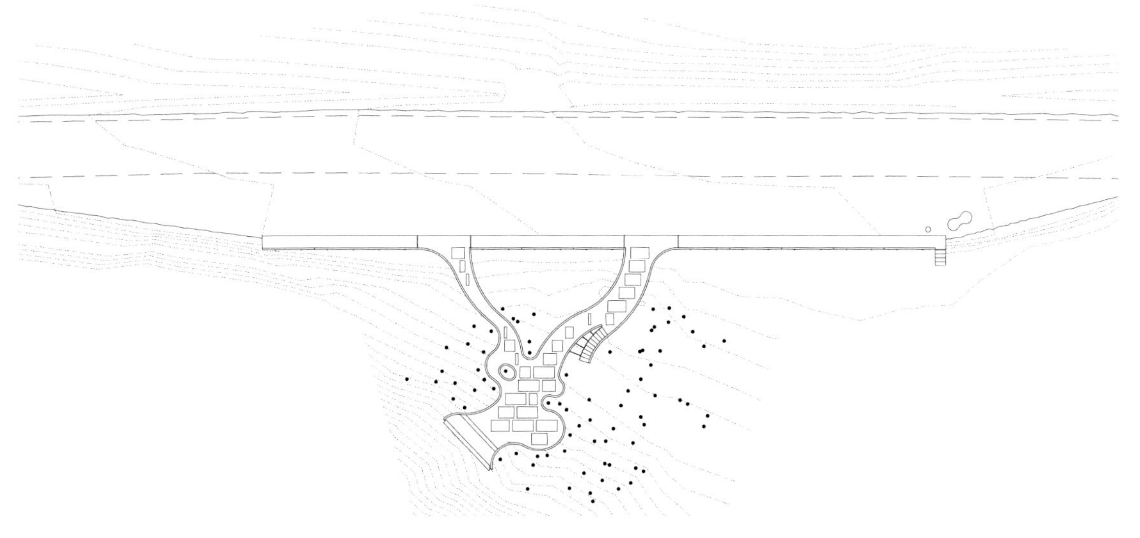

Plan

Site plan

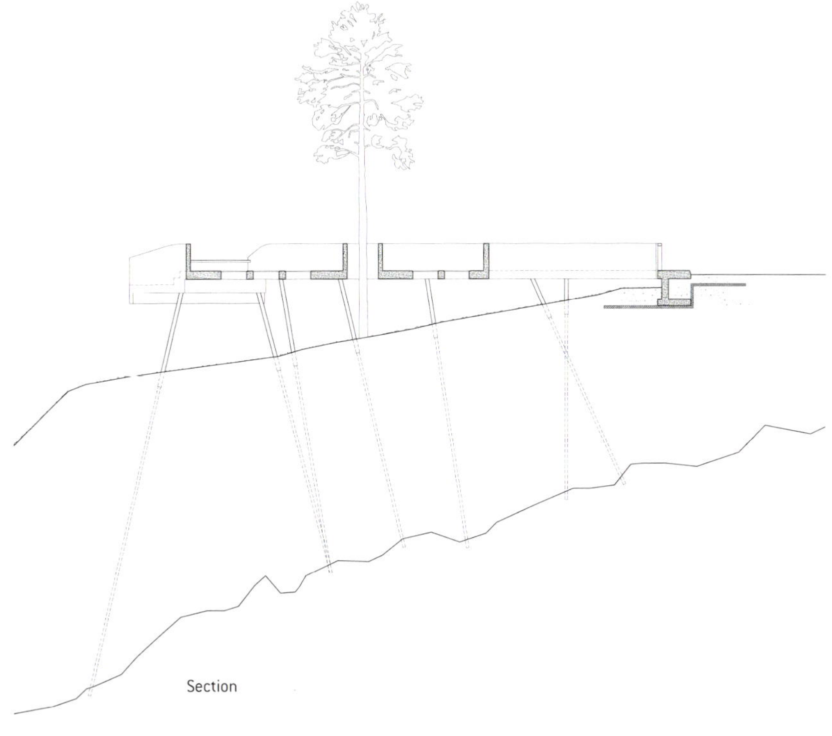

Section

Aurland Lookout

Aurland, Norway

The large number of tourists coming to enjoy the views of the spectacular Sognefjord forced the authorities to find a solution that was not aggressive with the environment. The landscape architects decided to build a delicate pinewood structure some 100 ft above the highest point of the fjord, suspended by a steel frame anchored in a concrete base.

La grande affluence de touristes attirés par les vues spectaculaires du fjord Sogn og Fjordane a contraint les autorités à rechercher une solution paysagère respectueuse de l'environnement. Les paysagistes ont opté pour la création d'une structure fragile en bois de pin située à 30 m du point culminant du fjord et suspendue à une structure en acier ancrée dans une base en béton.

Der große Touristen-Andrang aufgrund der spektakulären Aussicht auf den Fjord Sogn og Fjordane zwang die Behörden, eine umweltfreundliche Lösung zu suchen. Die Landschaftsgestalter wählten eine leichte Pinienholz-Struktur, 30 m über dem höchsten Punkt des Fjords, die durch eine in Beton verankerte Stahlstruktur gestützt wird.

De grote toevloed van toeristen die willen genieten van het spectaculaire uitzicht op de fjord Sogn og Fjordane, heeft de autoriteiten ertoe aangezet om een milieuvriendelijke oplossing voor het landschap te zoeken. De landschapsarchitecten kozen voor de aanleg van een broze grenenhouten structuur op 30 m van het hoogste punt van de fjord, opgehangen aan een in een betonnen basis verankerde stalen structuur.

Todd Saunders/Saunders Architecture, Tommie Wilhelmsem/Sivilarkitect MNAL
www.saundrers.no
www.tommiewilhelmsen.no
© Todd Saunders/Saunders Architecture

The viewing platform, located 2,000 ft above the fjord, allows the magnificent views to be appreciated for those reaching the end, where there is only a tempered glass panel.

La passerelle, située à 600 m du sol, permet d'accéder à son extrémité pour contempler les magnifiques vues du fjord. En ce point, seule une plaque en verre trempé a été installée.

Der 600 m über dem Boden angebrachte Laufsteg ermöglicht es, bis zum Ende zu gelangen, um die herrliche Aussicht auf den Fjord zu genießen. Dort wurde nur eine Platte aus Sicherheitsglas installiert.

De 600 m boven de grond aangebrachte verschaft een magnifiekuitzicht op de fjord. Hierop is slechts een plaat van gehard glas geïnstalleerd.

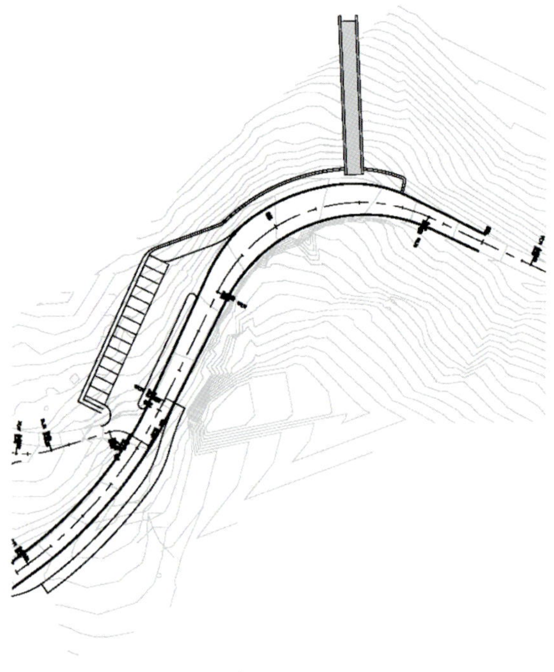

Site plan

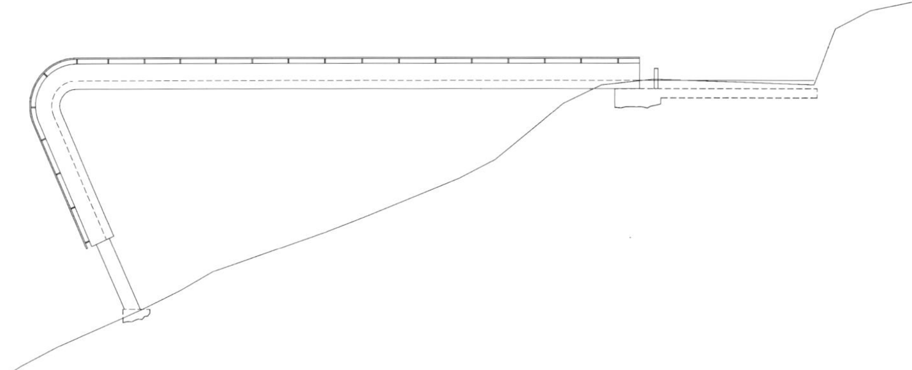

Elevation

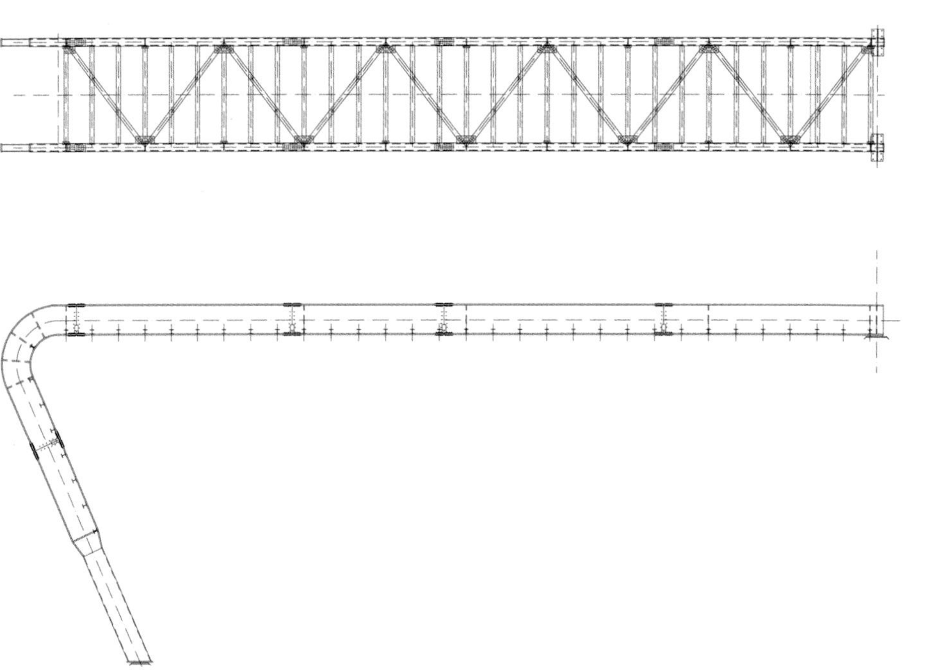

Plan & structural elevation

Gudbrandsjuvet Tourist Project

Gudbrandsjuvet, Norway

As a result of increased tourism to the Gerainger Fjord at Trollstigen, the Norwegian government decided to build walkways and footbridges for visitors. The platforms, footbridges, visitors' center, and a mountain lodge were built to blend in with the landscape and leave the area unharmed.

En raison de l'essor touristique enregistré sur l'itinéraire du fjord de Geiranger à Trollstigen, le gouvernement norvégien a décidé d'aménager des passerelles et des ponts pour les visiteurs. Les plateformes, les ponts, le centre de visiteurs et un hôtel ont été construits de sorte qu'ils s'intègrent au paysage sans dégrader la zone.

Aufgrund des Tourismus-Booms auf der Route vom Geirangerfjord nach Trollstigen, beschloss die norwegische Regierung, Stege und Brücken für die Besucher installieren zu lassen. Plattformen, Brücken, Besucherzentrum und Landschaftshotel wurden harmonisch in die Landschaft eingefügt.

Vanwege het bloeiende toerisme langs de route van de Geirangerfjord naar Trollstigen besloot de Noorse regering om loopplanken en bruggen aan te leggen voor de bezoekers. Er werden platforms, bruggen, een bezoekerscentrum en een landscapehotel gebouwd. Zij werden in het landschap opgenomen zonder het gebied schade te berokkenen.

Jensen & Skodvin Arkitektkontor
www.jsa.no
© Jensen & Skodvin Arkitektkontor

The walkway was cantilevered over the abrupt landscape of the Valldøla River. This structure makes passage easy and safeguards the rocky landscape.

La passerelle a été construite en porte-à-faux au-dessus de la géographie accidentée de la rivière Valldøla. Cette structure permet de faciliter le passage tout en conservant le paysage rocheux.

Der Steg wurde über dem zerklüfteten Gelände des Flusses Valldøla überhängend konstruiert. Diese Konstruktion erleichtert den Durchgang und schützt die felsige Landschaft.

De hangbrug werd boven het ruige oppervlak van de rivier de Valldøla gebouwd. Dankzij deze structuur kan men oversteken en wordt tegelijkertijd het rotsachtige landschap beschermd.

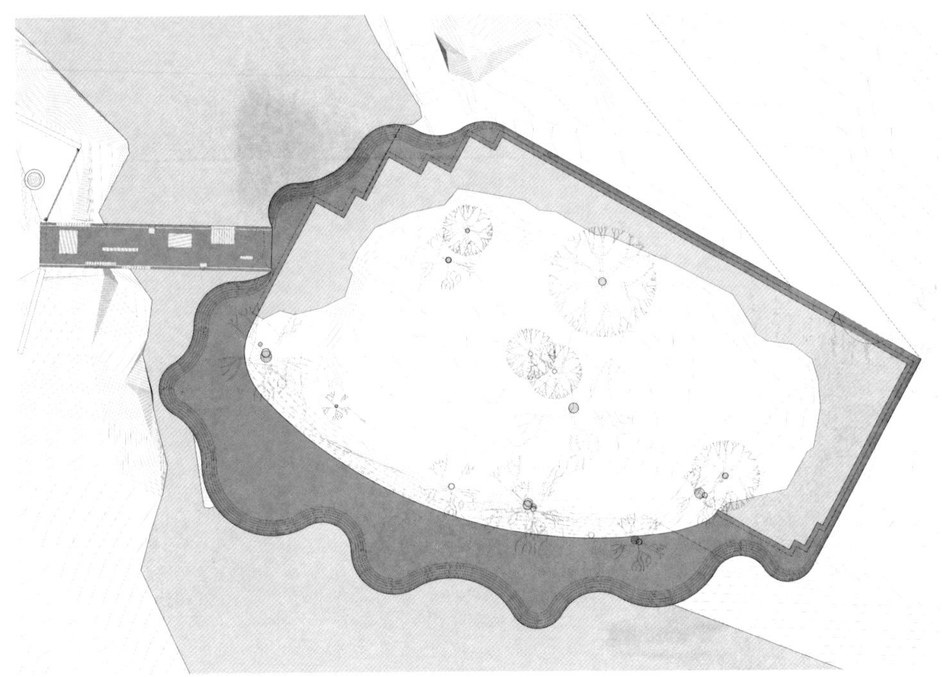

Platform plan

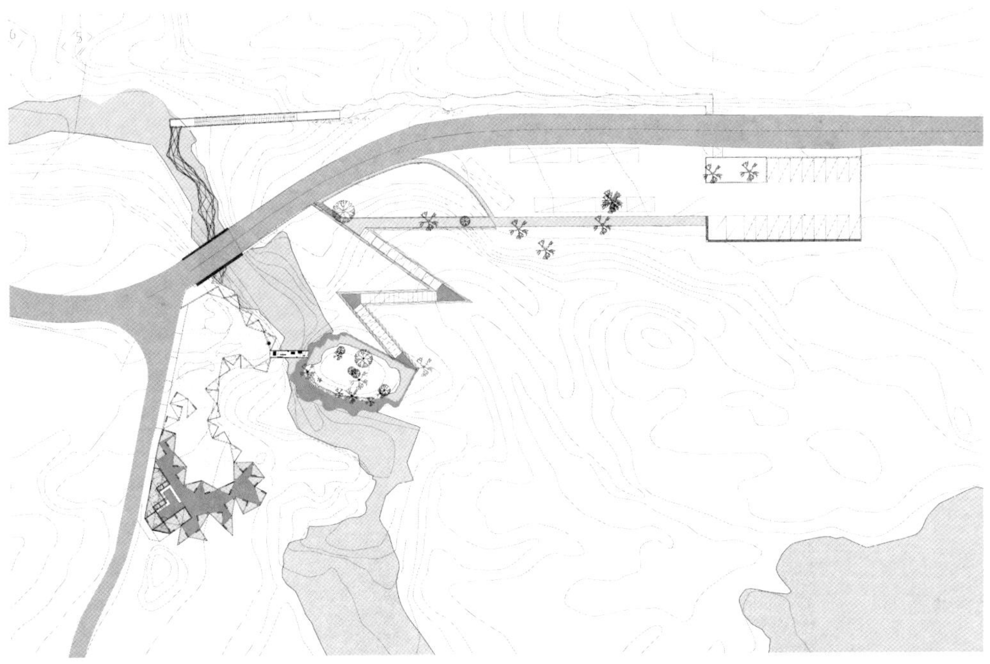

Site plan

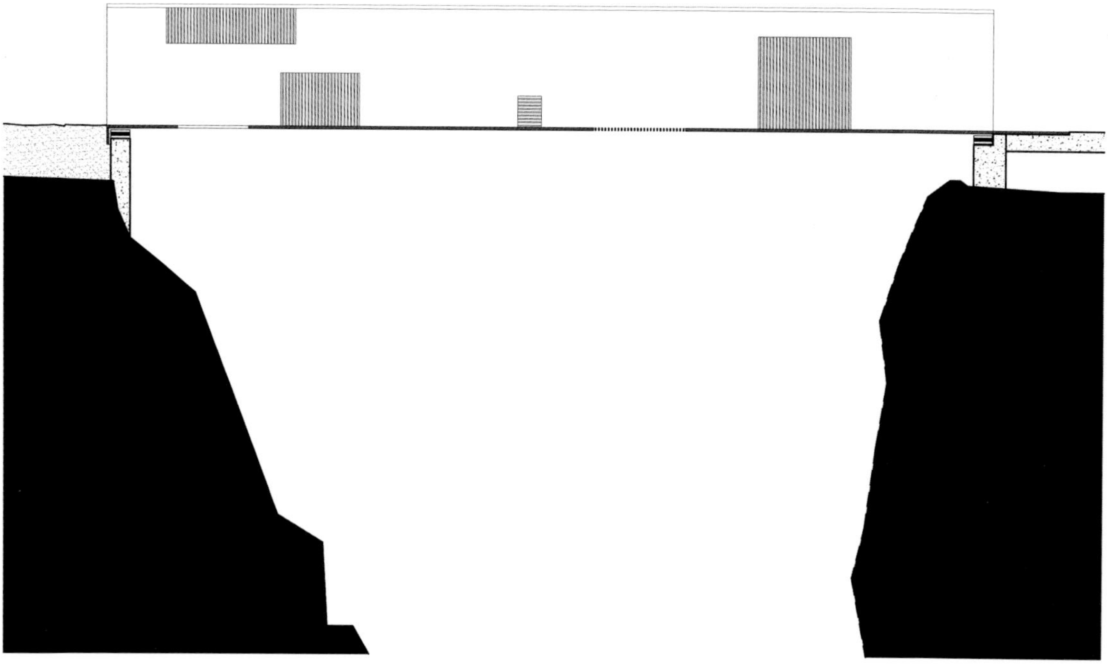

Bridge section

Platform section

Pedra Tosca Park

Les Preses, Spain

This park, located in the so-called volcanic area of La Garrotxa, is a natural space formed by an expanse of thousand-year-old volcanic rocks. It required landscaping as over time it had become an accumulation of volcanic rocks and thick walls, in addition to huts and fields.

Ce parc, situé dans la zone volcanique de La Garrotxa, est un espace naturel composé d'une étendue de pierres volcaniques millénaires. Une intervention s'est avérée nécessaire, du fait de l'accumulation avec le temps de roches volcaniques et de larges murs de pierre, ainsi que de l'apparition de baraques et de parcelles de culture.

Dieser Park im Vulkangebiet von La Garrotxa ist eine Naturlandschaft, die durch ausgedehntes, tausende Jahre altes Vulkangestein geformt wurde. Sie erforderte einen Eingriff, da sich mit der Zeit Vulkanfelsen, breite Mauern, Hütten und Parzellen für Anpflanzungen angesammelt hatten.

Dit park, gelegen in de vulkanische zone La Garrotxa, is een natuurgebied gevormd door eeuwenoude vulkanische stenen. Er was een ingreep nodig daar zich in de loop van de tijd vulkanische rotsen en brede muren hadden opgehoopt, alsmede barakken en landbouwpercelen.

 **RCR Aranda Pigem Vilalta Arquitectes**
www.rcrarquitectes.es
© Eugeni Pons, RCR Aranda Pigem Vilalta Arquitectes (drawings)

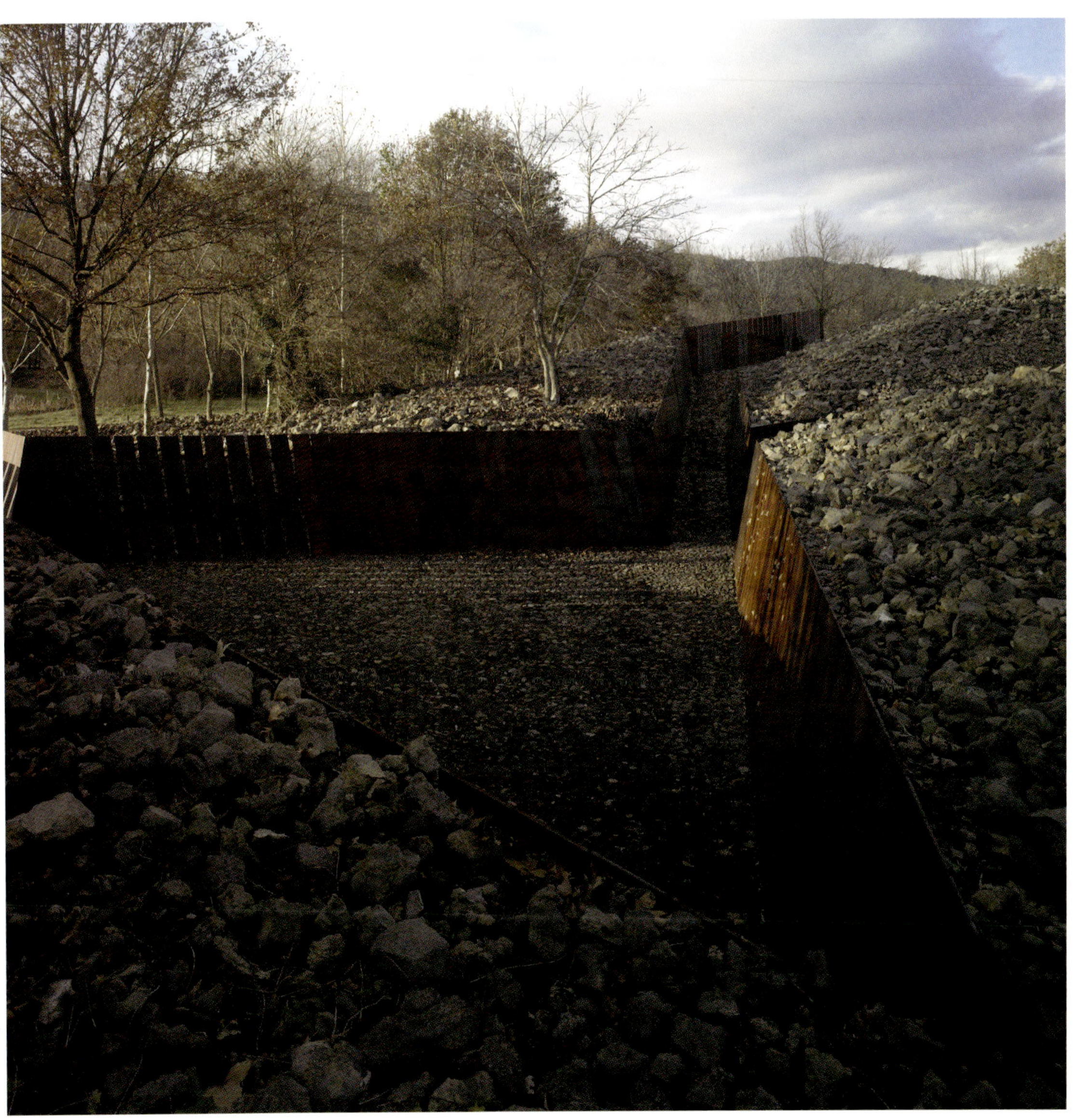

Visitors to the park travel along narrow paths between irregular mounds of volcanic rocks. These are kept in place by a continuous wall of treated steel.

Les visiteurs parcourent le parc en empruntant des chemins étroits entre des monticules irréguliers de pierres volcaniques. Ces dernières sont maintenues à l'aide d'une clôture continue en acier traité.

Die Besucher begehen den Park auf schmalen Wegen zwischen unregelmäßigen Erhebungen aus Vulkangestein. Diese werden durch einen Zaun aus behandeltem Stahl gehalten.

De bezoekers van het park lopen via smalle paden langs onregelmatige hopen vulkanische stenen. Deze worden tegengehouden door een onafgebroken afrastering van behandeld staal.

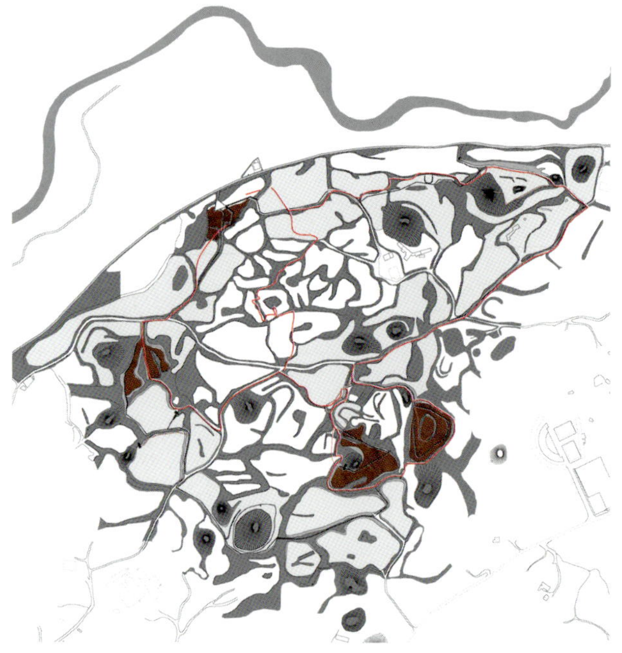

Site plan

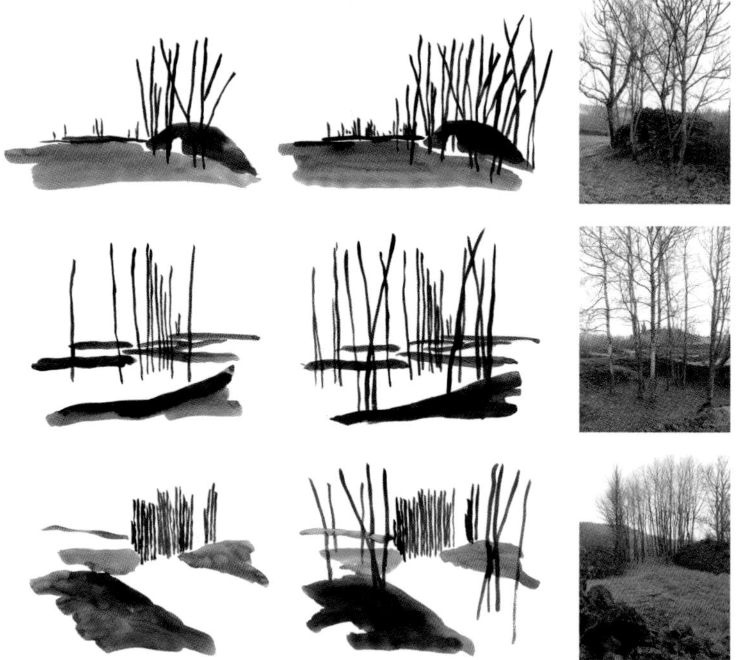

Conceptual sketches

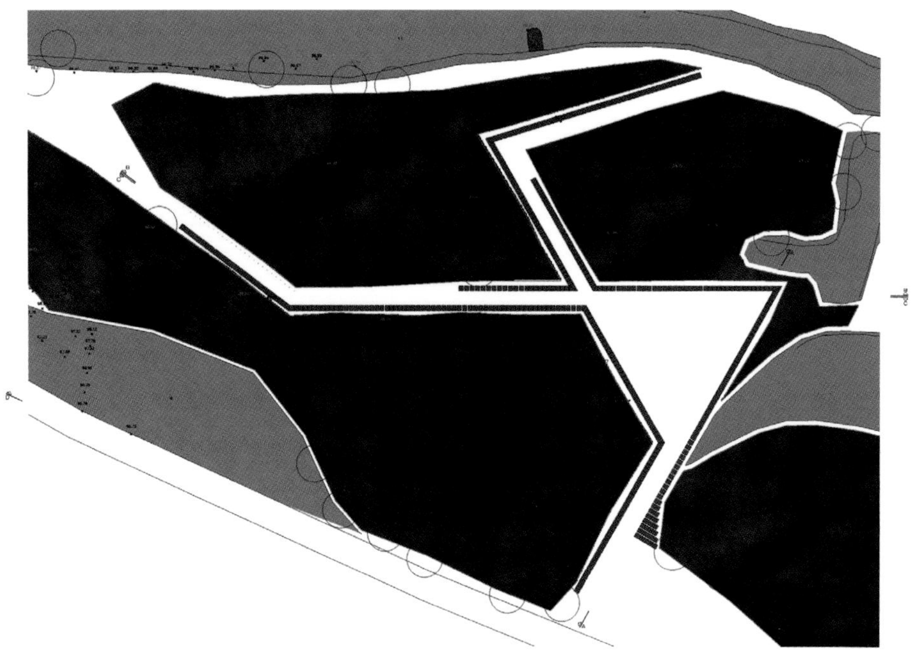

Plan

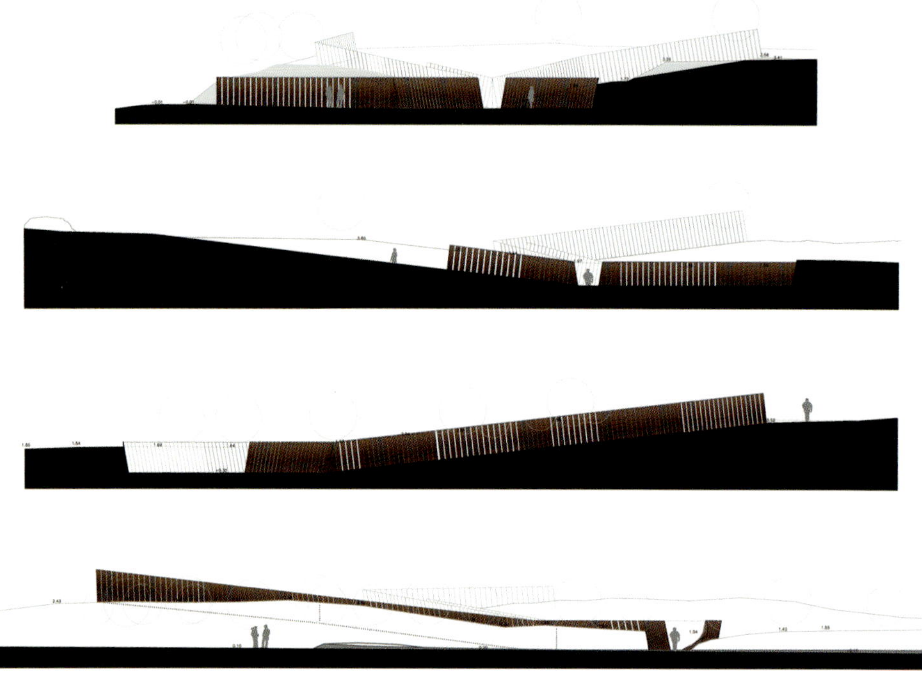

Sections

Zhongshan Shipyard Park

Zhongshan, China

This project consists of the transformation of a shipyard into a recreation area for the residents of Zhongshan. The park is also an educational space that commemorates the area's industrial past. Existing industrial features were preserved and restored by coloring them red. Different vegetation species were planted and pruned in geometric shapes.

Ce projet a permis de transformer un chantier naval en une zone de loisirs pour les citoyens de Zhongshan. Le parc est également une zone didactique qui rappelle le passé ouvrier industriel. Des éléments du tissu industriel existant sont conservés et restaurés en les colorant en rouge, alors qu'une végétation diversifiée a été plantée et taillée de manière à former des figures géométriques.

Dieses Projekt besteht aus der Umgestaltung einer Werft in ein Erholungsgebiet für die Einwohner von Zhongshan. Der Park ist auch eine didaktische Anlage, die an die industrielle Vergangenheit der Zone erinnert. Vorhandene Elemente der industriellen Struktur wurden erhalten und rot gestrichen. Es wurden verschiedene Pflanzenarten angepflanzt und zu geometrischen Formen beschnitten.

Voor dit project werd een scheepswerf omgebouwd tot een recreatiezone voor de inwoners van Zhongshan. Het park heeft eveneens een didactische functie en herdenkt het industriële arbeidersverleden. Bepaalde bestaande elementen uit het industriële verleden zijn bewaard gebleven. Deze werden gerestaureerd en rood geverfd. Daarnaast werd er diverse vegetatie geplant en in geometrische vormen gesnoeid.

Turenscape
www.turenscape.com
© Kongjian Yu, Yang Cao, Turenscape (drawings)

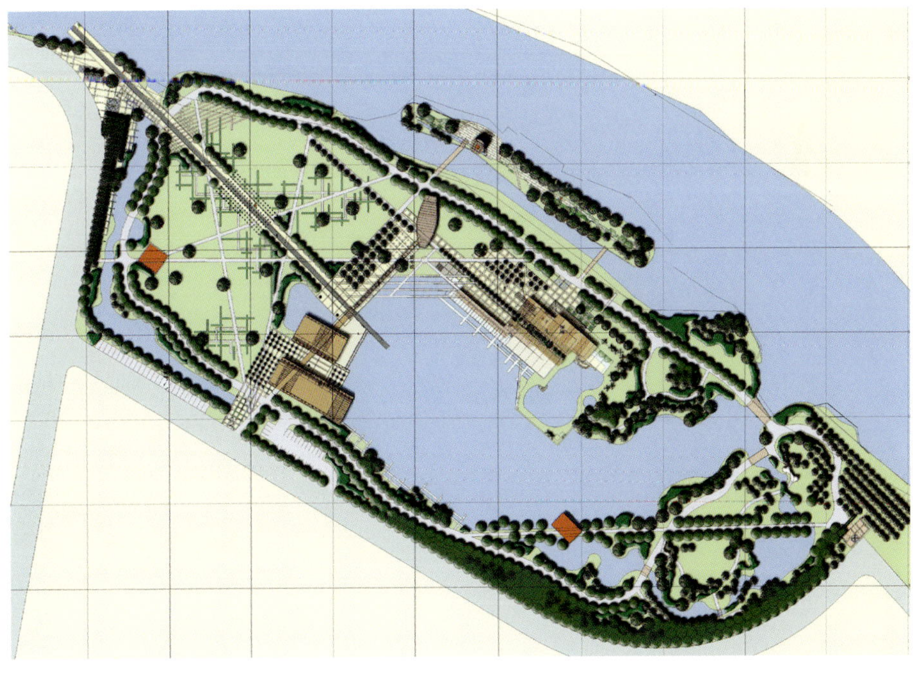

Plan

When designing the park, the landscape architects decided on the use of natural recyclable materials and remodeled some of the industrial structures for educational purposes.

Pour la création du parc, les paysagistes ont opté pour l'utilisation de matériaux naturels recyclables et certaines architectures industrielles ont été réhabilitées à des fins didactiques.

Die Landschaftsarchitekten wählten wiederverwertbare natürliche Materialien. Einige industrielle Anlagen wurden für didaktische Zwecke umgestaltet.

Bij de aanleg van het park hebben de landschapsarchitecten ervoor gekozen om recyclebare natuurlijke materialen te gebruiken en zijn sommige industriële architectonische elementen omgevormd voor didactische doeleinden.

Wernigerode State horticultural show

Wernigerode, Germany

The German town of Wernigerode was the venue for an international horticultural exhibition in 2006. This was the perfect opportunity to create a modern park adapted to the features of the terrain, laid out around a central walkway called "Fish Walk".

En 2006, la localité allemande de Wernigerode a accueilli le Salon international du jardinage. Un parc moderne adapté aux caractéristiques du terrain a pour l'occasion été créé, avec un sentier appelé « chemin du poisson » comme élément central.

Im Jahr 2006 wurde in der deutschen Stadt Wernigerode die Landesgartenschau veranstaltet. Das war ein perfekter Anlass für die Schaffung eines modernen, an die besonderen Merkmale des Geländes angepassten Parks, der die so genannte „Fischstraße" umgibt.

In 2006 werd in de Duitse plaats Wernigerode de Internationale Tuinbeurs gehouden. Dit was de perfecte aanleiding om een modern park aan te leggen, aangepast aan de eigenschappen van het terrein dat rondom een middenpad, de zogenaamde "lavisweg", is gestructureerd.

Hutterreimann & Cejka Landschaftsarchitekten, A_lab Architektur, Jens Schmahl (architectural follies)
www.hrc.net
© Christo Libuda, Franziska Poreski, Christine Trosin, Horst Bilek (renderings), Hutterreimann & Cejka (drawings)

7 TEICHE — DER-FISH-WALK-VERSUCHT

Sketches of Fist Walk

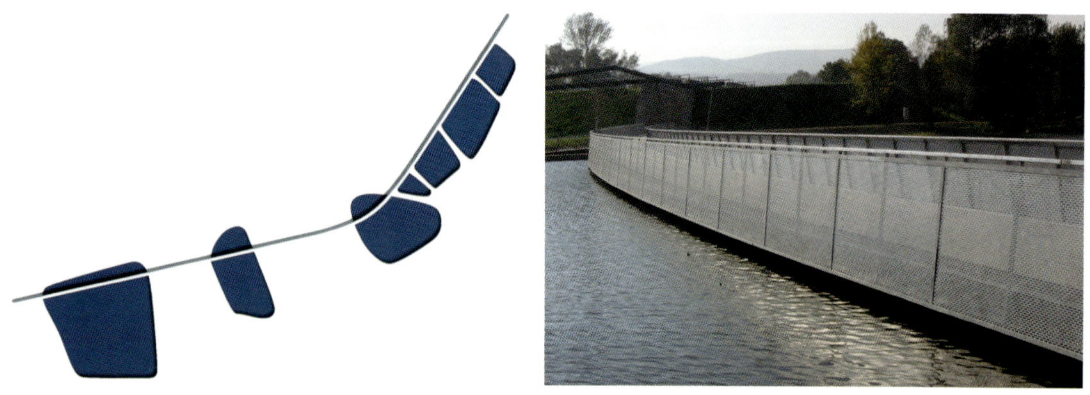

Rendering of Fist Walk

Limestone walls evoke the old mines of the region. The mountains surrounding the project are the inspiration for the different geological motifs incorporated in the design.

Des murs de pierre calcaire évoquent les anciennes exploitations minières de la région. Les montagnes qui entourent le site sont la source d'inspiration des différents motifs géologiques qui intègrent son design.

Kalksteinmauern erinnern an die frühere Bergbautätigkeit in der Region. Die umgebenden Berge dienten als Inspiration für die geologischen Motive.

Kalkstenen muren brengen de voormalige mijnbouw van de streek in herinnering. De bergen die het project omringen, vormen de inspiratie voor de verschillende geologische motieven die zijn opgenomen in het ontwerp.

Rendering of Fist Walk

Rendering of general view from bank

Rendering of general view from bank

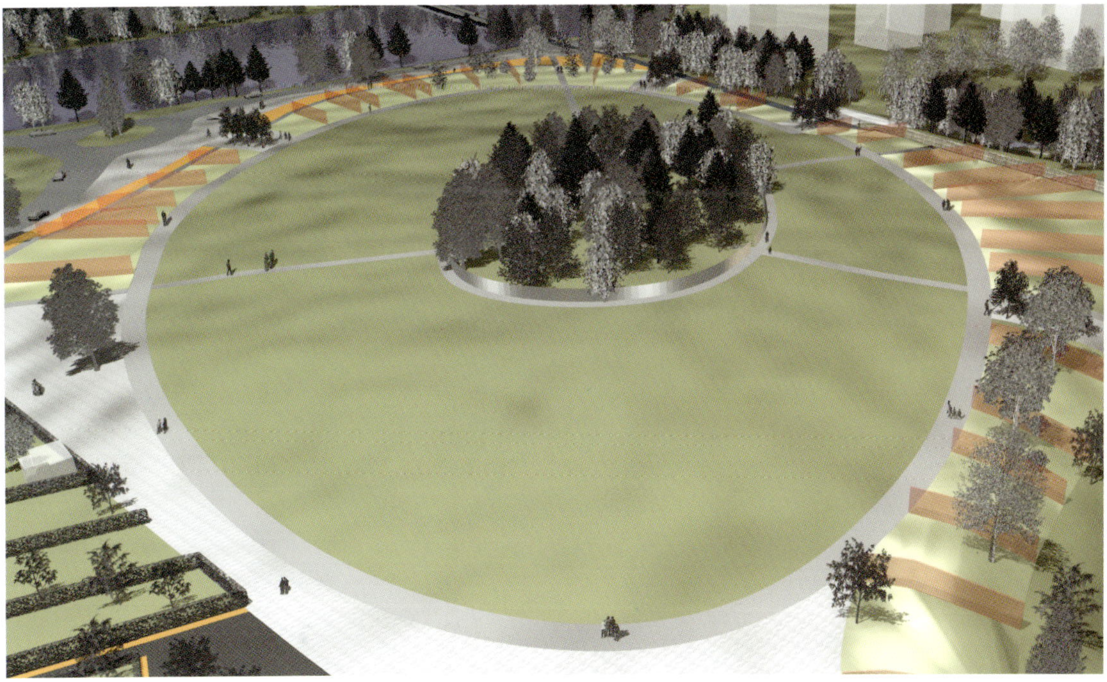

Rendering of air view

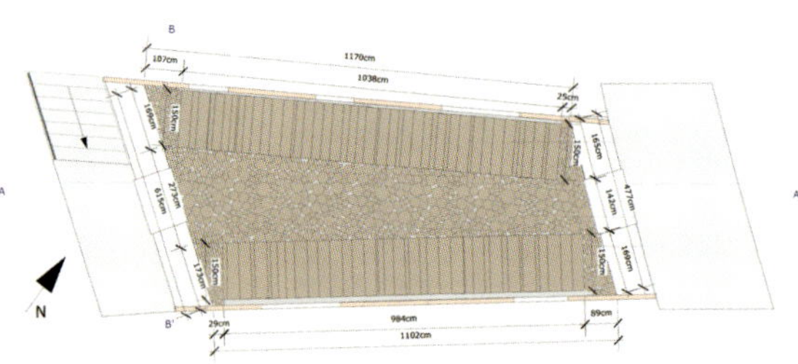

Rendering of mineral gorge

Floor plan 1:100

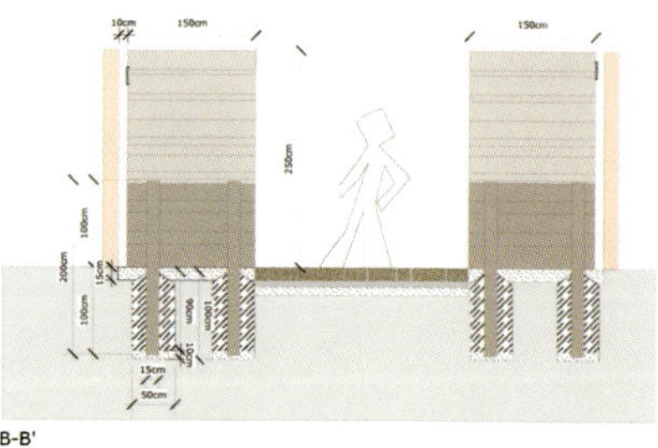

B-B'

Section 1:50

A-A'

Section 1:100

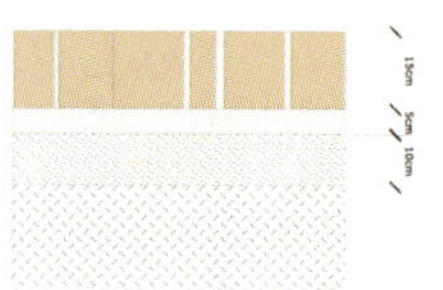

Assembly of wooden log paving

The Lake at Harnes

Harnes, France

The regeneration of mining land in the industrial region of Harnes in northern France was an opportunity to create a 17½-acre green space. Wastewater from the lake was treated by a series of plant-based systems.

La réhabilitation d'un territoire minier situé dans la région industrielle de Harnes, au nord de la France, a permis la création d'une zone verte qui s'étend sur 7 ha. Les eaux résiduaires de la lagune ont été épurées grâce à la plantation d'espèces végétales.

Die Sanierung eines Bergbaugebiets in der Industrieregion Harnes im Norden Frankreichs ermöglichte die Schaffung einer sieben Hektar großen Grünzone. Das verschmutzte Wasser der Lagune wurde durch die Anpflanzung spezieller Pflanzenarten gereinigt.

Dankzij het herstel van een mijngebied in de industriële regio Harnes, in Noord-Frankrijk, kon een groenzone van 7 ha worden gecreëerd. Het afvalwater van de lagune werd gezuiverd door middel van begroeiing met diverse plantensoorten.

Paysages
www.lascoppaysages.com
© Paysages Lille

0
100

Sections of water and plantation concept

1. Filtration in the willow saplings planted on gravel
2. Supply from the treatment station of Fouquières
3. Short rotation willow shoots
4. Blockhouse
5. Aquatic plantations
6. Lagooning in the basins planted with aquatic vegetation
7. Grassy bank
8. Wind pumps
9. Oxygenation and exposure to ultra-violet rays
10. Channelling of overflow
11. Water step
12. Riprap
13. Top soil
14. Shale backfill
15. Impermeability
16. Access to Montigny channel
17. Canal bridge
18. Variable sill spillway

While its industrial past is not denied, this region showed geographic and social commitment in regenerating an area as a green space for visitors.

Sans renier son passé industriel, cette région marquée géographiquement et socialement a été réhabilitée afin d'aménager un espace vert pour les visiteurs des lieux.

Ohne seine industrielle Vergangenheit zu leugnen, wurde ein sozial und geografisch heikles Gebiet wiederhergestellt, um eine Grünzone zu schaffen.

Zonder het industriële verleden te vergeten, werd een geografisch en sociaal geëngageerd terrein hersteld om de bezoekers een groenzone te bieden.

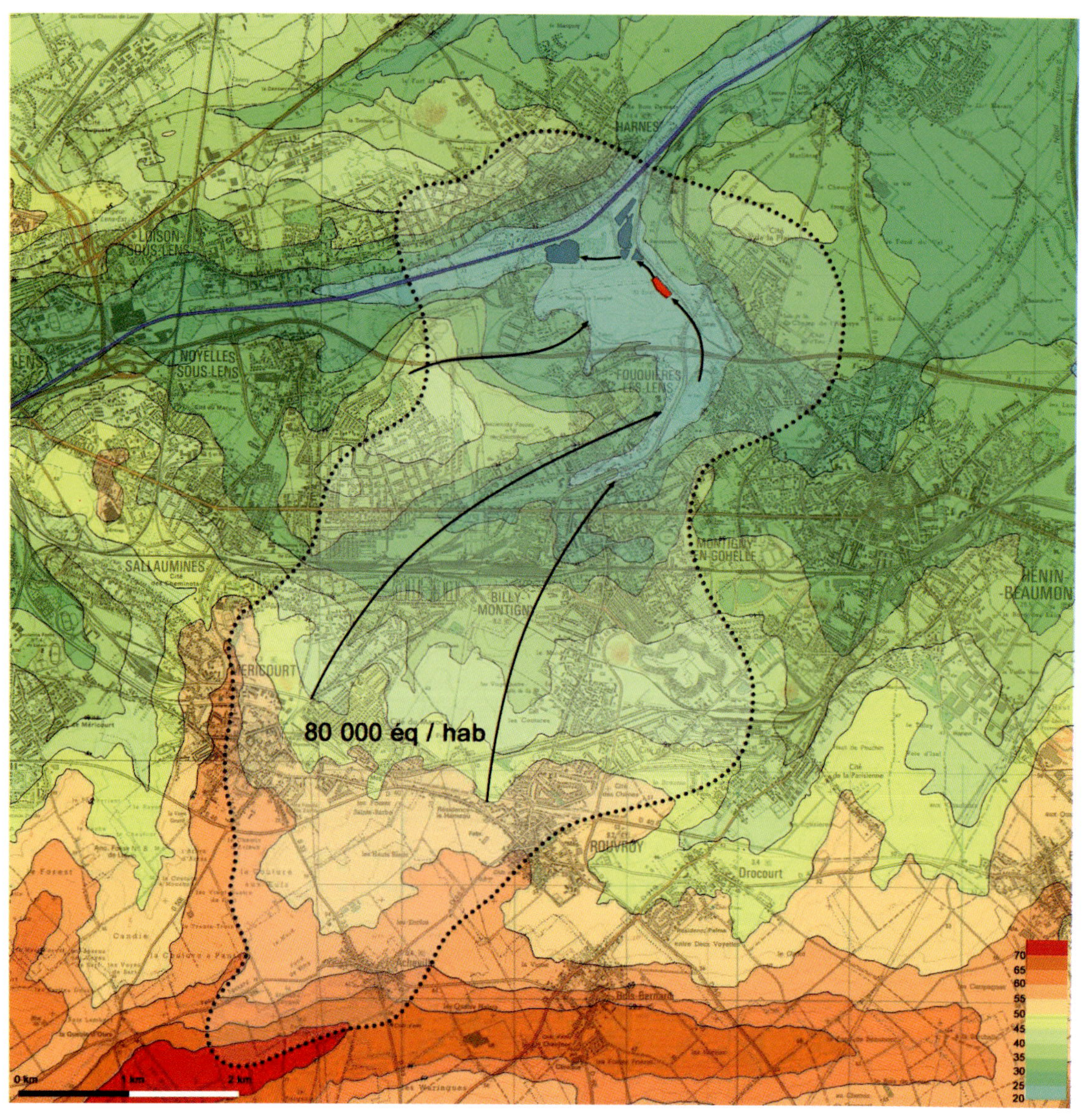

Situation plan

Intervention plan

1. Lagooning
2. Oxygenation exposure to ultra-violet rays
3. Lagooning in the basins planted with aquatic vegetation
4. Courrieres
5. Filtration in the willow saplings
6. Release from the treatment station
7. Lagoonage finish
8. Future dipping zone
9. Release into the Lens canal

Seefeld Lausitz

Lausitz, Germany

The IBA Fürst-Pückler-Land international exhibition commissioned Atelier Le Balto to create a minor works landscaping project for the Lausitz region. The design consisted of a field with the logo "See" marked out on the planted crop.

L'exposition internationale IBA Fürst-Pückler-Land a confié à l'Atelier Le Balto des travaux paysagers de second-œuvre pour la région de Lusace. Le projet réalisé est composé d'un champ cultivé sur lequel le logo « See » est dessiné.

Die internationale Bauausstellung (IBA) Fürst-Pückler-Land beauftragte das Atelier Le Balto mit einem kleineren Werk der Landschaftsgestaltung für die Lausitz-Region. Der ausgeführte Vorschlag besteht aus einem bepflanzten Feld, auf dem das Logo „See" zu erkennen ist.

De internationale tentoonstelling IBA Fürst-Pückler-Land heeft het Atelier Le Balto de opdracht gegeven om een klein landschapsproject te ontwerpen in de regio Lausitz. Het voorstel bestaat uit een stuk bouwland met daarin het logo "See".

 **Atelier Le Balto**
www.lebalto.de
© Rainer Prautsch, Steffen Rasche, Atelier Le Balto (drawings)

The crop field where the word "see" can be read is framed by a large mantle of blue flowers contrasting in color and geometry with the central field.

Le champ cultivé, où apparaît le mot « see », est entouré d'un grand lit de fleurs bleues, dont les tonalités et la géométrie contrastent avec ce motif central.

Das bepflanzte Feld mit dem Wort „See" wird von einem großen Beet mit blauen Blumen umrahmt, die sich in Farbe und Form vom Zentralmotiv abheben.

Het stuk bouwland waarin het woord "see" staat geschreven, wordt omgeven door een groot perk van blauwachtige bloemen die in kleur en geometrie een contrast vormen met het centrale motief.

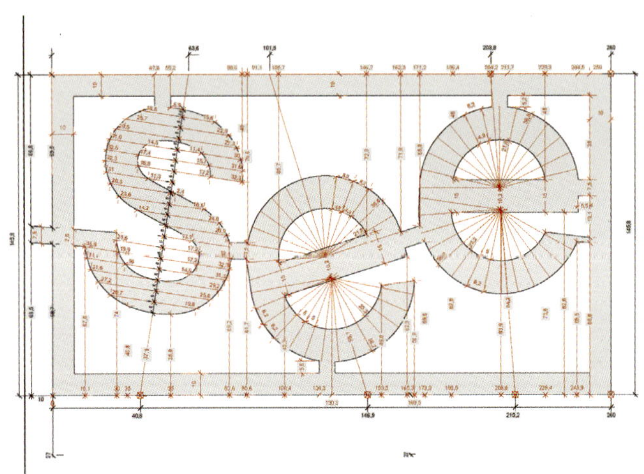

Detail plans

Schematic design study

Vertical Garden

London, United Kingdom

This project is a cultural representation questioning the world's current relationship with nature. The vertical garden consists of a ladder against a wall serving as a support for varied plant species.

Le projet est une représentation culturelle de la nature qui évoque le rapport de cette dernière avec le monde actuel. Le jardin vertical consiste en l'installation d'un escalier de secours sur un mur qui sert de support à la végétation variée.

Das Projekt ist eine kulturelle Darstellung der Natur, die die Beziehung der Welt von heute mit eben dieser Natur in Frage stellt. Der vertikale Garten besteht aus der Installation einer Feuerleiter an einer Wand, die als Stütze für die verschiedenartige Vegetation dient.

Het project is een culturele voorstelling van de natuur die de relatie tussen de huidige wereld en de natuur betwist. De verticale tuin bestaat uit een brandtrap tegen een wand, die verschillende plantensoorten ondersteunt.

GROSS. MAX., Mark Dion, Isabel Vaseur/Vicky Lewis of Art Office London (art director)
www.grossmax.com
© GROSS. MAX., Mark Dion

Native and exotic plants were chosen for their vigorous growth and cultural value. They are maintained by a drip watering system.

Des plantes autochtones et exotiques, dont l'entretien s'effectue par un système de goutte-à-goutte et d'arrosage, ont été sélectionnées en raison de leur croissance vigoureuse et leur valeur culturelle.

Aufgrund ihres üppigen Wachstums und kulturellen Wertes wurden einheimische und exotische Pflanzen ausgewählt, die automatisch berieselt werden.

Autochtone en exotische planten werden geselecteerd vanwege hun energieke groei en culturele waarde. Het onderhoud gebeurt door middel van een druppel- en bevloeiingssysteem.

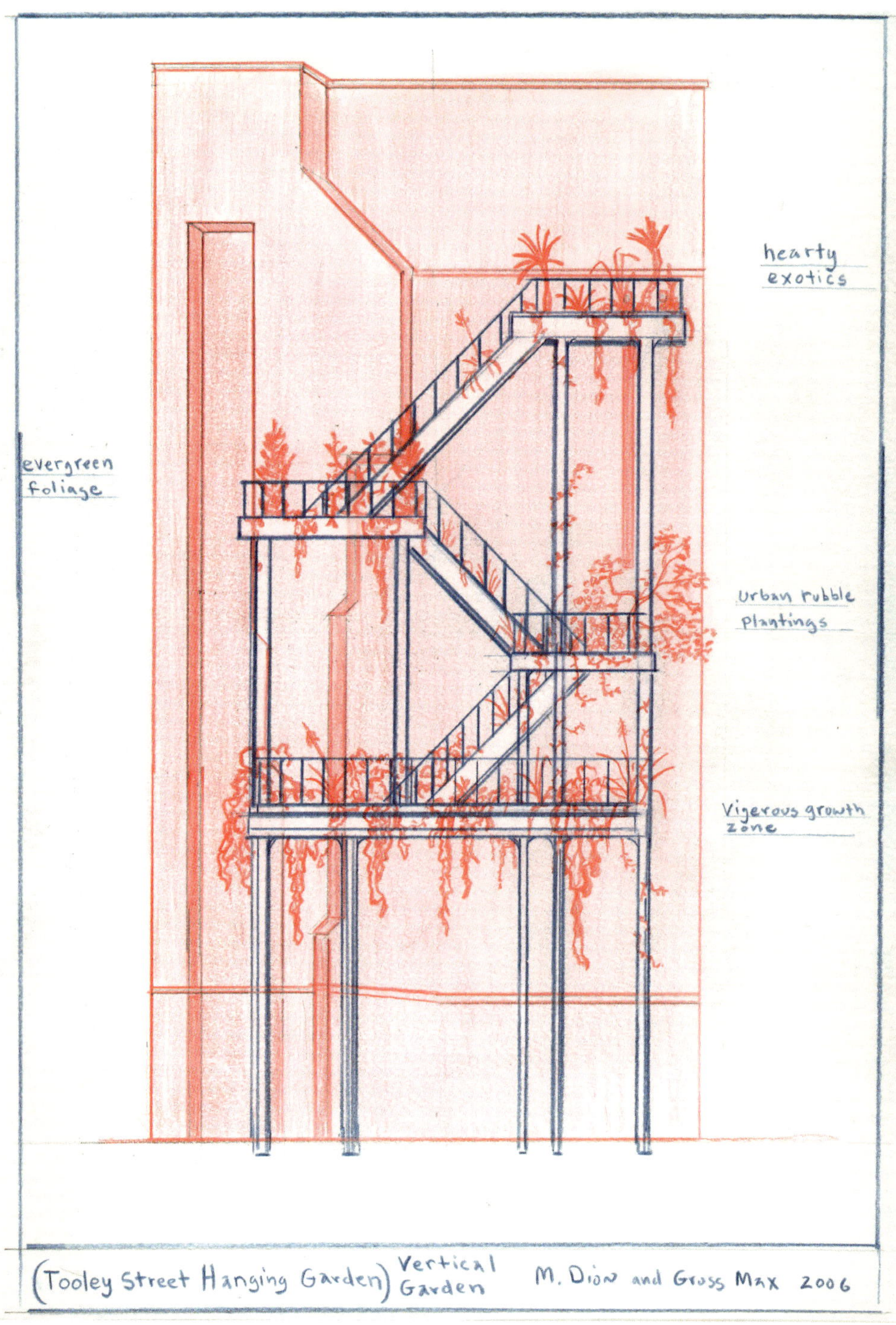

Preliminary sketch

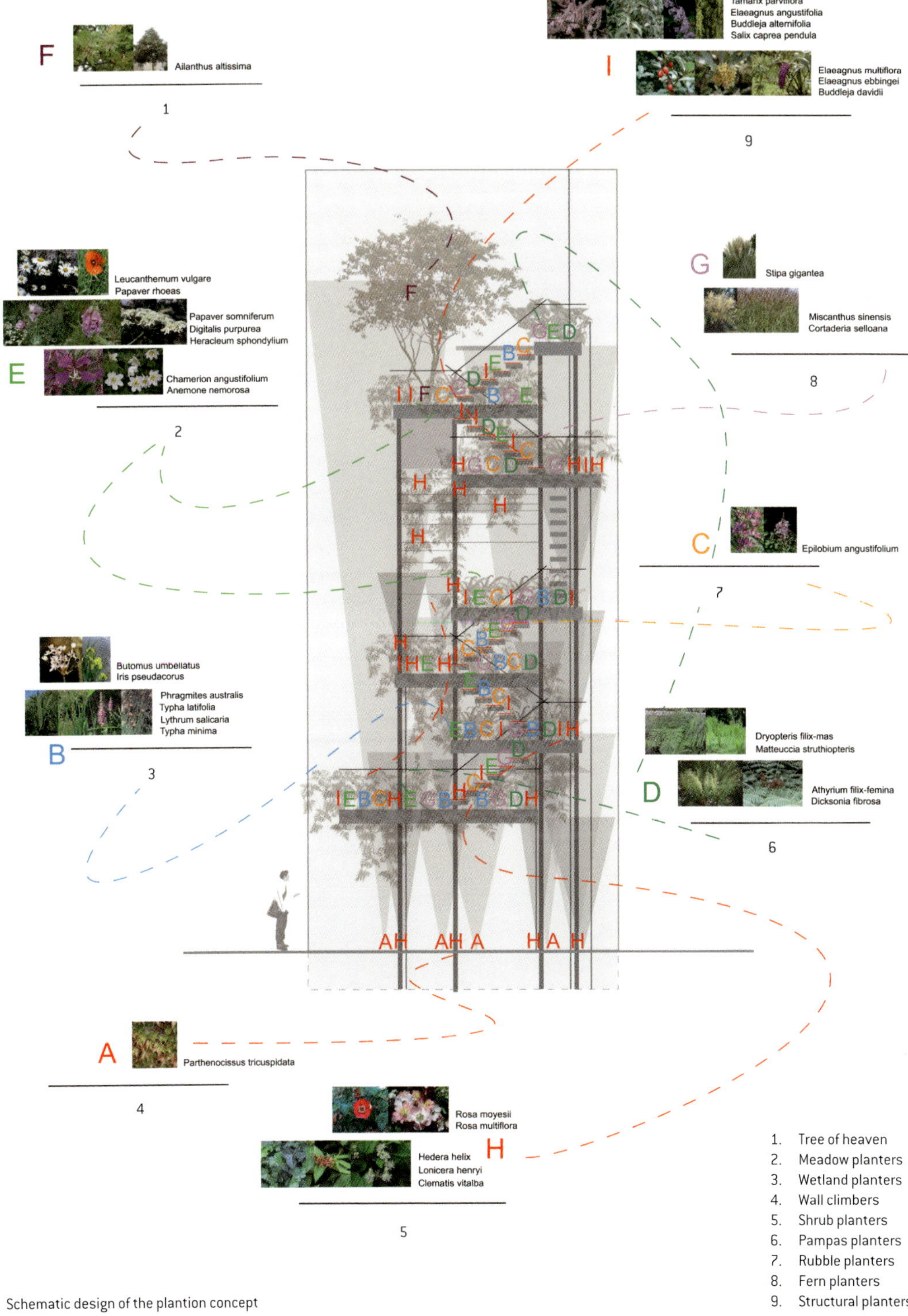

Schematic design of the plantion concept

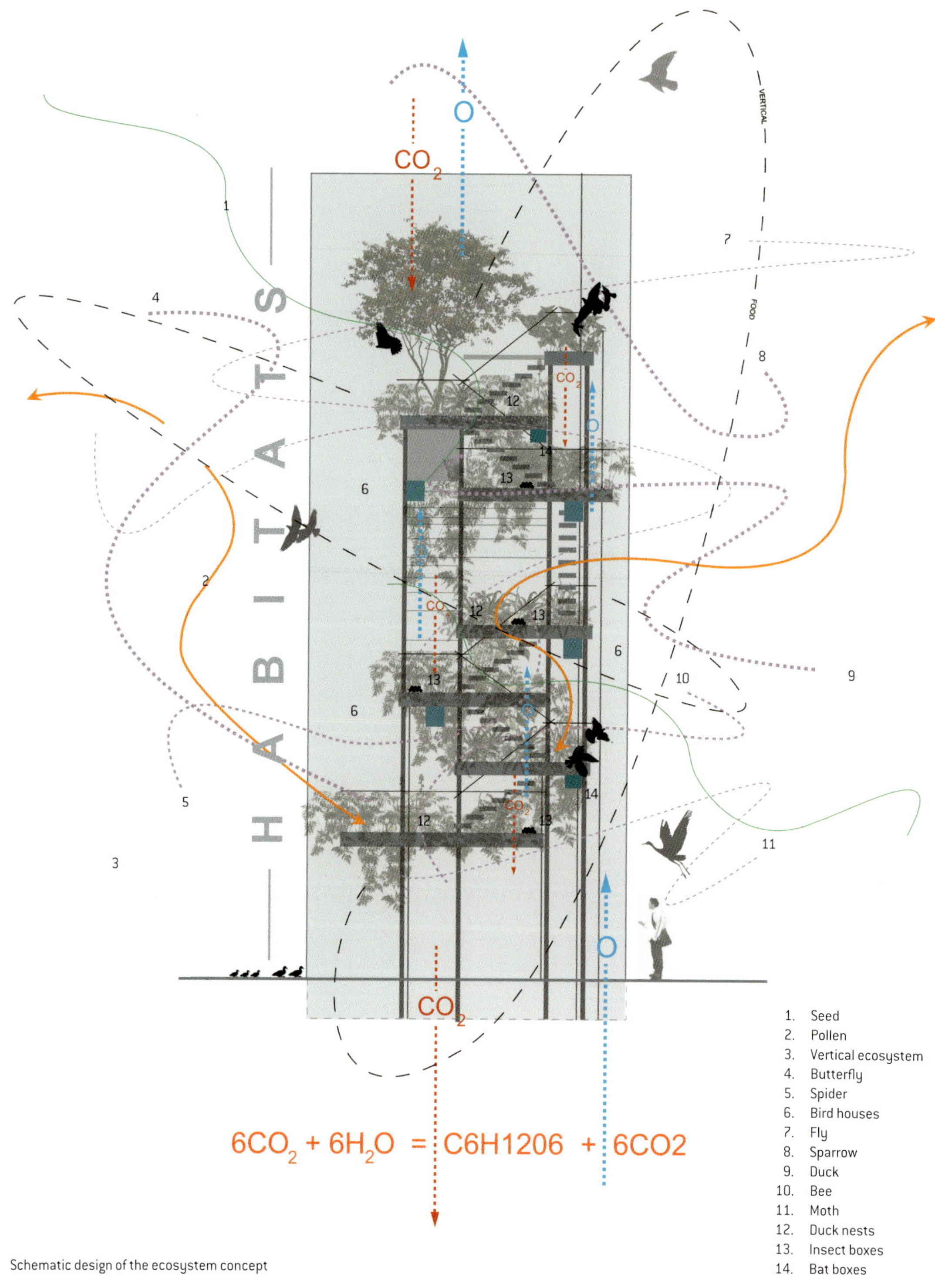

Schematic design of the ecosystem concept

1. Seed
2. Pollen
3. Vertical ecosystem
4. Butterfly
5. Spider
6. Bird houses
7. Fly
8. Sparrow
9. Duck
10. Bee
11. Moth
12. Duck nests
13. Insect boxes
14. Bat boxes

572

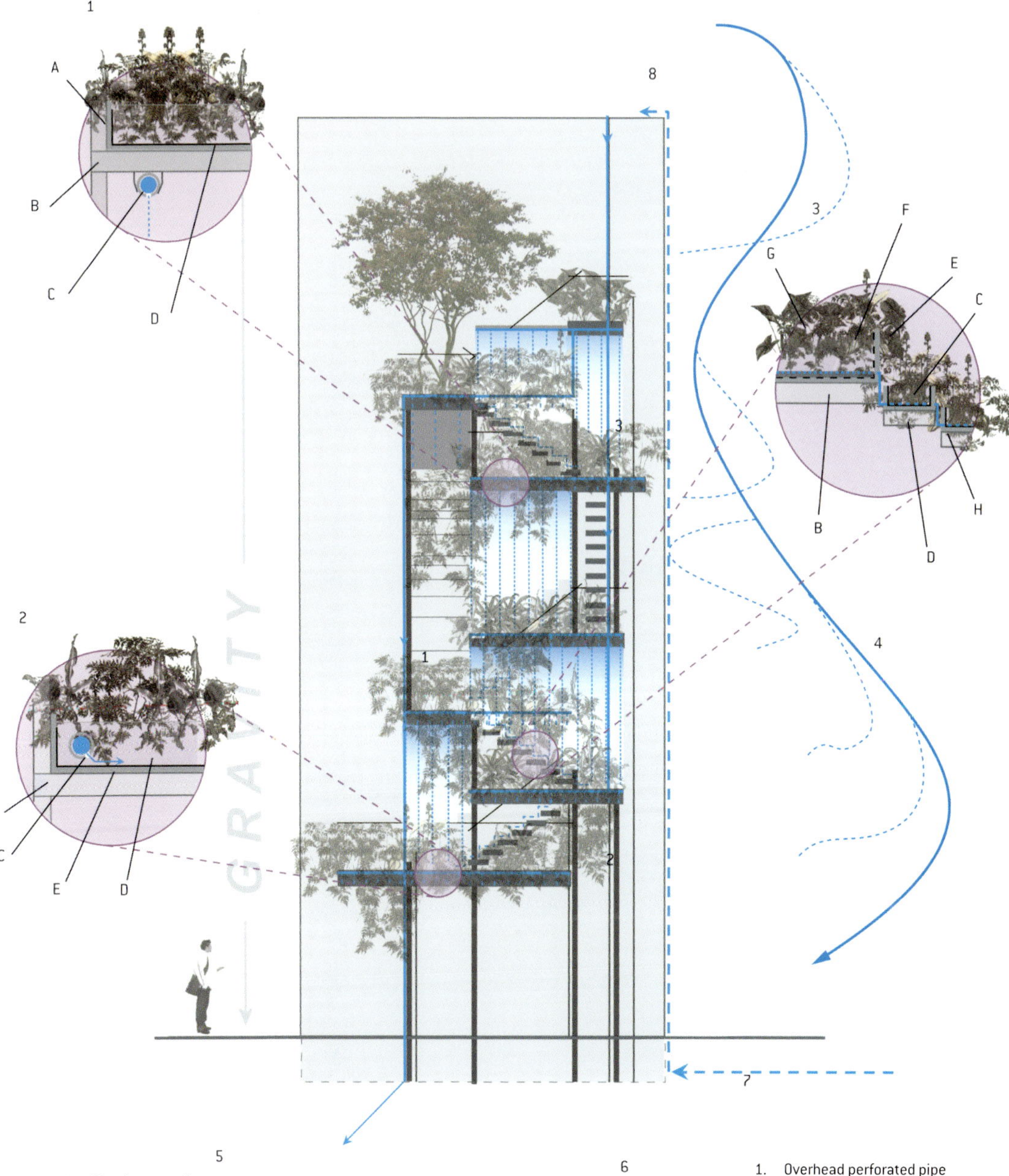

A. Planting container
B. Fire escape structure
C. Perforated pipe
D. Impermeable membrane / root barrier
E. Planting container
F. Excess water from planting collected by gravel strip and channeled to perforated pipe
G. Permeable membrane
H. Fire escape steps

Schematic design of the irrigation concept

1. Overhead perforated pipe
2. Embedded perforated pipe
3. Excess water irrigation
4. Drip irrigation
5. Overflow to mains drain
6. Mains water inlet – no pump required, water raised by mains pressure
7. p>1 bar . p=pressure . 1 bar rises water by 10 meters
8. Water storage / distribution regulator

Valladolid Masterplan

Valladolid, Spain

The growth of the city of Valladolid has created many projects offering expansion solutions. This design is a sustainability model that can be applied to other European cities. It consists of freeing up the old railroad track corridor, constructing new underground tracks and using the new space for public use.

La croissance de la ville de Valladolid a généré de nombreux projets offrant des solutions d'expansion. Cette conception est un modèle de durabilité exportable à d'autres villes européennes. Elle consiste à libérer le couloir de l'ancienne voie ferrée, enterrer les nouvelles voies et adapter la nouvelle surface à d'autres utilisations publiques.

Das Wachstum Valladolids hat zahlreiche Projekte hervorgebracht, die Lösungen für die Expansion bieten. Dieses Modell der Nachhaltigkeit kann in andere europäische Städte exportiert werden. Es umfasst die Freilegung des Korridors der alten Gleisfahrbahn, die unterirdische Verlegung neuer Gleise und die Ausstattung der neuen Fläche für öffentliche Nutzung.

De groei van de stad Valladolid heeft tot talrijke projecten geleid die uitbreidingsoplossingen bieden. Dit ontwerp is een duurzaamheidsmodel dat naar andere Europese steden uitgevoerd kan worden. Het bestaat erin de strook van het oude spoor vrij te maken, het nieuwe spoor onder de aarde te leiden en de nieuwe oppervlakte in te richten voor openbaar gebruik.

Vidal & Asociados Arquitectos, Richard Rogers Partnership
www.luisvidal.com
© Vidal & Asociados Arquitectos

ENTRADA
RENFE ESTACI
AVE
3
4

The creation of a new boulevard measuring 13,125 ft long and 197 ft wide will improve the social life and the new urban features in the city. Also six new neighborhoods with 5,900 homes will be constructed.

La création d'un nouveau boulevard de 4 km de long et 60 m de large enrichira la vie sociale et les nouveaux équipements urbains de la ville, de même que la construction de six nouveaux quartiers avec 5 900 logements.

Die Schaffung eines neuen, 4 km langen und 60 m breiten Boulevards bereichert das gesellschaftliche Leben und die Stadt mit neuen Einrichtungen sowie mit dem Bau sechs neuer Stadtviertel mit 5900 Wohnungen.

De creatie van een nieuwe 4 km lange en 60 brede boulevard zal, in combinatie met de bouw van zes nieuwe wijken van 5900 woningen, het sociale stadsleven en de nieuwe stadsuitrustingen verrijken.

Photomontage

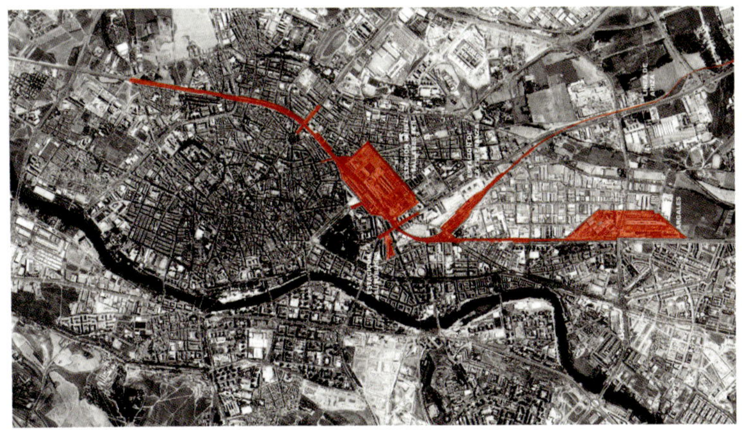

Aerial view of the intervention 1

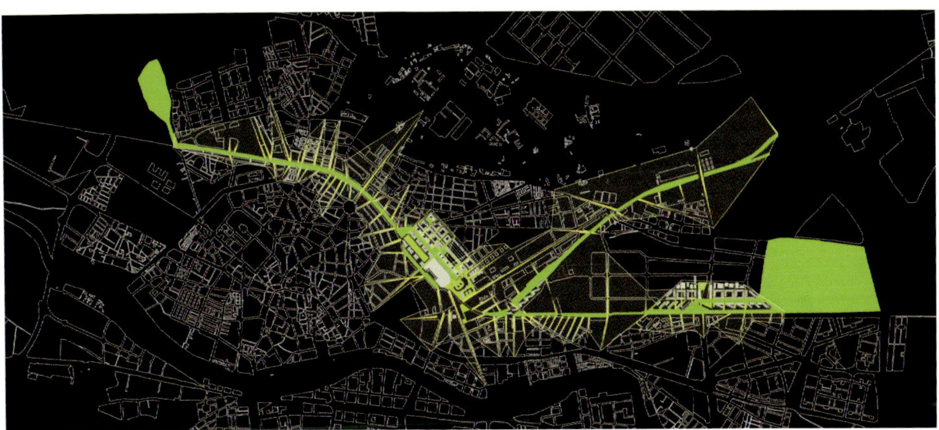

Aerial view of the intervention 2

Schematic section

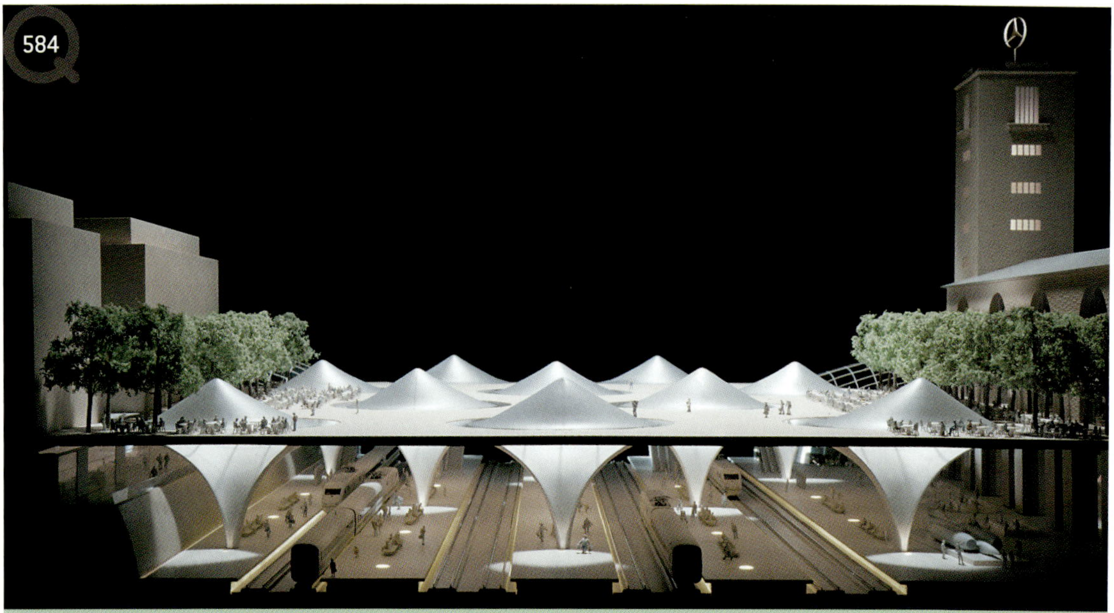

Stuttgart Main Station

Stuttgart, Germany

The project for the Stuttgart train station was designed to be built 40 ft underground. It will be integrated into a new residential district and the roof with skylights will form part of a large public plaza.

Le projet de la future gare ferroviaire de Stuttgart a été conçu pour être construit à 12 m du sol. Il sera intégré au sein d'un nouveau quartier résidentiel, de manière à ce que la toiture à lucarnes s'intègre à une grande place publique.

Das Projekt für den zukünftigen Bahnhof in Stuttgart wurde für den Bau in 12 m Tiefe entworfen. Das Dach des Bahnhofs, welcher zu einem neuen Wohnviertel gehören wird, wird mit seinen Oberlichtern Teil eines großen öffentlichen Platzes.

Het project voor het toekomstige station van Stuttgart werd ontworpen om op 12 m hoogte van de grond gebouwd te worden. Het zal geïntegreerd worden in een nieuwe residentiële buurt, en wel zodanig dat de dakbedekking met dakvensters deel gaat uitmaken van een groot openbaar plein.

Ingenhoven Architects
www.ingenhovenundpartner.de
© Ingenhoven Architects

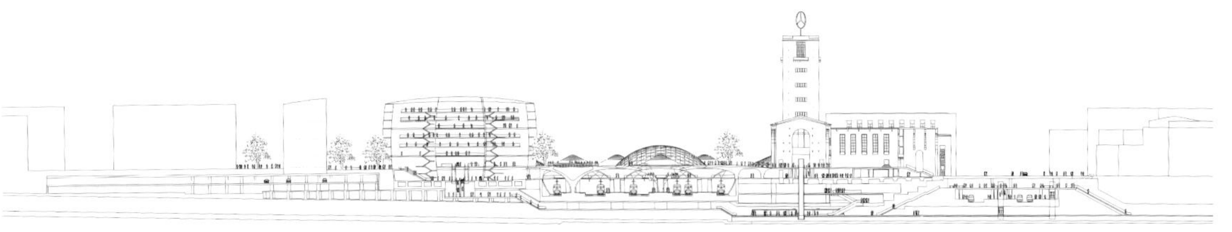

Section

Natural light will be provided by installing circular skylights in the roof of the station. The design has been subject to strict eco-friendly terms such as minimizing construction material and avoiding the use of heating.

L'installation de lucarnes circulaires sur la toiture de la gare fournira de la lumière naturelle au projet. Cette conception a été régie par des principes écologiques, comme la limitation des matériaux de construction et l'absence de chauffage.

Der Einbau runder Oberlichter bringt Tageslicht in das Projekt, das Umweltkriterien wie Minimierung der Baumaterialien und Vermeidung der Heizung berücksichtigt.

De ronde dakvensters in het dak van het station zullen het project natuurlijk licht verschaffen. Dit ontwerp werd bepaald door ecologische voorwaarden, zoals het minimaliseren van bouwmaterialen en het vermijden van verwarming.

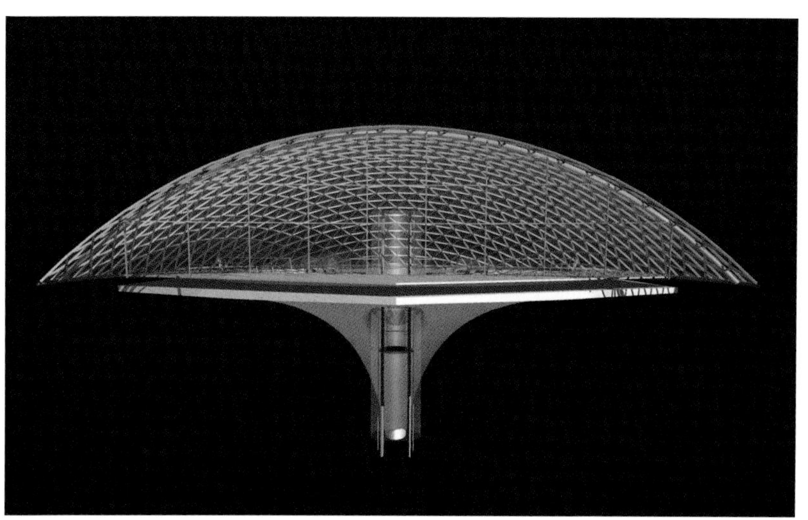

Computer generated 3D renderings

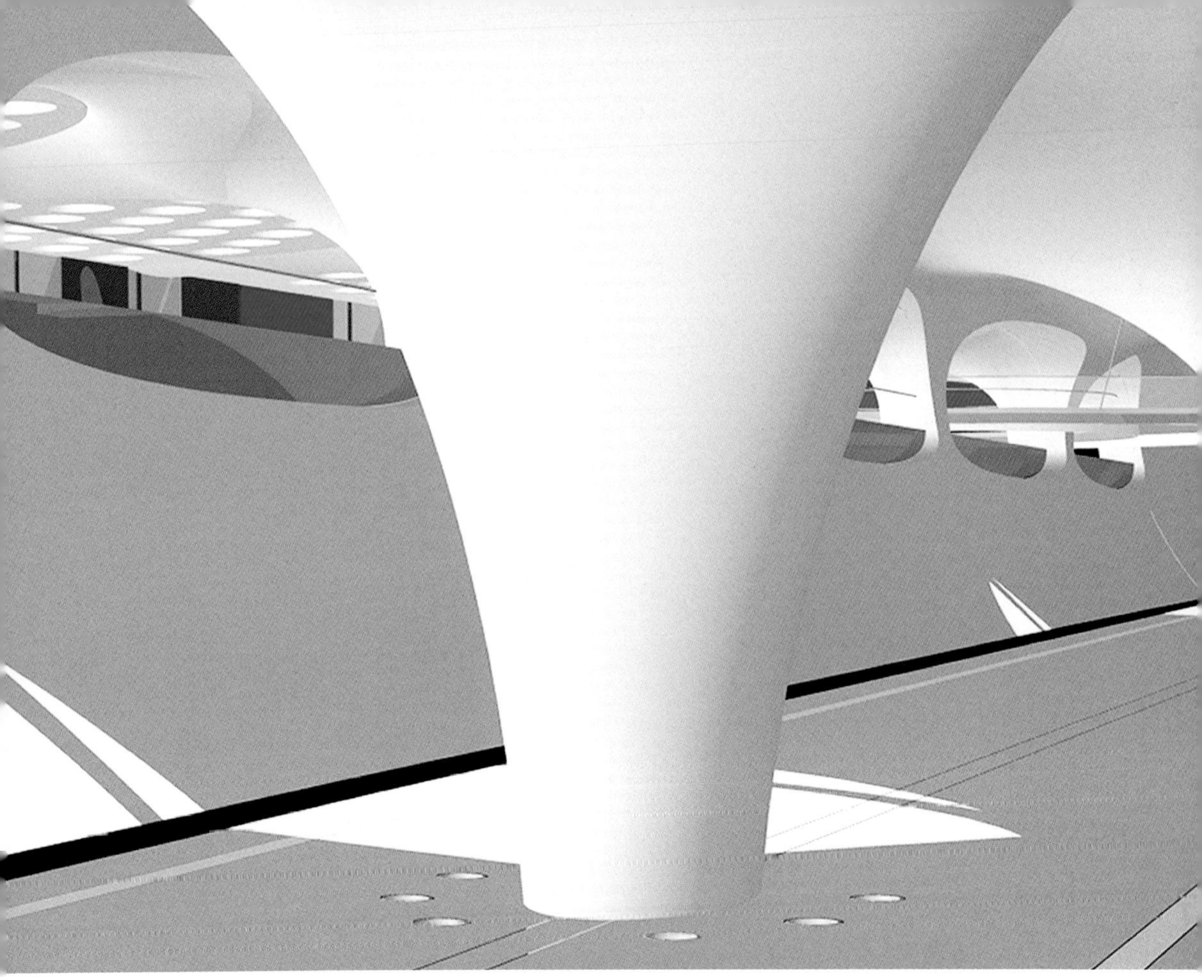

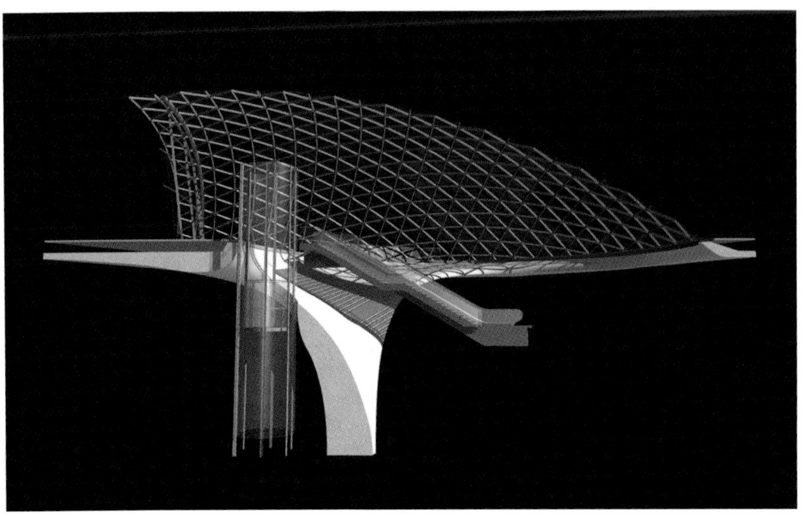

Computer generated 3D renderings

Schlossplatzareal Berlin

Berlin, Germany

The project was designed to occupy a site for the reconstruction of a Prussian palace. The design involved the construction of larch wood walkways raised 1 ft over an expanse of grass, and balustrades over an area where there were ruins of the old palace.

Le projet envisagé devrait occuper le terrain qui abritera, à l'avenir, la reconstruction d'un ancien palais prussien. La conception prévoit l'installation de passerelles en bois de cèdre, surélevées de 30 cm au-dessus d'un lit végétal, et équipées de garde-corps, au-dessus d'une zone abritant les anciennes ruines du palais.

Das vorgeschlagene Projekt soll auf dem Grundstück für die Rekonstruktion eines alten preußischen Palasts installiert werden. Das Design sieht die Einrichtung von Lärchenholz-Stegen 30 cm über einem grünen Teppich und Balustraden über einer Zone der Palastruinen vor.

Het voorgestelde project zal een perceel bezetten dat in de toekomst de reconstructie van een oud Pruisisch paleis zal vestigen. Het ontwerp voorziet de plaatsing van larikshouten vlonders die 30 cm boven een groen perk hangen, en balustrades boven een zone waar zich de oude ruïnes van het paleis bevinden.

 Relais Landschaftsarchitekten, Momentum3
www.relaisLA.com
© Relais Landschaftsarchitekten

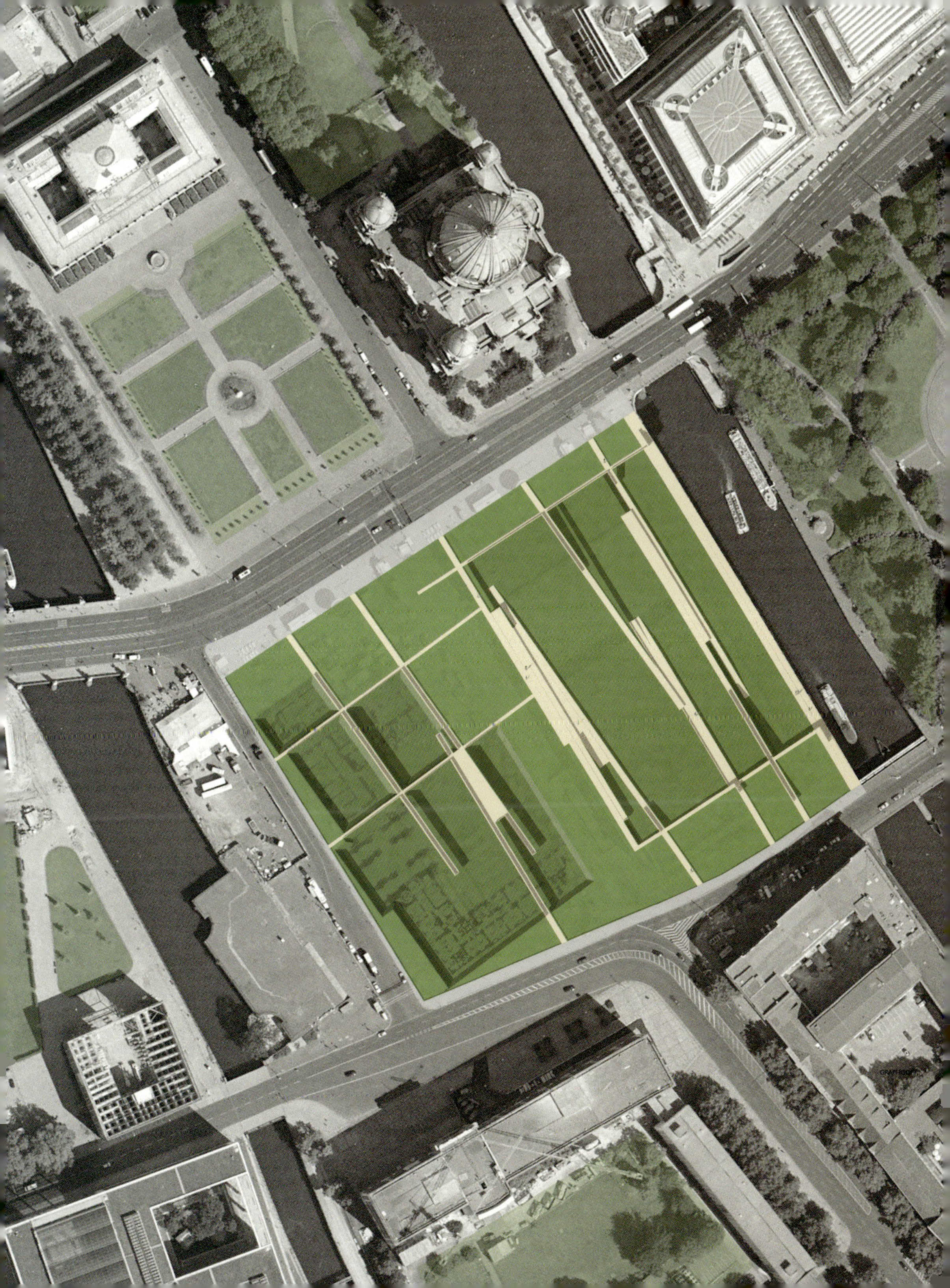

This temporary structure can be easily disassembled once work begins on reconstruction of the palace. A platform will be built for recreational purposes.

Cette structure éphémère pourra être rapidement démontée lorsque le palais reconstruit sera installé. Une tribune destinée à un usage ludique sera mise en place pour les visiteurs.

Die kurzlebige Struktur ermöglicht eine schnelle Demontage, sobald der rekonstruierte Palast errichtet wird. Es wird eine Tribüne für die Freizeitgestaltung der Benutzer gebaut.

Deze kortstondige structuur zal snel gedemonteerd kunnen worden op het moment dat het herbouwde paleis wordt geïnstalleerd. Er zal een tribune voor recreatief gebruik van de bezoekers worden gebouwd.

Computer generated 3D rendering

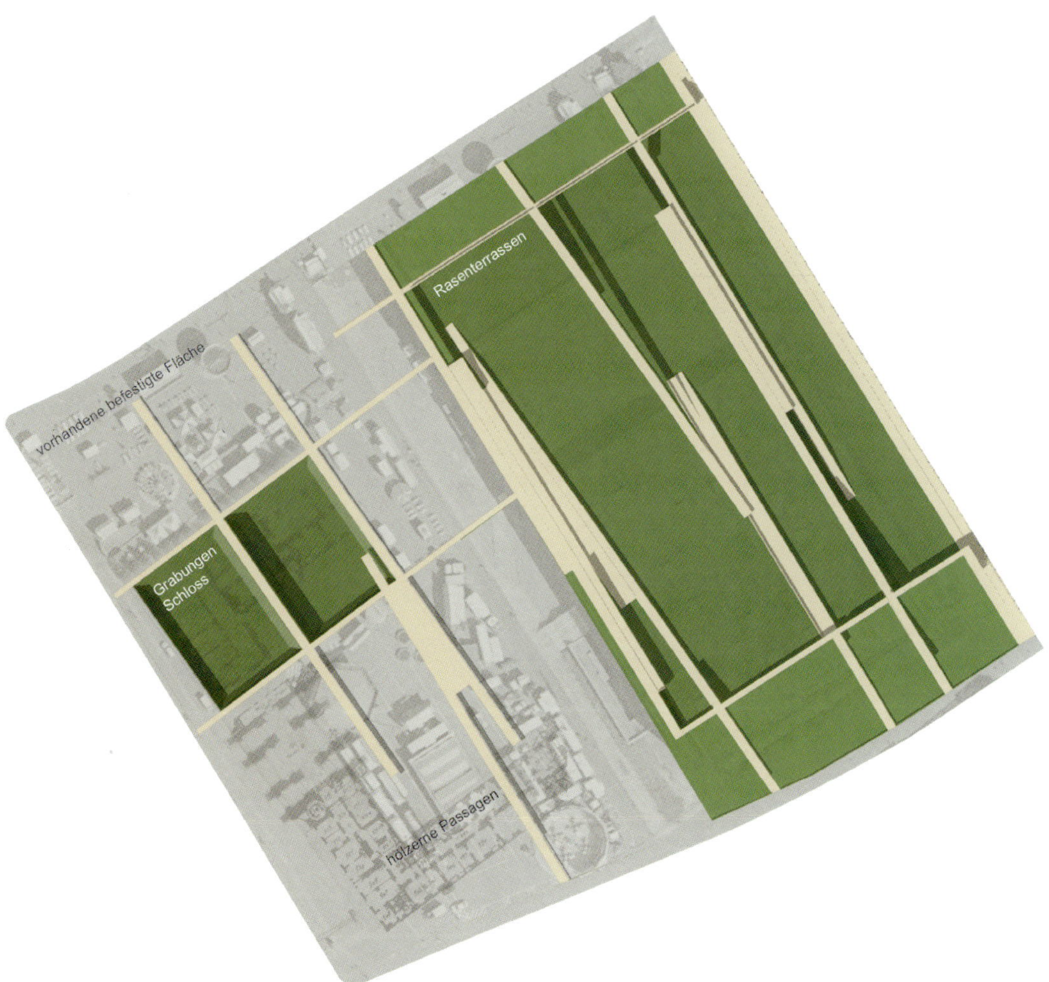

Plan 1

Humboldtbox
Rasenterrassen
Grabungen Schloss
Baustellen-einrichtung U-Bahn
hölzerne Passagen

Plan 2

Computer generated 3D rendering

ment Campus

Campa de los Ingleses

Bilbao, Spain

Balmori Associates won the design competition for the Abandoibarra plan, consisting of redeveloping the space between the Guggenheim Museum and Euskalduna Convention Center in Bilbao. The project placed special importance on spaces for relaxation and views over the river, the mountains, and the museum.

Balmori Associates a été désigné adjudicataire du projet d'Abandoibarra, consistant en la rénovation de l'espace situé entre le Musée Guggenheim de Bilbao et le Palais Euskalduna. Le projet accorde une importance particulière aux espaces destinés à la détente et à la contemplation du fleuve, de la montagne ou du musée.

Balmori Associates gewann den Wettbewerb für den Abondoibarra-Plan, der darin bestand, den Raum zwischen dem Guggenheim-Museum und dem Palacio Euskalduna in Bilbao neu zu gestalten. Das Projekt legt besonderen Wert auf Plätze, an denen man ausruhen und von denen man den Fluss, die Berge oder das Museum betrachten kann.

Balmori Associates won de wedstrijd voor het Abandoibarra-plan, dat de zone tussen het Guggenheim-museum van Bilbao en het paleis Euskalduna wil herstellen. Het project hecht bijzonder veel belang aan plaatsen men kan ontspannen en naar de rivier, de bergen of het museum kan kijken.

Balmori Associates
www.balmori.com
© Balmori Associates

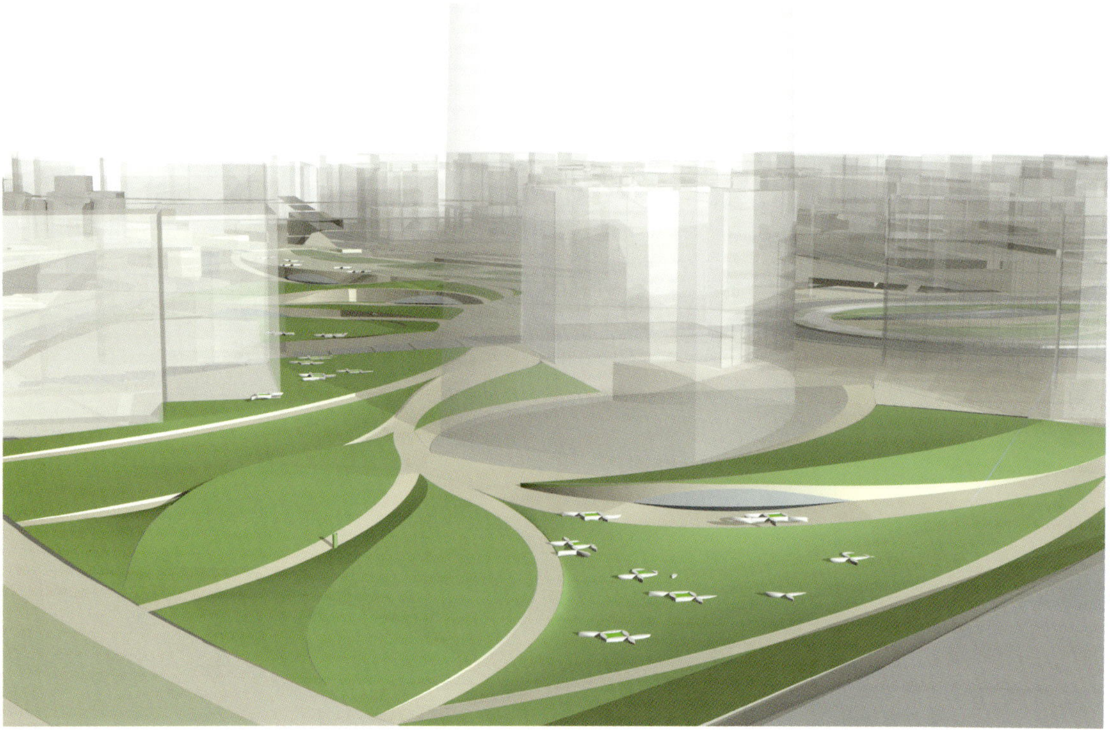

Computer generated 3D renderings

Computer generated 3D renderings

The combination of curved terraces creating a contoured landscape over a height of 33 ft, elliptical silhouettes, and pedestrian pathways characterize the project.

L'ouvrage est formé par une combinaison de terrasses courbées, aménagées comme un paysage en relief avec un dénivelé de 10 m, de silhouettes elliptiques et de passages piétons.

Die Kombination von Terrassen, die mit einem Höhenunterschied von 10 m wie eine Landschaft gewölbt sind, die ellipsenförmigen Umrisse und die Fußgängerwege sind Elemente des Projekts.

Het project bestaat uit de combinatie van gebogen terrassen als een reliëflandschap met een hoogteverschil van 10 m, elliptische silhouetten en voetgangersoversteekplaatsen.

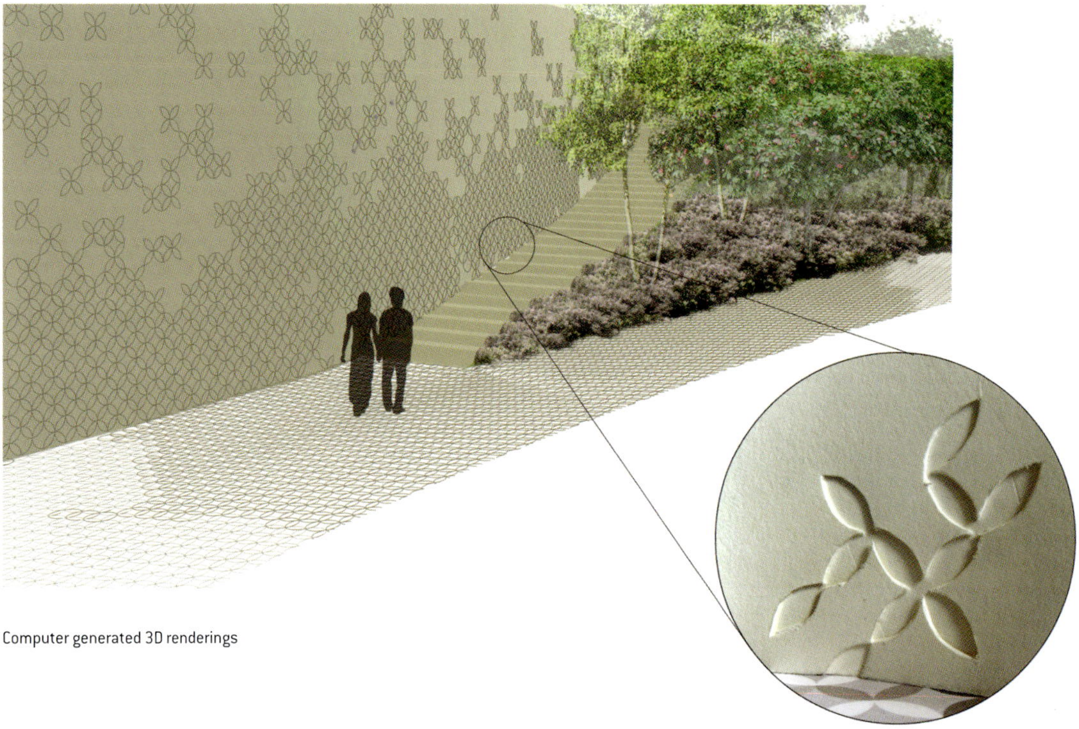

Computer generated 3D renderings

Remembrance Park

Camorino, Switzerland

This cemetery, located in suburban Milan, is Paolo Bürgi's personal project and poetic vision of burial. It was designed as a living landscape, a place for remembering, and for spiritual renewal. The tombs will be located in wooded areas, while a flat space will be kept as an open area.

Le cimetière, qui sera construit dans la banlieue de Milan, est un projet personnel de Paolo Bürgi, faisant preuve d'une vision poétique de la sépulture. Il a été conçu comme un paysage de vie, un lieu de souvenir et un espace de revitalisation spirituelle. Les tombes seront installées dans une zone boisée de surface plate, qui sera entretenue comme un site ouvert.

Der Friedhof am Stadtrand von Mailand ist ein persönliches Projekt von Paoli Bürgi mit einer poetischen Sicht der Grabstätte. Er wurde als Landschaft des Lebens aufgefasst, als Ort für die Erinnerung und die spirituelle Regeneration. Die Grabstätten befinden sich auf baumbestandenem Gelände.

De begraafplaats, die in de buitenwijken van Milaan zal komen te liggen, is een persoonlijk project van Paolo Bürgi met een poëtische visie van de begrafenis. Het kerkhof werd ontworpen als een levenslandschap, een plaats voor nagedachtenis en spirituele wederopleving. De graven zullen op het met bomen beplante terrein komen te liggen en een vlak stuk wordt als open ruimte gehandhaafd.

 **Paolo L. Bürgi/Studio Bürgi**
www.burgi.ch
© Paolo L. Bürgi/Studio Bürgi

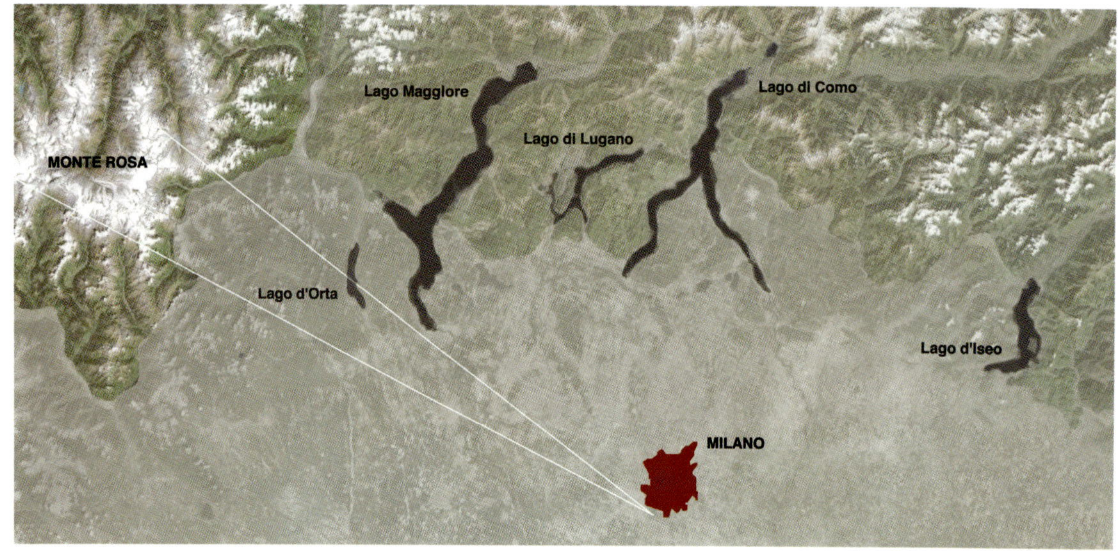

Location map

Diagramatic representation

The other paths lead to the central circle, which is the focal point of the landscape. The chapel and the terraced platform are the other features of the project.

La couronne centrale, d'où partent les autres chemins, constitue la colonne vertébrale du paysage. La chapelle et la plateforme en terrasse sont les autres éléments du projet.

Der zentrale Ring, von dem alle Wege ausgehen, bildet das Rückgrat der Landschaft. Die Kapelle und eine Terrasse bilden den übrigen Teil des Projekts.

De middenring van waaruit de rest van de paden start vormt de ruggengraat van het landschap. De kapel en het platform op een terras vormen de rest van het project.

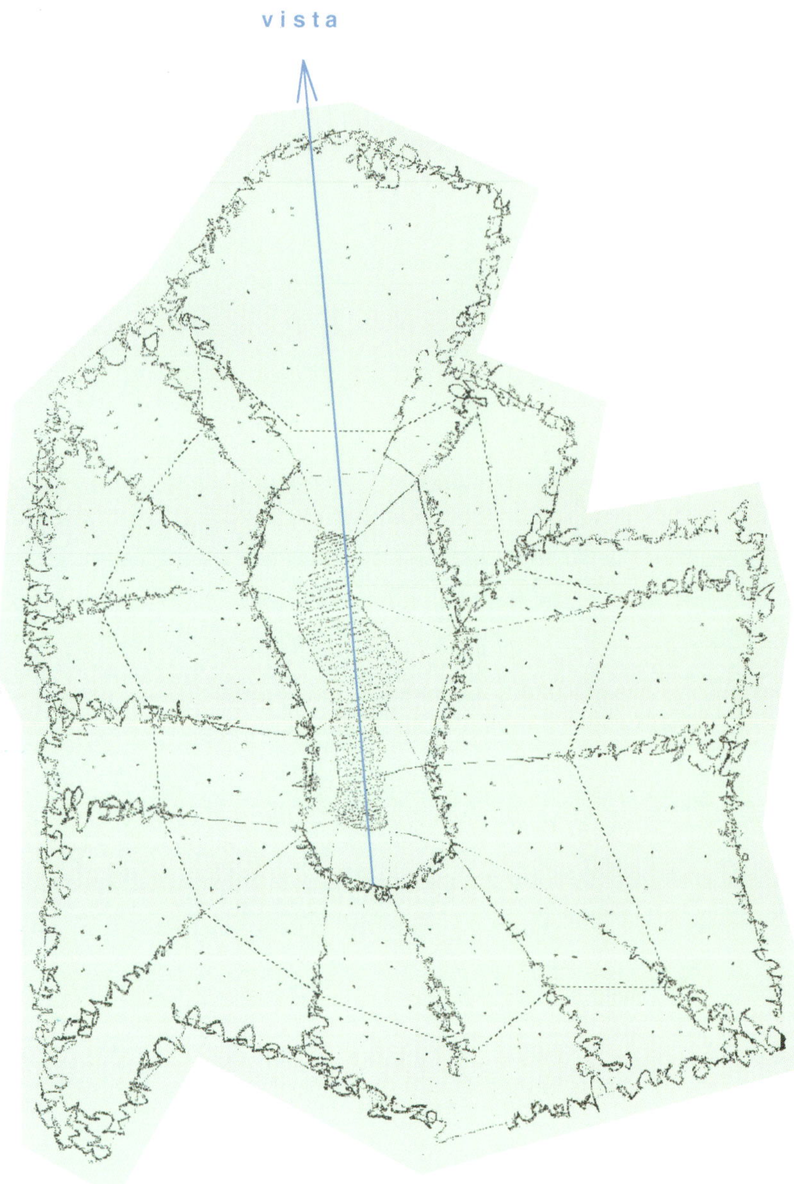

Orientation plan

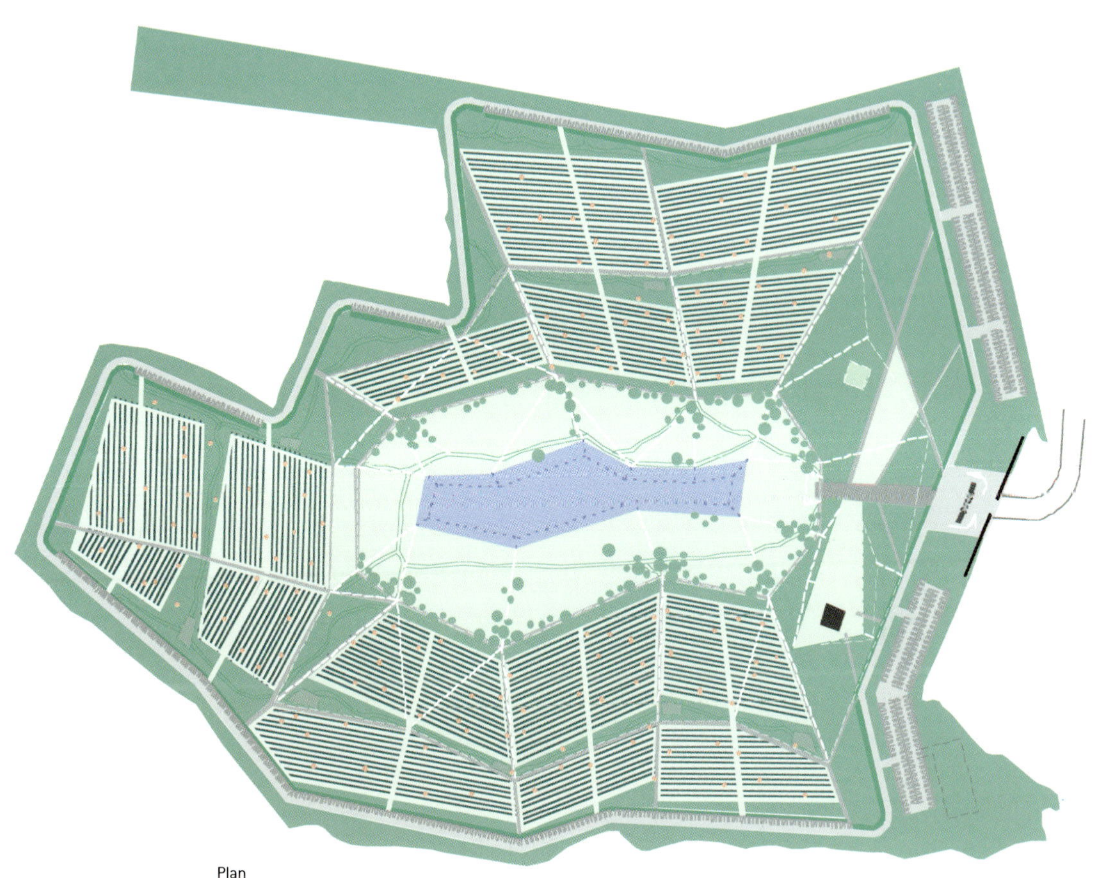

Plan

Federation Island

Coast of Sochi, Russia

The original artificial archipelago is inspired by the Russian Federation both in its form and in its surroundings: the rivers represent canals and the mountains are the relief of the islands. The archipelago is made up of seven main islands, twelve private and three which act as breakwaters.

Cet archipel artificiel original s'inspire directement de la fédération russe, tant dans la forme que dans le fond : les rivières représentent ici des canaux et les montagnes composent le relief des îles. L'ensemble se compose de sept îles principales, douze privées et trois autres en guise de brise-lames.

Die originelle künstliche Inselgruppe ist in Form und Hintergrund an die Russische Föderation angelehnt: Die Flüsse sind hier Kanäle und die Berge Inselreliefs. Die Gruppe besteht aus sieben Hauptinseln, zwölf Privatinseln und drei Inseln, die als Wellenbrecher dienen.

De originele kunstmatige archipel is direct geïnspireerd op de Russische federatie, zowel qua vorm als qua omgeving: de rivieren vertegenwoordigen kanalen en de bergen vormen het reliëf van de eilanden. De groep is samengesteld uit zeven hoofdeilanden, twaalf privé-eilanden en drie eilanden die dienst doen als golfbrekers.

EEA Architects
www.eea-architects.com
© EEA Architects

The project also contains dwellings, hotels, leisure, culture, and sporting installations, beaches, dunes, prairies, and forests. All of these above elements make up the artificial archipelago.

Le projet inclut également des résidences, des hôtels, des bâtiments de loisir et culturels, des installations sportives, des plages, des dunes, des prairies et des bois. Tous ces éléments composent l'archipel artificiel.

Das Projekt der künstlichen Inselgruppe umfasst Siedlungen, Hotels, Freizeit-, Kultur- und Sportanlagen, Strände, Dünen, Wiesen und Wälder.

Het project omvat naast résidences, hotels, gebouwen voor vrije tijd en cultuur en sportinstallaties eveneens stranden, duinen, weiden en bossen. Al deze elementen vormen samen de kunstmatige archipel.